Special Event Production

SPECIAL EVENT PRODUCTION

THE RESOURCES

Doug Matthews

AMSTERDAM • BOSTON • HEIDELBERG • LONDON • NEW YORK • OXFORD
PARIS • SAN DIEGO • SAN FRANCISCO • SINGAPORE • SYDNEY • TOKYO

Butterworth-Heinemann is an imprint of Elsevier

Butterworth-Heinemann is an imprint of Elsevier
Linacre House, Jordan Hill, Oxford OX2 8DP, UK
30 Corporate Drive, Suite 400, Burlington, MA 01803, USA

First edition 2008

British Library Cataloguing-in-Publication Data
A catalogue record for this book is available from the British Library

Library of Congress Cataloging-in-Publication Data
A catalog record for this book is available from the Library of Congress

ISBN: 978-0-7506-8523-8

For information on all Butterworth-Heinemann publications
visit our web site at books.elsevier.com

Typeset by Charon Tec Ltd (A Macmillan Company), Chennai, India
www.charontec.com

Printed and bound in Canada

08 09 10 11 12   10 9 8 7 6 5 4 3 2 1

Contents

Preface

Those readers who have already devoured Special Events Production: The Process will realize that my main goal in writing the books was to offer an advanced level of knowledge in event production that heretofore has not been available in industry-specific literature. The primary approach I have taken in striving to achieve this has been to present facts and details about theory and actual equipment and how it may be used. This is what I consider to be the core knowledge necessary for producers. These facts and details are not presented at an entry level, but rather the presentation presumes that, to begin with, the reader already possesses a basic knowledge about special events. I have been especially conscious of not repeating information that may be found in other books already written because it is from these sources that the basic knowledge may be obtained. After reading this book, and armed with the advanced core knowledge, producers should at the very least be able to discuss and determine the equipment required to achieve a specific look, effect, or end result for their events. There is no expectation that they will become technicians but there is an expectation that they will know where to go or what to do – with little or no supervision – to solve specific technical problems or challenges. In simple terms, they should be 'job-ready' and require minimal training to understand the technical details of event production.

As part of this approach, I have also strived to place the reader in the position of an actual producer in two ways. The first is to relate actual production 'war stories' that illustrate what can happen when something goes awry with the equipment used that is the topic of any particular chapter. Of course, it is seldom the fault of the equipment, but more often the fault of the producer, and therein lie the lessons learned. I and the other contributors of these stories have learned our lessons through the 'school of hard knocks' and pass on the lessons so that our mistakes will not be repeated. The final way in which I have tried to place the reader in the position of producer is to pose a number of 'production challenges' at the end of each chapter that test the reasoning skill of the reader by using the chapter's knowledge to provide solutions. In the majority of cases, these challenges are not solved by a simple regurgitation of the facts within the chapters, but rather by an application of the facts and details covered.

Although not one of my stated goals in writing these two books, but a logical outcome of taking the approach I have, is an emphasis on thorough, professional risk management. As the reader will quickly see, especially in Special Events Production: The Resources, I advocate placing a very clear responsibility on producers and suppliers to follow existing standards and regulations, of which there are many, and to commit to paper in contracts this responsibility. There is really nothing 'new under the sun' here, just an ethical duty to do the right thing, to take the time to learn the standards, and to insist that they be followed, sometimes to the detriment of profit. It is, in effect, raising the level of professionalism to that of other fields that must follow such standards and regulations, such as engineering, law, and medicine, among many.

I hope you enjoy the learning experience and continue to invent ever more creative, astounding, and memorable special events.

Doug Matthews
November 2006
Vancouver, Canada

Acknowledgments

One book tests the patience of authors and those close to them, but two books severely tighten the shackles to desk and computer, not to mention testing the friendships and loyalties of industry colleagues. Without these friendships and loyalties, this second book would not have come to fruition. I therefore wish to sincerely thank the following people for their part in its creation.

My publisher, *Elsevier*, and editors *Ms. Sally North*, *Ms. Jane Macdonald*, and *Mr. Dennis McGonagle*, for having the faith to work with me and to publish not one but two books in an untested area of the special events industry.

My wife, *Marimae*, for her patience, support, and faith.

Mr. Ben Kopelow, the founder of Pacific Show Productions, once again for the immense amount of knowledge he passed on to me in an era when special event production was in its infancy as an industry.

Ms. Julie Ferguson of Beacon Literary Services, for her extensive suggestions on writing, passed to me over many bottomless cups of coffee.

My colleagues in TEAM Net, the Total Event Arrangements and Meeting Network, for sharing their knowledge and for their numerous contributions to both books. I also want to single out *Ms. Dianne McGarey*, the Executive Director and Founder, for her positive attitude and boundless enthusiasm for this industry.

Mr. Jonathan Rouse, former Chair of the Faculty of Tourism and Outdoor Recreation at Capilano College in North Vancouver, BC, and *Mr. Casey Dorin*, Dean of the Howe Sound and Tourism Programs at Capilano College, for their encouragement in allowing me to revise the advanced program in special event management at the college, and also for allowing me to teach event production at an advanced level, much of the content for which is based on this book.

Mr. Mike Granek, the present owner of Pacific Show Productions, for his willingness to allow me to rummage through old files and photographs in search of interesting content for the books.

Mr. Tim Lewis, of Proshow Audiovisual-Broadcast, who has worked with some of the biggest names in show business and politics, for his review of the audio and visual presentation chapters.

My son, *Stephen Matthews*, of Q1 Production Technologies, for his assistance with and review of, the lighting chapter and the electrical power portion of the chapter on miscellaneous technical resources.

Mr. Chris Briere, of Briere Production Group Inc., for his assistance in explaining to me some of the finer details of audio systems.

Mr. Wilson Durward, of the Evergreen Cultural Centre, for his review of the entertainment chapter.

The many contributors from companies and countries around the globe who have been kind enough to provide photos and to share some of the wisdom gleaned from their years of experience.

All the employees and subcontractors of Pacific Show Productions over the years who helped to 'cause applause' and create memories.

Everyone else whom I may have missed but for whose assistance I am truly grateful.

Thank you one and all.

ENTERTAINMENT

LEARNING OUTCOMES

After reading this chapter, you will be able to:

1. Understand and describe the different forms of entertainment.
2. Understand the primary reasons why entertainment is used in special events.
3. Understand what comprises content in entertainment, from both the audience and performer points of view.
4. Describe and analyze what makes a good performance in the four main genres of entertainment.
5. Plan an effective entertainment program.
6. Understand how to work with performers.

'If man is a sapient animal, a tool making animal, a self-making animal, a symbol-using animal, he is, no less, a performing animal, *Homo performans*, not in the sense, perhaps that a circus animal may be a performing animal, but in the sense that a man is a self-performing animal – his performances are, in a way, *reflexive*, in performing he reveals himself to himself. This can be in two ways: the actor may come to know himself better through acting or enactment; or one set of human beings may come to know themselves better through observing and/or participating in performances generated and presented by another set of human beings' (Turner, 1988; p. 81).

This statement by renowned anthropologist Victor Turner succinctly summarizes what special event entertainment is all about: communications. It is about live performers understanding their craft well enough to be able to communicate powerful messages, be they subtle or obvious, to their audiences. The successful delivery of a well-designed entertainment program can evoke strong feelings, emotions, and memories, and can affect many of our senses. Indeed, it is the one part of an event people may remember long after the event is over. In that sense, it is arguably the one resource that can make or break the event.

Although many event producers purport to be experts in the field of entertainment (are we not all critics?), it is a complex field. Our goal in this chapter is to make it easier to understand. In doing so, we will explore: how entertainment is defined; how to effectively stage an entertainment program; and finally, how to work with performers. Along the way, we will delve into physiology, psychology, and creativity. By the end, all the pieces should fit together, making it easier for producers to create, plan, and execute a successful and exciting program, and more than anything, to understand why they are doing it.

1.1   DEFINING ENTERTAINMENT

Properly defining entertainment requires us to understand the whole package, the sum of the various components that go into making up a complete presentation. Any given entertainment, whether a single performer or a multi-act extravaganza, can be fully defined by an analysis of three components or characteristics: form, reason (or 'use' by another definition), and content. We will examine each of these defining characteristics separately.

1.1.1   Form in Entertainment

To really define form, we need to first briefly contemplate the origins of performance. Although it would be nice to have foolproof evidence of the beginnings of human performance, such may never be the case. What we do have, based on current research, is a general knowledge of past *eras* or time periods during which the archeological evidence strongly suggests that certain genres of performance were either just beginning or were clearly fully developed.

To start at the true beginning, physiologically, it is not hard to understand that humans were capable of utilizing two basic modes of communication: vocalization and physical movement. These were not always present. It is believed that one of our related ancestors, *Homo heidelbergensis*, had developed a hypoglossal canal of sufficient size and construction to be able to create actual speech by at least 500,000 years ago (Tattersall, 2006).

On the physical side, the best evidence for movement resembling modern humans lies with early footprints found in Laeotoli, Africa, of a much more distant relative, *Australopithecus*, who seemed to walk with a bipedal gait similar to today's version of humans. Those preserved footprints are 3.5 million years old (Feder, 1996).

At this point, we must take a leap of faith based on logic, and posit that at some point in the unrecorded distant past, these basic communication skills, vocalization and physical movement, further developed into the beginnings of entertainment, as illustrated in Figure 1.1.

Whether these all occurred at the same time is both unknown and unlikely; however we have to start somewhere, and lacking prehistoric archeological evidence, this is the best place. It is also not illogical to speculate that this process was taken a step further over time, so that each of the basic forms of entertainment in Figure 1.1 probably evolved – albeit somewhat loosely – into the more complex forms outlined in Figure 1.2.

This then, can be the starting point for defining form in entertainment. Form is actually another word for genre, but with the addition of sub-genres and categories. The use of form helps us understand the makeup of the entertainment itself and allows for ease of cataloguing. The proposed classification system outlined below is not necessarily the only one or the 'right' one, but it is one that allows for easier understanding of how genres are related to each other, and it is the only one that follows most logically from the origins of each form of entertainment.

1.1.1.1 Genres and Categories

Again, it seems logical to follow the original evolution of entertainment as outlined in Figure 1.2 and base form on that. We thus arrive at the

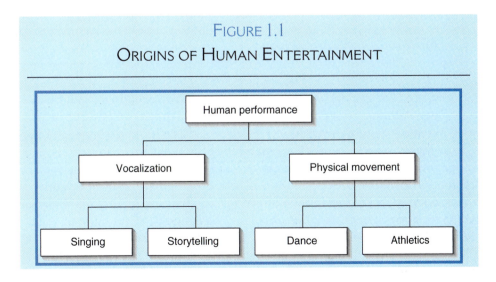

FIGURE 1.1
ORIGINS OF HUMAN ENTERTAINMENT

Courtesy: Doug Matthews

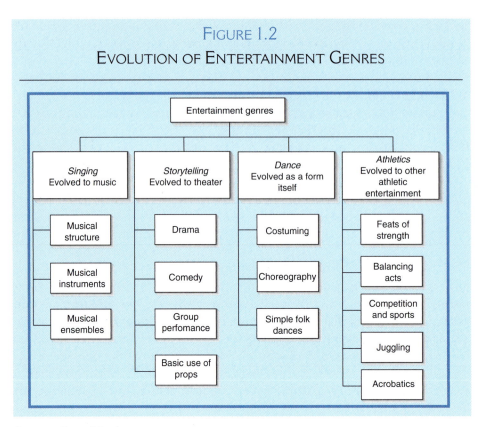

FIGURE 1.2

EVOLUTION OF ENTERTAINMENT GENRES

Courtesy: Doug Matthews

following primary genres and sub-genres:

- *Music*: Music in general can be considered a primary entertainment genre with sub-genres of vocal and instrumental.
- *Theater*: Beeman (1993; pp. 381–383), among others, has attempted to codify theater itself into a number of different genres based on the type of media used, the performers, and the content. However, his approach does not look at all entertainment genres together, thus making it difficult to arrive at any sort of common classification. I propose here that theater include the sub-genres of comedy, tragedy, and general speech. This allows for the inclusion of keynote speakers and similar spoken theatrical presentations that we use in special events.
- *Dance*: Throughout my own experience of working with every type of dance in special events, the sub-genres break down easily into cultural (e.g. folk, ethnic, traditional by other names), ballet, and modern or contemporary (e.g. tap, jazz, hip-hop, ballroom).
- *Other athletic entertainment*: This primary genre covers all other physical entertainment and includes the two sub-genres of sports and physical entertainment (e.g. acrobats, jugglers, magicians, stunt people, and stilt walkers). It thus includes most modern variety acts.

In order to further define any given form of entertainment, we need to add non-performative classifications that allow the form to be specified exactly. These we can term categories, as follows:

- *Size*: Size places the entertainment form in the context of a group performance. The sub-categories of size are large group (i.e. more than 10), small group (i.e. less than 10), and solo.
- *Prop-assisted*: This covers a wide range of possibilities and breaks down into sub-categories of large props and small props. Examples could be stilts (i.e. large props) for a stilt walker, balls and knives (i.e. small props) for a juggler, or roller blades (i.e. small props) for a roller blade demo team.

1.1.1.2   *Classifying and Cataloguing Entertainment*

Of course, any of the genres, sub-genres, categories, or sub-categories can be combined with any others to arrive at a specific entertainment form. This can work in reverse as well, taking an entertainment form and tracing it back to its primary genre, sub-genres, and categories. Let us look at some examples:

- *A juggler*: The primary genre is other athletic entertainment, sub-genre physical entertainment, size category solo, and prop-assisted category small props.
- *Rock band with a vocalist*: The primary genre is music, sub-genres instrumental and vocal, size category small group.
- *Famous musical comedian Victor Borge*: He is a combination primary genre of music with sub-genre instrumental, and theater with sub-genre comedy, size category solo.
- *A steel drum band accompanying limbo dancers*: This would also be a combination of dance as the primary genre with sub-genre cultural, and music with sub-genre instrumental, size category small group, and finally prop-assisted category of small props (e.g. the limbo bar).
- *A keynote motivational speaker using a laptop computer onstage*: The primary genre would be theater, sub-genre general speech, size category solo, prop-assisted category small props.

Using this system, any given entertainment form can be defined and, if need be, catalogued. Many entertainment agencies and event producers use their own system of cataloguing entertainment using slightly more familiar terms, although the end result is still the same. All the acts available to a producer somehow need to be catalogued in order to be retrieved easily when needed. Some of the more common categories used by producers and agents are:

- *Celebrity talent*: These include nationally and internationally known performers, who can be singers, musicians, comedians, speakers, or any of the other genres.

- *Musical variety*: These include comedy music, background music such as instrumentalists and soloists, symphony orchestras, and marching bands.
- *Dance bands*: These can be everything from duos to big bands.
- *Variety*: These are the unusual types of entertainers such as jugglers, magicians, ventriloquists, clowns, stilt walkers, and cirque-type acrobatic acts. Comedians are sometimes categorized with this group.
- *Cultural or ethnic*: This group includes Native Indian, Asian, Latin, and all other cultural performances that stress heritage.
- *Interactive*: This covers anything in which the main goal is for people to participate such as virtual reality games, table acts (e.g. fortune tellers, caricaturists, handwriting analysts), and strolling acts who interact with people.

Rutherford-Silvers (2004; p. 278) has an extensive list of entertainment resources, most of which can be categorized according to the genre and category system proposed above.

It is really only by classifying and cataloguing entertainment forms that entertainment as a resource can be useful. Most event producers and entertainment agents have enormous databases of performers of every conceivable form. Without a cataloguing system, easy retrieval is almost impossible, but it is invariably required when an event proposal must be prepared on short notice. Although most producers devise their own system for cataloguing, the genres and categories outlined above may be a good starting point.

Databases are now all automated using one of the more common programs such as Act, Maximizer, or Microsoft Access, and these are customizable to suit individual company needs. There are, however, some commonalities. Most use an alphanumeric cataloguing system of some sort (like any library), and the system proposed above easily lends itself to that. For example, a dance band with a vocalist might have the initial letters 'MIVSS' for 'music instrumental and vocal, small group size.' After that could come the name of the group (possibly abbreviated) and/or a number that might indicate the date they were posted in the date base. A combination entertainment form may have two or more catalog numbers to allow them to be part of different lists. This is useful when say, a comedy act is also a musical act, and both may be called upon for different events, so they need to be listed as both genres. These are only very rough examples but the concept is that a catalog number is what permits easy retrieval using the search function of the database program. Of course, other necessary information for the performers must be included, such as contact information (e.g. name, phone, fax, e-mail, and address) and details of the act itself (e.g. what it includes, length of normal show, standard cost, rider requirements, and promotional material). Considering that this is at the heart of what makes entertainment resources effective, it is well worth spending time to develop an effective system.

1.1.2 Reasons for Entertainment

The reason for any given entertainment concerns the overall message delivered by a performance. It is the 'why' question answered. The performance must satisfy the audience and client and deliver the promised results based on the original reason for the entertainment. For special event production purposes, the audience's interests are usually represented by a single person (e.g. a client or event manager) or a small number of persons (e.g. an organizing committee) during the planning process, and it is this person or these persons who must articulate the reason for the entertainment to the producer. Here, then, are the main reasons we produce entertainment shows for special events.

1.1.2.1 *Education*

A powerful reason is the imparting of knowledge to an audience; it may be based entirely on learning or may be a small part of a larger show with multiple goals. Here are some typical examples that have proven successful in my own and my colleagues' experiences.

- *Scripted show*: This occurs when entertainment is used with the main goal of providing – or helping to provide – knowledge to the audience. I have done this for a scripted variety show format in which we created a show that told part of the history of Canada through segments that incorporated singing, dancing, comedy, and acting, thus telling the audience in an interesting way about the country's history. Another way is to partially script a show to augment a corporate presentation and to thereby explain more about the company goals, such as for a sales meeting, or for the explanation of a complicated concept. I have done this through the use of improvisational comedians who performed semi-scripted, humorous problem scenarios for an audience of financial planners who then had to workshop solutions for the scenarios presented.

    Dianne McGarey of Atlanta-based Axtell Productions (McGarey, 2004) has had considerable experience with this type of show and states,

    'To do this successfully, it is vital to have a professional scriptwriter who will work closely with you to incorporate all the vital information, and agree (up front) to do "rewrites" as needed. A theatrical director and rehearsal hall for the cast will also be required.'

- *Existing act*: Knowledge may also be imparted through the inclusion of performers who use education as part of their act, such as cultural dance groups who explain the origins of their dances (e.g. Chinese, Native American, African), storytellers, or handwriting analysts (personal knowledge), among many. My company frequently used a world champion gold panner who would not only teach guests how to gold pan, but would also teach the history of gold panning and gold rushes while they were doing it.

1.1.2.2   *Physically Moving People*

There is no more impressive method of physically moving crowds than to have them follow highly visual and loud performers. Using a marching band or other 'noisy' entertainment to lead people can save considerable time, especially with a large audience, and can be a nice segue from a reception to dinner or between event segments. In my career I have used marching bands, Swiss alpine horns, drum groups, color guards, cowboys on horses, fanfare trumpets, a town crier, stilt walkers, a Chinese lion, Dixieland bands, dancers of various types, clowns, old cars, and more I can't remember. In almost all cases, guests automatically followed the entertainment without having to be told what to do, thus making my job as a producer a little easier (not to mention negating the need for a costly add-on audio system in a remote location).

Following musical performers or noisy acts is not the only way to move people. Also possible is creative hosting. For example, we once designed an

Evening in Paris night for an important client at which we used a dozen male and a dozen female dancers dressed in traditional French attire and all very outgoing. They greeted and cheered guests as they arrived and individually escorted each guest to their table, then appeared later to perform a can-can dance routine after which they went into the room full of seated guests to bring them up to the dance floor. This concept of participative 'party starters' has gained tremendous popularity in recent years.

1.1.2.3 *Emotionally Moving People*

Psychologists define the primary emotions as fear, anger, sadness, joy, surprise, disgust, and contempt. An emotion is considered a response to stimuli that involves characteristic physiological changes – such as increase in pulse rate, rise in body temperature, greater or less activity of certain glands, change in rate of breathing – and tends in itself to motivate the individual toward further activity (Emotion, 2004). People tend to confuse emotions with feelings and even psychologists are not united in definitions. 'By one estimate, more than 90 definitions of "emotion" were proposed over the course of the 20th century' (Plutchik, 2001; p. 344). For simplification, we will assume that emotions are the primary ones stated above and feelings are what emanate from these. For example, one might feel guilty about not contributing to a charity for starving children as a result of watching a movie that stirs the emotion of anger in the observer because so much food is being wasted due to corruption in poor countries. One might feel exhilarated and proud because of the emotion of joy experienced when hearing one's national anthem played as an Olympic champion stands on the podium. Any performance that is able to trigger strong emotions and subsequent feelings, to stir the audience inside, will be memorable, no matter what the performance genre (e.g. music, dance, comedy, acting). Emotional content is a direct reflection of the skill of the performers in choosing appropriate material, combined with their abilities to deliver it. We will explore this in depth in the next section.

I was once given the task of providing after-dinner entertainment for a black-tie gala of a national association. The organizer and her committee were not too happy with my suggestion of a harmonica player as they thought it was not befitting the occasion; however, because they were longstanding clients, they allowed me to proceed. The show went very well and after it was over several people came up to me and thanked me profusely because they were moved to tears by the performance, which had managed to hit them deep inside. The choice of performer was purposeful, in that he had a tremendous ability to deliver emotionally charged songs (his own) that I knew would work. He was also adept at playing over 20 different mouth instruments and had won numerous awards.

1.1.2.4 *Motivating and Inspiring People*

Motivating an audience is distinctly different from emotionally moving them, although they will undoubtedly experience some strong feelings when being motivated. As opposed to **only** trying to stir inner feelings, motivation's goal is to give the audience a reason to take some action. This might be to buy a product, to improve one's life, to become closer to God, to work harder, to give to charity, to sell more cars, or a host of other reasons. Motivational entertainment takes emotional performances and adds a specific message and call to action. For example, if one is producing a fundraising event for special needs children, the entertainment might incorporate a moving song performed live by an onstage celebrity with video clips of the special needs kids in the background. At the end, a request is made for donations. For more excellent examples of this type of persuasive entertainment, one only has to watch the many charity telethons that raise millions of dollars annually. Almost any form of entertainment can achieve motivation if the content and timing are correct. Other examples of when it might be used are for incentive groups and teambuilding activities (e.g. with drum circles), for sporting events (e.g. with cheerleaders or loud rock music), and for conference opening and closing sessions (e.g. with motivational speakers). Inspirational entertainment differs from motivational primarily by the fact that there is not necessarily any call to action, only a general uplifting of the spirit.

1.1.2.5 *Decoration*

A novel and frequent use of entertainment in events is as decoration. The performer(s) take on the persona of decorations that can be either stationary or moving, interactive or inactive. Costumed living statues, interactive entertainers (e.g. stilt walkers, mimes, dancers, and others in themed costumes who move amongst guests anywhere but on a stage), and look-alikes are typical of decorative entertainment. Figure 1.3 is representative of an extremely novel interactive, but decorative, performer.

My company produced many events using this form of entertainment. At some, we placed dancers in spotlighted statuesque poses amongst tables as guests entered an event space. Once all were seated, the dancers then gradually came out of their poses and began an introductory dance routine. At another beach party event, we actually hired bodybuilders to pose and lift weights as if on 'Muscle Beach.'

1.1.2.6 *Announcing, Introducing, or Advertising*

For this use, performers may announce, introduce, and advertise people, products, services, and activities. These reasons are lumped together because the concept for each is similar. Some examples best illustrate this concept:

- Celebrities as masters of ceremonies.
- Herald trumpets to sound a call to dinner, to introduce another segment in an event, or to draw attention to a speaker.
- A personalized video greeting from a celebrity or from an automated talking head as part of a product introduction.

FIGURE 1.3

EXAMPLE OF A PERFORMER AS DECORATION

Courtesy: Designs by Sean, www.designsbysean.com

- Strolling 'robots' used at a trade show to draw attention to a particular booth or product.
- A magical 'reveal' created by a magician for introducing a product or person.
- Fireworks at midnight used to 'introduce' the New Year.

Perhaps the best results occur when producers get creative with 'off-the-wall' concepts. Here are some examples from my own personal experience.

- We once introduced a new Vancouver to Boston airline service by photographing a Paul Revere character riding a horse in front of a taxiing 747 while holding a huge banner announcing the service.
- One of our clients (a gas company) made the front page of the local newspaper when we dressed up two actors as a new baby and Father Time and had them lighting a giant 15 ft tall gas torch like an Olympic flame (it was an Olympic year), just before New Year's.
- For the introduction of a version of Microsoft's Flight Simulator computer program near Christmas one year, we provided about a dozen Santa

Clauses all playing the game at a bank of computers, an advertising gimmick that successfully drew a lot of attention and garnered press coverage.

- A new dollar coin was introduced using an 18 ft diameter flying helium 'space ship' inside a convention center ballroom that made a surprise entry flying over the heads of assembled guests and dropping a giant replica of the coin onstage to a VIP speaker who proceeded to make a speech about the occasion.

1.1.2.7   Creating Ambience

Particularly in theme events, establishing the right ambience for the event is one of the first considerations producers have. The ambience can be so much more than static décor or lighting, even if the lighting is automated. Adding other sensory input in the form of live entertainment helps to set a 'living' mood. This can be done for any number of reasons, such as providing an atmosphere for easy discussion, for conducting business, or for relaxing. The proper choice of music can accomplish this with perhaps a jazz trio that enables unstrained conversation. As a side note, the importance of establishing and maintaining this relatively 'quiet' ambience should not be passed over lightly. At far too many special events, the background noise level is excessively high, caused by poor room acoustics but exacerbated by music that is supposed to be background but is too loud. Producers tend to believe that volume equates to having a good time which in turn equates to a successful event and they could not be farther from the truth. In the majority of corporate events, guests attend because they want to dialog with long-lost colleagues, and in many such events, to consummate business deals. This cannot be done if talking is uncomfortable.

At the other extreme, atmosphere can be high energy. For example, a group of 'paparazzi' greeting guests at the event entrance sets a lively ambience. One prime example from my own experience was adding to a beach party ambience by having a surf band enter the party in an authentic 'Woodie' car complete with honking horn, surfboards, and girls in bikinis.

1.1.2.8   Rewarding Performance and for Image Purposes

Frequently, producers are called upon by clients to 'just give me something really good.' This would seem to yield the conclusion that not all entertainment needs to have a deep reason. Realistically, there usually is one if the event manager or client is asked the right questions. For example, an incentive client may make just that statement, although the real reason for the entertainment is as a 'reward' for top sales people (i.e. meaning motivational content). Likewise, a client may not state a reason but in reality wants to impress his or her clients by providing great entertainment. If budget presents a problem, producers may have to find performers or perhaps a single act, who can deliver an 'all-round package' at a reasonable price. Such performers tend to exhibit three key characteristics. First, they are absolutely perfect at their craft (entertainment form) whether it is music, comedy, dance, athletics, or any combination. Second, they incorporate a component of comedy into their act and make it seem natural and spontaneous, not forced. Typically, though, it has been rehearsed, proven, and refined over the course of time. Third, they incorporate a component of audience participation into their act, again making it seem unrehearsed and spontaneous, and again it will have been proven to work over the course of dozens or hundreds of performances. Such acts, in my experience, regularly receive standing ovations and make producers and clients alike look good.

Celebrity performers can also be ideal as 'rewards' or as image enhancers. Dianne McGarey (2004), a producer with considerable experience in this area states, 'Of all the things I do on a regular basis, celebrity events are my favorites. Over the span of 23 years, I have produced Smoky Robinson, Natalie Cole, Jim Belushi, The Four Tops, The Temptations, The Steve Miller Band, The Doobie Brothers, and Kenny Loggins . . . to name just a few. In almost every case, the client who chose these acts did so for the express purpose of creating a company image. They wanted to impress as well as entertain those in attendance whether they were employees, their own key clients, or potential customers.' For clients with good budgets, this is undeniably the best way to gain prestige.

Once the reasons for entertainment are known as expressed by the client, it is time to turn attention to the chosen performers and allow them to develop the content necessary to achieve the goals set by the client and producer.

1.1.3 Content in Entertainment

Content is the third of the three characteristics (form, reason, content) that define entertainment.

Beeman (1997) states, 'performance is the means – perhaps the principal means – through which people come to understand their world, reinforce their view of it and transform it on both small scale and large scale. It can be employed for conservative and for revolutionary uses. As a conservative force, it reinforces the truth of the world and enacts and verifies social order. As a transformational force, performance behavior has the power to restructure social order through the persuasive power of rhetoric, and through the power of redefinition of both audience and context.' What he is saying is that it is content that drives the success of the performance.

It is in the content of entertainment programs that special events – particularly private corporate events – and the relationship of performer(s) to audience, differ from most other platforms for performers (e.g. concerts, TV). First, in many cases, performances are restricted to short segments for any individual performers or acts, often 15 min or less, necessitating an informed selection of material on the part of the performer(s) that will provide the desired content and will meet the goals of the client. Second, audiences are 'captive' in that they have paid for their attendance at the event, the primary purpose of which may very well **not** be to observe entertainment. Third, they are watching the performances with no prior knowledge of the performers or content and have not had any previous opportunities for evaluation (i.e. they must rely on the skills of the main client or event producer to make informed choices on their behalf). Fourth, audiences have often been subjected – in a positive or negative manner – to lengthy proceedings prior to the entertainment program, including the use of alcohol, which can inhibit their objective appreciation of the perform-ance. Lastly, the performance setting in terms of acoustics, visibility for all audience members, staging, rehearsal opportunities, and timing, is not always as ideal as in other platforms for performers, which can in turn, place undue stress on the performers. It is under these constraints that performers must operate with their advertised and expected skill and aplomb.

Success all boils down to this. The performer must deliver the expected content to an audience that is presumably untrained in the art form, under the constraints explained above. Whether this is achievable will depend on the choice of material and the manner in which it is delivered. It is the pro-ducer's job to act on behalf of the client to ensure that this is done effec-tively. Therefore, it behooves the producer to understand what makes a good or bad performance, to become in essence an 'entertainment critic.' We begin by trying to 'get into the head' of a performer, looking at why one would choose this profession, and then looking at the general ways that per-formers connect with audiences. We finish this section by actually becoming performance critics and analyzing what makes a good performance in the different genres.

1.1.3.1   Why Performers Perform

Loosely interpreting the pioneering work of Turner (1988) and later of Schechner (2002), performance in complex societies is a three-phase process consisting of a rehearsal period (*proto-performance*, from Schechner), a per-formance period, and a cooling-down or post-performance period (*aftermath*, from Schechner). These periods form the core of performers' existences, and although they move occasionally outside the phases, they inhabit them most of the time if performing is their chosen profession. It is a lonely place to be, especially during the rehearsal period, a place where the only feed-back may be a mirror, a director's or choreographer's comments, the playing back of a recorded song, or a spouse's friendly encouragement. Validation comes with group rehearsals and eventually from a real audience. Why, then, would anyone choose such an existence? There are several reasons:

- *To enter flow*: Czikszentmihalyi (1974), and later Turner (1988) are credited with bringing the term *flow* into the lexicon of psychology. Flow refers to 'an interior state which can be described as the merging of action and awareness, the holistic sensation present when we act with total involvement, a state in which action follows action according to an internal logic, with no apparent need for conscious intervention on our part.' Most performers at some point in their careers will experience this. If they are highly trained, it will undoubtedly occur on a regular basis. For the performer, it is a very desirable mental state, somewhat metaphysical and even transcendental. For them, it is a feeling of wanting to remain 'in the moment.' It happens particularly with group performances and only when members are completely 'in synch' and performing together, each sensing what the others are doing as if they were a single, totally blended unit. It does not happen for every performance and it does not necessarily happen for an entire performance. When it does, however, it is magical for the performer.

- *To connect with the audience*: Connecting with an audience is the ultimate validation for their existence that performers seek. It means that first, the audience has indeed 'received the message,' and second, the art form and method of delivery are appreciated. Most of the time, this will be either sensed by or obvious to, the performers (e.g. through the audience's rapt attention or applause/laughter at appropriate times). Of course, negative connection is also possible and if it is obvious to them, performers must make immediate changes to try to re-establish a positive connection.

- *To receive recognition*: What better job satisfaction can there be than the instantaneous gratification obtained by sustained applause or a standing ovation? For performers, this beats the endless pushing of paper in an office, the constant struggle to climb the corporate ladder, and the frustrations of company personality clashes. The occasional accolade letter or annual corporate personnel reviews do not come close to the ecstatic screams of an adoring audience. Why else would the Rolling Stones still be performing after 40 years? They certainly do not need the money!

- *To receive remuneration*: Unfortunately, performers have to live and, unlike the Rolling Stones, most of those who work in special events are not highly paid, contrary to the opinion of some uninformed clients and the general public. While the psychology of performing may be their main reason for choosing this career path, they do need to be compensated for doing it.

1.1.3.2   *Connecting with the Audience*

Beeman's statement about 'performance being the means through which people come to understand and transform their world' can only happen if the performer can connect with the audience. Although performance strategies vary amongst genres and amongst individual performers, there appears to be a more or less universal set of criteria that combine to define the skill set necessary for an effective performance: charisma or stage presence, technical proficiency, and choice and interpretation of material. We will explain these in detail.

1.1.3.2.1 Charisma

Webster's dictionary defines charisma as 'a special charm or allure that inspires fascination or devotion.' Beeman (1997) suggests it is 'the ability to engage and hold the attention of an audience.' In other words, it is *stage presence*. It is not necessarily a gift performers are born with, but more often a skill that must be nurtured and developed. How then, can good stage presence be achieved? Most top performers with charisma use one or more of the following techniques. For simplicity, we will use a single performer for explanations but the same information applies to group performances.

- *Placement*: Being close to the front edge of the stage (*downstage*) brings the performer into a seemingly more intimate relationship with the audience. Likewise, working the entire downstage area including both corners ensures that as much of the audience will be brought into this relationship as possible.
- *Eye contact*: Periodic direct eye contact with audience members is considered very positive and enhances the feeling of intimacy. Again, this should not always be front and center but vary from side to side as well. Done too much, however, eye contact can get distracting, so the 'default' look should be slightly over the heads of the audience.
- *Facial expressions*: This is one of the more difficult skills to master for good stage presence. Basically, the facial expression of a performer should mirror the material that is being performed: sad song = sad expression; upbeat song = smile; and so on. Of course, in comedy this theory falls apart as it is often the incongruity of mixed emotions that wins the laugh. It is, however, even in this situation, necessary to master the correct expression (think the exaggeration of Jim Carrey, the ridiculousness of Red Skelton). Usually the expression of choice is the smile, especially in special events where the audience must almost always leave with a feeling of having had a good time.
- *Costuming*: No matter what the circumstances of the performance, good costuming is essential in helping to establish a 'professional' look. Too often this is the last thing that performers – and producers – think about. Even if the trite, all-black ensemble must be used, it should be made clear to performers that shoes must be polished, dresses and pants must be pressed, and everything must be immaculately clean. Costuming is all about first impressions, just as it is in job interviews, and poor costuming onstage is magnified a hundred-fold thanks to lighting and the fact that the performer is the focus of all attention. If possible, something bright, unusual, or attention grabbing should be used rather than black, within the bounds of good taste dictated by the event. Liberace, Cher, Elton John, Elvis, and many others were and are masters of this aspect of performing.
- *Interaction with other performers*: In some situations that do not include group interaction as a choreographed or rehearsed part of the performance,

onstage performer interaction can signal to the audience that the performers are having a good time and help to transfer that feeling to the audience. Examples might be when two guest singers work spontaneously together or when musical band members interact.

- *Audience participation*: This is one of the most powerful and effective ways to gain audience support and enhance charisma. It is not, however, only a simple matter of asking the audience 'how they are doing.' The more rehearsed and controlled the situation, the more effective it will be. Participation can take place in the audience (i.e. offstage) or it can take place on the stage. By going into the audience, a performer is in the audience's territory and had better be well prepared for anything that may happen. Therefore, for this type of situation, all circumstances should be covered. That means that a set routine should be rehearsed (e.g. exact dialog and participation actions), with escape plans for any eventuality, be it vocal inappropriateness (e.g. audience member swearing at the performer or no reaction at all), or physical abuse (e.g. audience member grabbing or touching the performer inappropriately). Proper technical preparation must be in place as well (e.g. adequate audio and lighting). Just 'winging it' when a peformer is in the audience makes the performance appear amateurish. See Figure 1.4 for an example of a charismatic performer working an audience.

FIGURE 1.4
CHARISMA: MICK JAGGER WORKS AN AUDIENCE

Courtesy: http://www.flickr.com/photo_zoom.gne?id=101664714&size=1

Audience participation onstage brings the audience into the performer's territory and puts the performer more in control of the situation, although removing some of the intimacy of direct contact with a larger portion of the audience. Onstage participation can take several forms: rehearsed, unrehearsed, controlled, and uncontrolled. Once again, the more rehearsed and controlled, generally the better will be the performance. By rehearsed is meant that the routine is tested and perfected over the course of many performances (including all jokes, questions, and dialog) so that the outcome is more or less standard, thus defining what may be considered a controlled situation. This type of routine might include anything from a set of questions and answers between performer and audience members (still in their seats), to an entire onstage performance by a group of audience members (e.g. dance number, hypnotism show, victims of a pickpocket, ventriloquist's dummy). At the other extreme, is the completely unrehearsed and uncontrolled situation. Someone is invited to the stage to sing a song or to be interviewed by the performer. Because the routine has not been rehearsed and never been done before or perhaps tried once successfully (without rehearsal), the performer assumes that it will be successful again. Unfortunately, human nature often turns ordinary people into caricatures once they get on a stage and they suddenly want to take over a microphone or act up to their friends (one of the basic rules of performing is never give the microphone to someone else unless it is rehearsed). This is not a situation that endears a performer to the audience, but rather it makes the performer look even more inexperienced. I once employed a celebrity performer before he became famous who thought it would be a good idea to invite a friendly guest to the stage. The guest was drunk and refused to leave the stage, resulting in our having to find several very burly guests to remove him physically from the stage. It was embarrassing for the performer and undoubtedly became a valuable lesson for him on his road to the top.

1.1.3.2.2   Technical Proficiency

We will deal with this aspect of performing in much more detail in Section 1.1.3.3, when we analyze the different entertainment genres. However, let us look here at some of the universal considerations for technical proficiency. To some extent, technical proficiency is a reflection of the audience's knowledge of the genre. If a violin virtuoso is hired for a corporate dinner, will the audience appreciate the performer's virtuosity because of only the performance or because of the association of the performance with the name of the performer? Will a performance by a Beatles clone band receive a standing ovation only because of the perfect delivery of the material or because of the stage presence of the performers and the fact that everyone in the audience likes Beatles songs? These are difficult questions to answer, and the results are never consistent. Perhaps rather than trying to analyze what makes a technically proficient performance, it is easier to analyze the universal difficulties encountered by performers in striving to achieve proficiency, as postulated by Beeman (1997).

- *Pushing*: This is the obvious effort shown in the interpretation of symbolic materials. This effort can be seen by the audience and can distract them from finding the message of the performance. An example might be the exaggerated facial expression and body movements of a singer trying to interpret a love song, or a jazz musician trying too hard to impress by 'over playing.'
- *Losing concentration*: If the performer is not totally engaged with the task of performing, it can also provide a distraction. Examples here might include the distracting glances of dancers at each other that are not part of a performance, unnecessary dialog between band members, or inappropriate facial expressions as part of the material presented.
- *Underpreparation*: The lack of adequate preparation and rehearsal makes it impossible to present material in a smooth and spontaneous way. This is usually obvious and takes the form of forgotten lines in scripts, incorrect dance moves, wrong notes in music, and such.
- *Overpreparation*: Similarly, too much rehearsal or preparation dehumanizes the performance, and makes it less believable. Many seasoned performers believe that once they stop feeling the butterflies and nervousness before a performance, they will no longer be good at their craft. There is some truth to this in that experienced performers can sometimes appear to be performing 'by rote' and without feeling.

1.1.3.2.3   Choice and Interpretation of Material

How well material for a show is chosen and interpreted will be partly determined by how successfully the producer has conveyed to the performer the goals of the event and the demographics of the audience. At one end of the spectrum, as noted by Beeman (1997), 'the performance may fail due to miscalculation of context, resulting from several causes. The performer may misread the audience, and present something that they already know and will be bored with, or that is so esoteric that they cannot comprehend it. Another possibility is presenting offensive material, or material that is insulting to persons of importance. The performer may also misread the circumstances of the performance and present material that is inappropriate, although the same material might be effective on other occasions (e.g. off-color comedy that works in a club but not in a corporate environment – author).'

At the other extreme, the successful choice and interpretation of material may lead the audience to mutually share the experience of 'flow' that the performer is feeling. This is the ideal situation and it often results in the standing ovation so sought by performers. An audience member might experience this physically as a 'lump in the throat' or a 'shiver down the spine,' both indications that the performance has touched very deep emotions and feelings.

Armed with adequate knowledge of the event and the audience, the performer can make informed decisions on content and interpretation based on several considerations.

- *Relationship of the material to audience demographics*: Demographics of course, refer to age, sex, language, occupation, and special interests. Appealing to only one or two aspects of demographics rather than their totality can mean choosing incorrect material. For example, assuming that anyone over 50 only likes big band era music is an incorrect assumption because that demographic grew up in the rock and roll era. Assuming that because another culture may not be as demonstrative as North Americans they will not like audience participation is incorrect because they enjoy it as much as anyone. It helps in this regard to determine what sort of entertainment has worked for a particular audience in the past so that this can be integrated with knowledge of their demographics.
- *Relationship of the material to the goals and reasons for the event*: Although this may seem obvious, it is not. Often, a client may tell a producer that they only want a great show. It may be necessary to read between the lines of this statement. It may mean that because the event is an incentive for sales persons, there should be some subtle inclusion of the company products in the show. Perhaps it becomes a customization of comedy material, a slight changing of song lyrics or the dedication of a song to the company president, or a small sign, logo, or corporate colors that become part of an act. This simple gesture of going beyond expectations can turn the show into a success, based purely on a knowledgeable interpretation of the event's goals.
- *Universality of material*: If evoking emotions is desired, nothing does it better than using subject matter that has universal appeal. This includes good versus evil, family values, love and honesty, striving to improve, and patriotism. Music or stories with any of these as their main theme will almost always be greeted with positive audience reaction. For example, a performance my company once gave for Canadian troops serving the United Nations in Cambodia climaxed with a series of patriotic songs that turned the audience into a screaming, ecstatic, mass of fans totally at one with the performers.
- *Suitability for the genre*: This essentially means that a performer should exercise caution if choosing material that may cross genres. For example, if a popular song evokes memories of teen love in the audience, will a satirical, comedic form of the same song be successful? Can dance be turned into theater, can dramatic theater be turned into physical comedy, and so on? One of many examples of this is West Side Story, a Broadway musical form of Shakespeare's Romeo and Juliet.
- *External enhancement of the performance*: Any performance can usually be enhanced by technical wizardry. Proper lighting cues (e.g. fading stage lights to black after a routine or performance segment and waiting exactly the right amount of time before fading back up), proper audio

(e.g. using the correct microphones and speaker placement), special effects (e.g. pyrotechnics, confetti cannons, fire), or augmenting the show with dramatic visuals on large screens can add to the effectiveness of the performance. Experienced performers know this and usually have certain audio and lighting requirements for their shows. For those who do not, a producer should consider adding them to a show whenever possible.

- *Interpretation*: Also sometimes considered as the *style* of the performer, this involves many factors and its success is often governed by the audience's personal tastes. Successful interpretation usually means that the audience empathizes with the performer or performance situation. Zillman (2006b) states, 'With regard to the type of presentation, it seems likely that the effective impact on an observer increases with the fidelity of the portrayal of the circumstances that foster emotion in a model.' In other words, the more realistic the performance, the more an audience will empathize and so take on the same emotions as the performer. A life story dramatically told, a piece of music played from the heart with a story that the audience relates to (e.g. teenage angst), a dance with a story line using a protagonist and antagonist, will all bring the audience to more strongly empathize. Timing also plays a role in interpretation. Beeman defines it as 'the ability to display symbolic elements precisely at a time when they will most effectively convey an intended meaning.' This can mean minutely *pushing* (i.e. coming in a fraction of a second early) or *holding back* (i.e. coming in a fraction of a second late) on such things as musical phrasing, dance moves, or dramatic statements, or even the very slightest but subtle change in facial expression. Lastly, freshness and spontaneity or the ability to 'display symbolic materials in novel and unexpected ways' as Beeman says, are additional means by which the audience's attention may be captured. Playing a song in a style not used before (e.g. turning a ballad into an upbeat reggae piece) or creating a musical about the tearing down of the Berlin Wall are two examples of such new approaches.

1.1.3.3   *Analyzing Performance*

Before performers are chosen for special event entertainment, someone must decide which act is 'right' for the particular event (e.g. it matches the reasons and goals of the event, the audience demographics, etc.). This task invariably falls to the event producer who must make an informed decision about the quality and value of the act and their ability to deliver on advertised promises. The key phrase here is 'informed decision.' This means that the producer must understand what makes a good or bad performance and further extrapolate that performance into a successful – perhaps modified – performance for the special event being planned. It has been my experience that although many producers come from entertainment backgrounds, many do not, and as a group, producers are ill-informed and under-educated about what constitutes a good or bad performance in entertainment of all genres. It is hoped that this section will help to ameliorate this situation, albeit even if only in a small way. Now we become critics and analyze performance in detail for the four main genres of entertainment that we postulated in Figure 1.2 have evolved from our early ancestors, namely music, theater, dance, and other athletic performance.

1.1.3.3.1 Music

At the risk of oversimplifying a complex subject, we will attempt to review the most important aspects of musical performance as they pertain to special events. These can loosely be divided into technique, psychology, and presentation.

- *Technique*: Whether vocal or instrumental, good technique is necessary for good performance. Music schools and competitions abound that critique technique, but not too many producers are aware of it. Here is a list of the important evaluation criteria:
  - *Pitch and harmony*: For instrumentalists, this begins with a well-tuned instrument. For vocalists, it refers to their vocal range (typically soprano and alto for females, and tenor, baritone, and bass for males), and whether they can move effortlessly though their range. It further refers to the ability of the musician or vocalist to hit the correct notes within musical phrases without wavering to one side or the other of the target note's pitch. For vocalists, the ability to harmonize or correctly sing different notes of a chord when in a group situation is essential to a smooth-sounding performance. Note that this analysis refers to our western major and minor scales and not to the many other scales with differing intervals that exist in other cultures.
  - *Rhythm and tempo*: This refers to the appropriateness of the rhythmic interpretation of the piece, and how well the musician, group, or vocalist sustains the rhythm through complex passages. For example, if it is a samba, can the group and vocalist keep to the rhythm even when the words to the song get complicated and may not be right on the beat? Tempo refers to the ability of the musicians and vocalists to keep time. In other words, do they speed up or slow down when playing or singing, rather than maintaining constant timing?
  - *Dynamics*: Dynamics means relative loudness. Good technique is reflected in a wide range of dynamics from very soft to very loud, which leads to an improved interpretation of the music.
  - *Tone quality*: By tone is meant the clarity and quality of an instrument's sound or the quality of a voice. Good tone is generally smooth throughout an instrument's or a voice's entire range with no harshness anywhere. For vocalists, this can also be affected by the type of resonance used (i.e. does the voice seem to come from the head, chest, or throat and which is most effective).

- *Practical technique*: For musicians, this refers to manual dexterity and flexibility and how well difficult passages appear to be played. If they are played with ease, then dexterity is good. For vocalists, practical technique also involves proper breath control and diction. For proper breath control, the vocalist uses the abdominal muscles and diaphragm to control breath and push out air from the very bottom of the lungs rather than using the throat muscles and only the top part of the lungs. Proper diction means that the words to a song are clear and easily understandable. If they are not, poor diction is likely the cause (in spite of some vocalists claiming that the audio system is to blame). Jones (2001) has a good review of damaging vocal techniques for those interested.
- *Style*: Style refers to the style of music and how well a musician or vocalist can consistently interpret it. For example, can they give a consistent and non-mechanical rendition of New Orleans jazz, reggae, country and western, baroque, big band, rock, or other styles? Not all professional musicians can effectively interpret all styles of music. More importantly, interpretation in the case of vocalists refers to their sensitivity to the words.

- *Psychology*: It is well known that music profoundly affects human beings on a deep, emotional level. How it does this is studied in the vast field of music psychology. We will be limiting discussion to only a few pertinent concepts that may help in the analysis of musical performance at special events.
  - *Sonic entrainment*: Goldman (2000) explains entrainment as 'an aspect of sound that is closely related to rhythms and the way these rhythms affect us. It is a phenomenon of sound in which the powerful rhythmic vibrations of one object (e.g. a dance band – author) will cause the less powerful vibrations of another object (e.g. an audience member – author) to lock in step and oscillate at the first object's rate.' Furthermore, within our own bodies, 'our heart rate, respiration, and brain waves all entrain to each other.' To make a long story short, it is possible, although not proven conclusively through rigorous scientific research, that playing music at certain frequencies may induce entrainment of an audience's brain waves. In other words, the comment that 'this music is hypnotic' may not be far from the truth. It is also a plausible – but not completely proven – explanation for the popularity of music with a particularly good beat (e.g. raves, continuous dance music, rap, reggae, etc.). Musical performers who understand this concept can construct their programs to take advantage of it (e.g. continuous music with the same rhythm or heavy beat). One very popular example of sonic entrainment at work is a participative drum circle. Figure 1.5 illustrates a motivational and participative drumming presentation that uses the principle of sonic entrainment for success.
  - *Excitation transfer*: As postulated by Zillman (2006a; pp. 215–238), this concept basically translates into the fact that there is residual

FIGURE 1.5
A PARTICIPATIVE DRUMMING PRESENTATION

Courtesy: Drum Café, www.drumcafe.ca

excitation created whenever a realistic portrayal or situation occurs that generates an arousing emotional response in an audience. Although studies have been done mostly for cinematic presentations, it is not unreasonable to make a logical leap to music and theatrical drama or comedy. Some examples that have been found by Zillman are that residual arousal from scenes of distress can facilitate subsequent sexual excitement, and residue from fearful scenes can intensify feelings of sympathy and support. Transferring this to music could lead to residual strong emotions after a powerful song about death which in turn could heighten the effect of a subsequent song that might be about love, or an upbeat rock song. Generally, excitation transfer is best the closer together the two scenes, or supposedly in the case of music, the songs. In other words, the more unarousing the songs that are placed in between the emotionally strong ones, the less will be the residual effect. In summary, it is best to keep music strongly emotional and the stronger are the emotions generated, the closer together the music should be for maximum effect.

- *Tonal sensitivity*: Campbell (2000) uses this term when he states, 'With the introduction of electronic sounds, our tonal sensitivity is evolving. We are learning not to judge new sounds as evil and uncharged.' In the same article, he also makes the point that other cultures such as Chinese, Indian, and Balinese have music that uses quartertones and microtones (i.e. sounds that are not in our 'western' scale and which our 'western ears' are unaccustomed to hearing), and that these have been entering western music for the last few decades. In short, with new cross-cultural music and new electronic music, we had better be aware of these new sounds and learn to adapt to them. Astute musicians are already creating new music with them. Thus, producers should be aware of such new sounds and not be too quick to judge them as inappropriate for events or simply as 'poor musicianship.'

- *Presentation*: Our earlier discussion of charisma did not fully explore the totality of musical presentation, especially in a group situation. For musical groups used in special events, there are other criteria to consider. Here are some pertinent questions:
  - Is the group one that relies on reading music (e.g. a symphony orchestra)? If not, as in the case of a dance band, is the group *off-book*? In other words, have they committed their entire stage presentation musical repertoire to memory? Usually, the best dance bands for special events will have been together long enough to have done this. It makes for a more professional, spontaneous presentation and removes unsightly music stands from the stage. It also enables the group to make sudden changes to their set lists without any problems. In addition, all vocalists must know their material by memory.
  - Is the group capable of moving directly from one song into the next with no pauses in a logical sequence that builds to a climax at the end of their set or program? This is in keeping with our previous discussion about excitation transfer and sonic entrainment.
  - Does the group or musical show successfully set up an inviting and exciting environment around them or in the total event space? An exciting environment means that they themselves, rather than the producer, have considered costumes, staging, backdrops and room décor, audio, specialized lighting, special effects, and choreography.
  - Is the group capable of changing direction in their material based on audience reaction? As a simple example, if nobody is dancing to a band, can they 'switch gears' and play slower or faster music?
  - Do all members of the group 'buy into' the show? In other words, are they all smiling – or frowning – at the same time, do they all project charisma, do they all make coordinated moves, do they know exactly when and where to play for solos or group parts, and are they obviously having fun? If any of these things are absent, they may have to change members, rehearse more, or reconsider their approach to the show.

1.1.3.3.2   Theater

In this section, we are concerned with dramatic acting, comedy, and speaking (e.g. keynote speakers), as well as the effective use of the stage for them. For special events, pure acting and full theatrical presentations are rare, but smaller scripted acting and speaking segments are often worked into a larger variety or musical stage show. Again, because this is such an extensive field, we will only mention the parts most relevant to special events.

- *Theatrical direction*: There are some fundamental elements to watch out for when evaluating the presentation of a play or any staged entertainment. They include:
  - *The use of props*: Clutter in the form of too many props should be avoided and the strategic center stage position should never be occupied by large props. Props should be varied in color, theme, and material in order to avoid monotony. Set pieces should be placed in at least three horizontal planes (e.g. foreground, middle, and background) to create the illusion of depth. Finally, the rules of good design should apply to the overall arrangement of props so that the entire composition is visually pleasing (Bloom, 2001; Pollick, 2002).
  - *Blocking*: Blocking is the choreography of actors' movements throughout a play. It is the job of the play's director to determine where the actors should go, or in the case of special event entertainment, where the performers should go, actors or otherwise. Some key points noted by Bloom (2001) are:
    - the upstage (toward the back) position is always the strongest when two or more actors are working;
    - a downstage actor looking at the audience is also in a strong position;
    - standing is a stronger position than sitting;
    - intimate moments require closeness of the actors and if they are shared moments, they are best done with the actors in profile to the audience;
    - powerful actions require more stage space;
    - movement should be minimized when complex language or difficult concepts are being presented;
    - the eye attaches more importance to the center of the stage and so any movement away from here should be deliberate and express change or it will be purposeless;
    - western audiences read the stage from left to right so entrances and exits should follow that pattern;
    - compositionally, when more than a single actor are onstage, diagonals or any arrangement other than straight lines works best;
    - as a rule of thumb, every audience member should be able to see at least one actor's face at all times.

As mentioned, these guidelines can also apply to any staged presentation of entertainment whether actors, comedians, variety acts, or musical shows.

- *Drama and acting*: There are many schools of acting and even kinds of acting. Schechner (2002; p. 148) for example, has broken acting into five kinds: realistic, Brechtian, codified, trance, and objects (masks, puppets). In our daily lives in North America, we are subjected to a bombardment of realistic acting in movies and television, so that is the type we will concentrate on in this section. Again, we are most concerned with analyzing performances so are interested in what constitutes a good performance. In special events, this will likely manifest itself on a regular basis as keynote speaker presentations. Here are some things to watch for in good actors and presenters:
  - They do not become distracted by the audience or let the audience's body language keep them from staying centered. All their concentration is on playing the part. In other words, they 'own the role' (Stevenson, October 2004).
  - They understand the importance of language and use it to evoke imagery and emotion. The language is in complete congruence with the topic and what is being said. It is first about communicating, not about actual words or their meanings. This understanding includes the use of verbal language (i.e. the words), vocal language (i.e. rhythm, tempo, volume, inflection, attitude, silence), physical language (i.e. physical movement and non-verbal cues), and emotional language (i.e. the actor's feelings and emotions) (Stevenson, June 2005).
  - They know how to use their voice. The most effective speaking pitch range is in the 2000–4000 cycles per second frequency band. Anything lower tends to 'discharge' the listener and detracts from the presentation (Wilson, 2000). The voice must also be clear and easily heard with good breath control (see Section 1.1.3.3.1).
  - They use tempo to illustrate anxiety or tension by speeding up their speaking, and to illustrate shock or confusion by slowing down.
  - They understand how 'silence speaks' by using it after delivering a profound or thought-provoking statement to allow the audience to process the concept and hopefully learn or be transformed. Stevenson (January 2005) makes the following comments when teaching speakers, 'You must determine in advance where in your presentation you are going to say something powerful, profound, or stimulating. After you say it, pause and let it sink in. Let your audience speak. Give them time to talk to themselves. You've just made a powerful or provocative statement. Hopefully you were standing still when you said it. Movement during powerful statements distracts from their power. After you make the statement, stand still for 3 s. Let the words hang in the air. Then, as if to gather your thoughts, turn and walk slowly to the right or left four or five steps. You may keep your eyes on the audience or bring them down into a private rumination. This movement fills another 3–5 s. Keep in mind, you must fill all silences with thought and/or emotion.'

- They are good storytellers. They use 'in and out' (i.e. in and out of first person character) moments of personal stories to illustrate their presentations. The 'in' moments are short bursts of first person acting out of a story. Stevenson (January and June 2005) is a master practitioner of this technique.
- Their presentations are precise and replicable. Although there may be some spontaneity due to changing audiences, their presentations are precisely honed and rehearsed when it comes to delivering the key points. This replicability includes full content, jokes, gestures, tempo, volume, moments of silence, spirit, and emotion. The speech can be given anywhere at anytime and it will remain the same. 'Winging it' and 'ad libbing' are never options (Stevenson, 1999).

- *Comedy*: Before being able to analyze comedy, one has to understand its *structure* and the importance of *delivery*. According to Beeman (2000), the structure of humor involves four stages, 'the *setup*, the *paradox*, the *dénouement*, and the *release*. The setup involves the presentation of the original content material and the first interpretive frame. The paradox involves the creation of the additional frame or frames. The dénouement is the point at which the initial and subsequent frames are shown to coexist, creating tension. The release is the enjoyment registered by the audience in the process of realization and the release resulting therefrom.' Here is a simple joke to illustrate, from Jessel (1980):

  'Two drunks accidentally wandered into an amusement park and boarded a roller coaster. The ride was fast and furious, but it didn't seem to make much of an impression. As they were getting off, one drunk was heard to say, "You know, we may have made good time, but I have a feeling we took the wrong bus".'

In this case, the setup is the first sentence, which establishes a situation. The second sentence is the paradox, which helps to fix a set of assumptions in the minds of the audience (i.e. that the roller coaster ride did not have any effect on them). The third sentence is the dénouement (the *punch line*), and the one that is the surprise, that points out the incongruity of the whole situation. The release is the expected laughter of the audience. By laughing, the tension created by the paradox is released. Generally speaking, setup lines should be short (i.e. no more than one or two short sentences) and punch lines should end with a punch word if at all possible. In the case above, the punch word is 'bus', which is the last word, making this a strong joke.

Of course, part of the structure of comedy is the subject matter, the concept. Typical comedians will spend many hours making notes of life's situations and making lists of funny ideas and phrases which can be further refined through ridiculous combinations. For comedy at special events, subject matter is often extremely important because audiences may be cross-cultural or from specialized occupations. Obviously, different cultures may not understand certain jokes and specialized occupations may prefer tailor-made material. Off-color material is normally not part of special event comedy unless specifically requested. Most good standup comedians will go into their show with jokes loosely based on subject matter. If one set does not work, they may switch to another. The first part of their show is usually devoted to ascertaining how the audience will react to certain jokes based on subject matter.

Delivery is what makes comedy successful. It involves rhythm, tempo, volume, inflection, and timing – besides all of the traits we examined earlier on charisma and stage presence. Similar to the excitation transfer we discussed in music psychology, comedians may try to build on successful jokes by either adding more incongruities and further punch lines to a good joke or by adding more jokes at a faster pace. In doing so, they may incorporate higher or lower volume in their voices, different facial expressions, and body movements. Timing though, is the key to delivery. A short pause before the punch word or line can make the joke. In delivering jokes, comedians may also use different *types* of comedy. According to Stevenson (September 2005), there are 29 disciplines of comedy, including selfdeprecating humor, hyperbole (extravagant exaggeration), the tongue tie, physical comedy, alliteration, plays on words, characterizations, and many more. Most good comedians use several of these disciplines in their acts.

The best judge of any given comedy show is the audience, and as with all of the entertainment genres, watching them rather than the stage, will give the biggest clue as to how successful a comedy show will be.

1.1.3.3.3   Dance

There are numerous sub-genres of dance and we could fill several books trying to analyze all of them. The sub-genre most often encountered in special events is contemporary jazz dance and for the sake of brevity, that is the one on which we will concentrate. Analysis of jazz dance involves an understanding of choreography and technique:

- *Choreography*: Choreography uses the three basic elements of dance: space, time, and energy (Roston, 2000). Space includes both vertical and horizontal planes. In the vertical plane, choreographers will use low level (i.e. on the floor) moves to lower the energy level, medium level (i.e. standing) moves to travel in the horizontal plane and to work in different patterns, and high level to add energy and more spectacular moves such as leaps and lifts (Roston, 2000). All choreographers have different styles and will use space in different ways, but most will vary all three levels for variety and to match the mood or energy level of the music. Cooper (1998) discusses how the changes and shifts in vertical and horizontal planes are like 'moving sculptures,' some of which emphasize the individual line of the dancers through symmetrical and asymmetrical patterns (i.e. different placement of group shapes and sizes in the horizontal plane). She suggests the need for artistic variation in the number of dancers onstage, noting that too many dancers can often look tedious. Obviously, in any group patterns or movements, all dancers must be exactly placed and move precisely together as a single unit.

Time, according to Roston (2000), 'encompasses speed, rhythm, and syncopation of movements. For example, when dancers freeze in a position, they "stop" time.' For variety, some sections can be performed in half-time (twice as slow) or in double-time (twice as fast). Also, *canons* can be used. Roston (2000) explains how. 'A choreographic canon requires dancers to perform an identical phrase at specific intervals – 8, 12, or 16 counts apart, for example. Canons work best when the movement changes levels, remaining at each level for a while.' Generally, the more variety, the more interesting will be the routine.

Energy 'relates to the quality of the movement' (Roston, 2000). For example, leaps and lifts add energy, funky and upbeat jazz or hip-hop demands explosive energy, and rapid movement from upstage to downstage can add energy. Slower music (e.g. ballads, blues) usually requires soft and expansive qualities (Roston, 2000). Again, variety will always be perceived as more interesting. Any routine should have a beginning, middle, and end, and should build toward a climax, while always reflecting the lyrics and energy level of the accompanying music.

Figure 1.6 is a fine example of choreography. Note the different 'layers' in the vertical plane and the appearance of a 'sculpture.'

FIGURE 1.6
EXAMPLE OF CHOREOGRAPHY AT ITS BEST

Courtesy: Barkley Kalpak Associates, www.bka.net

- *Technique*: Diane Buirs, a creative director and choreographer with extensive experience in England and Canada, including several Royal Command performances, offers some enlightening comments on dance technique. She breaks down technique into essentially four components: flexibility, strength, focus, and appearance. Although probably not noticeable by the audience, poorly developed flexibility and low strength can cause a dancer to be unable to make the necessary moves. Lack of flexibility, for example, can result in improper foot placement or limb movement. Low strength can result in an inability to gain the elevation required for good leaps and lifts since leg strength and deep knee bends (*pliés*) control takeoff and landing. Focus is both psychological and physical. Psychologically, a dancer must **want** to leap. In addition, physically in leaping the dancer must lead the leap with an *eye line* that indicates the direction of the leap, by placing the head in a slightly higher position. Likewise, in turns or spins, the dancer must properly *head spot* to maintain balance and proper limb position. Lastly, appearance dictates that costumes, hair, and makeup must be perfect so that there are no distractions to the performance (Diane Buirs, Personal Communication, May 4, 2006).

1.1.3.3.4   Other Athletic Entertainment

This genre includes so much variety that specific analysis is virtually impossible. Some examples of athletic or physical entertainment, besides sports, include stilt walkers, acrobats, trampoline artists, illusionists, clowns, mimes, face and body painting, fire eaters, hypnotists, jugglers, knife throwers, living statues, mascots and costumed walkaround characters, motorcycle and bicycle trick acts, pickpocket artists, puppeteers, rollerbladers, stuntmen, and many others. For most of these, their success is dependent on several key criteria:

- *Originality*: Many of these acts have intense competition in their particular sub-genre. To stand out, they must be very original. Jugglers, for example, cannot just get by with juggling three or four balls; now they have to juggle chain saws, lamps, handkerchiefs, bottles, and other unusual items all at the same time. Illusionists can no longer amaze an audience by using Houdini's trunk illusion; they have to do it with a completely new twist (e.g. escaping from the trunk while underwater or some such idea). Living statues can no longer just stand or sit; they have to incorporate some unique movement or audience interaction into their performance.
- *Costuming*: Outrageous and 'over-the-top' are the new guidelines for costuming in this genre. Flashy, creative, and colorful costuming is becoming normal, and is one of the few ways that performers can stand out from the crowd.
- *Audience interaction*: A lot of these types of acts have managed to 'get by' in previous times by just 'doing their act.' An example might be stilt

walkers who may have been well costumed but really had no other skills with an audience other than walking around looking pretty. Now, it is almost required that most of the acts have good personal interaction with an audience. This is often not only the ability to speak to them in a friendly manner, but also to incorporate other skills such as comedy, balloon sculpting, or magic. Again, an example might be stilt walkers who can also deliver creative comedy routines in their interaction with the audience. Furthermore, acts that can do both roving sets and stage shows are more valuable and stretch a client's entertainment dollar.

- *Skill*: Fortunately, in this genre most audiences have seen so many examples in their lives that formal analysis of skill is not necessary. They know what is good and bad just by their experiences. Acts that do not measure up in terms of advanced skill simply do not get the business. Acrobats have to jump, contort, fly, twist, and maneuver themselves in ever more intricate ways, puppets have to be more outrageous, stuntmen have to perform as if they were in a Jackie Chan movie, bicycle trick acts have to balance on more bikes going faster, and so on. Before any such acts are hired, they should be seen ideally before another audience so the audience's reaction can be observed. Again, watching the audience and not the act is the best way to analyze their capabilities.

1.2   STAGING ENTERTAINMENT

Having defined the entertainment to be used, we now turn our attention to its effective presentation. In Section 1.1.3, we discussed the content of a performance from the standpoint of the performer in isolation. To now use this content effectively in a show, we must consider it in the context of other event parameters, namely the audience, the layout of the event space, the staging available or possible, the scheduling and timing, including length of the performance, technical support, and any required interaction with other acts or performers.

1.2.1   Number of Performers or Acts

Special event entertainment can be simple in presentation, such as a single act that has no requirements for rehearsals or special technical support. There is a fixed show length, a certain start time, and the show proceeds with little fanfare, particularly if the event is being held indoors. For example, a dance troupe might come fully prepared for their performance with costumes and backing music on a CD. They may not even require a rehearsal. Likewise, an outdoor event, such as a festival, may have a series of simple acts between which there is little or no interaction. They arrive, they set up and sound check at the appointed time, and no rehearsals are required. More often than not, however, special event shows involve more than a single act and frequently include scripts, complex rehearsals, technical support, and unique staging. In these cases, considerably more preparation and planning are needed to stage a successful show.

For a show with multiple acts, it is possible to create the illusion of a coordinated presentation through the use of common theatrical elements such as costuming or music. For example, if a show – let's say a 1970s show – is being presented that consists of a comedian, a dance troupe, and a dance band, all scheduled to perform at different times in the event schedule, they can be tied together by common costumes and music from the 1970s. The comedian can be linked by a costume and some reference to the 1970s in his material.

For most other shows with a number of acts, there may be a requirement for a full script, rehearsals with all performers and technical support, and the need to integrate the show into a larger program of speeches and/or awards.

Given all the event parameters (e.g. schedule, location, budget, demographics of audience), at some point during initial event planning, the producer and client will have to decide whether a single act, multiple acts, or a scripted show format works the best in achieving the event's goals and translating the reason for the event into a meaningful entertainment program.

1.2.2 Scheduling and Timing

For stage presentations, in terms of timing there are typically two options: a single continuous show or a show divided into multiple segments.

1.2.2.1 Single Continuous Show Format

A single show, particularly for corporate events, rarely exceeds 50 or 60 min in duration. This is because the audience has often been subjected to prior extended and unrelated event segments, namely reception, dinner, speeches, or award presentations, and lacks the necessary stamina for a longer show. Shows containing overly esoteric material should also be avoided in the interests of keeping the audience's attention. If a single continuous show has multiple acts of short duration, there is a much better chance of success due to the variety presented, in that more of the audience is likely to enjoy at least one of the acts. With a single act, there is a greater possibility of some of the audience not appreciating it.

1.2.2.2 Segmented Show Format

Fortunately, the problem of sustained audience attention can be minimized in several ways. Rather than having a single continuous show after dinner at the end of a long event, dividing up the entire show into short segments performed between meal courses works well. A show of this type can be divided up yet still maintain a storyline providing that there is a simple link or explanation between segments, such as a script with an *MC* (Master of Ceremonies) voiceover that can tie them together. The duration of such segments should be no longer than 5–10 min during which the event space must be completely clear of wait staff and food. This requires close coordination between the producer and catering or banquet manager in order to ensure all tables are cleared from the previous course and the following course is not served until the entertainment segment is complete. The other advantage this method of presentation has is that it permits an extended period for stage changeovers without the audience having to wait. This further enables all presentations to take place from a single stage instead of multiple ones if required. All presentations do not necessarily have to take place between all the courses. The timing is entirely at the discretion of the producer and the client. Perhaps one at the very beginning of the event as guests arrive or as they sit down to dinner followed by only one more after dinner is all that is needed for a varied program.

This method also is an excellent means of injecting interest into a lengthy standup reception event at which guests might otherwise only stay for a short time. Given periodic and unique entertainment segments at 15 or 20 min intervals throughout a reception can add an element of surprise that will make guests want to stay.

A segmented show has another dimension to it when a performance is sustained for a longer period of time. By this is meant a form of entertainment that is not used for a stage show per se, but rather strolls around or is stationary for a long period. Examples include solo musicians or a group of musicians (e.g. a dance band) who are hired either to provide background music during dinner and/or a reception, or to provide continuous dance music, or other performers with sustained performances. Examples here include table acts such as caricaturists, graphologists (handwriting analysts), tattoo artists, and fortunetellers, or strolling physical performers such as sleight-of-hand magicians, jugglers, mimes, stilt walkers, costumed characters, and such. At some point, all these types of performers will need breaks so they should be built into the schedule in such a way that not all are taking breaks at the same time. We will deal more with this aspect in the next section about working with performers.

1.2.2.3 *Show Setup and Sound Checks*

The last but by no means least critical aspect of scheduling and timing, excluding the show content itself, is the time and method of setup, sound checks, and rehearsals for performers. If the show is at all complex and involves several acts that are dependent on each other (e.g. a live musical group backing up dancers, a musical group playing *stings* or musical play ons and offs for awards, a comedian interacting with an MC, or a multimedia show as a component of the entire presentation), then at least one full technical rehearsal with audio, lighting, A-V, and complete performance, should be scheduled. Without one, the show has an increased likelihood of failure and an amateurish appearance. In special events, there is only one chance to get it right and for a complex entertainment show, that one rehearsal is critical.

For shows with unconnected entertainment presentations, a full rehearsal is usually not required; however, full setup and sound checks are still needed. If performances are to take place from a single stage and there are multiple acts sharing the stage during the course of the show, then there is a correct and efficient way to execute the setups and rehearsals for all the groups, and that is to work in 'backward performance order.' This means that the last act scheduled to perform will set up and sound check first, followed by the second to last act, and so on down to the first act which sets up and sound checks last in the production schedule. When the last act has completed setup and sound check, the stage is *spiked* or taped with small 'Xs' that indicate the correct placement location for pieces of equipment (e.g. amplifiers, microphones, monitors) and then their equipment is *struck* (removed) and stored, usually beside the stage on one side in reverse order to their scheduled performance so that their equipment is farther from the stage than the act before them. This same procedure is followed until all acts have completed setup and sound check. The last act to set up and sound check is thus the first act to perform and when their sound check is complete, their equipment remains onstage. When the actual performance time comes, and the first act's performance is over, the equipment is removed, usually to the other side of the stage. The next act's equipment is then set up, the group performs and exits in the same manner, and so on until the final act. In the same way, the performers themselves will enter from one side of the stage and exit from the other in order to avoid confusion. Figure 1.7 illustrates what this coordinated approach to setup and sound check looks like, with locations indicated for pre-show equipment storage after setup and sound check. Note the group numbers refer to the order in which the groups will perform in the program.

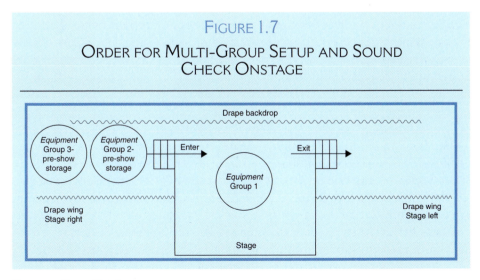

FIGURE 1.7

ORDER FOR MULTI-GROUP SETUP AND SOUND CHECK ONSTAGE

Courtesy: Doug Matthews

The length of time that setups and sound checks take is invariably under-estimated by producers and especially by clients. Here are some considerations for each of the primary genres of entertainment.

- *Theatrical presentations*: For most standup comedians, all that is required is a microphone sound check, as they normally come prepared with their material. This will take about 5 min. An improvisational comedy troupe may require wireless lavalier or wireless headset microphones that will have to be individually tested and equalized which will take somewhat longer, approximately 10 min per person. Other theatrical presentations and speeches such as for keynote or motivational speakers or MCs, may take longer as they typically require a check of their PowerPoint presentations or scripts either with their own laptop computer at a lectern onstage, with another remotely controlled computer, or with a teleprompter. As well, their microphones – which again may be wireless lavalier, wireless headset, wireless handheld, or wired – will have to be equalized and set up as discussed in Chapter 3. This can take up to 30 min or more per speaker if the speaker insists on a full run-through of their presentation.
- *Dance*: Most dance troupes come with their music on CDs or tapes and may require a short rehearsal to the music so they can become accustomed to the event staging. This may be one song or routine rehearsed one or more times, or their entire dance program, depending on: the quality of the stage surface and the ease with which they can maneuver; their ability to adequately hear their music (i.e. how well audio monitors have been placed on or near the stage); and how much their choreography must be changed to match the staging situation (e.g. the ease of their entrances and exits, the distance to the green room, the route to travel undetected by the audience from one side of the stage to the other, usually backstage). Sometimes this can take as little as 5 or 6 min for a single dance routine with an uncomplicated stage setup, to over 60 min for a complex dance program in which the dancers must perform several routines one after the other, complete with costume changes and travel between stage sides backstage, or must enter and exit through the audience. It can become even more complicated if the dancers are performing to live music and/or backing up singers, because then the entire show must be rehearsed onstage. Whenever this type of show is being performed, it is preferable to allow at least 2–3 h for rehearsal.
- *Music*: Whenever live music is part of a show, especially if the musical group is a large one or if they are accompanying other performers, sufficient time must be allowed for setup and sound check. As discussed in Chapter 3, the audio needs of a musical group can be quite complex. In addition to the main audio system, there is also the full monitor system that must be balanced and equalized for all musicians. It is the monitor system that often takes the most time to check as it is critical that each musician be able to hear exactly what he or she must in their individual

monitors, as there is no other way for them to tell if they are playing correctly for the other musicians. As well as the sound check, the preceding setup itself may take a long time due to the need for the musicians to be conveniently positioned onstage for audience visibility and for visual connection with each other. A minimum of 30 min and ideally 60 min should be allowed per musical group for complete setup and sound check.

- *Other athletic and variety performers*: Most other acts will have unique setup and sound check requirements. Hypnotists, jugglers, physical comedians, magicians, acrobats, and such, all must be given time to become accustomed to the stage and the space in which they will be working. Stage magicians, often called illusionists, may need considerable preparation time to construct their illusions and place them in exact positions onstage. Acrobatic and cirque-type performers may need time to check the rigging for their act and to rehearse their act in its entirety. Jugglers and hypnotists may need to try out the stage and ensure there is sufficient space for their act. The list goes on. Usually, an average of 30 min should be allowed for this type of act, longer if it is known to be complicated such as a magic show with large illusions.

With any show, no matter how many acts or how complex, there should also be an opportunity made to review lighting during the rehearsal time, as this enhances any show in terms of establishing a mood and assisting in segues between acts (e.g. fading to black after an act ends). It may also be critical if actors must hit marks onstage within a certain focused light's beam, or if performers will be moving around the audience – or offstage as with aerial acts – and need to be seen with followspots.

1.2.3   Using the Event Space

Considering that an event space is three-dimensional, it makes logical sense to stage as much of the entertainment in as much of the space as possible. After all, the audience occupies a considerable amount of that space, so why should they not all be given equal opportunity to have an optimum view of the show, rather than place it all on a single main stage that only those close enough can see well? Indeed, if space and budget permit, it is preferable to use one or more auxiliary stages for short segments of entertainment. This has several advantages. First, it permits more of the audience to feel 'included,' thus endearing the performers to them, and second, it permits easier main stage changeovers without undue attention so that the show in its entirety becomes more 'seamless.' Just as with stages, so too can doors play into the show. Having performers enter and exit from many doors rather than the same one all the time, allows the audience more opportunities to feel part of the show by being close to the performers. This can be done with any of the stage setups below.

1.2.3.1 *One Main Stage against a Wall*

We begin this discussion by assuming that there is always the option of a single stage against a wall with no other stages. This is still the most common method of presenting entertainment. The advantages include: lower costs for staging, audio, and lighting; one central focal point; lower costs for stage décor; and generally easier coordination of stage presenters and entertainment. However, adding auxiliary stages greatly improves 'performer–audience connection' and adds an exciting and more professional approach to the entire show. Figure 1.8 illustrates some optional locations that may be used in addition to a main stage in a typical hotel or conference center ballroom situation for an event. One or more of these stages can be used in the course of a single show. For example, a large act requiring a lot of stage area can be confined to the main stage while other smaller acts may be interspersed on one or more of the auxiliary stages. This works particularly well in a situation such as an event in which there

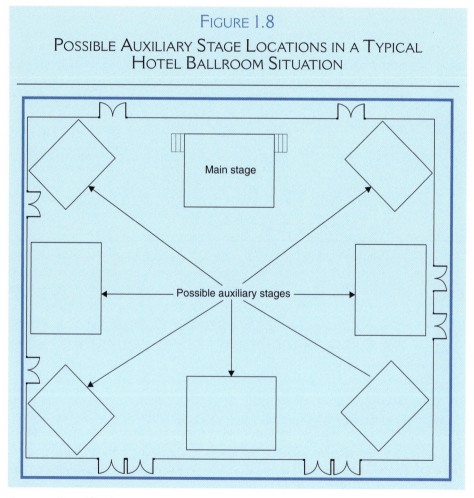

FIGURE 1.8

POSSIBLE AUXILIARY STAGE LOCATIONS IN A TYPICAL HOTEL BALLROOM SITUATION

Courtesy: Doug Matthews

is a dinner followed by a main stage presentation (e.g. speeches, awards, or show) followed by a dance band. It allows for the dance band to set up and prepare silently while the main stage activities are still ongoing, but allows for an instantaneous 'seamless' transition to dancing once the main stage activities are complete. Of course, there must be a dance floor already in place in front of or near the auxiliary band stage. This also brings up a second advantage to using two stages in a main stage/dance band situation, and that is it prevents a large 'gap' between audience and performers if there is only a main stage that must be used for a show preceding a dance. This is a deadly situation for any performer in that it disconnects the audience from the performer and sometimes this 'disconnection' cannot be repaired sufficiently, causing the main stage show to 'bomb.' This setup is especially bad for comedy. Note that in any case where there is more than one main stage, each of the auxiliary stages requires a separate technical setup for audio and lighting, although both systems may be tied into and operated from their respective main consoles and console location.

1.2.3.2   One Main Stage Centrally Positioned

Although a little awkward for technical setup in that lighting and audio must be multi-directional, a centrally located stage can be very impressive for focusing audience attention. Its big advantage is that it puts most of the audience on more of an equal footing than a stage against a wall. Technically, the multi-directionality can best be handled using flown audio and lighting systems or a box trussing system around and over the main stage. The disadvantage of a central stage is that any stage changeovers as part of a continuous show are viewable by the audience unless there is some intervening activity such as a meal course or unless there are auxiliary stages, thereby making the show a little less seamless. Figure 1.9 diagrammatically illustrates a central stage with some possible options for auxiliary stages. Of course, with a central stage, if the event is a sit-down dinner then dining tables have to be placed around the outside of the stage. Interestingly, this situation can also be achieved by having the dining tables and hence the audience on risers around the outside of the space with the central stage replaced by a central floor space as the performing area, although this requires considerable time, effort, and expense for renting and setting up risers of differing heights with safety railings installed. This setup resembles the old Greek amphitheater setting.

1.2.3.3   Floor Space as a Performing Area

Entertainment need not be confined to a stage. Often, for greater visibility and audience interaction, it is preferable to use floor space. This situation arises for performers who find stage work awkward such as large processions with giant puppets and stilt walkers, and costumed characters, marching bands, and certain types of athletic acts (e.g. bicycle stunt riders, roller bladers, gymnasts). For these acts, space can be designed in and amongst

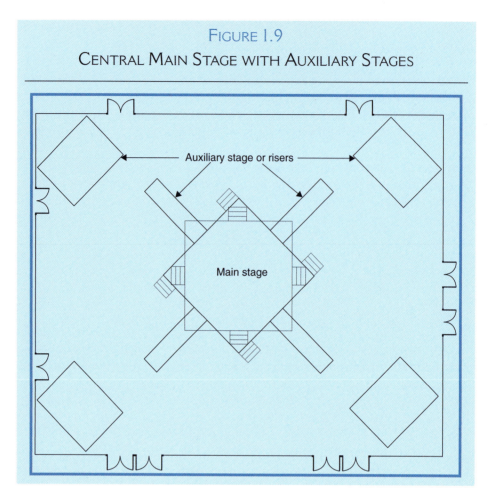

FIGURE 1.9

CENTRAL MAIN STAGE WITH AUXILIARY STAGES

Auxiliary stage or risers

Main stage

Courtesy: Doug Matthews

tables or around the periphery of a room. Of course, this can also be combined with one or more stages for even more variety in presentation. When performers are moving about a larger area however, they require adequate lighting and this usually takes the form of one or more followspots so that they may be lit equally on all sides and the entire audience may seem them clearly. They might also require wireless audio microphones if there is any spoken or sung component to their performance. Figure 1.10 illustrates some possible options for the use of floor space for performing. Almost any combination of floor areas and staging is possible and really a matter of how creative producers wish to be.

1.2.3.4 *Vertical Space as a Performing Area*

Although theater productions have used vertical space for many years, it has only been since Cirque du Soleil-type acts became popular in special events beginning in the late 1990s that performances using the third

FIGURE 1.10

POSSIBLE OPTIONS FOR USING FLOOR SPACE AS A PERFORMING AREA

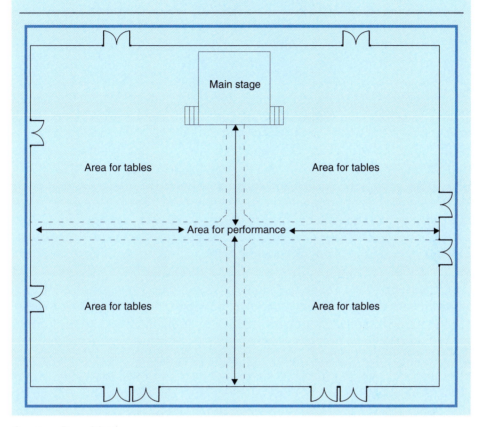

Main stage

Area for tables

Area for tables

Area for performance

Area for tables

Area for tables

Courtesy: Doug Matthews

dimension have become increasingly popular. This has necessitated more emphasis on proper risk assessment and proper rigging. We discuss these topics in detail in Chapter 7 of Special Event Production: The Process and Chapter 9 of this book, respectively. Acts of this genre include aerial silks, bungee, ropes, hoops, and trapeze among others, and all require rigging plus a large safety area beneath the performing location that is clear of people and objects. This may be on the floor or on a stage. The one consideration that always presents a creative challenge is finding a way to place performers in position prior to their act without drawing undue attention from the audience. This can often be done by using a distraction at another stage or with a roving performer to keep audience focus away from the aerial act. As with any roving performers, aerial acts require special lighting consideration. Usually followspots work well for these acts, but at least two may be needed to adequately light all sides unless the act takes place over a stage that is being viewed from only one direction.

1.2.4 Building the Show

Although a show relies on talented performers and exciting acts to be successful, it needs the loving, guiding hand of a masterful choreographer or director to pull them together into a finished product. Lynnette Barkley of event production company, Barkley Kalpak Associates in New York, has staged over 200 musicals and plays as an award-winning choreographer and director. About this process, she advises, 'Piece by piece the materials are pulled together, as scripts, arrangements, designs, floor plans, and costumes are developed. The show is rehearsed, tweaked, massaged, and adjusted to create a theatrical arc. Within that arc, you want balance, flow, pace, build, and surprises. *Balance* – a variety within the music and staging so that it is never monotonous. *Flow* – seamless transitions and segues from one moment to the next. *Pace* – keep it moving, even within a beautiful ballad, there is an underlying energy that must be maintained. *Build* – making sure each moment is enhanced from the moment before it. *Surprises* – never allow the audience to anticipate the next moment – keep their interest with variety and the unexpected' (Barkley, 2004). Let us briefly examine each of these.

It does not matter if the show consists of a single act or multiple acts in a variety format; all these elements can and should be used. As Vancouver-based choreographer Diane Buirs states, 'The audience needs to have a relationship with the performers as soon as possible from the outset of a show' (Diane Buirs, Personal Communication, May 4, 2006). This can be done by having balance in subject matter (e.g. a comedian who can discuss multiple topics), in repeat small appearances by the same performers but in different costumes or roles (e.g. dancers returning with different styles of dances and costumes), in different musical styles (e.g. an a cappella vocal group that varies singing styles among barbershop, Gregorian chant, and R&B), and in working different parts of the stage and the event space (e.g. using the entire stage or different stages, corners of the room, or different entrances).

We discuss flow in Section 1.2.5 in the context of beginnings, endings, and segues (different from the psychological interpretation discussed in Section 1.1.3). The key to flow is not to have any 'pregnant pauses' in a show. As soon as one act or performer finishes, the next is already coming onstage to perform, or indeed becomes part of the preceding act and moves directly into their performance with no abrupt start and end. This can be done by using different parts of a stage for one act and another part for the next act, or by using entirely different stages or parts of the venue. It can also be done by musical transitions. These are often specially written for a live orchestra or band and can involve no more than several bars of modulated key changes that correspond to stage changeovers. It can also be done by using audio effects operated by the audio engineer in the form of pre-recorded sound tracks such as fanfares or short musical interludes. Lighting can help to effect the changes and the flow of the show by changing colors, light levels (e.g. fading to black at the end of a dance number), direction, or focus.

Surprises are what help to keep audience interest and connection with performers. Sometimes, surprises can be very endearing to an audience. A wacky character that only appears for a minute, a wild costume, an entrance from a totally unexpected location, a prop or object that becomes part of the show, a waiter who turns into a performer, are all surprises that are beyond the audience's concept and expectations. Special effects also fall into this category and we will be explaining them in detail in Chapter 6.

Pace and build tend to work together in that they represent the overall energy level of the show. Pace is concerned with timing and the ability of the performers to sustain the audience's attention throughout the show. For example, it can be a 'fast-paced' or 'slow' show. For most special events, the overall pace must generally be fast. There can be short periods when it slows down, but no more than about two in a typical short 45 min show. Fast-paced means not necessarily that all songs have to be up-tempo or that all gags have to be delivered in rapid-fire mode. What it does mean, however, is that changeovers, performance styles, the number of performers onstage, the lighting levels, colors, and amount of automation, all cannot be static for too long but must be efficiently and purposefully changed. Any slowing down is for an audience 'breather' and only serves to bring them back refreshed and ready for even more. Likewise, build refers to being able to consciously relate to and improve upon what went before this point in the show. This is particularly significant toward the end of the show. There cannot be any 'down time' as Diane Buirs cautions, very close to the end, but rather a gradual build in energy level so that the show finishes on a high note that might incorporate all the performers, complete with special effects, all backed up by the strongest song of the show.

As an example to illustrate pace and build, Figure 1.11 depicts a hypothetical plot of the energy levels from 1 to 10 of a typical 45 min corporate event stage show. Let us assume that this show includes a contemporary dance troupe, a comedy variety act, and a small musical group with three lead vocalists that is also used to backup the dancers. The dancers would open the show strongly, backed by the band with what is called a *production number* in which all dancers and perhaps one or two of the vocalists are onstage (minute 0:00 to about 5:30). The singers and band might stay onstage for another one or two songs (minute 5:30 to 10:00). The comedy variety act could then take over, perhaps entering through the audience while the band exits the stage, and they perform for about 20 min (minute 10:00 to 30:00). The band returns with perhaps one vocalist or alternatively a single dancer for a solo routine (this is the 'breather' number for the audience before a final build, minute 30:00 to 33:00). The remaining vocalists then return for perhaps two or three songs (minute 33:00 to 42:00) before the final, high-energy production number with the entire dance troupe, full band, vocalists and perhaps even the variety act if they can be choreographed into the routine (minute 42:00 to 45:00). This would be a show with relatively fast pacing, variety, and a good build to the finale.

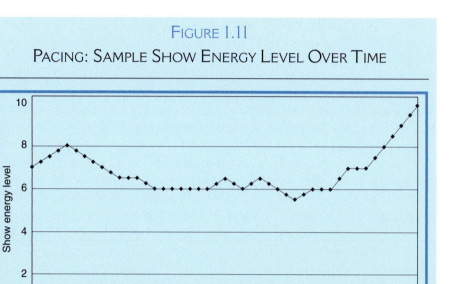

FIGURE 1.11

PACING: SAMPLE SHOW ENERGY LEVEL OVER TIME

Courtesy: Doug Matthews

Being cognizant of how a show should be structured is the first step to success. The second is knowing the right people to make this happen. Although producers may decide to tackle this on their own if they feel they have the talent, it is never a bad idea to seek out exceptional choreographers or directors with theater experience to help the process. Now we will turn our attention to what really makes the difference: beginnings, endings, and segues.

1.2.5 Beginnings, Endings, and Segues

'Visualize this thing you want. See it, feel it, believe in it. Make your mental blueprint and begin' so said Robert Collier, and nothing could be truer when it comes to staging entertainment. A **good** producer will coordinate acts. A **great** producer will coordinate a concept. It takes effort on the beginning, the ending, and the *segues* between acts to coordinate a concept. It is more than simply throwing acts onstage one after the other in the right order. A method of introduction is required to begin, a method of acknowledgment is required to end, and a method to tie all the acts together with segues (smooth transitions) is required to produce a show that exudes professional finesse.

1.2.5.1 *Beginnings*

The question of how to introduce a show or individual acts is always a challenge for any type of entertainment. The beginning of the show is the 'first impression' and sets the tone for what will follow. Let us look at the possible options for beginning a show, whether it is a single act or scripted show comprising many acts.

- *Live introduction*: This comes in two forms: professional or amateur MC, the amateur form often being the client or a client representative. Although it saves money, using an amateur MC, even with the insistence of a client, can be a disastrous way to start a show. Why is this? First, the amateur usually has no formal training and very little public speaking experience, thereby making a demonstrative, expressive, 'showbiz-type' introduction highly unlikely, rather more likely very stilted. Second, there is a good possibility that, because the amateur is not familiar with the act, the introduction will probably be read, making it sound completely unnatural. Third, invariably a name is mispronounced or left out entirely. Professional MCs, on the other hand, will ensure none of these happens because they will check scripting and voice intonation, and will ensure that all names are pronounced correctly.
- *Onstage introduction or voiceover*: Onstage introductions have their place and seem to work well if the MC is familiar with the audience or if the event is not too formal. Otherwise, it can appear to be unnatural and outdated, resembling the old vaudeville days and the stiffness of Ed Sullivan. It may work if there is only a single act and no need to continually keep popping up to the stage to introduce multiple acts. Otherwise, a voiceover or 'God-voice' using the house audio system and a microphone set up at the *front-of-house* (FOH) position (audio control console position) gives a very professional feel to introductions and can allow for proper voice inflection and intonation by a professional MC reading a script. In fact, it is the best form of introduction when a script must be read. It also allows for clean stage changeovers and segues between acts when there are multiple acts, eliminating messy entrances and exits of performers and MC at the same time. For example, it permits the stage to go dark while one act exits and the next act takes the stage, during which time the MC can read the scripted intro at a speed suitable to allow the stage changeover. Thus once the intro is finished, the act is completely ready to begin on the last word of introduction, with no pauses.
- *No introduction at all*: With the advent of more theatrical style shows in special events that incorporate multiple acts and a storyline, a beginning fashioned after the theater can lend a professional feel to the production. House and stage lights can be dimmed, a musical introduction can be employed, and the event can begin with no spoken introduction, thereafter just being allowed to flow one act into the other, with lights and/or music being used for scene or act changeovers. The success of this approach usually depends on the strength and understandability of the storyline in combination with the strength of the overall presentation of the acts and how well they relate to the storyline and reason for holding

the event. If there is no obvious connection or if the connection is too esoteric, there is a chance that the point of the show will be lost on an audience with other distractions (e.g. alcohol, conversation), so the totality of the show should be considered before deciding that no spoken introductions are required.

1.2.5.2 Endings

The ending is what leaves a 'lasting impression' and will be the strongest memory the audience carries away. Much like the beginning, it cannot be simply allowed to happen on its own with no forethought. Whether the show is a single act or multiple acts, there must be an acknowledgment of them, ideally as a voiceover or an onstage acknowledgment. This is the opportunity to bring all the performers back onstage in a professionally choreographed ending with proper rehearsed bows. It is worth taking the time to gather all acts together at the sound check and have a short rehearsal of this ending so it appears rehearsed and planned. The audience will always appreciate that a little extra effort above and beyond the call of duty has been given to the show. If it is too awkward to acknowledge each individual act after they complete their portion of the show, then this final bow is that opportunity.

What about encores? They present a unique and unpredictable case in that every show is different. It is usually the producer's call whether an act or acts return to the stage for an encore performance. This can depend on several factors. The most important one is obviously audience reaction. An extended standing ovation is the best thanks that any performers can be given and usually means an automatic encore if they have the material. At least one strong song or routine should be kept at the ready for this. However, if applause is sustained but there is no standing ovation, the decision is a little harder. I used to watch for signs such as shouts of 'More!' or rhythmic clapping before I would bring an act back. Another factor is show length and how long the show – and the event (e.g. dinner, speeches, awards, etc.) – have already lasted. If it has been a marathon of 4–6 hours, it may not be worth extending the show, no matter how good it has been. It is best to 'leave them wanting more.' How long should an encore be? Not long is the best answer. If it is for a musical act ideally one song, with two at most if the show has been fairly short (e.g. 30–45 minutes). Anything longer has a negative effect on the audience and they sense they are being 'milked' or forced to enjoy against their will.

1.2.5.3 Segues

Segues or transitions between acts are what 'glue' the show together. As producers like to say, they are what make the show 'seamless.' They depend on a number of factors, including where the stage(s) and performance spaces are located, where doors are located for entrances and exits, where the green rooms are located, what lighting is available, whether there will be act introductions (e.g. onstage or voiceover), and what other event programming may be before or after the act (e.g. another act and what type it is, speeches, meal course, awards, auction, and such). Sometimes, exact segues cannot be finalized until the entire event setup is complete and the producer has a chance to check where and how acts will get to and from the stage(s). Here are some possibilities for segues.

- Verbal introductions and acknowledgments by a live onstage MC or by a voiceover. As explained, a live onstage MC tends to make for a disjointed show due to the need for him or her to continually take to the stage for short periods. It also means that any exits or entrances by performers are seen by the audience and, if they are not clean, will give the show an amateurish appearance. A voiceover allows for lighting to be used to hide stage transitions so they can be done in the dark. In the end, it depends on personal preference. It may also depend on whether the live MC is a celebrity, in which case it makes sense to have that person seen as much as possible, or if the MC is a comedian who can continue with an act as part of the transition.

- *Changing audience focus*: This requires that the producer employ a method to distract the audience while acts are in transition. It often is used when there are not going to be any verbal introductions. If there is only one stage used for performances, it may mean that acts enter the event from a door at the farthest end of the venue and make their way up to the stage through the audience, either interacting with them (the audience) or performing in some way as they move, thus allowing sufficient time for the previous act to exit cleanly and unseen from the main stage. It may also mean changing focus to an auxiliary stage or performance area (e.g. a section of floor or an aerial act suspended from the ceiling) if there is more than one stage so that the main stage may be changed over.

- *Interaction of acts*: This is the most theatrical of any method of transition. It means that either the producer or the acts in the show must devise a short, scripted interplay that will in itself become the transition between them. For example, a comedy act might call on a dancer to join them onstage for some simple banter which in turn leads to the start of a dance routine that enables the comedy act to exit. A band playing an opening overture might be stopped midstream by a comedy musical performer who then joins the band and begins his act accompanied by them. There are endless possibilities, with the only requirement being the willingness of the acts to cooperate and take the time to rehearse together. Of course, this often necessitates extra remuneration to them.

Beginnings, endings, and segues are all a matter of timing, of knowing the exact second when to begin to act or play, and the exact second when to stop. It means that as the applause is just starting to die out for the previous act, the next act begins (or is introduced), not after the applause is over and not too soon **during** it, but just at the moment that 'feels right.' It follows from this statement that for great segues, all performers must know where to be and when to be there so that there is no last minute panic before taking the stage. This is covered in more detail in Chapter 8 of Special Event Production: The Process.

1.3   WORKING WITH PERFORMERS

It is amazing how many clients I have encountered in my career who treat performers like lower class hired help. They wonder why they are so expensive (e.g. 'Why is so-and-so charging $1000 for 30 min? I'm in the wrong profession.'), they wonder why they need 2 h to set up and sound check (e.g. 'It's only a dance band with some singers. Why all the fuss?'), they wonder why they need coffee and sandwiches and a comfortable changing room (e.g. 'That is going to cost $300 extra and it is not in my budget. You will have to cover it.'), and then they wonder why the show was not very good! I am hoping that producers and their clients of the future will read this section and reconsider this way of thinking. The reasons should become obvious as we progress through the section and consider the key points in working with performers from **their** perspective.

1.3.1   Mindset

Mindset – frame of mind – zone – headspace. These terms describe a utopian psychological state inhabited by performers, elite athletes, motivational speakers, and anyone who must be at their absolute peak of ability performing before a live audience. It is a place where their body, mind, and spirit meet in harmony in readiness for the task at hand. Only those who visit can understand how necessary it is to find it in order to give a successful performance.

Different performers have different ways of achieving this state. Some pace, some pray, some joke, some drink coffee, some intently review scripts, some practice, some stretch or do exercises, some just talk, but everyone does it, either consciously or sub-consciously. Indeed, some performers have onstage personalities completely different from their offstage personalities and people are often astonished by this. Really, it is only their inhabitation of a performing mindset that is happening. If the two personalities are extremely different, then performers may need some extra time to get into that performing mindset.

Anthropologist Turner (1988; pp. 54–55) understood what is happening. Any performance, as he noted, involves 'frame, flow, and reflection.' By 'frame' he was referring to 'that often invisible boundary around activity which defines participants, their roles, the "sense" or "meaning" ascribed to those things included within the boundary, and the elements within the environment of the activity,' in other words, for our purposes, an event entertainment show. Performers recognize that the show (or 'frame' according to Turner), is a distinct activity outside the norm of everyday life, and can be treated as such, so that they are free to be who they want or need to be. They can only get to this state by being given time to be on their own away from distractions.

What does this mean for producers? It means that performers, no matter who they are, must be given quiet time before their performance, on their own, to find the right frame of mind. Therefore, it behooves the producer to provide such an environment. This topic is listed at the very top of this section because it is considered the most important aspect of working with performers.

1.3.2   Creature Comforts

Along with the need to provide a welcoming environment is a need to provide creature comforts for performers. This will mean some standard amenities in the form of:

- *Changing rooms*: Also called *green rooms*, these are areas or actual rooms in a venue – or perhaps a tent at an outdoor event – set aside for the use of the performers only. They can take many forms. I have had to put performers in everything from presidential suites to tiny washrooms. Ideally, they should be heated, well lit, and large enough to comfortably contain all the performers. They should also be close to the performing area(s) or stage(s). If possible, washrooms should be close by and not require performers to be seen by the public or the audience when visiting them. Lastly, if there are multiple performing groups, or single groups with both sexes, different rooms should be assigned to each group or to each sex, out of respect. At the very least, if separate rooms are not possible, a single large room can be divided using pipe and drape. Occasionally, some groups such as dance troupes require secondary quick-change or preparation areas close to the stage where they will be performing. This can be a small curtained area behind or beside the stage, which should be well lit and invisible to the audience.
- *Other amenities*: Common sense dictates that if it is a changing room, then performers will need something to hang their clothes on, as well as other amenities to assist them in preparing to go onstage. This means that sufficient chairs, tables, movable clothes racks, coat hangers, mirrors, and electrical outlets for hair dryers, razors, and other appliances will be needed for all the performers.
- *Refreshments*: Although refreshments are not always a necessity, they are especially appreciated if performers must remain onsite at an event for a period of 2 h or more, including their performance time, but are virtually a necessity if this period extends over a meal hour. Although they do not have to eat the same six-course meal that the event guests

will be fed, they will expect and appreciate at minimum a substantial sandwich tray, along with perhaps crudités and cookies, plus a selection of water, soft drinks, juice, and coffee. They should not expect any alcoholic beverages although occasionally one drink may be allowed after their performance as long as they will not be driving and consumption takes place out of sight of the event guests. Food or drinks should never be consumed by performers in front of event guests or by taking food or drinks prepared for the guests, without the very clear and express permission of the client or event producer.

It should be noted that all the amenities listed, particularly refreshments, also apply to technical personnel working onsite at the event (e.g. audio, lighting, A-V technicians, and stage managers) if they will be there over meal hours, which is often more likely to happen for them than for performers. They will also need the changing space as they must change from their work clothes into more formal attire for the event itself and may need to change back to work clothes after the event for the strike.

1.3.3 Unique Preparations and Performance Needs

Inexperienced producers cannot always understand why performers prepare in certain ways. To understand this, one first has to understand that a special event is a temporary and 'shifting' performance situation. It is one that has unusual demands for performers, including: the need to often shorten or rearrange their performance to suit the length of the overall show, sometimes at a moment's notice; the need to wait for extended periods of time, often well past the stated performance start time; and the need to begin their performance immediately when called, having prepared themselves completely notwithstanding any lengthy wait. Because of this, every performance genre has unique needs.

1.3.3.1 Musicians and Vocalists

Musicians and vocalists anywhere in the world have common needs because music is a universal language. As well, many instruments have their own quirks to deal with. Here are some of the common considerations, not including technical needs (e.g. audio and lighting), for musical performers.

- *Vocalists*: Vocalists need to warm up their voices alone and together and can only do this in a room where they and others will not be disturbed. They also need water onstage, normally in individual glasses and without ice in order to keep lubricated and hydrated. Water can be delivered to the stage and placed in an inconspicuous location before the performance begins.
- *Musicians*: Many musicians – and vocalists – belong to the AFM (American Federation of Musicians) or 'union' and must abide by their

regulations, which stipulate maximum play times and minimum fees for contracted types and lengths of performances. For example, technically the union maximum time that a musician or group can play is 90 min before taking a break. This must be borne in mind when the event is planned, especially if a client expects a continuous performance of a dance band or musician playing background music. Most breaks should last no longer than 15–20 min, often depending on the length and energy level of the preceding performance. Typical dance band or background music sets last from 45 to 60 min.

- *Equipment and instruments*: Musicians also require time to perform last-minute tuning of their instruments (guitars, violins, and other stringed instruments are particularly susceptible to going out of tune when the ambient temperature varies even slightly) before taking the stage or beginning their performance. Some instruments require a lot of warming up, such as bagpipes, and pipers or pipe bands will expect an area out of audible range of any guests to warm up, tune, and practice. Acoustic pianos (e.g. uprights, baby grands, or full grands) need to be tuned after extensive moving (slight moving is acceptable without tuning) such as being lifted onto a stage, and this should be done prior to a sound check. It usually takes about 2 h. Musicians, especially symphony musicians, require music stands and lights for these stands, and they do not always bring their own, so this question has to be settled prior to contracting.

1.3.3.2 *Actors, Comedians, and Speakers*

The biggest concern for this group is remembering their lines, so they need a quiet area to reflect and review. Their second concern is getting into character and this also requires a quiet space away from distractions. Occasionally, they may have special props that are used as part of their performance and that must be pre-placed on the stage prior to the performance.

1.3.3.3 *Dancers*

Dancers must have their bodies in perfect working order to perform. Hence, they need a green room or area large enough to warm up with stretching exercises and perhaps to do last-minute run-throughs of their routines. This might be extremely important if their performance space (i.e. stage area) is not as planned or not the size that they were initially told, and they have to make last-minute adjustments to choreography onsite. To the chagrin of choreographers everywhere, this happens far too often in special events due to lack of communications between producers and performers. Dance troupes will often bring CD or tape players to their events to do these run-throughs. Dancers will also need to adjust their routines for entrances and exits and may have to make several unobtrusive visits to the stage area to determine how to do this once all dancers are onsite prior to their performance.

1.3.3.4 Other Athletic and Variety Entertainment

This group encompasses all other variety-type entertainment and their needs run a broad gamut. Some of the more common ones used in special events are jugglers, magicians, hypnotists and mind readers, stilt walkers, acrobatic acts, table acts, fire performers, a variety of cultural performers, and occasionally animal acts. Many of these have props (e.g. jugglers, fire performers, magicians) that may need pre-placing onstage prior to their performance. Some such as fire performers or magicians using flash pots and indoor pyrotechnics (see Chapter 6), need fire extinguishers close by with operators at the ready, as well as a safety zone clearly demarcated. Stilt walkers need assistance negotiating doorways and stairs (some can use them, some cannot, but they should be avoided if possible). Table acts (e.g. caricaturists, masseurs, graphologists, temporary tattoo artists, fortunetellers, cardsharps, and others) normally only need an area with good lighting but may also require their own tables and chairs for guests, plus some water for themselves. Acrobatic acts are similar to dancers in that their bodies are their performing instruments and they must stretch and warm up, often immediately before taking the stage, so a heated space near the stage may be needed (this is important for contortionists especially). In the occasional jurisdictions that permit animal acts at special events, special care, and thorough risk assessments are required, as well as safety enclosures and areas for the animals to heed the call of nature, preferably not inside on a carpet! In my career, some of the funniest and scariest moments have involved animals and they have invariably been the hit of any show, but they also must be treated humanely and with the utmost respect.

Those athletic and variety acts that perform onstage have varying average lengths of shows: 5 to 6 min for acrobatic acts and fire performers; 5–15 min for animal acts; 15–30 min for jugglers; 30–45 min for magicians if using large illusions; up to 60 min for large cultural performances; and 60–90 min for hypnotists. Those that are roving or table acts have average performance durations that are more a function of their physical and mental stamina than anything else: 20–30 min for jugglers or stilt walkers; 30–40 min for sleight-of-hand magicians; and up to 2 h for table acts. For most, a break of 15–20 min is expected after these performances and then they are able to perform another *set* of the same length.

1.3.4 Communications

Regular communication with performers is absolutely necessary for optimum performances. This begins with the first phone call, moves to a contract, and ends with the performance.

1.3.4.1 General

From the very first request to use their services, performers will be expecting to know: the time, date, venue, and address of the performance; duration of the performance(s); type and theme of the event; who or what precedes and follows them in the show or event program; audience size; and audience demographics (ages, genders, nationality, languages, type of business, or organization). Of course, remuneration will also be discussed and tentatively agreed upon. From this information, the performers will be able to adjust and mold their shows to relate to the audience and event parameters. They may also want to know, prior to contracting, what amenities will be provided, including green rooms with their own needs considered as outlined above, costume or attire requirements, where and how load-in will take place, rehearsal and/or sound check details, and whether parking fees will be covered. As outlined by Rutherford-Silvers (2004; pp. 286–288), there may also be a number of other considerations that need to be confirmed such as eating and drinking policies, book-back policies, whether guests are allowed, and such.

1.3.4.2 *Contracting and Follow-up*

We discuss contracting at length in Chapter 6 of *Special Event Production: The Process*, and Sonder (2004; pp. 165–172) goes into some detail about it, as does Rutherford-Silvers (2004; pp. 277–290). Suffice it to say, all the performance details discussed during initial contact and any leading up to the contract, need to be put into the contract with the performer, including such things as overtime performance and remuneration policies, payment schedules, cancellation policies, and such. Along with the contract, a tentative event schedule and show running order, plus a floor plan and stage plot, should be sent to the performer or act so that they have the latest information.

The time between the contract date and performance date can be lengthy, often months. Producers sometimes forget that they need to keep performers informed of changes to a show. Start times, rehearsal and setup times, and show length changes can all affect an individual act's ability to give an optimum performance. Therefore, any changes to the event that impact on the show should be given to all performers whenever they occur, right up to the performance date. A day or two out from the event itself, all performers should be called and all performance details reconfirmed. It is at this time that the load-in information, green room assignments, parking details, meal arrangements, and setup and sound check expectations are provided in their final form.

1.3.4.3 *At the Event*

As we have alluded to throughout this section, performers must be treated with courtesy and respect. Nothing can undermine this more than having them frustrated on arrival at an event site by a locked door and no visible way to enter the event space. They must be given exact directions about how to load-in and enter the venue, or navigate through an outdoor event and fencing. Sometimes this entails getting though security barriers such as doors with pass codes or live security guards. If it is impossible to give them codes to enter a venue, then someone must be assigned to meet them at a specific location on arrival. Otherwise, there is a chance that they will be late for setup, sound check, or rehearsal. Once onsite, they should be escorted to their green room, or if it is not ready, at least to a location where they can temporarily leave valuables and equipment safely.

From the moment they arrive onsite to the time they perform, they must be kept fully informed of what is happening at the event, including any changes to their start time or to the length of their show. As they will undoubtedly be confined to the green room once setup, sound check, and rehearsals are over, this means regular updating of their estimated performance time. I personally like to give approximately 60, 30, 15, 5, and 1 min warnings. At the 15 min mark prior to their performance, they should be moved to their standby location at or near the stage or other performing area, such as an entrance door, to await their cue to enter.

After their performance, they should be personally thanked and paid. If the show was great, they should be told, but if it was not, this is not the time to dwell on the negative. This can be saved for later discussion as they will usually clearly understand what went wrong without being told.

1.3.5   The Special Case: Celebrities

Celebrities draw people to events. However, while they are wonderful as a draw, they can be expensive to accommodate and sometimes come with complex contract riders outlining technical and personal requirements. These last may extend to the type of transportation, accommodations, and meal arrangements that are acceptable, but may go much farther and detail green room requirements, some of which can get into the ridiculous. Often, fulfilling riders costs as much or more than the basic contract. However, most are quite reasonable and result from years of experience and often inadequate treatment at the hands of inexperienced show producers and promoters. Sonder (2004; pp. 183–184) also discusses this topic. Dianne McGarey (2004) of Axtell Productions in Atlanta has spent many wonderful hours and days working with celebrities. She offers the following advice:

- Determine your client's budget up front. You simply must know whether you are buying a Cadillac or a Ford before you start shopping!
- Determine whether a 'meet and greet' is key to the success of the event. If so, you will need to do your homework to see which artists are gracious and eager to accommodate. Much better than to find out the day of the show that they will only meet for 5 min and permit five photographs! (Yes, this has actually happened!)
- Determine the 'type' of act that will best suit your client.
- Obtain a list of available acts in the price range desired. (Remember the cost can easily double or even triple when rider requirements and expenses are added in.)
- Present the list to your client asking them to narrow their choices to the top three in order of preference, so that you can do your homework to

nail down exact bottom line prices (including production at the intended location). I normally do a line item cost analysis for each of the three acts.

- Be sure your client understands that availability is good 'at this writing' since most celebrity acts will not hold dates until a written offer is in their hands! This way, if the client procrastinates and loses their first choice, you cannot be held responsible.

- Be sure that your client understands that once the written offer is made, they are committed! I've had to demand a minimum 50 percent payment on more than one date where the client changed their mind after the written offer was made. In some cases, a full 100 percent payment was made after a decision to 'cancel the order.' When you play with the big boys, there is very little room for mind changing without penalty!

- Be sure that you have access to the venue no later than the morning of the evening event. Better yet, if possible, try to negotiate a setup time the night before. This can give you the 'breathing room' you need in case of technical difficulty the day of the show.

- Be sure to schedule a production meeting the day before your celebrity event with all the key players including hotel or venue contacts, sound and lighting contractors, A-V supplier, decorators, caterers, and ground arrangements personnel. Provide each of them with a contact list so that in case you are not available at a critical time, they can call the person needed to address the problem.

- Stay calm. The day of the screaming, out-of-control producer is past! You will gain much more respect from your client and your co-workers if you work through each challenge without throwing around a lot of attitude. Delegate responsibility from the beginning so that you will not be inundated with trivial questions on event day. Once sound checks are done, you should be able to relax and enjoy the event along with everybody else!

We have spent a lot of time in this chapter discussing entertainment from the performer's perspective, and that has been on purpose, because so many books and articles consider only the entertainment consumer's perspective. In summary then, given that the performers for a special event have been treated well, that they have been fully informed of the reason for the event and the content they must deliver, and that all other preparatory concerns have been satisfied, what can the event producer or manager expect in return? First, because the vast majority of performers follow this calling out of sheer love for their craft, they can be expected to deliver a professional performance filled with emotion and passion. In more practical terms, it should be delivered on time, be of the correct length, and communicate the messages and content discussed and contracted prior to the event. Stage attire and costuming should be of the highest quality, deportment should be respectful at all times before, during and after the show, and language and content should be above reproach. Any performer who is incapable of fulfilling and meeting these minimum expectations should not be seriously considered for future employment in special event entertainment.

1.3.6 Risk and Safety

Most of the risk associated with performers and entertainment in general, assuming that all the technical equipment is correctly used, surrounds their being where they should be at the right time, and performing according to their contract for the length of show promised. Therefore, as discussed throughout this chapter, if contracts are followed and performers treated appropriately, there should normally be no risk involved from their side. From my personal experience, the most risk has been associated with having performers arrive on time and knowing where to go. Even with the best directions and allowing enough time for getting lost, traffic jams, or parking problems, there were still instances when fate intervened and a performer was late. Producers sometimes have to accept that probabilities tell you that this is inevitable. However, having a backup plan such as rearranging the order of performances, or calling an alternate performer, is always a good idea, as is keeping a list of performer contact information at the ready while onsite.

The physical safety of performers and the audience is paramount as well. Ignoring the obvious crowd management problems of large concerts which we deal with to some degree in Chapter 9, there may be potential for harm depending on the performance content. For example, I once became an onstage 'volunteer' for a strong man act and ended up standing on his shoulders thinking to myself, 'I sure hope you have liability insurance, my friend.' Usually, these types of audience participation routines are relatively harmless but just in case, producers should ensure that such an act has a contract holding the producer harmless for any injuries incurred to audience members, that the act carries sufficient CGL insurance, and that the act names the producer as an 'additional insured.' On the other side of the coin, performers may get injured just moving through an audience or venue or by an audience member. These cases are covered by Workers' Compensation and producers should again ensure that all acts and performers are registered for coverage by providing copies of their certificate of registration. Double-checking routes that performers will use in getting to or from a stage or in performing their act is critical, especially with respect to trip hazards and proper lighting.

PRODUCTION CHALLENGES

1. Briefly describe the different forms of entertainment.
2. Name six reasons for entertainment. Give examples of an event that might be organized for each reason.
3. You have a client who would like to motivate and educate his company's sales force, using lots of emotion in a show. Suggest two specific options of content and form of entertainment that would achieve this and explain why and how it could be done.

Continued

---

4. You are to produce an entertainment show for a standup reception for 3000 convention attendees in a large convention center ballroom. The event lasts 3 h and your client would like to keep the attendees there for as long as possible. Plan a show that will be exciting and highly visual and that will keep attention for the full event. Suggest at least three different layouts for stages or performance areas and how the entertainment could be staged for maximum effect.

5. An awards show for which you are the producer will have periodic entertainment segments throughout the event, including performances by a standup comedian, a backup band for the awards program, a three-member female vocal group, and a keynote speaker. Detail the concerns that must be addressed in looking after these performers and suggest ways to take care of them throughout the event, which will last for 5 h (6:00 p.m. to 11:00 p.m.). They will all have had to be at a rehearsal at 4:00 p.m. and will need to stay on the premises from then until the end of the event at 11:00 p.m.

REFERENCES

Barkley, L. (2004). Building a Show from Scratch: From Inspiration to Execution. *Hot Tips for Events that SIZZLE*. Vancouver: Total Event Arrangements and Meeting Network, pp. 7–11.

Beeman, W.O. (1993). The Anthropology of Theater and Spectacle. *Annual Review of Anthropology*, 22, 369–393. Retrieved May 18, 2006, from http://www.brown.edu/Departments/Anthropology/publications/Theater.pdf.

Beeman, W.O. (1997). *Performance Theory in an Anthropology Program*. Retrieved April 25, 2006, from http://www.brown.edu/Departments/Anthropology/publications/PerformanceTheory.htm.

Beeman, W.O. (2000). Humor. In A. Duranti (Ed.), *Linguistic Lexicon for the Millenium. Journal of Linguistic Anthropology*, 9(2). Retrieved May 18, 2006, from http://www.brown.edu/Departments/Anthropology/publications/Humor.htm.

Bloom, M. (2001). *Thinking Like a Director: A Practical Handbook*. New York: Faber and Faber, Inc.

Campbell, D.G. (2000). The Overtones of Health. In D. Campbell (Ed.), *Music: Physician for Times to Come*. Wheaton: The Theosophical Publishing House, pp. 89–94.

Cooper, S. (1998). *Staging Dance*. London: A&C Black Limited.

Czikszentmihalyi, M. (1974). *Beyond Boredom and Anxiety*. San Francisco: Jossey-Bass.

Emotion (2004). *The Columbia Encyclopedia*, Sixth Edition. New York: Columbia University Press. Retrieved April 27, 2006, from Questia database: http://www.questia.com/PMqst?a=o&d=101242680.

Feder, K.L. (1996). *The Past in Perspective: An Introduction to Human Prehistory*. Mountain View: Mayfield Publishing Company, pp. 84–87.

Goldman, J.S. (2000). Sonic Entrainment. In D.Campbell (Ed.), *Music: Physician for Times to Come*. Wheaton: The Theosophical Publishing House, pp. 217–233.

Jessel, G. (1980). *George Jessel's Funniest Jokes*. Toronto: Coles Publishing Company Ltd.

Jones, D.L. (2001). Damaging Vocal Techniques. *The Voice Teacher*. Retrieved May 16, 2006, from http://www.voiceteacher.com/damaging.html.

McGarey, D. (2004). Creative Ways to Reap ROI From Your Entertainment Program! *Hot Tips for Events that SIZZLE*. Vancouver: Total Event Arrangements and Meeting Network, pp. 65–72.

Plutchik, R. (July 2001). The Nature of Emotions. *American Scientist*, 89, 344. Retrieved April 28, 2006, from Questia database: http://www.questia.com/PMqst?a=o&d=5000081731.

Pollick, M. (2002). Basic Stage Blocking Techniques for Play Directors. *Pagewise*. Retrieved November 14, 2005, from http://www.wy.essortment.com/stageblocking_rbua.htm.

Roston, J. (June 2000). So You Want to Choreograph. *Dance Spirit*. Retrieved November 15, 2005, from http://www.dancespirit.com/backissues/may_june00/feature01chorg.shtml.

Rutherford-Silvers, J. (2004). *Professional Event Coordination*. Hoboken: John Wiley & Sons, Inc.

Schechner, R. (2002). *Performance Studies: An Introduction*. London: Routledge.

Sonder, M. (2004). *Event Entertainment and Production*. Hoboken: John Wiley & Sons, Inc.

Stevenson, D. (1999). *Acting Technique*. Colorado Springs: Story Theater International. Retrieved May18, 2006, from www.storytheater.net.

Stevenson, D. (October 2004). The Paradox. *Story Theater Newsletter*, 5(9). Colorado Springs: Story Theater International. Retrieved May18, 2006, from www.storytheater.net.

Stevenson, D. (January 2005). Let the Audience Speak. *Story Theater Newsletter*, 6(1). Colorado Springs: Story Theater International. Retrieved May18, 2006, from www.storytheater.net.

Stevenson, D. (June 2005). The Four Types of Language. *Story Theater Newsletter*, 6(6). Colorado Springs: Story Theater International. Retrieved May18, 2006, from www.storytheater.net.

Stevenson, D. (September 2005). Get More Laughs. *Story Theater Newsletter*, 6(8). Colorado Springs: Story Theater International. Retrieved May18, 2006, from www.storytheater.net.

Tattersall, I. (September 19, 2006). How We Came to Be Human. *Becoming Human: Evolution and the Rise of Intelligence. Scientific American*, Special Edition, pp. 67–73.

Turner, V. (1988). *The Anthropology of Performance*. New York: PAJ Publications.

Wilson, T. (2000). Chant: The Healing Power of Voice and Ear. In D.Campbell (Ed.), *Music: Physician for Times to Come*. Wheaton: The Theosophical Publishing House, pp. 11–28.

Zillman, D. (2006a). Dramaturgy for Emotions From Fictional Narration. In J. Bryant and P. Vorderer (Eds.), *Psychology of Entertainment*. Mahwah: Lawrence Erlbaum Associates, Inc., pp. 215–238.

Zillman, D. (2006b). Empathy: Affective Reactivity to Others' Emotional Experiences. In J. Bryant and P. Vorderer (Eds.), *Psychology of Entertainment*. Mahwah: Lawrence Erlbaum Associates, Inc., pp. 151–181.

DÉCOR

LEARNING OUTCOMES

After reading this chapter, you will be able to:

1. Understand and explain design theory, specifically the elements and principles of design, and how they relate to event décor design in a three-dimensional space.
2. Describe the different categories of décor and how they can be used in a special event.
3. Understand the importance of correctly planning for the setup and strike of décor at an event.

Special events are emotional and sensory experiences. The more an event can appeal to the emotions and the five senses, the more memorable and successful it will be. People attend events to be transported into an environment that is different from their everyday life, whether it is a concert, a championship football game, or a formal dinner. Frequently, these events are held in what would ordinarily be venues that are not conducive to such a fantasy environment unless they are transformed through the magic of well-designed décor. Successful event décor design takes talent and considerable thought to be effective. It has become a specialty in itself and the designer is a key member of the production team, with the producer and designer working together to bring the 'wow factor' of décor into the event.

This 'wow factor' often takes the form of a *theme event*. [   ] pter is intended to provide knowledge of the resources that may b[   ] create such an event without detailing what might go into any sp[   ] me, as several other authors (Malouf, 1999; Goldblatt, 2002; Mon[,   ]5) have given excellent interpretations of the process.

In this chapter, we will review design theory and how good event décor designers use it, we will explore the main categories of décor that designers use for events, and lastly, we will discuss the myriad details that a designer and a producer must consider when integrating a décor setup into the event production schedule. This is not intended to be an exhaustive treatment of this subject, but only enough to acquaint producers with the essentials.

2.1   DESIGN THEORY

Design theory crosses all artistic boundaries. Whether it is interior decorating for a home, planning for a store window display, landscaping, creating a web page, conceiving a stage set for a rock star's world tour, or decorating a special event, similar theory comes into play. Design theory incorporates *elements of design* and *principles of design*.

2.1.1   Elements of Design

These are the raw ingredients of design. They are very general but form the basis of the design in that different functional or visual effects can be achieved by working with them. Although they are sometimes called by other names in different artistic disciplines, we will examine each one and how it relates specifically to event décor. Several excellent web resources explain most of these in detail (Adler, 1998; Lovett, 1999; Skaalid, 1999; Saw, 2001; Arts Connected, 2006).

2.1.1.1   *Space*

Three-dimensional space is the most obvious element of design that one notices when first walking into a large room such as a convention center hall or a hotel ballroom with nothing in it. Space is something we cannot touch but it touches us. It surrounds us and envelops us and any other object in it. Luckily, we are able to 'sculpt' it and change its appearance, and therein lies one of the secrets of good décor design. That cold, cavernous hall can be changed from an empty, echoing void into a warm, intimate dining room and theater. The challenges faced by an event designer, unlike artists in other disciplines, are that this transformation must be temporary, it must be accomplished relatively quickly, and it must make use of all three dimensions in the most effective manner.

Making use of space successfully means being aware of negative and positive space. Positive space is where shapes and forms occur within the three dimensions. Negative space is where they are absent. For the designer, this necessitates striking a balance between the amount of negative and positive space. Novice event designers often mistake three-dimensional décor as being a combination of wall coverings (the two dimensions of height and length or width) and tables, chairs, and centerpieces (the two dimensions of length and width with minimal height). They neglect to extend into the third dimension in both cases, thus leaving too much negative space in one dimension. For example, the vertical plane can be better filled by using very high table centers extending **up** from the tables, or by using ceiling mounted, matching décor pieces extending **down** from the ceiling above the tables. Likewise, extending themed props outward into the room from murals or wall coverings can fill the horizontal plane. In this way, all three dimensions are more effectively utilized.

One key point must be made that is well known by good designers, and that is that in any event space indoors or outdoors (where the vertical dimension is infinity!), people quickly fill the bottom 6 ft of the vertical dimension. That means any décor placed below this level is virtually ineffective and will not be noticed. The general rule-of-thumb is to place all essential décor above eye level (i.e. above approximately 5–6 ft from the floor or ground).

Accomplishing quick three-dimensional event space transformation necessitates the designer being aware of the raw materials available that can be set up easily. Some of the latest décor pieces that enable this to happen will be discussed in the section on types of décor, but include large inflatables, tensile fabric structures, banners, and murals or backdrops.

Having reviewed what can be done with a space, it is also necessary when first analyzing an event space, to be aware of what is **already** there. Three-dimensional architectural or other elements such as columns, obstructive corners, overhanging balconies, unmovable furniture, or practical fixtures (e.g. bars, fixed seats, tables, or open kitchen), might require some sort of workaround, as may doors and windows. The key point here is that the designer wants to avoid any extra costly construction or time-consuming cover-ups of these elements in order to achieve the desired design. Rather, it is better to work **with** them and incorporate them into the design. Likewise, unsuitably patterned or colored wallpaper, carpets, and lighting can clash with a designer's concept and may have to be brought into the design to be successful.

2.1.1.2 *Form*

Form is the basic tangible element of design. It has substance and shape. In two-dimensional disciplines such as painting, forms are made up of combinations of basic rectangles, triangles, and circles. In three-dimensional design, such as event décor design, the forms take on volume and mass, and the combinations of shapes are limitless. Geometric forms such as boxes, cones, balls, tubes, and many others are used to create event décor. By combining the basic geometrical forms in different ways, new free-form or abstract shapes emerge.

With the advent of new materials in recent years, designers have realized that event décor can be revolutionized by incorporating unique design forms that can be erected and taken down easily, inexpensively, and efficiently. Examples include tensile fabric décor, air tubes, and the integration of structural-type forms such as scaffolding or trussing, with fabrics and lighting. These are often used to transform mundane shapes into attention grabbing, colorful sculptures.

In terms of the practical use of forms for events, if they are intended to be functional, forms should be appropriate for their intended use. In terms of the use of forms for pure design, varying shapes adds excitement to the overall design, such as combining new table and stool shapes created with spandex coverings, with other forms (e.g. perhaps air tubes), but still keeping within the event's color scheme and theme in all the forms. We will be exploring color and themes later in this chapter.

2.1.1.3 *Line*

As a design element, line has two meanings. The first and most obvious is that it serves to outline form and separates it from the surrounding space. For example, one might say that an automobile or a dress or a piece of furniture have nice lines, meaning that their shapes, as defined by their outlines, are well designed.

The second meaning of line is an abstract one. It describes the separation between areas of change, when objects are aligned, or when the repetition of objects creates visual movement. The line leads our eye from one point in the overall design to another, and thus helps to unify the design by bringing various objects together. Furthermore, the direction of the abstract line has more subtle, inherent meanings. Horizontal lines suggest calmness, vertical lines suggest a potential for movement, and diagonal lines suggest actual movement, giving vitality to the design.

Figure 2.1 illustrates both these meanings. It first illustrates the clear way in which lines outlining forms separate the forms from their surrounding space. The brightly lit shapes are well defined and separated from the dark background. Secondly, it illustrates how the horizontal line of the objects – actually a compositional diagonal in the photograph – leads the eye along the dark corridor and into the next room.

2.1.1.4 *Texture*

Texture is the surface quality of form. It is always present in three-dimensional space because everything has a surface. The term is often misused to refer only to rough surfaces, but it can mean smooth like the surface of a mirror, coarse and rough like burlap, or variations in between. Actually,

FIGURE 2.1
EXAMPLE OF LINE IN DESIGN

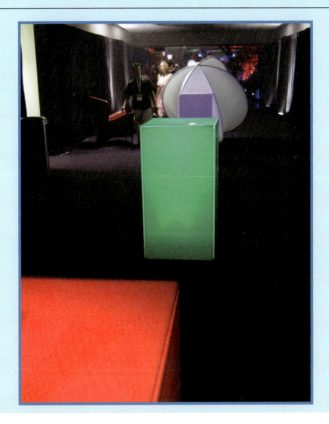

Courtesy: Doug Matthews

texture can be either tactile (i.e. the actual physical feeling of an object's surface) or visual (i.e. the illusion of a surface's texture in two dimensions, exemplified by the angle of light falling on a surface in a photo). In special events, we deal primarily with tactile texture.

Two other terms are related to texture. The first is *ornament*. Ornament is an extension of texture and gives visual interest to the form. For example, an ornament may be a single logo on a plate or cup, it may be the chrome bumpers on an old 1950s car, or it may be the decorative top of a Corinthian column. If ornament is repeated on a surface, it becomes a *pattern*. It should be noted that an ornament is normally physically attached to and part of a surface. The second term associated with texture is *accessory*. An accessory is an addition to a form, and is physically separate from it, although it could appear to be part of it. For example, it may be a napkin ring, a chair tie, or in the case of our 1950s car, simulated leopard skin seat covers.

In designing events with texture in mind, it is considered good practice to vary textures and hard goods, while still keeping within the event color scheme and theme, as with variations in forms. For example, variations in linens and soft goods could encompass mixing crushed velvet table covers with smooth spandex chair covers. Variations in hard goods could mean using a mixture of metal, wood, stone, and plastic, all in the same event.

2.1.1.5   *Value and Light*

Value is considered to be one of the main elements of design, even though it is related to color. It refers to the relative lightness or darkness of a certain area within a space. For an event, this is also related to the amount of light in that certain area. Variations in value (*value contrast*) can be used for emphasis (a *principle* of design) to create a focal point in a room. Depending on the color and texture of a form in an event space, the amount of light thrown on it can also highlight the *color contrast* of the object against its background.

2.1.1.6   *Color*

Color, like space, is all around us. It is unquestionably the most powerful design element for event décor. Because we deal extensively with color theory in Chapter 5 on Lighting, we will focus our attention in this chapter on color meaning and the various color schemes that may be used with décor to create an event environment. In doing so, we will demonstrate how color may be used to dramatize an effect, tie a variety of objects together, create a subtle understated look, or create a mood.

2.1.1.6.1   Color Meaning

To fully understand how important color is in event design, one should have a basic knowledge of how color affects us as human beings. This enters the realm of *design psychology*. It affects our bodies and it affects our minds, but our culture and sex determine how we interpret it. An examination of the meaning of color will assist us in making the correct choices for event color schemes. Here is a review of how we interpret colors, courtesy Color Wheel Pro, which is a software tool that helps one create harmonious color schemes based on color theory (QSX Software Group, 2005):

- *Red*: Red is the color of fire and blood, so it is associated with energy, war, danger, strength, power, determination as well as passion, desire, and love. Red is a very emotionally intense color. It enhances human metabolism, increases respiration rate, and raises blood pressure. It has very high visibility, which is why stop signs, stoplights, and fire equipment are usually painted red. This color is also commonly associated with energy, so it can be used when an event involves games, cars, items related to sports, and high physical activity.
  - Light red represents joy, sexuality, passion, sensitivity, and love.
  - Pink signifies romance, love, and friendship. It denotes feminine qualities and passiveness.

- Dark red is associated with vigor, willpower, rage, anger, leadership, courage, longing, malice, and wrath.
- Brown suggests stability and denotes masculine qualities.
- Reddish-brown is associated with harvest and fall.

- *Orange*: Orange combines the energy of red and the happiness of yellow. It is associated with joy, sunshine, and the tropics. Orange represents enthusiasm, fascination, happiness, creativity, determination, attraction, success, encouragement, and stimulation. To the human eye, orange is a very hot color, so it gives the sensation of heat. Nevertheless, orange is not as aggressive as red. Orange increases oxygen supply to the brain, produces an invigorating effect, and stimulates mental activity. Orange is the color of fall and harvest. Orange has very high visibility, so it can be used to catch attention and highlight the most important elements of design.
  - Dark orange can mean deceit and distrust.
  - Red-orange corresponds to desire, sexual passion, pleasure, domination, aggression, and thirst for action.
  - Gold evokes the feeling of prestige. The meaning of gold is illumination, wisdom, and wealth. Gold often symbolizes high quality.

- *Yellow*: Yellow is the color of sunshine. It is associated with joy, happiness, intellect, and energy. Yellow produces a warming effect, arouses cheerfulness, stimulates mental activity, and generates muscle energy. Yellow is often associated with food. Bright, pure yellow is an attention-getter, which is the reason taxicabs are painted this color. When overused, yellow may have a disturbing effect; it is known that babies cry more in yellow rooms. Yellow is seen before other colors when placed against black; this combination is often used to issue a warning. Yellow can be used to evoke pleasant, cheerful feelings. Yellow is very effective for attracting attention, so it can be used to highlight the most important elements of a design. Light yellow tends to disappear into white, so it usually needs a dark color to highlight it. Shades of yellow are visually unappealing because they lose cheerfulness and become dingy.
  - Dull (dingy) yellow represents caution, decay, sickness, and jealousy.
  - Light yellow is associated with intellect, freshness, and joy.

- *Green*: Green is the color of nature. It symbolizes growth, harmony, freshness, and fertility. Green has strong emotional correspondence with safety. Dark green is also commonly associated with money. Green has great healing power. It is the most restful color for the human eye; it can improve vision. Green suggests stability and endurance. Sometimes green denotes lack of experience; for example, a 'greenhorn' is a novice. Green, as opposed to red, means safety; it is the color of free passage in road traffic. Green can be used in any event that has a component of nature as part of the theme, or with any component that concerns money or wealth, such as the color of gaming tables.
  - Dark green is associated with ambition, greed, and jealousy.
  - Yellow-green can indicate sickness, cowardice, discord, and jealousy.

- Aqua is associated with emotional healing and protection.
- Olive green is the traditional color of peace.

- *Blue*: Blue is the color of the sky and sea. It is often associated with depth and stability. It symbolizes trust, loyalty, wisdom, confidence, intelligence, faith, truth, and heaven. Blue is considered beneficial to the mind and body. It slows human metabolism and produces a calming effect. Blue is strongly associated with tranquility and calmness. It can be used in any event that involves air, sky, water, or sea. As opposed to emotionally warm colors like red, orange, and yellow, blue is linked to consciousness and intellect. Dark blue is associated with depth, expertise, and stability; it is a preferred color for corporate America. When used together with warm colors like yellow or red, blue can create high-impact, vibrant designs; for example, blue-yellow-red is a perfect color scheme for a superhero.
  - Light blue is associated with health, healing, tranquility, understanding, and softness.
  - Dark blue represents knowledge, power, integrity, and seriousness.

- *Purple*: Purple combines the stability of blue and the energy of red. Purple is associated with royalty. It symbolizes power, nobility, luxury, and ambition. It conveys wealth and extravagance. Purple is associated with wisdom, dignity, independence, creativity, mystery, and magic. Purple is a very rare color in nature; some people consider it to be artificial. Light purple is a good choice for a feminine design in events.
  - Light purple evokes romantic and nostalgic feelings.
  - Dark purple evokes gloom and sad feelings. It can cause frustration.

- *White*: White is associated with light, goodness, innocence, purity, and virginity. It is considered to be the color of perfection. White means safety, purity, and cleanliness. As opposed to black, white usually has a positive connotation. White can represent a successful beginning. It can be used for events using high-tech or futuristic themes. White is an appropriate color for charitable organizations and hence, non-profit events; angels are usually imagined wearing white clothes. It can also be used as a neutral color to offset others in an event color scheme. White has a negative connotation in some Asian cultures, as it is associated with death.

- *Black*: Black is associated with power, elegance, formality, death, evil, and mystery. Black is also associated with fear and the unknown (e.g. black holes). It usually has a negative connotation (e.g. blacklist, black humor, Black Death). Black denotes strength and authority; it is considered to be a very formal, elegant, and prestigious color (e.g. black tie, black Mercedes). Black gives the feeling of perspective and depth, but a black background diminishes readability. Black contrasts well with bright colors. Combined with red or orange – other very powerful colors – black gives a very aggressive color scheme for an event.

2.1.1.6.2 Color Schemes

In Chapter 5, we also explore color theory, specifically how colors are mixed in the *visual color wheel* (also called the *lighting or RGB [red, green, and blue] color wheel*). In this chapter, we will examine the *pigment color wheel* (also called the *mixing color wheel*), and how the colors in it can be used alone or in combination to create attractive event color schemes, because most décor is constructed of pigment-based materials.

In traditional color theory, there are three pigment colors (i.e. colors found in paint and fabrics) that cannot be mixed or formed by any combination of other colors. These are red, yellow, and blue, known as primary colors. All other colors are derived from these. Secondary colors are formed by mixing the primary colors, and are green, orange, and purple. Tertiary colors are formed by mixing the secondary colors and are yellow-orange, red-orange, red-purple, blue-purple, blue-green, and yellow-green. All these colors can be represented in a color wheel for pigments, as in Figure 2.2.

As opposed to the **pigment** color wheel, the **visual** color wheel is based on the primary colors red, green, and blue (RGB). The RGB primaries are used for computer monitors, cameras, scanners, and such. The secondary triad of the visual (RGB) wheel is CMY (cyan, magenta, yellow), which is a standard in printing. Also, the human eye contains RGB receptors (QSX Software Group, 2005), hence the name 'visual.' Because of this fact, many artists believe that the visual RGB color wheel should be used instead of the traditional pigment (RYB) wheel to create visual complements, and indeed they are occasionally used in events. However, for purposes of this chapter we will stick to the pigment color wheel.

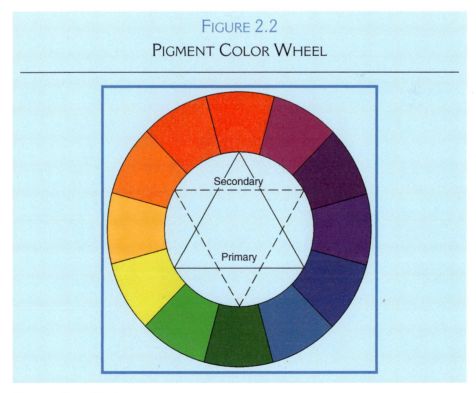

FIGURE 2.2
PIGMENT COLOR WHEEL

Courtesy: Doug Matthews

Given the color wheel and the meaning of color, we can now proceed to develop specific event color schemes. There are six classic color schemes: monochromatic, analogous, complementary, split complementary, triadic, and tetradic (QSX Software Group, 2005).

2.1.1.6.2.1 *Monochromatic color scheme*

In this scheme, one hue is dominant and variations in lightness and darkness of the single hue are used. The scheme looks clean and elegant but lacks contrast. It is relatively easy to manage, and works well with neutrals such as white or black. Figure 2.3 demonstrates a very good monochromatic event that has used black chairs and a black and white stage set to offset the bright red of the tables, centerpieces, and drapes.

2.1.1.6.2.2 *Analogous color scheme*

These are related colors from a pie-shaped section of the color wheel, usually colors adjacent to each other. It is always a good idea to strive for one color to be the dominant one and allow the others to enrich it. This scheme is relatively easy to create but lacks contrast, although it is very rich.

2.1.1.6.2.3 *Complementary color scheme*

This scheme uses colors that are *complementary* or directly opposite each other on the color wheel. It offers the highest contrast of any of the color schemes, but is harder to balance than others. The best results are achieved by placing warm colors against cool ones.

FIGURE 2.3
MONOCHROMATIC COLOR SCHEME

Courtesy: Nat Raider Productions, www.natraider.com

2.1.1.6.2.4 *Split complementary color scheme*

This is a variation of the complementary scheme and uses a single color combined with the colors adjacent to its complementary. It provides high contrast but is harder to balance than the monochromatic or analogous schemes. It is best to choose a single warm color and place it against cool colors.

2.1.1.6.2.5 *Triadic color scheme*

Any three hues equally spaced on the color wheel can form a triadic color scheme. This scheme looks very balanced and offers strong visual contrast and richness. It is best to choose one color to be used in larger amounts than the others and to subdue the use of gaudy colors. Figure 2.4 illustrates such a scheme in a 'Hot! Hot! Hot!' club theme, using the colors CMY in table linens, with black acting as a neutral to offset the others. In this example, yellow would be the most dominant color, as it is in both the linens and the lighting. Note that this example is actually based on the **visual** color wheel's secondary colors so those on the pigment wheel do not correspond perfectly.

2.1.1.6.2.6 *Tetradic color scheme*

This is the richest of all the color schemes. It brings together two pairs of complementary colors. While offering more variety, it also is the hardest scheme to balance and for this reason, it is recommended that one color be chosen as the dominant one and set against the others. This is about as far

FIGURE 2.4

TRIADIC COLOR SCHEME

Courtesy: Current Affairs, www.current-affairs.net

as most event designers will go in working with color schemes, as anything more can easily become an unattractive jumble.

2.1.2 Principles of Design

While the elements of design are the raw ingredients, the principles of design provide flexible guidelines for the effective combination of these elements. Once again, they transcend all artistic disciplines. They include proportion, balance, rhythm, emphasis, and harmony.

2.1.2.1 *Proportion*

Proportion is the relationship between *size* and *scale*. Size is absolute. It is how large-or small-an object (form) is and is a measurable quantity. Scale is relative. It refers to how small-or large-an object seems to be in relation to the space it occupies. For example, for an event in a large room or outdoors, the décor will need to be of very large size because the scale of the event space is very large. If the ceiling is 50 ft (15 m) from the floor, a 4 ft (1.2 m) high banner will be lost (i.e. 'out of proportion') when suspended from it. This vertical height will demand a banner of at least one-third of the total height (16.7 ft or 5 m) to be in good proportion and esthetically pleasing. Likewise, an overly large décor piece in a very small room will be out of proportion because the size of the piece does not match the scale of the event space.

One interesting aspect of proportion that is often not known by designers but that usually comes out naturally in their designs is what is sometimes referred to as the *golden* or *divine proportion*. This refers to a ratio of sizes between two objects that is 1:1.62. It is also known as the number Phi. Although adequate explanations are scarce, it turns out to be the most pleasing ratio of sizes used not only in human designs but also in the natural world. For example, the ratio of a violin's neck to the length of the violin body is 1:1.62. The distance between the edge of some butterflies' wings to the first colored mark compared to the distance to the center of its body is 1:1.62. Good art, photography, interior design, and advertising, among others, all recognize this ratio, although sometimes not overtly. There is no reason why it cannot be applied to the three-dimensional space of an event. Hence, the ideal height for the banner in our example would probably be just over 19 ft (5.7 m) instead of 16.7 ft (5 m), also dependent of course on its width, the readability of its graphics, and the total number and placement of other pieces of décor.

When working with event décor, some other general rules also apply. When in doubt about the exact proportion, oversize almost always impresses. Why? Because having décor larger than the scale demands gives the psychological impression that there is more of it, and it is usually easier to take some away than to add some at the last minute. Secondly, for visual variety, it can be more interesting to mix the scale in patterns if there will be more than one pattern. For example, large patterns in table overlays could be mixed with smaller patterns in chair covers.

2.1.2.2   Balance

Visual balance is related to the size of objects (forms) and also their value, such as lightness or darkness, termed visual weight. One part of a design should appear equally weighted or visually balanced with another. There are three categories of balance.

2.1.2.2.1   Symmetrical Balance

This is usually considered to be mirror image balance, meaning that in two dimensions, both sides of the design are identical. It can also mean that both sides of a design are equal in terms of numbers, colors, and sizes of objects or forms (Skaalid, 1999). In three dimensions, symmetrical design is more difficult to achieve, particularly in an event space where doors, windows, and other features may prevent perfect symmetry. In general, symmetrical balance is more formal and orderly, and 'conveys a sense of tranquility, familiarity, or serious contemplation' (Howard Bear, 2006). Typical symmetrical balance at an event would refer to both sides, or even four quarters, of a venue being decorated with identical numbers and sizes of props in close to similar positions in the space, although the subject matter and material need not be the same. Approximately equal color value would also enhance the symmetry.

2.1.2.2.2   Asymmetrical Balance

This is considered to be informal balance. Each design half is different yet appears to be of equal importance visually. As Skaalid (1999) states, this is achieved when 'several smaller items on one side are balanced by a large item on the other side, or smaller items are placed further away from the center . . . than the larger items. One darker item may need to be balanced by several lighter items. It is usually harder to achieve (than symmetrical balance) because the artist must plan the layout very carefully to ensure that it is balanced.' Sometimes, by intentionally avoiding balance, a designer can 'create tension, express movement, or convey a mood such as anger, excitement, joy, or casual amusement' (Howard Bear, 2006).

2.1.2.2.3   Radial Balance

The third type of balance is radial balance in which all elements radiate out from a center point (although not all designs are exactly circular). 'It is very easy to maintain a focal point in radial balance since all the elements lead your eye toward the center' (Skaalid, 1999). This can work particularly well in stage backdrop designs.

2.1.2.3   Rhythm

Rhythm in design refers to the manner in which one's eye is drawn into the design. Some designs 'move you throughout in a connected, flowing way much like a slow, stately rhythm in music. Others move you from one place to another in an abrupt, dynamic way much like a fast, staccato rhythm in

FIGURE 2.5
EXAMPLE OF RHYTHM IN DESIGN USING REPETITION

Courtesy: Freddie Georges Production Group, www.freddiegeorges.com

music will give you the impression of movement' (Skaalid, 1999). Rhythm is produced through *repetition* and *transition*. 'Repetition is the use of the same element more than once. Transition is the relative change in size from large to small; the gradation in color from light to dark, from dull to bright, and from color to color; and in texture from rough to smooth or coarse to fine' (Adler, 1998). Figure 2.5 illustrates an impressive entrance to an event that demonstrates good rhythm through the use of repetition in neon lighting.

2.1.2.4 *Emphasis*

Emphasis, also known as *dominance*, is all about controlling the attention of a viewer. According to Adler (1998), 'it creates a focal point or center of interest within the design and attracts the eye to a central outstanding feature or idea to which all else is subordinate. One kind of line, shape, direction, texture, or color needs to dominate or the design falls apart.' Emphasis is achieved through *contrast, placement*, or *isolation*.

2.1.2.4.1 Contrast

Contrast can be by color or value (i.e. lightness or darkness). Generally, bright colors of the same hue stand out more than dull colors (value), but different colors that are the same value do not stand out as much from each other. Contrast can also be by shape and texture. A single geometric shape, for example, will stand out against a backdrop of free-form shapes, a vertical line against horizontal lines, and a silver truss grid against a painted wall.

2.1.2.4.2 Placement

Correct placement of décor in the context of a special event is key to creating a focal point. In the three dimensions of a special event, creating one or more focal points becomes a design challenge due to the many options available. Let's look at what can affect the placement of décor to create a focal point:

- *Type of event*: This will be the first determinant in choosing a focal point. For example, if the event is a dinner with only dining tables in a room, multiple focal points could be created as spectacular, 8 ft tall table centers each individually lit from above. If the event is an awards show with a stage, the main focal point will have to be the stage and most effort should go into designing an attractive and practical stage set. If the event is a standup reception with multiple buffets, the decorating effort should go into making the buffets the focal points in order to attract guests to them, best done by designing very tall and well-lit buffet centerpieces. Perhaps it is an interactive event in which there are multiple themed rooms or areas. In this case, it would be best to design entrance décor, perhaps in the form of themed vignettes, to lead guests to that location. Lastly, if it is an outdoor event such as a festival with crowds spread out over a large area, the focal points will necessarily have to be extremely high and well lit in order to act as 'beacons' for people to go to them. These might be tents with large banners on top, stages with huge graphics over speaker wings, an entrance with a tall arch, and so on.
- *Number of attendees*: We have briefly mentioned the necessity of placing décor above the average height of a human being in our initial section on space as a design element. This again is a factor in designing a focal point. Anything that is intended to be a focal point will have to be above this height. One interesting exception is that the floor can be a focal point. This can be done by using certain lighting effects like *gobos* or *automated lights*, on the floor, by using a colored *LED* (*light-emitting diode*) dance floor (see Chapter 5 for more explanation), or by placing actual décor on the floor. Many great designers have used a variety of floor coverings to achieve a certain effect. These have included live rose petals for a romantic setting, sawdust for a western theme, peanuts for a Cuban-themed restaurant or a baseball theme, leaves for an outdoorsy theme, artificial turf for a sports event, sand for a beach theme, and many more. In these cases, the number of attendees becomes irrelevant.
- *Budget*: If money is tight, there are key areas that, if decorated well, will still make a focal point. In approximate order of descending importance, these are:
  - *Stages*: If there is no more at an event than a performance stage – or multiple stages – it can be made a focal point by the simple placement of a drape or curtain behind it to offset the action onstage from the wall or scenery behind.

- *Entrances*: An appealing entrance gives a good first impression and sets the theme for the entire event.
- *Tables*: If the event involves a sit-down meal, attractive dining tables can override all other décor as a focal point. High, well-lit table centers, and well-chosen table linens can draw the eye immediately to them. This also applies to buffet tables.
- *Corners*: If budget allows after the other key areas have been decorated, then we move to corners where décor vignettes can be built out of props or backdrops, then subtly illuminated. These work well for themed events.
- *Walls*: Now the budget gets bigger. Wall coverings in the form of murals, complete draping, or giant projections can form spectacular focal points but are expensive.
- *Ceilings*: Lastly, ceiling draping, hangings (e.g. banners or balloon sculptures) complete coverings, or ceiling lighting can be focal points and complement the other décor, but tend not to 'grab' attention as much as some of the other areas. They also tend to be very costly due to the extra time and labor involved for installation.

Once the focal point has been established by placement, what is noticed next as either part of that same point or the next focal point, is governed by *proximity, similarity*, and *continuance* (Saw, 2001). Proximity refers to the fact that near or overlapping objects will generally be seen next. For example, if the main focal point is a stage set with a large graphic, the panels surrounding the graphic will be seen next. Similarity means that an object that is of the same color, size, and/or shape will be seen after the nearest one. In our stage set, if a frame surrounds the graphic and there are other frames surrounding A-V screens, they will be seen third. Continuance means that if the primary object points or looks at another object, it can direct the viewer's attention. This could be especially important in the design of multimedia shows. In the case of our stage set, if there are two A-V screens with similar frames, the image on one could be used to direct the audience's attention to the second screen, or to any other object on the stage or in the event.

2.1.2.4.3 Isolation

This is fairly obvious as a method of controlling emphasis. Everyone is acquainted with the giant inflatables used for advertising. For example, think of a giant Elvis on top of a used car dealership. This is a very obvious example of how isolation can work to create a focal point. Similarly, for an outdoor event, a stage strategically placed with no other similar stages or décor of comparable size around, will be the focal point.

2.1.2.5 *Harmony*

'Harmony is achieved when different forms and colors have a feeling of *unity*' (Skaalid, 1999). In essence, for an event it is an almost intangible

FIGURE 2.6

EXAMPLE OF HARMONY

Courtesy: Designs by Sean, www.designsbysean.com

sense that the design is complete and that all the elements and principles have been successfully followed. It is pleasing visually and psychologically. Figure 2.6 illustrates an event décor installation that has achieved harmony by applying design elements and principles correctly. Note the symmetry of form placement, the good use of a color scheme, and optimum sizing relative to the event space.

2.2   CATEGORIES OF DÉCOR

A successful event designer not only has to know design theory, but must also be intimately familiar with the ingredients that can be used to put the theory to practical use and build the design. By this we mean the actual décor itself. There are almost endless choices for décor with new inventions added annually. To assist with understanding what they are, we will break these choices down into categories and explain what each one is and how the types of décor within it can be used.

2.2.1   Backdrops

In the special event world, backdrops (also called *murals*) are used for theming. By definition, they are often used as backdrops for stages (where they make excellent focal points) and as decorative murals mounted on or in front of walls. Because of their size, sometimes measuring over 40 ft (12 m) in width and up to the ceiling of a venue in height, they are ideal for creating a total surround, themed environment. Realism is often enhanced by the addition of smaller props to extend out into the third horizontal dimension in front of the backdrop.

Although in the past most backdrops were constructed of canvas and the designs used oil-based paint, today they are constructed of lightweight, 100 percent polyester and the designs are airbrushed on. Bev Pamensky-Murray, President of Dreamworld Backdrops in San Diego, California, notes that in the past, the old painted canvas was subject to drying and cracking whereas today's lightweight polyester cotton material with better paints applied, can be easily folded and transported without any damage. Today's material also receives fire-retardant treatment as standard procedure (Bev Pamensky-Murray, Personal Communication, February 22, 2006). Most backdrops are constructed with a top sleeve and/or fabric ties that allow for easy suspension on pipe and drape hardware (horizontal poles supported by vertical poles), trussing, or any other horizontal support available in a venue. Standard sizes of backdrops range from 10 to 20 ft (3–6 m) in height and 10–40 ft (3–12 m) in width. Some newer themed backdrops are painted onto smaller horizontal sections that can be joined together vertically by means of heavy-duty zippers, to form larger murals, thus providing flexibility for fitting into venues with differing ceiling heights.

Correct lighting is the key to a backdrop having optimum decorative power. Even lighting over the entire surface of the backdrop is recommended to eliminate shadows. Luminaires are best placed well downstage – or in front of – the backdrop surface to avoid any burning of the fabric (Pamensky-Murray, 2006). Figure 2.7 illustrates a Parisian-themed backdrop in use as a main décor component of a themed dinner. Note how it creates a realistic total environment.

2.2.2 Themed Sets

Set pieces for special events generally mean large décor pieces. Sets have traditionally been designed as part of theatrical stage productions. For example, think of any major Broadway play and a spectacular stage set usually comes to mind (e.g. the immense street junk of Cats, the theater of Phantom of the Opera, etc.). It is not much different for special events. Sets tend to be constructed of wood with various adornments such as window frames, signs, mock stairs and doors, or roofs. Although spectacular if used in the right space, these sets can be extremely cumbersome to set up, and nowadays they are often rejected in favor of lightweight fabric décor, backdrops, lighting, and projection technology. There is, however, still a place for them in events such as trade shows and often as spectacular focal points on a stage or room entrance. They also work well if setup time is not at a premium, in a large space with high ceilings, especially if an element of realism is sought.

FIGURE 2.7

EXAMPLE OF PARISIAN-THEMED BACKDROP

Courtesy: Dreamworld Backdrops, www.dreamworldbackdrops.com

Set pieces are usually constructed of thin wooden plywood sheets affixed to a wood frame (together called *flats*), painted realistically on their front surfaces or covered with material, and supported by triangular wooden bracing screwed into the frame, upon which sandbags or other weights are placed to hold them sturdy and upright. They can also be supported by L-shaped steel brackets, especially good for two-sided scenic flats. Part of the difficulty with using sets for special events is that they are large and this can pose problems if venue access is difficult or tight, especially freight elevators and hallways where the pieces must be carried. As with backdrops, realism may be enhanced by the addition of smaller props in and around the larger set.

2.2.3 Props

Prop is a shortened version of the word *property* and derives from theater terminology, wherein *stage properties* constitute the smaller items that are used by actors in a play. This terminology has also crossed into the movie industry as well as special events. In theater, props have traditionally been divided into three categories: set props, hand props, and decorative props.

Set props are considered to be larger movable items not built into a stage set, such as furniture, floor lamps, rugs, stoves, tree stumps, and others (Gillette, 2000). We can categorize these items similarly in special events but include much larger items such as classic columns, cars, wagons, models, machinery, and others. They often are used to embellish large sets as described above. In my personal event career, I have utilized a great variety of unique large props in events, such as large model trains and airplanes, boats of varying sizes, antique cars and hot rods, real race cars, real western buckboards, robots, miniature space ships, jukeboxes and pinball machines, and totem poles. Set props, if used correctly, especially authentic ones like jukeboxes or antique cars, can become good focal points for an event, often acting as a surprise component. They work best when combined with thematically matching large sets as described above (e.g. a western buckboard placed within a false-fronted western street scene), so that the realism of the scene is enhanced. As with backdrops, due to their size and attractiveness, these items demand proper lighting, as well as safekeeping and adequate insurance, since many are on loan or rented from private collectors.

Hand props are smaller items that are literally handled or carried by actors. Decorative props are ones that enhance a setting visually but are not actually handled by actors (Gillette, 2000). In special events, these two categories tend to be lumped together as *small props*. Sometimes they are handled by guests at the event, sometimes they are handled by performers, and sometimes they are pure decoration with nobody touching them. Typical small props are such items as mock ice cream sodas and old signs at a 50s diner, surfboards at a beach party, carved masks at a northwest coast native potlatch, a suit of armor at a medieval feast, a real ice carving as a table center or as a larger sculpture, or an old movie camera at an Academy Awards-type dinner. Small props and set props add a degree of realism to events.

Often, real props cannot be found and replicas must be made or new creations manufactured. Suffice it to say that any and all materials are used, including Styrofoam (e.g. simulating large boulders), foam-cor (simulating many different shapes in lightweight material), wood, metal, Plexiglas, rubber (e.g. knives, swords), and plastic (e.g. those fake ice cream sodas). Designers will either make them themselves or subcontract to have them built as required for a specific event.

2.2.4   Fabrics and Soft Goods

Arguably the category of décor that has revolutionized the appearance of special events more than any other over the last 20 years has been fabrics. Dinner tables with stark white tablecloths and practical but ugly chairs have been replaced by free-form structures with shapely fabric table and chair covers of every imaginable color and design, creating event venues bursting with energy and life. Cavernous convention center halls have now become fantasy environments through the use of giant tensile fabric structures. The choices and uses of different fabrics increase each year. We will examine the main types of fabrics and how they are used for events.

2.2.4.1   Linens and Napery

This sub-category includes tablecloths, table runners, table overlays, table skirting, chair covers, chair sashes or bands, napkins, tray and tray stand covers, and placemats. The options of material, sizes, colors, and patterns available are almost endless, making it easy to coordinate a color scheme or event theme. As an example, some of the materials available in most of these products include polyester, spandex, cotton, damask, crushed velour, satin, lace, burlap, and denim. Prints vary from red and white checks to themes of space, sports, stars and stripes, racing, leopard, jungle, and many more. According to Marion Van Keken-Rietkerk, owner of linen supply company Table Trends in Vancouver, Canada, recent novel additions to linen lines even include appliquéd fabrics with rhinestones and fully customized linens created uniquely for events, such as corporate imprinted linens used to assist in putting across a specific message (Marion Van Keken-Rietkerk, Personal Communication, March 9, 2006). These fabrics are used to cover almost every type of table and chair, including round dining and cocktail tables, rectangular dining or buffet tables, serpentine tables, regular dining chairs, Chivari chairs, fold-up chairs, and stools. Table 2.1 details linen sizes generally required to properly fit the most common table sizes.

For these sizes, note the following:

- Table size refers to table diameter in inches for round tables and the width and length in inches for rectangular tables.
- Cloth size refers to the cloth diameter in inches for round tables and the cloth length and width in inches for rectangular tables.
- Drop point refers to the point below the tabletop where the cloth ends in inches. For rectangular tables the points are the drop below the sides followed by the drop below the ends. The formula to find the drop point is:

$$\text{Drop point in inches} = \frac{\text{Cloth size in inches} - \text{Table size in inches}}{2}$$

- Skirting refers to the total length of skirting required to fully skirt the table (in feet) with one extra foot added for safety. The formula to find the total length is:

$$\text{Length of skirt in feet} = \frac{\text{Table size in inches} \times 3.1416}{12} + 1$$

- Overlay dimensions are in inches and refer to the size of a square overlay (dimension of a single side) that will at minimum fully cover the table surface. For many, two options of sizes are given, separated by a slash.
- No metric conversion has been provided because most linens in North America are still based on tables sizes in Imperial units.

One important consideration when working with linens, especially chair covers is that installation can take much more time than expected, particularly if the covers must be individually fitted, such as spandex covers, and if the chairs also require the addition of sashes or bands. It should be determined at the outset by the designer who will be doing the installation (and strike) of these items, either catering staff or decorating staff, and the

TABLE 2.1
LINEN SIZING CHART

Table Size (in.)	Seating	Cloth Size (in.)	Drop Point (in.)	Skirting Required (ft)	Overlays (in.)
Round					
30	2–4	90	30	8	48/54
36	4	90	27	9.5	48/54
42	4–5	90	24	11	48/54
48	6	72	12	13	54/72
		90	21	13	54/72
		100	26	13	54/72
		108	30	13	54/72
54	6–8	72	9	15	54/72
		90	18	15	54/72
		100	23	15	54/72
		108	27	15	54/72
60	8–10	72	6	16	72/82
		90	15	16	72/82
		100	20	16	72/82
		108	24	16	72/82
		120	30	16	72/82
66	8–10	72	3	18	72/82
		90	12	18	72/82
		100	17	18	72/82
		108	21	18	72/82
		120	27	18	72/82
72	10–12	90	9	19	82
		100	14	19	82
		120	24	19	82
		132	30	19	82
Rectangular					
36 × 36	4	54 × 54	9	13	
		82 × 82	23	13	
48 × 48	4	54 × 54	3	17	
		82 × 82	17	17	
30 × 48	4–6	60 × 96	15 × 24	14	
30 × 72	6–8	60 × 96	15 × 12	18	
		72 × 120	21 × 24	18	
30 × 96	8–10	72 × 120	21 × 12	22	
		72 × 144	21 × 24	22	
		90 × 156	30 × 30	22	

appropriate labor planned. Venues do charge for the installation of linens so costs should be compared.

Van Keken-Rietkerk also notes that care must be taken when handling linens in order to keep them unwrinkled. Normal packing and transportation will necessarily result in fold lines. If these are unsightly, then they are best removed through steaming, especially if they are synthetics made of polyester

FIGURE 2.8

HIGH STOOLS WITH DOUBLE FABRIC BACK COVERS ONLY, COORDINATED TABLE LINENS AND OVERLAYS

Courtesy: Doug Matthews

or nylon, such as lames and organzas. Sometimes, however, steaming is wasted because most of the linen's area ends up being covered by tableware and the only part of chair covers seen are the backs. Linens do wrinkle when held by a hand though, so wait staff in particular need to be made aware.

Figure 2.8 illustrates a typical coordinated combination of patterned table overlay, solid color tablecloth, and solid and patterned chair sash/back cover.

2.2.4.2 *Drapery*

Thanks to an array of sturdy and flexible support hardware, drapery has become commonplace as an attractive and inexpensive means to isolate stage areas and to hide equipment and undesirable sections of a venue. In addition, drapery fabrics are used extensively in decorating entrances, ceilings, walls, and augmenting other décor pieces such as props and backdrops. We will examine the main uses and types of drapes and materials.

2.2.4.2.1 Stage Draping

Event managers frequently neglect to consider what a stage presentation will look like when a stage is placed against a bare wall. Because the stage is relatively low in height, it tends to get lost against the larger area of wall behind it. For this reason, to assist in creating a focal point, placing a simple drape backdrop behind the stage can make a tremendous difference. Besides the need for creating a focal point, sight lines in a venue often necessitate drapery being used to *mask* or hide backstage areas and equipment such as lighting. We will cover stage draping in detail in Chapter 7.

2.2.4.2.2 Room Draping

Drapery is often used to dress up or hide other areas of an event. For example, it may be swagged over entrance doors to give a classy appearance when guests arrive, it may be mounted on pipe and drape hardware to hide changing and technical areas, entrances, exits, and kitchens, or last but not least, suspended from ceiling-mounted piping or trussing to form floor-to-ceiling masking of the entire venue walls. These drapes are often the same velour or commando cloth of stage backdrops, but can also be the more lightweight *banjo cloth*, which is a textured, medium weight, synthetic, inherently flame-resistant fabric available in a wide range of colors, that is typically used for trade shows. A better fabric for highly visible, decorative uses such as entrance swags is *crushed velvet*. Crushed velvet is a medium weight synthetic fabric that is full of texture and bright with luster, and feels luxurious. It is ideal when draperies must 'show' and reflect light. While the overall effect is of a 'heavy' fabric, it is actually quite light in weight and therefore can be used for pipe and drape panels. It comes in a variety of colors. Figure 2.9 shows an entire venue – in this case an armory-masked off using 250 ft (75 m) of burgundy velvet velour swag. This is a good example of how an impressive transformation can be made using drapery.

To complete a theme if budget permits, effective ceiling treatment can be spectacular and swagged draping is often the means to accomplish this. Because of the heights and weights, the material used for ceiling treatment is usually lightweight sheer, voile, or satin made from 100 percent polyester that can be treated for flame resistance. The material is typically suspended from trussing, piping, or wires that have previously been rigged from ceiling hanging points. As a cautionary note, ceiling draping can be very time-consuming and labor-intensive, and also must be accomplished while there are no interfering obstacles such as dining tables or chairs underneath. This means that it must usually be done before any other equipment or décor has been set up for the event, often in the early morning hours.

Draping and fabric décor is used for multiple other purposes in embellishing props, florals, or in isolating areas of a room or a décor vignette. The material, as for ceiling draping, can be sheers, velour, crushed velvet, satin, and silk in any color. It can be used in various ways on tables, risers, people, and other props.

FIGURE 2.9
EXAMPLE OF DRAPERY USED TO MASK A VENUE

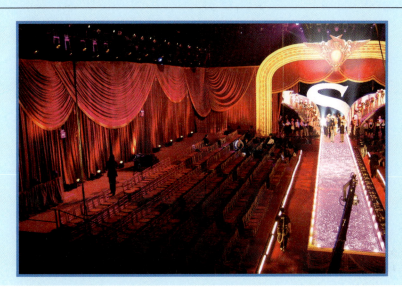

Courtesy: I. Weiss, www.iweiss.com

2.2.4.2.3   Specialized Draping and Soft Material

Besides stage and room drapes made of ordinary material, there are several specialized types of drapes and materials used in events in a drapery format:

- *Cyclorama*: This is usually only used on large stages. Also called a *cyc*, it encircles or partially encloses a scene to form a background. It's most familiar use is as a sky or void backing a setting or elements of scenery placed in the foreground. It provides an excellent surface for lighting and multimedia effects. It is usually made of cotton muslin.
- *Scrim*: A scrim is a commonly used piece of stage curtain magic. Due to the scrim fabric's unique capabilities, when lit correctly from the front, a scrim appears opaque. When the front light is turned off, however, and objects behind the scrim are lit, the fabric appears transparent. It is made of cotton or polyester.
- *Star drop*: This is a black fiber optic curtain with two layers of heavy-duty, fire-retardant cloth (usually commando or velour). Fibers enter the cloth in gathered bundles and then are distributed in individual random or designed order over the entire curtain to give the appearance of a starry night sky.
- *LED backdrop*: Soft-LED (see Chapter 5) backdrops are lightweight and flexible, fabricated much like fiber optic curtains, inherently flame retardant and wrinkle-free. Each Soft LED backdrop contains a grid of LED nodes interlaced with thin, flexible wire cable. Nodes can be compared to

FIGURE 2.10

EXAMPLE OF A SOFT LED BACKDROP

© David Morrell. *Courtesy:* XL Video

computer pixels with regards to image quality. The tighter the spacing of the nodes, the higher the resolution of the image and the closer the viewer can get to the drop without the image 'separating.' Current high-resolution LED backdrops have a node spacing of 4 in. and this spacing is expected to decrease in the future. The advantage of LED backdrops, of course, is that they are essentially a giant fabric computer screen that can be programmed to project anything that can go on the computer, be it a graphic, photo, or video. They are controlled using DMX (digital multiplex) control protocol (see Chapter 5 for an explanation). See Figure 2.10, one of the first large soft LED backdrops used in a concert setting.

- *Mylar curtain*: Sometimes referred to as a *rain curtain*, a Mylar curtain consists of narrow strands of Mylar with finishes that are wet look, metallic, iridescent, fluorescent, neon, or holographic. These curtains are mostly used as stage backdrops to give a very 'glitzy' appearance.
- *Holographic film*: This is an extremely thin, polyester-based film that can be laminated to various substrates such as paperboard, vinyl, or plastic to give a multi-colored, almost three-dimensional appearance. It is effective as a stage backdrop, stage or table skirting, and wall or floor covering.

2.2.5   Banners and Signs

Material and printing technologies are now at the point where gigantic, crystal-clear photo reproductions and graphics can be printed on a variety of durable materials and suspended from large buildings or other structures, both indoors and outdoors, to be viewed from great distances. These are not the old-style painted billboards, but superior quality, easy-to-install signage. These banners and signs have become commonplace in the special event world as décor and signage at trade shows, exhibitions, sporting events, and festivals, not to mention all types of smaller events. We will review the different materials available for signs and banners, the methods of printing, the requirements for graphic artwork, and finally, the methods of suspension.

2.2.5.1 Materials

Materials for signs and banners are varied, with some long-lasting fabrics that are suitable for indoor or outdoor use, and many flexible or rigid options. Note that all materials used for graphic displays need to be tested for fire safety and should come with a fire certificate, especially for fabric prints. The following list is a summary of materials, including the applicable methods of printing on each, the sizes available, the colors available, and whether they can be used indoors or outdoors (AAA Flag & Banner Mfg. Co., 2000).

2.2.5.1.1 Specialty Fabrics
- *Sunbrella*: Durable, high-quality, indoor/outdoor use, multiple colors. Up to 60 in. (151 cm) wide. Can be screen printed.
- *Satin*: Lustrous, elegant, indoor use. Up to 60 in. wide. Screen or digital printing.
- *Polyester*: Matte finish, indoor use. Up to 60 in. wide. Screen or digital printing and appliqué.
- *Canvas*: Heavy material with coarse texture and stiff look, matte finish. Up to 16 ft 4 in. (4.9 m) wide. Screen and digital printing, or hand-painting.
- *Knit polyester*: Cost-effective fabric with glossy, mesh-like finish, indoor/outdoor use. Up to 60 in. wide. Screen or digital printing.

2.2.5.1.2 Flexible Substrates
- *Vinyl*: Economical indoor/outdoor use, smooth finish, multiple colors. Up to 16 ft 4 in. wide. Seaming will create larger sizes. Comes in different weights. Screen or digital printing, appliqué, hand-painting, computer-cut vinyl letters or graphics.
- *Polyethylene*: Cost-effective, indoor/outdoor use, many colors, short-term use. Up to 60 in. wide. Comes in different weights. Screen or computer-cut vinyl printing.
- *Nylon*: Rich look with bold, saturated colors, indoor/outdoor use, many colors. Up to 60 in. wide. Comes in different weights. Screen and digital printing, or hand-painting.
- *Mesh*: Economical, indoor/outdoor use, multiple colors, multiple styles, good for windy areas. Up to 16 ft 4 in. wide. Seaming will create larger sizes. Comes in different weights. Screen or digital printing, hand-painting, computer-cut vinyl letters or graphics.

2.2.5.1.3   Rigid Substrates

- *Sintra*: Durable, indoor/outdoor plastic, many thicknesses and colors. Up to 5 ft × 10 ft (1.5 m × 3 m) sheets. Screen or digital printing, hand-painting, computer-cut vinyl letters or graphics.
- *Styrene*: Cost-effective, indoor/outdoor plastic, white only, different thicknesses. Up to 4 ft × 8 ft (1.2 m × 2.4 m) sheets. Screen or digital printing, hand-painting, computer-cut vinyl letters or graphics.
- *Coroplast*: Lightweight, corrugated plastic, indoor/outdoor use, many thicknesses and colors, good for short-term use. Up to 5 ft × 10 ft sheets. Screen or digital printing, hand-painting, computer-cut vinyl letters or graphics.
- *Gatorboard and Foamcore*: Durable, lightweight paper and foam product, many thicknesses, several colors. Up to 5 ft × 8 ft (1.5 m × 2.4 m) sheets. Screen or digital printing, hand-painting, computer-cut vinyl letters or graphics.
- *Aluminum*: Lightweight, durable sheet metal, variety of thicknesses, can be coated to any color. Up to 5 ft × 10 ft sheets. Screen or digital printing, hand-painting, computer-cut vinyl letters or graphics.
- *Plywood*: Durable wood, indoor/outdoor use, variety of thicknesses, can be coated to any color. Up to 5 ft × 10 ft sheets. Screen or digital printing, hand-painting, computer-cut vinyl letters or graphics.
- *Masonite*: Light, less-durable, cost-effective pressed wood, variety of thicknesses, can be coated to any color. Up to 5 ft × 10 ft sheets. Screen or digital printing, hand-painting, computer-cut vinyl letters or graphics.
- *Showcard*: Coated cardboard paper product, variety of thicknesses and colors. Up to 40 in. ×60 in. (100 cm × 151 cm) sheets. Screen or digital printing, hand-painting, computer-cut vinyl letters or graphics.

2.2.5.2   Printing Methods

Many options exist for getting graphics and photos onto materials. Here is a brief listing and what they can do.

2.2.5.2.1   Digital Printing

Digital printing techniques are generally used for printing short-run graphics, especially banners and signs for special events. The three main processes are regular photo printing, inkjet or ultraviolet (UV) printing, and dye sublimation or fabric printing. The assistance of Image Options and the Freddie Georges Production Group in California is gratefully acknowledged in compiling the information in this section (Morgan Salmon and Freddie Georges, Personal Communications, February 2006).

- *Regular photo printing*: This uses a traditional style processor to produce photo panels that are then laminated with a variety of offerings for finish. Printing with this method requires a high-resolution image of 150–300 *PPI* (*pixels per inch*) at full size be provided to the printing company. In order to work with smaller files, it is possible to proportionally downsize the file given to the printing company to 300–600 PPI at half the final print size. Note that PPI refers to the resolution of a photograph in a digital file, while *DPI* (*dots per inch*) refers to the resolution of a photograph from a printer.

- *Inkjet or UV printing*: This method is slightly lower in resolution but costs less for printing large graphics. Heated dyes with raised images press a thin plastic film carrying colored pigments against the paper. The pigments transfer from the film to the paper; heat and pressure assist in the bonding process. Using new UV flatbed printers allows graphics to be printed directly onto substrate material instead of printing on paper first then laminating and mounting the print onto the substrate, thus saving on labor and material. Files for the inkjet print process should be 75–150 PPI.
- *Dye sublimation printing*: Sublimation is a process that imprints color on a variety of surfaces using heat and pressure. Sublimation is performed by using specially formulated inks printed on paper, and then applying the print to receptive surfaces. Unlike screen printing, the sublimation process produces permanent images that will not crack or fade. Dye sublimation is cost efficient and popular for short-run customization of fabrics. Special logos, pictures, and designs can easily be created or scanned into the computer. Transfer paper can be generated and custom prints finished in a matter of minutes. Files for this process should also be 75–150 PPI.

2.2.5.2.2 Screen Printing

Screen printing is a very old process that is the most economical method of producing thousands of images from a single one onto a variety of substrates, especially textiles such as nylon, cotton, wool, silk, and canvas. Ink is expressed through a stretched fabric mesh by a squeegee blade to reproduce the original image onto the substrate below. It is ideal for such things as multiple advertising banners and signs (e.g. for a festival or large public event).

2.2.5.2.3 Appliqué

Appliqué is a decorative design made of one material attached to another (e.g. sewn or glued). This can be very attractive for single designs for special events but does not make sense for large runs of signs or banners.

2.2.5.2.4 Hand-Painting

Like appliqué, hand-painted designs are great for one-off pieces of decorative artwork, but prohibitively expensive for multiple copies. Occasionally, hand-painted designs have made their way into special events, especially for such unique items as T-shirts, clothing, or other artwork created by well-known artists as part of an event entertainment program or fundraising auction.

2.2.5.2.5   Computer-Cut Vinyl

This refers to small lettering and graphics that are cut out of sheets of vinyl with adhesive on one side, using special cutting machinery controlled through a computer interface. These letters or graphics are then applied to larger banners or signs of almost any material that will allow them to adhere.

2.2.5.3   General Requirements for Graphic Artwork

In addition to the resolution sizes mentioned for graphics in Section 2.2.5.2 on printing methods, there are several other general requirements that most printing companies have (Salmon and Georges, Personal Communications, February 2006). Knowing what they are will save time and effort for designers, producers, and managers.

- Vector files (e.g. what is known as *line art*, including logos and geometric shapes) produced by such software as Adobe Illustrator and Corel Draw, are ideal for large format reproductions because they can be scaled to larger sizes without losing any image resolution. In other words, one can start out with a small image file and it will be just as good when blown up.
- Raster files (e.g. file formats for photographs, such as TIFF, BMP, GIF, and JPEG) produced by such software as Adobe Photoshop, are dependent on resolution and require higher-resolution files if the image is to be blown up to a large size.
- Files should be provided with all editable elements, including fonts and actual images.
- Color references should be included for consistency. This means giving the printing company color matching *PMS numbers*. PMS stands for Pantone Matching System, which designates every color in a standardized industry set by a unique number. Alternatively, there should be enough time allowed for a proof of all files before final printing is done.
- Printed image resolution or DPI must be adjusted for viewing distance. If the originating file resolution in PPI is high, usually the resulting printed image will be better, but not always. An 8 ft × 10 ft (2.4 m × 3 m) image on a wall does not need the same DPI at full size as a 2 ft × 3 ft (0.6 m × 0.9 m) image. The smaller image will probably be viewed from 1 to 8 ft (0.3–2.4 m) away, whereas the larger image will probably be viewed from 6 to 25 ft (7.5 m) away. A simple formula can be used to determine an approximate resolution for the final image as follows:

Standard resolution in DPI = 300/Viewing distance

High resolution in DPI = 600/Viewing distance

In other words, if a blown up, 8 ft × 10 ft photo will be viewed from a 10 ft distance in a trade show booth and you need the highest resolution possible, the DPI would be 60. A good rule-of-thumb is to provide raster (image) files at 72 DPI for the final output size.

2.2.5.4 Methods of Suspension

Most fabric banners and signs are constructed with a method of suspension built in. These methods are simple and usually consist of one of three types: a stitched hem with a metallic grommet and hole at corners and key points along a hem to allow for rope, wire, plastic, or other ties to be inserted; a series of fabric ties stitched to the banner along the top and/or bottom hems to allow the banner to be tied onto a support; and a sleeve or pocket stitched to the top and/or bottom hem of the banner to permit horizontal support poles such as those used with draping to be inserted.

Actual suspension mechanisms vary considerably. For larger fabric banners, a horizontal pole inserted in the top sleeve of the banner is the preferred method and allows for the easiest installation on a large structure or from ceilings or trusses. A horizontal pole also inserted into a bottom sleeve helps to keep the banner hanging straight. Fabric ties are also used. For smaller signs, especially ones made from rigid or semi-rigid material, there are many different freestanding support bracket and sign holder combinations available. Occasionally, male and female Velcro patches placed on the back of signs and on the mounting surfaces work well for temporary signage, as do flexible magnets (e.g. like refrigerator magnet material) on the back of the signs if they will be mounted on metal surfaces.

2.2.6 Tension Fabric Structures

Modern technology has given the events industry a new look in the form of tension fabric structures over the last 20 years. By definition, the fabrics used are stretched into a final shape in one of two ways: the first is by anchoring lines tied on one end to reinforced corners of the fabric and on the other end to an architectural structural component such as a wall, ceiling, or floor; the second is by forming around a freestanding or self-forming structure made of aluminum, PVC (polyvinyl chloride – a widely used plastic), or fiberglass tubing. The freestanding structures are supported by vertical poles (pipe and drape hardware) that fit into heavy metal bases for anchoring. For indoor use, the fabric is typically nylon spandex that can be cut into limitless shapes, colors, and sizes and can be imprinted with graphic designs (e.g. advertising, logos, photos) using a dye sublimation or silkscreen process. Single-color tension fabrics, especially white, are perfect for use as projection media for video and multimedia, and for lighting effects, and are so used in many event applications. Fabric structures are most impressive when well lit. According to Debra Roth of New York-based tension fabric company Pink Inc., the best form of lighting is front and up lighting because it causes the structures to glow. She also notices more and more LED lights being used because of their low cost and safer cool operation, and the fact that they can safely be used for inner lighting of the structures (Debra Roth, Personal Communication, March 15, 2006). Figure 2.11 illustrates a

FIGURE 2.11

EXAMPLE OF TENSION FABRIC DÉCOR

Courtesy: Pink Inc., www.pinkincdesign.com

spectacular event at which tension fabric structures were the main type of décor and formed a focal point at a buffet.

Besides indoor uses, tension fabric structures play a major role in the latest designs of tenting but are constructed of more durable, weather-resistant material that we will be discussing in Chapter 8 on Tenting.

2.2.7   People and Other Creatures As Décor

There is nothing that raises the participation level and excitement of an event more than having the action amongst the guests. If the guests **are** the action or, at the very least **interact** with the action, they feel empowered and tend to enjoy the event more than if they are only observers. This is done by using people as décor. People – and creatures – as décor can take three forms: functional, interactive, and decorative.

Functional refers to using the actual participants in the event as décor. These include wait staff, bar tenders, technical personnel, and guests. It is relatively easy to rent costumes for technical personnel, wait staff, and bar tenders. Add guests to the mix of costumed participants and suddenly a venue is transformed into a sea of moving decorations. Costuming in this manner has several advantages. First, costuming is relatively inexpensive when compared to other décor. Second, even a simple hat can transform the most reticent guest into a gregarious personality. Third, setup time is non-existent.

Interactive refers primarily to entertainment and the different genres and categories that can interact with guests in thematic costumes or as special characters. This includes robot characters, strolling celebrity look-alikes, magicians, silt walkers, jugglers, musicians and others in theme costumes, and table acts such as caricaturists, graphologists, and fortune tellers who can be in character and costume but interact from a fixed position.

Besides people, this category can include 'other creatures,' specifically animals. Until not so long ago, before animal rights advocates pushed for changes in municipal laws, animals were a popular highlight of events. My company frequently put a variety of live Canadian wild animals on 'decorative display' for guests, such as bear cubs, cougars, eagles, moose, and deer, and sometimes more exotic ones like pythons, panthers, tigers, and spiders. Two necessary conditions that we always insisted on were that they be properly caged or penned for safety and that qualified handlers be present at all times. Although this form of display is rare now, if and when it is still possible under the strictest of safe, sanitary, and humane conditions, it can represent a unique opportunity for guests to interact with creatures they would never see close up. Although we had the occasional sanitary mishap, because precautions were taken, no guests or animals were ever harmed.

Decorative refers again to entertainment but in this case not as interactive. Decorative entertainment is there to actually be visual and to be a passive part of the décor. Although the performers do move, they generally do not interact. Examples are living statues and performance art.

2.2.8   Floral Décor

Nothing evokes memories or joyful gasps from guests on first entering an event than the scent of fresh flowers in bloom. In keeping with the designer's dictum to use the five senses, nature never fails when called upon to assist.

Many volumes have been written about floral design and many schools and classes exist. Because of this, we will not go into detail about floral design in this section. See Malouf (1999) and Monroe (2006) for excellent treatments of this subject. However, we will briefly refer to how and where florals may successfully be used in events and review general guidelines for integrating their use into the event production.

2.2.8.1   *Where and How is Floral Design Used?*

Nature has endowed humans with a love of flowers. Our senses of smell and sight react to them in a positive way, very seldom negative. For this reason, their use is almost unrestricted, and a special event is no exception. For the remarkable, memory-evoking scents mentioned above, real flowers arranged creatively and timed to bloom at the event, cannot be beaten. Also running a close second visually but without the scent, are silk and artificial flowers. If seasonal flowers are not available and/or if maximum impact is required for minimal budget, either a design using all artificial flowers or a combination of real and artificial can work well. Also not to be forgotten, are other forms of plants categorized with florals, such as trees, mosses, grasses, cacti, and vines, all of which can be real or artificial. Armed with this knowledge, let us now look at where and how both these types of florals may be best used.

2.2.8.1.1 Part of Event Focal Points

Earlier in the section on design we discussed the principle of emphasis, or creating a focal point, and referred to several locations within an event space that would be considered focal points. Some of these form perfect settings for the use of florals to achieve this emphasis. These include tables (including buffets), entrances, stages, and corners, or décor vignettes. Floral arrangements placed in these areas will be the most obvious.

- *Entrances*: Colorful, large, surrounding, and aromatic are the key words when placing florals at entrances. Large vases with high, full arrangements, and colored but hidden lighting work well. Topiary trees with pin lights work, as do many other possibilities. The idea is to be spectacular since the entrance is the first impression of the event.
- *Dining tables*: For many events in which a meal is served, the dining tables occupy the largest proportion of the event space, so to use this space and that above the tables makes sense if visual impact is sought. High table centers with a floral component extending as much as 6–10 ft (1.8–3.0 m) above the table surface can be truly spectacular. Heights should be adjusted to accommodate sight lines for guests if they must view a stage or presentation of some sort, as must conversational barriers in the form of table centers that are too wide. Usually, a short table center should be under about 1 ft (30 cm) in height while tall centers can extend much higher as long as their bases are narrow and guests can still see each other across the table.
- *Buffet tables*: The guidelines for dining tables do not apply to buffet tables. For buffets with a floral component, spectacular is the way to go. High, wide, and oversize is best if space permits, because each is a focal point.
- *Stages*: Florals are often used to dress stages. Typical placements are on downstage corners, upstage corners, as rows along the downstage edge, as rows along the upstage edge or under a backdrop, in front of lecterns, or on the floor in front of the stage. Generally, any of these arrangements should be large and oversize as long as they do not obstruct sight lines of the audience. This is because distances to the stage are often considerable, and what at the front of a room may appear large, will

appear very small 200 ft (60 m) away at the back of the audience. Also, these arrangements are isolated and as such need to be large to create an impact and to help focus attention.

- *Corners or décor vignettes*: Florals can become part of décor vignettes in isolated locations such as corners or smaller themed rooms. Again, scent, color, freshness, and size determine how effective the arrangement will be.

2.2.8.1.2 Total Environments

Probably the ultimate in event design with florals is to completely transform the event space using florals. Good event designers can use all three dimensions to do this. Consider the impression created by filling the ceiling with hanging vines and subdued lighting for a jungle atmosphere, completely covering the floor with rose petals to instill a candlelit dinner with an ambience of romance, or covering the walls with giant floral murals. What the designer is really doing is using architecture to advantage, and instead of trying to match or coordinate with the room colors or designs, is choosing to ignore the designs and create a totally new space. My company frequently produced events in which we brought into a ballroom up to 300 or more live evergreen trees to create a west coast rainforest theme.

Alternatively, if a venue's existing architecture is so unique and attractive, it may invite the designer to bring florals into it without disturbing the basic esthetic but rather augmenting it for a totally new look. I have seen this done in an 800-year-old Norman cathedral in England in which floral arrangements were creatively worked into doorways, windows, pews, and other sections of the cathedral.

2.2.8.1.3 On People

The act of wearing flowers has always been an important one for human beings, whether it is as an expression of love as with corsages or boutonnieres at weddings, or simply as an expression of individualism as in hair bands of the 'free love' generation. This begs the question, 'Why not more?' Indeed, event designers have already been there in some very unusual ways. People can become décor unto themselves and florals can be the way to do it. Figure 2.12 illustrates a person completely covered in florals as part of a 'living garden' concept. Actors or dancers so costumed can stroll around or be part of a design like this garden. Individuals have also been used as buffet table centerpieces and have become part fruit or vegetable and part human, the so-called 'talking centerpiece.' Combined with props, this concept makes for some very interesting approaches.

2.2.8.2 *General Guidelines for Integrating Florals with Event Production*

To successfully integrate floral design with an overall décor design and to accomplish the installation of florals at an event in a timely fashion that fits

FIGURE 2.12

EXAMPLE OF A PERSON AS FLORAL DÉCOR

Photo by Photo Tech. *Courtesy*: Event Solutions

into the production schedule, there are some key points with which a producer or event manager should be concerned.

- Florals can and should be integrated with any theming in keeping with the event's overall décor design. This is mentioned because the floral supplier is often not the overall event décor designer. Themed props and other décor should be considered to be part of the design, whether it is table centers, stage arrangements, people as décor, or entrance décor. Props can be added to florals or florals can be added to props. For example, this can include using miniature cars in floral table centerpiece for a racing theme, old wine barrels or giant oversized wine bottle props as part of a wine-tasting event integrated with a floral vineyard, or adding large classical urns of florals on top of tall Greek columns on a stage at an awards ceremony.

- Sufficient time and space must be allowed for final preparations of florals onsite. This means having a room or large vacant area set aside to do the final builds of table centers or the final arranging of large pieces. This room should preferably have access to fresh water and be well lit.

- The floral designer must communicate with the producer and vice versa in order to obtain florals that match the event design and that can be obtained for optimum freshness in that particular season. This communication should include a discussion of the temperature of the event environment in order to time the arrival and setup of florals to minimize harm to them. Hazel Egerton of Barwick Designs in Vancouver, Canada, states, 'Have your florist deliver the flowers the day of the event, a few hours before the start time. Flowers are often one of the last things to be set up, after the rush of lighting, room décor, table placement, and linens. Because you can never predict the temperature of the venue, it's possible that the flowers could wilt quickly once the event begins, although not common under normal circumstances, and you want the freshest flowers possible. Fresh out of the florist's cooler or off the design table works best because both situations will help prolong the florals' lifespan. An example of a hot venue in which one should be careful about adding florals too soon is a summer tent that can get incredibly warm inside. If you can't avoid the risk of storing the florals before the event or even overnight, they must be kept cool (not cold) and out of the sun. Ask the venue contact person if they can be kept temporarily in the venue's empty fridge. Some types of flowers will die in the cold like delicate orchids, but others will appreciate the cold' (Hazel Egerton, Personal Communication, March 31, 2006).

- Static floral designs **must** be properly illuminated. This can include everything from individually lighting table or buffet centers with pin spots or automated fixtures, to subtle hidden ambient lighting of entrance or corner vignettes. A meeting of the lighting designer, décor designer, and producer is essential to accomplish this. Sufficient space should be allowed on buffets or around vignettes and other arrangements to allow for lighting, typically with *PAR (parabolic aluminized reflector) lamps* (usually PAR36s up to PAR64s – see Chapter 5).

- Finishing touches are critical to successful florals. Edges and the underneath of floral designs have to be finished with embellishments such as moss, grass, sand, or dirt or at least a neat enclosed border.

2.2.9 Inflatables

The term inflatables covers a number of different products: air and helium-filled regular latex balloons; balloons made out of foil and other materials in regular and odd shapes; reinforced poly air tubes; and other oddly shaped blowups made of various materials such as foil, latex, and lamé. Inflatables have been a staple of event décor for a long time, and with new concepts coming along regularly, will continue to be. We will briefly examine each type of inflatable and how it can be used.

2.2.9.1 Balloons

According to Leigh Jones, President of Inflated Ideas in Vancouver, Canada, 'balloons are ideal as decoration when one wants to create a whimsical look, or for any festive event such as a carnival or life celebration like birthdays' (Leigh Jones, Personal Communication, March 1, 2006). The lowly balloon is the grandfather of inflatables. Balloons now come in every color and style imaginable. Surface finishes include metallic foil, jewel tones, solid and at last count, up to more than 30 types and names, each with at least one or more shapes. They can be filled with helium to float or with air to hang. The following are some of the most common types used in events:

- *Animal balloons*: These are the long, narrow balloons used by entertainers to create animals, flowers, and other sculptures. They are identified by two-part numbers such as '260' in which the first digit (2) refers to the diameter (in inches) of the balloon fully inflated, and the second two digits (60) refer to the length fully inflated. Also called pencil or twisty balloons, they are made of latex, a form of rubber. Animal balloons are used in small sculptures and as embellishments in helium-filled balloon bouquets or clusters on tables and around rooms.
- *Foil balloons*: Often incorrectly called Mylar (a trademarked name for a certain type of polyester film) balloons, the balloon industry refers to them as 'foil' balloons, because they are made of nylon sheet, coated on one side with polyethylene and metallized on the other. They are generally used in helium bouquets or clusters.
- *Giant balloons*: This refers to balloons that are greater than about 16 in. (40 cm) in diameter. They are now available outside North America to over 10 ft (3.0 m) in diameter. The smaller sizes are usually latex, the larger made of vinyl. They are most often filled with helium and used to make a visual statement over tables or as the tops to balloon columns.
- *Round balloons*: These are the standard latex balloons that are most used in balloon bouquets, arches, clusters, and drops. They come in a variety of finishes and diameters. They are often customized by imprinting with logos or names.
- *Odd shapes*: Other common shapes of latex balloons, sometimes used with bouquets or clusters, include:
  - *Airships*: Same shape as a blimp but small.
  - *Flying saucer*: A flat, round balloon with a nozzle coming off the edge at an angle. It spins as it deflates.
  - *Geos*: Donut shaped or flower blossom shaped.
  - *Hearts*: Heart shaped, sometimes made of foil.

- *Knobbies*: Long skinny balloons that inflate into a series of bulbous segments, rather like a caterpillar.
- *Mouse head*: Shaped like a cartoon mouse head.

Balloons can be used in several novel ways for event décor. The common ones include:

- *Arches*: Arches are built by tying helium-filled round balloons to strong (e.g. 50 lb) fishing line and weighting the line down at both ends using attractively wrapped bricks or other weights. Arches can be single balloon or multiple balloon spirals. If used with a mixture of colors, the effect of a spiral arch can be quite spectacular. Arches are perfect for covering vertical space at an event as a grand entrance or over entire areas of a room or stage. The size of the arch can be determined by using the formula:

$$L = W + 1.5H$$

where L is the required total length of the arch, W is the width of the arch opening, and H is the height of the arch at its highest point (usually the center). This will give the most esthetically pleasing shape. Multiple arches of decreasing size on the same vertical plane can be used together to create a backdrop or wall cover, or multiples of the same size on a horizontal plane can be spaced to create a tunnel effect. The opposite of arches in the form of balloon swags can be created using air-filled balloons suspended from the ceiling.
- *Columns*: Columns are built of air-filled round balloons supported by an internal PVC frame or of freestanding, helium-filled balloons. Most columns are topped with a large helium-filled, giant round balloon. As with arches, multiple colors used in a spiral effect works well. Columns are very effective in key locations in an event space, such as the edges of dance floors, the corners of rooms, or the corners of stages.
- *Clusters or bouquets*: These are arrangements of helium-filled round balloons often mixed with some of the differently shaped ones, and tied to decorative ribbon, then weighted down. They are commonly used as table centers in which they can also be mixed with small props, flowers, custom Foamcore cutouts, or fabrics, or they can be standalone centers themselves. The benefit of helium bouquets is that their height can be easily adjusted by changing the length of the ribbon. Large bouquets or clusters can be freestanding around a room as well, and of any height. They are good for augmenting arches in key locations such as entrances, stages, or dance floors.
- *Ceilings, floors, and walls*: Masses of free balloons can be used to cover ceilings (helium-filled), floors (air-filled), or walls (frame-supported helium or air-filled).
- *Sculptures*: Although not quite as popular in recent years as in the 1990s, balloon sculptures can be impressive. Giant three-dimensional

depictions of life-sized machines, buildings, animals, people, logos, and artwork have been constructed out of balloons. These are often suspended from a ceiling and attractively illuminated to act as a décor focal point in an event. They are usually constructed out of air-filled round balloons, but can bring in other shapes and types as well. Similar two-dimensional art can be used to fill walls and built using a preformed frame and small 5 or 6 in. balloons.

For any of these creations, the balloons may be augmented with rope light or pin lights woven throughout the bouquets or sculptures, by external illumination, or even by small, battery-powered lights placed inside some of the balloons.

Using masses of balloons, certain special effects can be created. These include:

- *Reveals*: This is industry terminology for an effect that hides an object or person and then instantly reveals them using a special effect. Balloons can do this in several ways, including:
  - An exploding wall in which air-filled balloons are arranged close together as a wall supported by an internal PVC framework and hiding the person/thing. At the appropriate moment, key balloons with small charges in them are exploded and the entire wall instantly falls apart revealing what is behind.
  - A floating reveal in which a similar wall of helium-filled balloons is created but anchored to a supporting bottom frame. At the key moment, the frame support is loosened and the balloons float up to reveal what is behind.
- *Drops*: A large number of air-filled balloons is enclosed in a light netting and suspended from a ceiling with a length of filament or string coming down to the floor in a key location. At the appropriate time, the string is pulled releasing the netting and the balloons fall. Like any special effect, this is best timed to emphasize a key point in an event or program. This same effect can also be achieved by building an upside down pillar and filling it with small air-filled balloons capped with a giant one. Once the giant one is released (ideally as an exploding balloon), the insides spill out.

There are several insider tips about balloon décor that every producer and designer should know in order to get the most out of the balloons (Leigh Jones, Personal Communication, March 1, 2006).

- Air-filled balloons are best for long-term displays due to the fact that air molecules are heavier than helium and do not escape as rapidly. Air is generally good for up to 7 days and helium for 24 h. However, a helium retention product called 'Hi Float' can be used to coat the inside of helium balloons to make them last up to five times longer.

- Oxidation dulls the outside finish of balloons, particularly jewel tones (transparent balloons), so the length of display time should also be judged by the appearance of the balloons based on this oxidation. If a longer term is needed, a different choice of finishes should be made.
- Nitrogen makes a good inflation medium as an alternative to air when large quantities of small balloons are required. It is faster because of higher pressure, and cheaper than air.

2.2.9.2   Air Tubes

Originally created by Doron Gazit of Air Dimensional Design, air tubes are long, tubular inflatables, best used when an abstract display is needed. They fill visual space very well and can be used to wind around permanent or temporary architectural structures, both indoors and outdoors, such as buildings and bridges, scaffolding and fences, stages and columns. Air tubes are constructed of heavy, flame-retardant polypropylene and are sold in long rolls of flat uninflated material. They must be unrolled and cut to length before installing in their uninflated state. One end is then attached to a high-powered, steel-encased, 110 V, 3 amp fan that must constantly blow air to keep them inflated, and the other end is sealed. They can remain inflated indefinitely. They are available in inflated diameters ranging from 4.5 in. (11.3 cm) to almost 18 in. (45 cm) and multiple colors.

2.2.9.3   Other Blowups and Air-Supported Décor

The ingenuity of inventors combined with strong new materials has resulted in a plethora of different inflatable and air-supported products that can be used for event décor. One such inventor, Ashley Ramage, President of UK and San Francisco-based Blowupthings, takes a distinctly refreshing approach to the design of events using inflatables. Because of the ability of inflatables to do so much with so little, he likes to take an event space and use it to 'enhance, conceal, or distract, and also to arrest people's sensibilities; in other words, make them stop and think' (Ashley Ramage, Personal Communication, March 28, 2006). He has made walls, suspended décor, stage backdrops, and trade show booths out of unique, customized inflatables and is on the cutting edge of this expanding category of décor. His and most of the other new inflatables are made of lightweight fabrics other than latex, such as rip stop nylon, and most require an electric-powered, low-voltage fan to keep them inflated, and/or at least one external suspension point. Some of these exciting products include:

- Architectural pieces such as stage backdrops, entranceways, and trade show booths for indoor use.
- Giant portable movie screens as large as 100 ft × 45 ft (30 × 13.5 m) for outdoor use.
- Smaller air or helium-filled abstract shapes for hanging or mounting on the ground. See Figure 2.13.

FIGURE 2.13

EXAMPLE OF UNUSUAL INFLATABLE SHAPE FOR FLOOR MOUNTING

Courtesy: Air Dimensional Design, www.airdd.com

- Wearable inflatable products to permit a human interactive component to be added.
- Wind-movable products such as Fly Guys that come in heights up to 60 ft (18 m) and require two fans to keep inflated and moving, and Air Flames, made of less resilient metallic fabric, but also require fans for movement. Doron Gazit of Air Dimensional Design originally invented both these products. Note that they need to have dry weather if used outdoors.

PRODUCTION WAR STORY: A PREMATURE SURPRISE

A beautiful and highly creative balloon wall was installed in front of the band stage that would magically burst and reveal the band once it was time to dance. It would be an incredible ending to an evening of good food, fun, and camaraderie. Unfortunately, someone forgot to tell Mother Nature. The room was fully encircled by floor-to-ceiling windows looking out to the west and this event was held late in June near the day when sunlight lasted until very late in the evening. The event day was quite hot and the sunlight beamed through the

Continued

windows, eventually making its way to shine on the balloon wall. Just as dinner was underway, we heard the first explosion, followed in fairly rapid succession over the course of the next 20 min by a periodic, unrehearsed exploding balloon wall that was soon left in tatters, ragged pieces of balloons hanging from the wall supports like broken flesh. Although somewhat comical while happening, this premature balloon wall explosion did not make our client very happy. The balloon experts were called in and the remaining pieces of the wall were dismantled to leave a clean look, but the damage had been done.

In this case, communication with the client was immediate and consisted of an apology and an explanation. This was a situation that could only be described as a true Act of God. It may have been avoidable but we were never sure exactly how. During the site inspection days before, the weather was cloudy and an estimate was made of where the sun would be at a certain time and whether it would strike the balloon wall. This was only a guess and even with this, nobody – even the balloon experts – expected or anticipated that the sunlight would overheat the balloons and their tethers, which we could only surmise expanded at different rates and caused the premature explosions. The client was not charged a penny for the wall and seemed to be happy with that settlement, but nothing could bring back the planned excitement that had been lost.

What lessons were learned? This was a difficult case. The most obvious one that we learned was not to use a balloon wall or any balloon structure in situations where weather – or excessive heating or cooling of any sort – could be a factor.

Courtesy: Doug Matthews

2.2.10   Other Unique Décor

Every year, someone invents a new type of décor that does not fit within the categories laid out in this book, so more than likely we will not have covered it all. However, in an attempt to bring it all in, here are some other categories that do not fit the traditional mold.

2.2.10.1   *Nature As Décor*

The ancient world was considered to be composed of the elements earth, wind, fire, and water. Special event designers still use these elements in various ways. Fire is still popular in the form of candles. Earth and sand are sometimes used in floral displays or artificial beaches. Water is used for florals and sometimes in special displays for boats and in the form of ice carvings. All of it can enhance any event if used properly. However, some cautions pertaining to risk management are in order:

- Candles, especially tall ones, tend to drip wax and should never be used in a drafty room. Furthermore, all flammable material in close proximity should be treated with flame retardant or the candles not used at all. Tall candles on candelabra are particularly susceptible to drafts and if flame is used, it should be sustained by gas and not the candle itself.

- Earth or sand especially in large quantities such as for an artificial beach and beach volleyball games, can be a nightmare for venue staff to clean up. It almost always requires several large dump trucks full of sand to provide enough. The event will likely be a big success providing arrangements have been made for cleanup before the event is finalized.

- Ice carvings are spectacular when sculpted by a master. There are even companies that carve to music as a form of entertainment. Carvings can be used as food dishes, bars, table centers, buffet centers, and just plain décor focal points. The cost usually depends on the size, which is governed by the number of standard ice blocks that will be used. They must be delivered just before the event begins and will last at least 2 h and still look good. However, they do require proper lighting and proper drainage, whether it is a small tray placed beneath a table center or larger trays on a buffet for a giant ice carving. For ponds and other water displays, tarpaulins or waterproof ground sheets should be used as well as leak-proof containers.

2.2.10.2   Other Sensory Décor

Up to this point, we have mostly concentrated on only two of our senses, sight and touch. A successful event will encompass all the senses if possible, and that is where other sensory décor comes in. Apart from food (our sense of taste), which is usually the purview of catering, there are two other senses we need to think about.

2.2.10.2.1   Smell

The Proust effect, or Proustian memory, named after French author Marcel Proust who first described it in writing in the early 1900s, is the phenomenon of a particular smell or odor bringing a memory to mind. It has been proven that the part of our brain that handles memory is the same part that interprets smells, so we have a built-in link. Thus, smell is a very powerful sense and one that can lead directly to an emotional interpretation of time and place. It has not been used to its full potential as part of special event décor, but the tools are available to use it.

Certainly, the catering side of an event uses appropriate food choices to stimulate our olfactory receptors, but artificial scents are also available to help. There are several companies that provide different scents to retailers to stimulate sales, and to events to create sensory environments. For example, North Carolina-based ScentAir offers over 1000 scents ranging from environmental ones like ocean, rain, sagebrush, and redwood forest, to exotic and unusual ones such as musty, oily machinery, and dinosaur breath. They are delivered using a dry-air technology that releases a fragrance from undetectable locations such as ceilings, without sprays, aerosols, or heated oils. A single scent delivery system is very small, operates on adapted 110 VAC, covers up to 4000 ft^2 (364 m^2) of space, and even includes a motion sensor. A scent cartridge lasts up to 300 h.

2.2.10.2.2 Hearing

Several authors talk about 'soundscaping' for events (Goldblatt, 2002, p. 213; Rutherford-Silvers, 2004, p. 209) and how it adds to the experience of being encompassed by a total environment. Put simply, soundscaping is the ability to control the aural environment at an event. Although some event sounds cannot be controlled such as people (talking, eating, moving, etc.), other ambient sounds can be. Soundscaping is included in this section because it should be considered as part of the event designer's arsenal of décor options.

There are two main ways to control the aural environment: live sound such as musical groups or people making real-time sounds through an audio system, and recorded sound. It's easy to say to the audio engineer, 'Just put on some mellow walk-in music' or 'Crank up the volume when they start dancing.' This is not soundscaping and it is far from properly controlling the aural environment. Successful control considers timing, volume, and content, and often must be coordinated with other resources such as lighting and catering.

Timing means that a conscious effort has to be made to change the ambient sounds at predetermined moments at an event. For example, a popular form of entertainment for convention opening ceremonies in Vancouver has been a West Coast Native Talking Stick Ceremony, and our company produced many. During walk-in, we would carefully choose appropriate new age music with an environmental flavor such as flutes with light drumming at a low volume to set the mood, then at the start of the ceremony, we would dim all the house lights and initiate a grand entrance with the room dark and only the sound of crashing thunder and the rain forest for ambience. The thunder was at a volume high enough to shake the floor, thus creating a realistic feel, and demonstrating the power of dramatically changing volume at a precise moment to gain attention.

Volume is also important when sounds are being played in the background to only create ambience. Many events have been ruined because volume was not controlled. Whether it is the sound of ship's foghorns set amongst a rolling fog and a gangplank at an event entrance, or a live quartet playing background jazz, either one could be too high or too low to be effective if not continuously monitored. It is necessary to monitor guest reactions to background sounds by physically being where the sounds are. The audio engineer or producer has to literally go to the entrance or walk amongst the diners to see if people can hear or are complaining about volume. People watching is critical to successful soundscaping.

Content, as we have discussed in Chapter 1, is arguably the most powerful variable in generating emotional and physical reaction to entertainment. This is where many producers do not take enough time to consider what the effect of sound will be. This is particularly true of background music or other sounds. Let us take an example of a sports-themed event in which guests walk around to different themed rooms to participate in activities and partake of different foods. Consider a 'baseball-themed' room. What would be more conducive to an exciting and emotional reaction in that room, background rock music or playback of a live radio broadcast of a world series winning game, complete with play-by-play action, and the sound of the cheering crowd? If you had been watching that game 20 years ago, wouldn't the radio broadcast bring back more memories than simply rock music? Time needs to be taken to choose content.

2.3   SETUP CONSIDERATIONS FOR DÉCOR

Setting up or installing décor can be a stressful undertaking, not only for the designer but also for the event producer who must coordinate with venue staff and other suppliers. There are literally hundreds of details that have to be considered and probably equally as many things that can go wrong. Of course, every event and every type of décor presents unique problems and challenges, so it is virtually impossible to predict or list every one. Throughout setup, however, constant monitoring for potential risks and safety hazards is essential. Although there are no specific safety or design standards for décor, many venues have a number of restrictions on what can and cannot be done. Monroe (2006; pp. 104, 105, 109, 133, 174–175) outlines several potential risk areas for the various types of décor, such as structural stability, flame retardancy, and toxicity. Producers should be fully aware of all restrictions on décor and of all potential risks by thoroughly reviewing the event décor plan with the designer. Here are some of the general considerations necessary prior to and at the event.

2.3.1   Prior to the Event

These happen from the moment the event is being considered right up until move-in.

- A preliminary site inspection should be made by the producer and designer to ascertain:
  - Load-in access from the loading dock to the event space, including exact measurements of the freight elevator if there is one, sizes and lengths of any connecting corridors, door sizes, and timing restrictions to movement of décor caused by necessity to go through public areas.
  - Accessibility of the actual loading dock, including size and number of docks, whether there is a ramp, parking restrictions for trucks and/or parking areas.

- The number, location, and load rating of ceiling hanging points in the event space if rigging and suspended décor will be used.
- The location(s) and rating of house power in volts and amperes, plus which outlets are on which circuits.
- The location of doors and windows and any effect daylight might have on event décor and lighting.
- The exact measurements of the event space and preliminary locations for décor placement.
- Whether there will be any stages, tables, dance floors, or other furniture in the space, plus the planned number and sizes of everything.
- Who will be responsible for providing ladders or scissor lifts.
- Any restrictions on scheduling caused by other activities in the same or adjoining space, including noise restrictions.
- Any restrictions on nailing, screwing, or otherwise affixing décor to venue property.
- Any pertinent restrictions relating to fire and the flammability of décor.
- Requirements for cleanup before and after the event and whether it will be done by contracted decorators or by venue staff.
- Existing venue color scheme and whether it must be covered or can be worked into the event color scheme.
- Availability of dedicated preparation areas or rooms for décor staff such as florists.
- Availability of a crew break area and availability and cost of refreshments.
- Planned setup schedule for venue staff such as power tie-in, stage setup, and table placement.
- Any restrictions from the venue for strike of décor after the event, including loading dock accessibility, noise, or staff.

- The designer should create a preliminary décor design plus a rough floor plan using the venue information and all the resources necessary.
- The designer should create a setup schedule of deliveries and timing for all suppliers that should be reviewed by the producer for integration into the overall production schedule and for possible cost savings by using existing suppliers such as lighting who can light décor as well as stages.
- The designer should calculate staff needs for setup and strike based on the approved schedule ensuring that sufficient staff plus a contingency factor are included.
- The designer should review and plan for all necessary tools, including portable electric saw, screw gun, and electric drill and selection of drill bits, duct tape in a variety of colors, 50 ft measuring tape, hammers, variety of nails and screws, glue gun and glue, zap straps, pencils, paper, and paint, brushes, and cleaner if onsite painting is to be done. If sets and hard props form a large part of the décor, it can be useful to have a carpenter onsite for last minute changes.

- The designer should arrange for all transportation for setup and strike.
- The designer and producer should review safety procedures and risk, including:
  - Any setup or strike procedures that could incur a risk or injury to workers, event staff, clients, or venue staff and ensure all involved are aware of the hazards.
  - Safety attire (e.g. steel-toed boots, hard hats, gloves) and that it will be used by setup and strike personnel as required.
  - Flame retardancy rating of all materials.
  - Qualifications for equipment operation if designer personnel will be operating it, such as scissor lifts.
  - All WCB (Workers' Compensation Board) certificates are current and payments are up to date.

2.3.2   At the Event

These happen during onsite setup and strike.

- The producer and designer continuously monitor all work for safety, risks, and adherence to regulations.
- The producer and designer continuously monitor the setup schedule and liaise with venue staff immediately to overcome problems as they arise.
- The producer and designer ensure all décor setup is coordinated with other suppliers such as lighting and A-V to ensure they can work around each other and that their components fit the décor as planned (e.g. lighting décor).
- The designer should ensure finishing touches are applied to all décor elements, such as:
  - Edges of floral displays are finished with moss or grass or edging.
  - Any battery-operated equipment has new batteries.
  - All electrical cords for décor are either hidden or taped down safely, preferably using duct tape in the color of the venue carpet or floor.
  - All electrical hazards such as lights close to flammable material are moved to safety.
  - Any support mechanisms for large décor such as pipe and drape hardware for backdrops or wooden bracing for set pieces is hidden by other décor, specially manufactured returns, or drapes.
- The producer and designer together should conduct a final 'idiot check' at least 1 h prior to the event commencing to ensure there are no safety hazards and all décor as planned and contracted is in place.

Mention must be made at this point of the importance to plan for décor strike after the event. This is a time, usually very late at night, when many problems occur, often unseen by either the producer or the designer as new crews are in place to accomplish the strike. For this reason it is absolutely necessary for the designer and producer to: establish crew call times for strike; assign a supervisor for strike; give special instructions about the handling of all décor and the exit routing out of the venue; and provide the supervisor with venue and client contact information. This will ensure that the strike is smooth and coordinated.

PRODUCTION CHALLENGES

1. You have a client who wants you to produce an event in which the venue is completely transformed into a jungle. Suggest three different ways to cover the walls, including methods of support or mounting for the décor.
2. You and your designer are having a debate about which color scheme will best combine richness and high contrast for an event. What would be your choices as the best two schemes and why? Which would be easier to coordinate?
3. You and an event designer are brainstorming ideas for table centers for a theme of 'The Old West Meets the 21st Century.' What are three different types or combinations of types of décor that could be used to depict this theme? How high would you make the table centers if the diners will be watching a stage show and how high if they will only be eating dinner followed by dancing to a DJ?
4. You are attending an initial meeting with a potential client who wants a 50s Rock and Roll event. Describe some specific creative décor for her that would appeal to all five senses and would sell her on using your company to produce the event.
5. Give 10 items that should be discussed with a venue manager before proceeding to organize the décor setup for an event, and explain why they must be agreed upon and finalized ahead of time.

REFERENCES

AAA Flag & Banner Mfg. Co. (2000). *Information Re-summarized by Author*. Retrieved February 24, 2006, from http://www.aaaflag.com.

Adler, L.M.A. (1998). *Centerpieces and Table Decorations*. Retrieved February 17, 2006, from http://www.ca.uky.edu/fcs/FACTSHTS/HF-LRA.093.PDF.

Arts Connected, The Minneapolis Institute of Arts (2006). *The Artists' Toolkit: Visual Elements and Principles*. Retrieved February 17, 2006, from http://www.artsconnected.org/toolkit/explore.cfm.

Gillette, J.M. (2000). *Theatrical Design and Production: An Introduction to Scene Design and Construction, Lighting, Sound, Costume, and Makeup*, Fourth Edition. New York: McGraw-Hill Higher Education.

Goldblatt, J. (2002). *Special Events: Twenty-First Century Global Event Management*, Third Edition. New York: John Wiley & Sons, Inc.

Howard Bear, J. (2006, About Inc.). *Symmetrical Balance*. Retrieved February 20, 2006, from http://desktoppub.about.com/od/designprinciples/l/aa_balance1.htm.

Lovett, J.(1999). *Design and Colour*. Retrieved February 17, 2006, from http://www.johnlovett.com/test.htm.

Malouf, L. (1999). *Behind the Scenes at Special Events: Flowers, Props, and Design*. New York: John Wiley & Sons, Inc.

Monroe, J.C. (2006). *Art of the Event: Complete Guide to Designing and Decorating Special Events*. Hoboken: John Wiley & Sons, Inc.

Pamensky-Murray, B. (2006). *Care and Handling of Our Backdrops*. Retrieved February 22, 2006, from http://www.dreamworldbackdrops.com/care_handle.htm.

QSX Software Group (2002–2005). *Color Meaning*. Retrieved February 17, 2006, from http://www.color-wheel-pro.com/color-meaning.html.

Rutherford-Silvers, J. (2004). *Professional Event Coordination*. Hoboken: John Wiley & Sons, Inc.

Saw, J.T. (2001). *2D Design Notes. Part V: Design Elements*. Retrieved February 17, 2006, from http://daphne.palomar.edu/design/part_v.html.

Skaalid, B. (1999). *Classic Graphic Design Theory*. Retrieved February 17, 2006, from http://www.usask.ca/education/coursework/skaalid/theory/cgdt/designtheory.htm.

AUDIO SYSTEMS

LEARNING OUTCOMES

After reading this chapter you will be able to:

1. Explain how the acoustics of an event space affect the quality of sound produced by an audio system.
2. Understand the primary uses of an audio system for special events.
3. Understand and be able to explain the general working of the main groups of equipment in a special event audio system and the components within these groups.
4. Know where in an event space the groups of audio equipment are normally located.
5. Understand the reason for an audio sound check and what it entails at an event.

Whenever an event has more than a bare minimum number of people in a small room (e.g. 100 people maximum, probably far fewer!), there will be a requirement for sound reinforcement in order that any speeches or entertainment can be heard. Poor sound quality can be catastrophic for an event, especially if an important speech cannot be understood or a high-cost celebrity artist's sound mix is totally inadequate.

Audio systems and their design tend to be one of several technical areas of specialization within the events industry that event managers prefer to leave to the experts, often relying on the event producer to oversee the installation and operation of the systems. For that reason, the producer **must** understand the basic theory and functioning of these systems so that the optimum system can be designed for a specific event, and the best return on investment made. This chapter will therefore explore the following key topics:

- Basic acoustic theory and how it is applied to the event space.
- Uses of an audio system.
- Main audio system groups, their components, and their basic theory of operation.
- Signal path and equipment locations within the event space.
- The pre-event sound check and system operation during the event.
- Risk and safety.

Except where noted, the explanations, tables, and figures in Sections 3.1.1.1 through 3.3.1.1.6 are provided courtesy Shure Inc. and used with permission.

3.1 ACOUSTIC THEORY AND ITS APPLICATION TO THE EVENT SPACE

In order to understand why music or the spoken word can either be well heard or completely unintelligible, we must first understand the part that acoustics play in a venue and how they react to the room's architecture.

3.1.1 What Is Sound?

Sound is produced by vibrating objects such as musical instruments, loud-speakers, and human vocal cords. These vibrations in turn produce pressure variations in the air immediately adjacent to the object, which cause a 'wave' effect of high and low pressure much like a wave in water. This is a sound wave and it travels through the air exactly like a wave in water, radiating outward from the sound source. A complete wave is a complete pressure change, or *cycle*, and takes the air pressure from rest, to maximum, to minimum, and back to rest again. Figure 3.1 shows how a wave forms alternating regions of rarefaction and compression as it radiates.

There are several important characteristics of sound waves that one needs to know in order to understand the basics of an audio system. They are frequency, wavelength, and loudness. The following explanations of these characteristics, unless otherwise noted, are provided by Shure Inc. and used with permission (Waller et al., 2005).

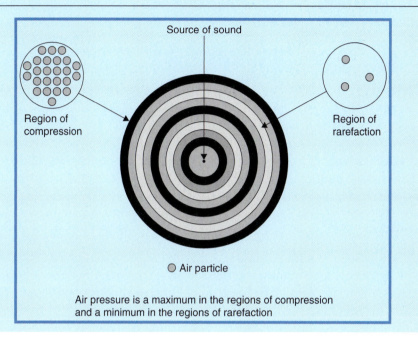

FIGURE 3.1

SOUND WAVE CAUSING A CHANGE IN AIR PRESSURE

Source of sound

Region of compression

Region of rarefaction

○ Air particle

Air pressure is a maximum in the regions of compression and a minimum in the regions of rarefaction

Courtesy: Doug Matthews

3.1.1.1   *Frequency*

The frequency of a sound wave indicates the rate at which the sound pressure changes occur. It is measured in Hertz (Hz) or cycles per second, where 1 Hz equals 1 cycle per second. As an example, human hearing extends from about 20 Hz (very low sounds) to about 20,000 Hz or 20 kHz (very high sounds).

3.1.1.2   *Wavelength*

The wavelength of a sound is the physical distance from the start of one cycle to the start of the next cycle. Wavelength is related to frequency by the speed of sound, which at sea level is approximately 1130 ft/s or 344 m/s. The following formula shows this relationship:

$$\text{Wavelength} = \frac{\text{Speed of sound}}{\text{Frequency}}$$

For example, for a 500 Hz sound source, such as the upper ranges of a tenor voice, the upper range of a tenor saxophone, or the middle to low range of a flute, the wavelength is 1130 ft per second/500 cycles per second or 2.2 ft. Of course, any particular frequency will have a unique corresponding wavelength. Table 3.1 gives some more examples of common frequencies and their corresponding wavelengths.

TABLE 3.1
SAMPLE OF WAVELENGTHS AT DIFFERENT FREQUENCIES

Frequency (Hz)	Wavelength
50	About 23 ft or almost 7 m (low range of a bass drum)
100	About 10 ft or 3 m (low range of a tenor saxophone, mid-range of a bass drum, low range of a bass male voice)
1000	About 1 ft or 0.3 m (upper range of a female soprano voice or mid-range of a flute and violin)
10,000	About 1 in. or 2.5 cm (the very highest notes of a pipe organ)

This relationship is important to know because shortly we will be discussing what happens when sound waves of certain lengths hit objects of a certain size.

3.1.1.3 Loudness

The loudness of a sound is directly related to the variation of air pressure, in other words, the amplitude of the sound. The greater the pressure change or amplitude, the louder the sound. Loudness is commonly measured in *decibels sound pressure level* (dB SPL); 0 dB is the threshold of hearing and at the other extreme, 120 dB is the threshold of pain. A loud rock band heard from 10 ft away is in the 110–120 dB range of loudness, and a quiet whisper is around 30 dB. Most special event environments are in the 80–110 dB range of loudness.

3.1.2 Sound Propagation and Its Relationship to the Event Space

Now that we know how sound waves are generated and travel through the air, the next thing to understand is that sound can actually be altered by its environment as it travels. There are four basic ways that this can happen: *reflection*, *absorption*, *diffraction*, and *refraction*. Let us examine each of them and relate them to the environment of a special event. The explanations in this section, except where noted, are provided by Shure Inc. and used with permission (Waller et al., 2005).

3.1.2.1 Reflection

A sound wave can be reflected by a surface or other object if the object is physically as large or larger than the wavelength of the sound. The reflected sound will have a different characteristic than the direct sound if all frequencies are not reflected equally.

Reflection is also the source of *echo*, *reverberation*, and *standing waves*. Echo occurs when a reflected sound is delayed long enough (i.e. by a distant reflective surface) to be heard by the listener as a distinct repetition of the direct sound. Considering the typical indoor special event environment, all but the very lowest frequencies (e.g. a bass drum) will normally be reflected by a room's walls and ceiling. If the room is a large one such as in some conference centers, there may even be an obvious echo, particularly of low-frequency sounds. Important to note, though, is that higher-frequency sounds can be reflected by a lot more hard surfaces than the low-frequency sounds. For example, again in our special event room, even dining tables, chairs, staging, and some items of décor will reflect higher frequencies, such as the human voice, or the high notes of instruments. See Figure 3.2.

Reverberation consists of many reflections of a sound, maintaining the sound in a reflective space for a time even after the sound has stopped. For enclosed special event environments, particularly large ones like conference centers, this has the effect of making listeners feel like they are inside a giant cavern.

Standing waves in a room occur for certain frequencies related to the distance between parallel walls. The original sound and the reflected sound will begin to reinforce each other when the distance between two opposite walls is equal to a multiple of half the wavelength of the sound. This happens primarily at low frequencies. For example, in a small room that is say 60–65 ft wide, a standing wave could form when the low notes of an electric bass are

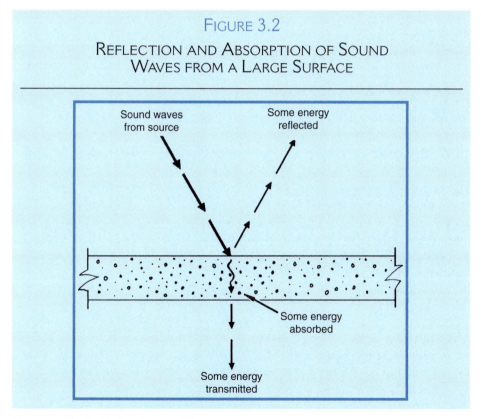

FIGURE 3.2

REFLECTION AND ABSORPTION OF SOUND
WAVES FROM A LARGE SURFACE

Courtesy: JBL Professional, www.jblpro.com

played. Let us look at how this works. At a frequency of say 90 Hz, one of the bass notes would result in a wavelength of about 12.6 ft. Half this figure is 6.3 ft. Therefore, with a width of 63 ft, the room would be a 10 times multiple of half the wavelength, resulting in a standing wave, or overly loud bass sound. This standing wave has to be eliminated during the sound check by adjusting the frequencies coming out of the main system speakers, a process called *equalization* (EQ) (see Section 3.5.1).

3.1.2.2   Absorption

Some materials absorb sound rather than reflecting it. The amount and efficiency of absorption are again dependent on the frequency of the sound. Thin material such as acoustic ceiling tiles or clothing on humans will absorb middle to high frequencies, while thicker material such as pile carpets, padded furniture, and heavy velour drape will absorb lower frequencies (Figure 3.2). It is this absorption that helps to control reverberation in an event space. It is also the reason why the sound in a room will be completely different during a sound check compared to during the event when the room is filled with people.

3.1.2.3   Diffraction

A sound wave will typically bend around obstacles in its path, which are smaller than its wavelength, and this is known as diffraction. The resulting effect in an event space is for low-frequency sounds to fill a room while high frequencies tend to be blocked by most small objects, particularly people. That is why audio engineers place large bass speakers (low frequencies) on the floor, as they will be heard everywhere in the room, even with people sitting or standing in front of them. Likewise, the middle and high-frequency speakers will be placed either on top of the bass speakers or ideally, flown from the ceiling in order to be in a position to reach the entire audience without these frequencies having to go **through** the audience (see Figure 3.3). As an example, from Table 3.1, if an acoustic trio of flute, bass, and guitar are playing for a stand-up reception in a crowded room with only a localized, small audio system to amplify them, as one gets farther away from the trio in the crowded room, only the lower registers of the bass will be heard because the shorter wavelengths of the other instruments will be stopped by the people in the room.

3.1.2.4   Refraction

A sound wave will bend if it must pass through a change in air density. This is most apparent outdoors, particularly at large distances, when the sound from loudspeakers passes through temperature and wind gradients (see Figure 3.4). As well, there is more sound attenuation in drier air (i.e. lower relative humidity) for frequencies above 2 kHz. This means that high frequencies will be attenuated more with distance than will low frequencies (Eargle, 1999).

FIGURE 3.3

DIFFRACTION OF SOUND AROUND OBSTACLES

Obstacle large compared with wavelength acts as effective barrier; substantial shading results

Sound waves

Obstacle small compared with wavelength; sound flows around as if it were not there

Courtesy: JBL Professional, www.jblpro.com

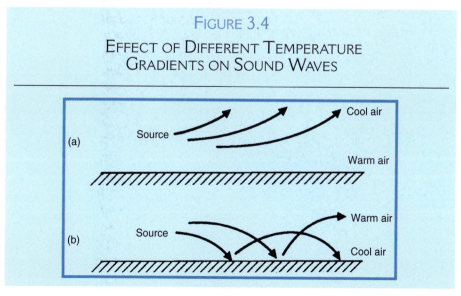

FIGURE 3.4

EFFECT OF DIFFERENT TEMPERATURE GRADIENTS ON SOUND WAVES

Cool air

Source

(a)

Warm air

Warm air

Source

(b)

Cool air

Courtesy: JBL Professional, www.jblpro.com

In summary, the audio quality at an event will depend on the dimensions of the room, the materials present in walls and other structures and equipment, the number of audience members, the seating or standing arrangements of the audience, the layout of the room, whether or not audio system speakers will be flown or mounted on the floor, and lastly, whether the event is outdoors or indoors.

3.2   USES OF AN AUDIO SYSTEM

Armed with knowledge of acoustic theory, we now turn our attention to the actual audio system and how it is used to amplify the human voice and the sounds of musical instruments or recordings for special events. Patil et al. (2000) have provided parts of the explanations in this section.

3.2.1   Audio for Speech

Often if speech is the main component of an event, the audio system takes on a different appearance from that for a concert or musical entertainment stage show. It must provide extremely crisp and clear reproduction of the spoken word. The spoken word generally demands specific types of microphones and speaker systems that are different from those used for music. Microphones, which we will explore in depth shortly, are primarily of four main types when the spoken word is to be amplified. These are *wireless handheld*, *wireless lavalier*, *wired lectern*, and *wired handheld* microphones. Occasionally, *wireless headset* microphones will also be used, but these tend to be more for a theatrical setting that uses the spoken word.

What is called a *distributed system* of speakers is most often used for speech. This type of system consists of multiple smaller speakers that amplify mid-range voice frequencies. These speakers are placed on stands distributed usually around the periphery of the event space. This distribution permits clear sound coverage throughout the audience without any single location being too loud. It presents a more appealing and unobtrusive look to the equipment, and one that does not block sight lines. It is also better suited to improving the sound quality of the range of speech frequencies in acoustically challenging spaces with a lot of hard, reflective surfaces (e.g. glass-walled buildings), as the placement of speakers allows for easier adjustment of critical frequencies and generally less reverberation to eliminate. Lastly, it permits what is known as more *gain before feedback*, which essentially means that sound attenuation is not as serious and the volume may be increased without feedback. Speech generally does not need speakers for sub-frequencies below about 80 Hz, although for a warmer and fuller sound, some audio engineers add small *sub-woofer* speakers (also called *bass bins*) near or even under the stage to handle the very low- to mid-range frequencies.

3.2.2 Audio for Entertainment

Most special event entertainment, particularly musical acts and bands, operates within a much more demanding range of frequencies than the spoken word, as well as a large fluctuation of loudness levels. An audio system must deliver clearly and audibly to an entire audience, no matter how large, everything from quiet whispers to loud rock music, and from high-pitched violin solos to booming bass lines. This wide range of frequencies and volumes can come from many different sources, some live, some already amplified, and some pre-recorded. To do this acceptably requires a much larger variety of microphones and a different package of speakers with different capabilities than those systems used only for speech.

Microphones used for entertainment include wireless handheld, wireless lavalier, wireless headset, wired handheld, plus a wide variety of specialized ones for picking up musical instrument sounds.

Speakers for entertainment must be able to amplify frequencies covering the entire spectrum of audible sounds. This cannot be done acceptably by any single type of speaker as for speeches. The spectrum of frequencies has to be amplified using at least two or even three different types of speakers. These speaker systems, especially the bass bins used for low or sub-frequencies, tend to be large, cumbersome, and intrusive to sightlines, and must be placed judiciously within the event space to keep this sight line intrusion to a minimum. Likewise, the speakers that amplify the middle and high frequencies are better placed as high above an audience as possible in order to avoid reflection, absorption, and diffraction of the higher frequencies. Therefore, they usually perform better *flown* or rigged from the ceiling if the venue structure and setup times permit. Both sound quality and sight lines are improved by doing this. If the event space is very large, with an audience that goes a significant distance back from the stage, delay speakers are also needed to compensate for the time delay in the sound reaching the rear of the audience. These are best also 'flown.'

In addition to the larger speaker groupings, musical entertainers usually require a monitor system so they can hear themselves and the other musicians play. This system may be quite complex. It consists of a number of different monitors (e.g. small, floor-mounted speakers and increasingly, in-ear monitors) and *mixes* which combine certain performers and instruments into one monitor. The monitor mixing board is normally positioned beside the stage and is typically operated by a dedicated, trained *monitor engineer*.

3.3 MAIN AUDIO SYSTEM GROUPS AND THEIR COMPONENTS

An audio system includes three groups: input group, signal processing and routing group, and output group, each with its own set of equipment components and standard locations (Patil et al., 2000). Let us take a long look at each one and try to explain exactly what all this equipment does and how it works.

3.3.1 Input Group

It might help in gaining an understanding of an audio system by thinking of the entire system as the 'flow' of an audio signal, much like a river, from its origin as a sound wave from an instrument, a voice, or a recording, downstream toward its final destination, the ocean, otherwise called speakers. The sound wave, at its origin, is converted to an electrical signal within the first main group of sound system components called the input group, most of which is normally located on the stage at a special event. This group consists of a number of standard pieces of equipment, all of which, in some manner, convert sound waves into electrical signals. They are:

- Wired vocal and instrument microphones.
- Transmitters of wireless microphones.
- Direct input boxes or DIs.
- Keyboard mixers.
- Onstage CD players, tape decks, or drum machines.
- CDs, DVDs, tape players, and audio inputs from video or PowerPoint located near the main mixer.

Except for wireless microphone transmitters and the other inputs located near the main mixer, these are all connected to a common onstage connector or junction box. This box forms one end of the *snake* or cable between the stage and the signal processing and routing group (where the main mixer is located). Since the resultant electrical signal from this equipment is the essence of the audio system, we will first examine each of these components and explain how this conversion takes place.

3.3.1.1 *Microphones*

A microphone is 'a generic term that is used to refer to any element which transforms acoustic energy (sound) into electrical energy (the audio signal). A microphone is therefore one type from a larger class of elements called *transducers*, devices which translate energy of one form into energy of another form' (Davis and Jones, 1990; p. 113).

The most important characteristics of microphones for live sound applications are their operating principle, frequency response, and directionality. Secondary characteristics are their electrical output and physical design. It is these characteristics that an audio engineer uses to choose the appropriate microphone for a specific event application, such as speeches or picking up the sounds of certain instruments. The choice of microphone based on these characteristics can mean the difference between a successful event and audio disaster. Event producers should be aware of the choices available and what they mean. The explanations and diagrams in Sections 3.3.1.1.1 through 3.3.1.1.4, except where noted, are provided by Shure Inc. and used with permission (Waller et al., 2005).

3.3.1.1.1 Operating Principle

Also known as the method of transduction, this refers to the actual method whereby the sound wave is converted to electricity. There are several such methods:

- *Dynamic microphone*: This type of microphone employs a thin plastic diaphragm that vibrates in response to a sound wave and in turn sets up an electrical signal in a small, attached coil of wire (*voice coil*) within a magnetic field created by a small permanent magnet. This type of microphone is extremely robust and is the most widely used in special events (Figure 3.5).
- *Condenser microphone*: This type of microphone employs a thin metal diaphragm mounted in front of a metal *backplate* and this entire miniature assembly (otherwise known as a *condenser*) is continuously charged electrically. When the sound wave hits the front diaphragm, the space between the two diaphragms changes and the resultant electrical signal also changes (Figure 3.6). The power used to maintain the continuous electrical charge within the microphone is known as *phantom power* and is provided by a mixing board that sends the small voltage required (typically 12–48 V DC) back through the microphone cable to the actual

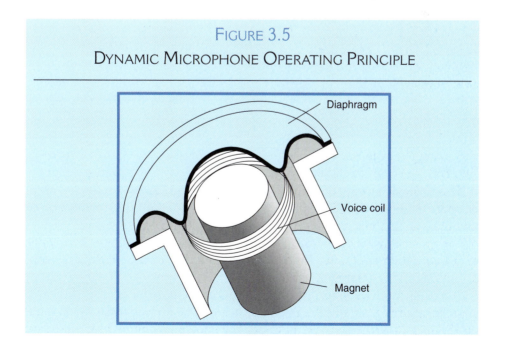

FIGURE 3.5

DYNAMIC MICROPHONE OPERATING PRINCIPLE

Diaphragm

Voice coil

Magnet

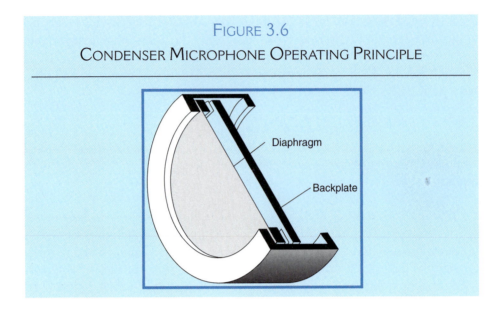

microphone. Condenser microphones are more complex and costly than dynamic microphones, and are not as robust, but are more sensitive and provide a smoother, more natural sound, especially at higher frequencies.

■ *Others*: Other principles include an *electret condenser*, a *ribbon*, a *carbon*, and a *piezoelectric* type of microphone, all with unique characteristics. Davis and Jones (1990; pp. 114–116) provide excellent explanations of these types, most of which are seldom used in special events.

3.3.1.1.2   Frequency Response

This refers to the sensitivity of the microphone over a certain frequency range. A microphone whose output signal is equal at all frequencies has a 'flat' frequency response, and is typically used to reproduce instruments with a wide range of frequencies such as guitars or pianos. One whose response has dips or peaks in signals at certain frequencies has a 'shaped' response, and is typically used for close-up vocals.

3.3.1.1.3   Directionality

This is the sensitivity of the microphone to sound relative to the direction or angle from which the sound arrives. The three basic directional types of microphone are *omnidirectional*, *unidirectional*, and *bidirectional*.

■ *Omnidirectional*: This microphone has equal pickup sensitivity from all directions around it, a full 360 degrees (Figure 3.7). This means that the sound source does not need to be directly in front of it to be heard. It is used, for example, as a type of lectern microphone when there might be several speakers at a lectern, none of whom may be standing

FIGURE 3.7

OMNIDIRECTIONAL MICROPHONE PICKUP COVERAGE

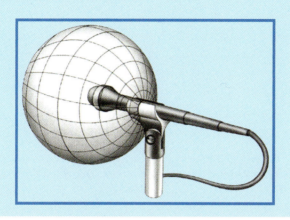

FIGURE 3.8

UNIDIRECTIONAL CARDIOID MICROPHONE PICKUP COVERAGE

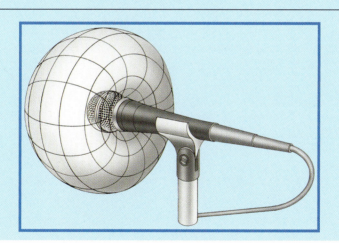

directly in front of the microphone, such as in an awards show with several winners of an award all surrounding the lectern. It is important to remember, however, that omnidirectional microphones can pick up ambient room sound as well and thus can be more susceptible to feedback.

■ *Unidirectional*: This microphone is most sensitive to sound arriving from on-axis and less sensitive to sound arriving as it moves off-axis (Figure 3.8). This type of microphone will allow higher gain levels (i.e. higher input volume) before feedback becomes a problem. There are two types of unidirectional microphones which derive their names from their pickup patterns. *Cardioid*s (upside-down heart-shaped pickup pattern) have a 130-degree pickup angle in front. *Supercardioid*s have a 115-degree pickup angle. The lower the angle, the less is the susceptibility to feedback.

- *Bidirectional*: This microphone is the last form of directional microphone. It has a pickup angle of 90 degrees, so that it essentially picks up sound coming from directly in front of it or directly behind it. It is not used much in special events but more in studio recording situations.

3.3.1.1.4 Electrical Output

The output of a microphone is usually specified by *output level, impedance*, and *wiring configuration*. Remember that small electrical signal that is generated by the microphone when a sound wave reaches it? That small signal is called the *sensitivity, output level*, or *microphone level*, and is measured in millivolts (mV). It generally falls between 0.1 and 100 mV, depending on the intensity of the sound and the type of microphone. If a signal voltage is small (i.e. if a sound is faint or distant from the microphone), it may be of similar level to the level of noise in the circuit (e.g. thermal noise from amplifiers, hum, hiss, clicks). Microphone level signals therefore must be amplified to what is called *line level* before being processed or routed onward in order to overcome the effects of unwanted noise. This is done in the mixer, to be discussed later, but the line level voltage is approximately 1 V.

The output impedance of a microphone is roughly equivalent to the *electrical resistance* of its output: 150–600 ohms for low impedance (low Z) and 10,000 ohms or more for high impedance (high Z). For practical purposes, low-impedance microphones can be used with cable ('snake') runs of 1000 ft (300 m) or more with no loss of quality, while high-impedance types lose high frequencies with cable runs greater than about 20 ft (6 m). Most microphones used for special events are low impedance.

Finally, the wiring configuration may be *balanced* or *unbalanced*. A balanced output carries the signal on two conductors (wires with shield). The signals on each wire are the same level but opposite polarity so that only the difference between the two signals is amplified and any unwanted noise is rejected, since it is identical in each wire (Figure 3.9).

On the other hand, an unbalanced microphone output carries its signal on a single conductor (plus shield), which in turn amplifies any unwanted noise pickup up by the conductor (wire) (Figure 3.10).

Therefore, for the sake of the best sound quality, nearly all special event sound reinforcement systems use balanced, low-impedance microphones (Figure 3.11).

At this point, it is worth mentioning a unique but very important adaptation of the microphone as described up to now, and that is the *wireless microphone*. A wireless microphone is actually a system consisting of a

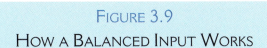

FIGURE 3.9

HOW A BALANCED INPUT WORKS

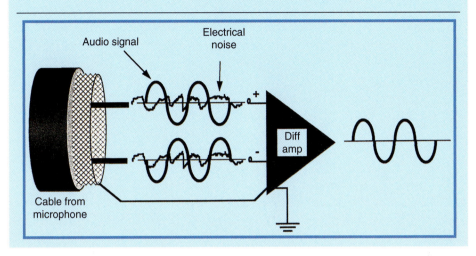

FIGURE 3.10

HOW AN UNBALANCED INPUT WORKS

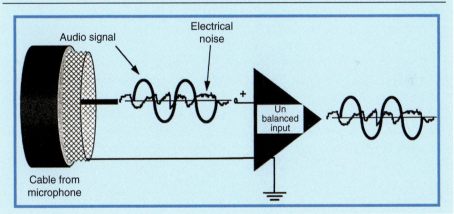

microphone, a radio transmitter, and a radio receiver. The characteristics of the microphone are all the same as for any microphone with one notable exception. The electrical signal produced by the workings of the microphone is converted into a radio signal that is broadcast by the transmitter to the receiver (usually across the event space or room to near where the mixer is located). This principle is called *frequency modulation* (FM) and is identical to that used by commercial radio stations. The combination of transmitter/receiver thus replaces the microphone cable.

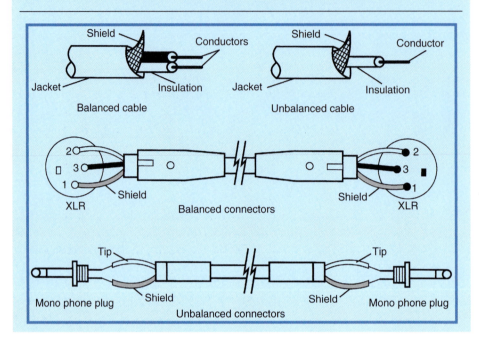

Physically, the transmitter takes two forms. One is a small box, called a body or *belt-pack* that can be clipped to a belt or otherwise attached to the user. The microphone is connected to the belt-pack via a small, thin wire. This form is most often used with lavalier or headset microphones for someone who must move around a lot, such as a keynote speaker or singer who also dances. The second form of transmitter is built into the body of the microphone itself and is used almost exclusively for speeches and for vocalists.

The receiver end of the system converts the radio signal back into an electrical signal and a regular audio cable connects the receiver output to the mixer, where the microphone is assigned a separate channel as for any wired microphone.

Wireless microphones operate in two main frequency bands: *very high frequency* (VHF) from 49 to 216 Hz and *ultra high frequency* (UHF) from 450 to 952 Hz. The VHF frequencies are shared with cell phones, walkie-talkies, radio-controlled toys, and other consumer electronic gadgets, thus making the wireless equipment using these frequencies prone to RFI or *radio frequency interference*. It is for this reason that most serious special event applications use only UHF wireless systems. It should also be noted that each wireless microphone must be assigned an individual frequency, which means that no two microphones can share the same frequency and each microphone must have its own transmitter and receiver. The transmitter and receiver should always be placed in line of sight of each other for proper functioning.

3.3.1.1.5 Physical Design

The physical design of a microphone is its mechanical and operational design. Types used in special event sound reinforcement include handheld, lavalier, headset, overhead, stand mounted, instrument and instrument mounted, and surface mounted. Most of these are available in a choice of operating principle, frequency response, directional pattern, and electrical output depending on the intended application. The correct selection of microphones is essential to good sound at a special event. The audio engineer must understand all details of the sound source in order to select the right microphones. Not only that, but if a person is using a microphone, he or she should know what the proper technique is for using that particular microphone. Correct placement of all microphones, no matter what the application, is also critical to avoid feedback and other potential problems. This is an area that is often overlooked in special events and it can result in disastrous audio problems. It is also an area about which many event producers are blissfully ignorant. We will review the main microphone designs and consider the optimum technique for using each design. Most of the explanations, images, and diagrams in this section, except where noted, are provided by Shure Inc. and used with permission (Lyons et al., 2005; Sigismondi, 2006).

Microphones used mainly for speech and vocals include:

- *Handheld microphones*: These come in both wired and wireless types and are normally used for speeches and by vocalists. The desired sound is the voice; the undesired sounds may be other talkers and, in the case of a musical group, other instruments, voices, or amplifiers. Dynamic microphones are the ones most often used in special events as they are more robust and will withstand frequent handling. The preferred frequency response is shaped, the directional pattern is usually unidirectional, and the output is balanced low impedance. Figure 3.12 gives an example of a handheld wired microphone (Shure SM58).

  Good technique for handheld microphone use includes:
  - Holding the microphone at the proper distance for balanced sound (4–12 in. for speech; touching the lips or a few inches away for vocals).
  - Aiming the microphone toward the mouth and away from all other sounds.
  - Using a *pop filter* to control breath noise.
  - Minimizing handling to avoid unwanted noise.

- Controlling loudness with the voice rather than moving the microphone.
- Using a microphone stand (for wired or wireless types) to reduce handling noise if the speaker or vocalist does not need to move around.

■ *Lavalier*: These come in both wired and wireless types, although the wireless forms are used almost exclusively in special events. The desired sound source is a speaking voice; undesired sounds include other talkers, clothing and movement noise, and loudspeakers. A condenser lavalier will give the best performance but only when phantom power is available. Otherwise, a dynamic is the choice. The most common directional pattern is omnidirectional but it may lead to more ambient noise. The frequency response is specially shaped to compensate for off-axis placement (e.g. speaker's head turns away from the microphone), and the output is balanced low impedance.

Placement of lavalier microphones is critical. They should be as close to the mouth as practical, usually a few inches below the neckline on a lapel, tie or lanyard, or at the neckline on a woman's dress, and never underneath any clothing. When they are used in theater applications on actors, they are best placed on or near the hairline, with the best method of holding it in place to be determined by the wig master. For this purpose, lavaliers come in white and tan colors to be more inconspicuous, and with an array of mounting pins and clips. Figure 3.12 gives an example of a lavalier microphone (Shure PG185).

Good technique for lavalier microphone use includes:
- Not breathing on or touching the microphone or its cable.
- Not turning the head away from the microphone.
- Speaking in a clear and distinct voice.

■ *Headset*: These come in wired and wireless forms, unidirectional and omnidirectional, condenser or dynamic, and with a choice of frequency responses. Most newer models have a lightweight frame that sits on the ears and wraps around the back of the head, with a short boom arm that holds the microphone at the corner of the mouth. They are the preferred microphone (especially unidirectional, wireless) for use in special event entertainment when a performer must both move and speak at the same time. They are used extensively for dancer/singers and for other variety performers moving around the stage (e.g. jugglers, physical comedians). The big advantage to these microphones is that they are directly in front of and close to, the sound source, resulting in optimum sound quality with minimum feedback possibilities. Figure 3.12 gives an example of a headset microphone (Shure PG30TQG).

■ *Overhead*: In the temporary world of special events, overhead microphones are rarely used except in venues that enable mounting of them above the stage area, such as in theaters. These microphones are most often condenser types, with unidirectional, cardioid pickup and flat, wide-range frequency response. They are balanced, low impedance, and

will worl
final mic

- *Direc*
  every
  feren
  locat
  close
- *Dyna*
  loude
  hand
  instru
  phon

Here are

- *Chor*
  tiona
  be co
  (0.6–
  row c
  Simila
  micro
  to the
- *Elect*
  1–4 in
  the s
  phone
- *Drum*
  quite
  ical m

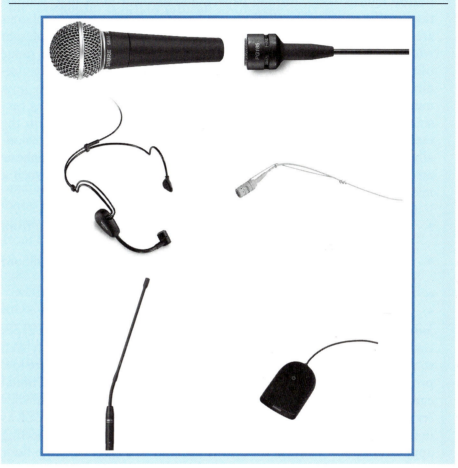

Courtesy: Shure Inc.

high sensitivity due to the distance from the sound source(s). Physically, they consist of a small condenser element mounted on a short goose-neck, which then leads to a thin cable that can be up to 20 or 30 ft (6 or 9 m) long. Figure 3.12 gives an example of an overhead microphone (Shure EZO Easyflex).

In these cases, if the desired sound reinforcement is of a large area of the stage (e.g. for a special play with multiple actors/performers), place-ment would be for the upstage area with the microphones suspended 8–10 ft (2.4–3 m) above the stage and aimed upstage. The pickup areas should not be overlapped.

PRODUCTION WAR STORY: UNCOOPERATIVE MICROPHONES

The president approaches the lectern for his welcome address and the lectern mics cannot be heard over the audience din. An embarrassing silence follows while a search ensues backstage for a handheld wireless mic. The handheld mic also does not function. Another long silence while a second wireless mic is found. This one works but the damage has been done and the president is thoroughly embarrassed and angry.

Since this happened at the beginning of a show, there was still some time to recover. The omnidirectional lectern mics were replaced with unidirectional mics on stands (less attractive but they worked) while the client was told what was happening. Unfortunately, the handheld mics had been hit with a bad case of RFI, which was unpredictable because of the preponderance of cell phones and radio frequencies of ships and planes in close proximity to the event location. As well, the audio engineer had placed the main mid-high range speakers too close to the lectern causing feedback from the omni mics.

Not only was the client given a substantial discount, but valuable lessons were learned about where and how to place microphones in relation to speakers, as well as the disruptive effects that can be caused by RFI.

Courtesy: Doug Matthews

(1000 ft/300 m or more). Certain instruments (e.g. guitars, keyboards, keyboard mixers) produce output signals which are already at the line level. This means that if these signals were to be fed directly into a mixing console – and there are inputs that accept line level signals – there would be a significant amount of noise and poor sound quality due to the length of cable that would be required to get the signal from the instruments to the mixer in almost every special event situation. For example, in a typical event, the stage is on one side of the room and the mixing console is on the other, sometimes as far as 100 or 200 ft (30 or 60 m) away, enough distance to degrade a line level electronic signal. This is where a DI or direct input box is used.

A DI is, in its most simple terms, a transformer that takes a line level signal (high impedance and unbalanced) and transforms it down to a lower or microphone level signal (low impedance and balanced) so it can be transported along that extended length of cable (the infamous 'snake') to the mixer and still arrive in good condition via an XLR connector at either end. A *passive* DI is one that is constructed of components such as capacitors and resistors, and an *active* DI is one that is constructed of active electronics such as integrated circuits, and must have continuous power applied from a wall outlet or battery.

The other main purposes of a DI are to balance the signal and to independently feed the same signal to a separate onstage amplifier (such as a guitar or keyboard amp) at the same time as the signal goes to the main PA system.

In most real event situations with musicians, it is, however, more normal to use a microphone for an electric guitar or electric bass amplifier rather than putting the signal through a DI, which tends to take away some of the warmth of the sound. On the other hand, a DI **is** used for acoustic guitars and also for an electronic keyboard mixer output.

3.3.2 Signal Processing and Routing Group

Normally located directly in front of the main stage but at least 30 ft (9 m) away and across the room, this group forms the audio console or mixer end of the 'snake' and includes:

- The house console or mixer.
- An effects rack.
- The snake (although not technically part of this group, it is included so that it can be explained properly).

The purpose of this group is to increase the strength of, and to manipulate, the signal arriving from the input group via the snake and then send it back to the output group via the snake. Let us examine exactly how each piece of equipment does this.

3.3.2.1 *The Mixer*

Also called a sound, house or audio *console* or *board*, the mixer to the uninitiated eye looks like the bridge of the Starship Enterprise – something to be feared and something far too complicated for the average event producer to comprehend. In actual fact, when broken down logically, it's not. Figure 3.19 shows a simple 20-channel mixer manufactured by Mackie.

The job of the mixer is really quite simple. It – with the guiding hand of a good audio engineer – performs the following tasks:

- Provides a separate channel for each input. Every single microphone, DI, CD/DVD player, keyboard mixer, and piece of sound-producing equipment onstage is assigned a separate input channel on the mixer. Mixers are usually identified by the number of input channels they have, with standard mixers coming in 4-, 8-, 12-, 16-, 24-, 32-, 48-, and 54-channel versions. Inputs are mic level (XLR) or line level (quarter inch phono plug).
- Increases or 'normalizes' the signal strength of the input signal. The mixer converts the input signal, if required, from the small microphone level (in the order of millivolts) to line level (0.1–2 V), so that all inputs have approximately the same signal strength before they move on.

FIGURE 3.19
EXAMPLE OF A MIXER (MACKIE CFX20.MKII)

Courtesy: http://www.mackie.com/home/showimage.html?u=/products/cfx20mkii/images/
CXF20MkII-3Qtr.jpg

- Integrates effects. It manipulates the sound of each channel and of the entire mix, before sending the mix onward in the system to the output group.
- Combines all input signals into a final mix and sends the signal on to the output group via the snake.

Let us now look at how the audio engineer uses the controls available on each separate channel. Here is a brief explanation of how each control works and what it does, using Figure 3.20, an example of a basic mixer's channel strips, as a guide.

- *Trim or gain control*: This boosts the input signal from microphone level to line level, or otherwise adjusts the signal strength to bring it to the same level as all others.
- *Auxiliary send (AUX)*: This sends the individual channel signal to other devices such as stage monitors or effects processors. This particular mixer has specific sends for effects (EFX) after the pre-fade listen (PFL).
- *PFL (or pre-fader)*: This button enables the audio engineer to check that the signal is present, at the right level, and of suitable quality before it goes to the fader (volume control) for the channel.
- *EQ*: This refers to equalization of bands of frequencies. The engineer can boost or diminish a particular frequency band for the individual channel to improve the sound quality of that channel. For example, the bass frequency band can be reduced on a lavalier microphone to reduce

FIGURE 3.20

EXAMPLE OF CHANNEL STRIPS ON A
MIXER (MACKIE CFX20)

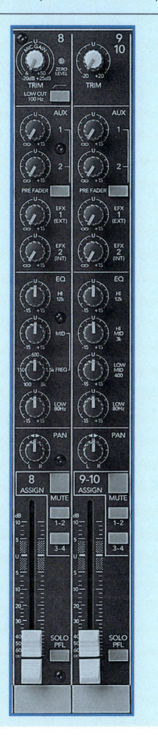

clunking sounds, or the high-frequency band can be reduced to prevent *sibilance* (excessive hissing through a microphone).

- *Pan*: This adjusts the amount of individual channel sound heard through the left or right speakers. Although each channel is actually in mono, this adjustment enables the simulation of stereo.
- *Mute button*: This mutes or silences the particular channel to prevent unwanted noise from impinging on the mix.
- *Assign*: Also known as the *bus section*, this assigns the input microphone or channel signal to the main output channels of the mixer, which can be anywhere from two to eight.
- *Fader*: This controls the individual signal or channel level (volume) sent to the output of the mixer.
- *Solo PFL*: This isolates the channel signal so that it can be heard by itself. This is useful for such things as cueing CDs or tapes.

A word must be mentioned at this point about digital mixers as they are coming onto the market rapidly. Digital mixers are replacing the large analog mixers described above. With digital mixers, all effects described below are built into the mixer, as well as dynamics control (e.g. compressors and gates) and output processing (e.g. EQ and time delays). They even include playback and recording of MP3 files. Most professional models have add-on capabilities so that a small mixer can be increased to 40 channels or more with little space added. The beauty of digital mixers is that individual channel settings can be preset, memorized, and instantly recalled when required. Of course, this also means that all settings can be stored and instantly recalled later from CD or from a hard drive, thus saving considerable time in sound checks. Storage, transportation, and setup are naturally much easier; however, operation requires a longer learning period.

3.3.2.2   The Effects Rack

Effects help to thicken or modify the sound that is going through the system. They are normally accomplished by setting up what is known as an effects 'loop' in which an individual channel signal is sent from the mixer post-fader (i.e. after the individual channel volume has been adjusted). The signal is then routed through a number of different effects, all mounted on what is known as a *rack* (just another term for a vertical arrangement of individual effects boxes in a traveling road case), and returned to the output of the mixer.

The effects that are most commonly used in special event audio systems are:

- *Delay and echo*: Echo is exactly that. It simulates the sound of a natural echo. Delay is basically the same. It is done by adding a time-delayed signal to the signal output. This produces a single echo, but multiple echoes can be achieved by feeding the output of the echo back into its input. Delay times from a few milliseconds to several seconds are common.

- *Reverberation (reverb)*: This is used to simulate the acoustical effect of sound in large rooms or concert halls, in particular the sound from all sources including reflected sound. It gives the impression of being in a very large space. It can be done digitally to lengthen the actual reverberation time within a small room to give it the feel of sound within a large room.
- *Chorus*: Chorus simulates the effect of more than one person singing. In other words, it can make a solo vocalist sound like two or more vocalists. It is achieved by adding in an echo to the original input signal; however, in this case, the echo's delay is continuously varied.
- *Flanging and phasing*: These are similar effects and are variations of the chorus effect. They make the sound appear to 'whoosh' or pulsate.
- *Noise gate*: This is used to prevent unwanted pickup of background noise such as hissing. It can be set to a certain threshold level so that any audio signal below that level will not pass through the gate, the result being a quiet channel.
- *Compressor*: A compressor simply reduces the difference between the loudest and quietest parts of a piece of music by automatically turning down the gain when the signal gets past a predetermined level. In this respect, it does a similar job to the human hand on the fader but it reacts much faster and with greater precision. In a loud environment say, for example a special event dinner, quieter passages will get lost unless the audio engineer 'rides' the channel fader for that instrument or vocalist to boost the volume during those quiet passages. The volume then needs to be reduced to prevent distortion or feedback when the instrument or vocalist gets loud again. A compressor allows the volume to be left at the 'boosted' level by reducing the peaks (loud parts) by a preset amount so they don't cause distortion. Two controls common to compressors are *threshold* and *ratio*. The threshold determines at what point the compressor function activates, and the ratio controls how much the signal is compressed. The compressor allows much more control by the audio engineer, and negates any reason for a vocalist – or person speaking – to move a microphone to control the volume level (Sigismondi, 2006).

Once all effects have been added to the mix, the signal is routed to the final output of the mixer and the main speaker volume level controlled directly from the master fader on the output panel of the mixer. It is normally comprised of one stereo or two single channel faders that correspond with the left and right main house speakers. It can also include outputs that correspond to monitor mixes for onstage performers.

3.3.2.3   The Snake

The purpose of the snake is simply to act as an extension cord that connects all the signals on the stage to the equipment the audio engineer uses at the audio console position, usually at least 30 ft across the room or event space from the stage. A professional snake can be up to 1000 ft (300 m) in length before there is serious signal degradation. It has a number (16 in Figure 3.21) of low impedance (XLR) female receptacles mounted in a box at the stage end that are connected directly to microphones and DIs as mentioned earlier, and each of these corresponds to a single mixer channel. At the console position, corresponding male XLR plugs go directly into the appropriate channel of the mixer. Some snakes also allow for a number of return signals (4 in Figure 3.21) to come back through the snake, such as with monitor mixes; however, for best audio quality, it is recommended not to use these returns for the mixer output going to power amps, and hence to main speakers, as feedback can occur due to *coupling* of signals going to and coming from the mixer (Davis and Jones, 1990; p. 289).

3.3.3 Output Group

This group is comprised of the audio system components that represent the final destination of the original audio signal that began away upstream as a

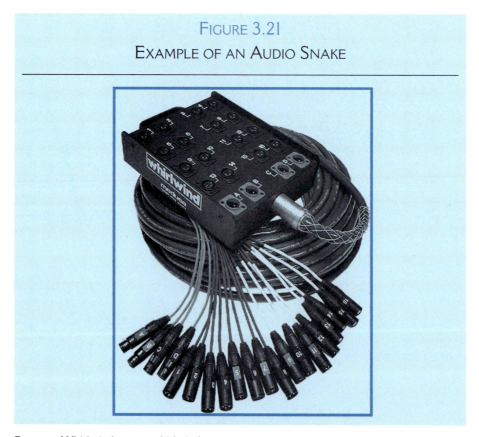

FIGURE 3.21

EXAMPLE OF AN AUDIO SNAKE

Courtesy: Whirlwind, www.whirlwindusa.com

sound wave going into a microphone on the stage. With the exception of two components, the equipment in this group is located either on or very close to the main stage. The equipment includes:

- A frequency equalizer system for the main sound.
- A limiter for the main sound.
- Crossovers to divide up frequencies going into the power amplifiers.
- Power amplifiers.
- The main speakers.
- The entire monitor system, also including EQ, amplifier, and stage monitors.

The purpose of this group is to prepare and deliver the output signal from the main mixer to the main or house speakers. The signal is first adjusted by a house equalizer and then by a limiter, both of which are located near the main mixer. The signal is then routed back through a snake (ideally separate from the main one) to the main stage area where it is divided up into frequencies that correspond to the different main or house speakers, amplified, and finally fed into the speakers. Let us examine how each of these components achieves this.

3.3.3.1 *Equalizer*

This equalizer system works exactly the same as the one for each individual channel except that this one adjusts the frequencies going to the main speakers in the house or event space after the audio signal has already been adjusted for each channel. In other words, this particular equalizer adjusts the entire mix.

Equalizers come in two basic varieties: *graphic* and *parametric*. The graphic equalizer is the most common. The controls on a graphic equalizer consist of rows of faders that are used to cut or boost specific frequencies. The more faders there are the more precise is the level of control. Hence the name 'graphic' as this refers to the 'graph' that is represented by the shape of the faders showing the frequencies that have been cut or boosted. Each fader itself corresponds to a small band of frequencies.

Parametric equalizers on the other hand, offer more precise control since they actually consist of three separate controls: frequency, boost/cut, and bandwidth. The frequency control permits the audio engineer to select a specific frequency, the boost/cut control selects how much that frequency is raised or lowered, and the bandwidth control selects how many adjacent frequencies are affected (Sigismondi, 2006).

The equalizer placed at the output of the mixer is used primarily to control the frequencies that are affected by the room or event space itself. For example, we earlier discussed the problems with low frequencies being dominant in a room by virtue of the fact that they 'bend' around small objects and are thus not absorbed as much as higher frequencies. Because of this, they can be minimized through the use of an equalizer at the output of the mixer, just as the high frequencies that tend to be absorbed by people filling the room can be boosted. This is especially important when a sound check is done in the afternoon before an event and before the room is filled with people. At the time of the event, with more people, the room behaves differently acoustically and the equalizer can compensate for this.

3.3.3.2   Limiter

A limiter is a specialized form of compressor (see the earlier section on effects) that uses a very high ratio to prevent any signal from surpassing the level set by the threshold. A limiter is primarily used as an overall system protection at the output of the mixer (after the equalizer), while compressors are typically used on an individual channel basis, although the actual hardware usually combines the two functions.

3.3.3.3   Crossovers

Crossovers are electrical devices placed in the path of the audio signal after the limiter. Their purpose is to divide up the audio signal into separate outputs of mid-, low-, and high-range frequencies. These separated signals are then routed to the appropriate speakers that are designed for them. *Passive* crossovers are located inside full-range speaker cabinets (i.e. speakers that cover all frequencies) and do this by dividing the signal after it leaves the power amplifiers. They tend to be inefficient in that all the speakers are working from the same power source, and the low-range speakers, which require more power, will rob power from the higher-range frequency speakers.

Active crossovers are located outside the speaker cabinets and before the power amplifiers. In this way, they make it possible to power the low-, mid-, and high-range speakers from different power amplifiers. This is a much more efficient use of power and enables the system to provide a more powerful and full sound covering all frequencies equally. It does, however, require more equipment and expense (Hysell, 2000). It is the system of choice for most special events with complex audio requirements and large audiences.

The practice of using an active crossover scheme in a system is known by several names, which depend on how many splits are being made in the audible frequency range. If the system is simply being broken into lows and highs, it is said to be *bi-amped*. If it is broken into low, mid, and high, it is said to be *tri-amped*.

The latest digital crossovers now have compressor/limiters built in to them so there is no need for a separate unit.

3.3.3.4   Power Amplifiers

The purpose of the power amplifiers is to boost the low-voltage line level signal coming from the limiter (or from the equalizer if there is no system limiter) to a higher voltage output signal capable of efficiently driving the loudspeakers. Power amplifiers are functionally simple units. All amplifiers have a set of line level inputs and a set of speaker level outputs. Most have a power switch and volume controls as well.

Appropriately, the power rating of an amplifier is its most important statistic. It is measured in *RMS watts* (RMS or root mean square is a mathematical expression used to describe the level of a signal) and should match the power-loading capabilities of the speaker it is driving. For example, for special event situations, it is not unusual to have amplifiers rated at 400 W or higher to amplify all the instruments and microphones. However, the matching speaker system must also be able to handle at least that amount of power.

It should be noted here **why** exactly so much power may be needed. The answer is quality and clarity of sound. If the required level for comfortable listening for a musical stage show is only 20 W, but there is a musical peak in the performance that is twice as loud, the laws of physics demand that the amplifier will require 10 times the power to make the music *seem* twice as loud. In other words, the amplifier must be capable of delivering 200 W of power to the speakers. Otherwise, the music will sound distorted and fuzzy. Not only that, but the speakers may also be damaged if the amplifier is incapable of providing that power level.

3.3.3.5   Main Speakers

Speaker design and the choice and placement of the correct speakers within the event space are critical to audio quality.

3.3.3.5.1   Design

A loudspeaker (speaker) is the final destination of the original sound wave that started onstage with a microphone or other electronic device. It simply converts the electrical signal back into mechanical energy in the form of a sound wave. The signal activates an electromagnet attached to the speaker frame. This electromagnet in turn generates a magnetic field that corresponds in intensity to the frequency and loudness of the electrical signal emitted by the amplifier. The variation in this magnetic field causes a *voice coil*, which is attached to the rear of a flexible cone-shaped diaphragm (also called a *membrane* and constructed of paper or synthetic material), to move the cone forward and backward in a pattern that mimics the frequency and loudness dictated by the electrical signal (Gillette, 2000). Figure 3.22(a) is a simple drawing showing basic speaker design, and Figure 3.22(b) shows how the electromagnet moves the cone to produce a sound wave.

Speakers are generally classified as low frequency (*woofers*), with a frequency range from approximately 20 to 1000 Hz, middle frequency (*midrange* or *mids*), with a frequency range from approximately 500 to 5000 Hz or more, and high frequency (*tweeters*), with a frequency range from approximately 5000 to 20,000 Hz. Manufacturers currently tend to be

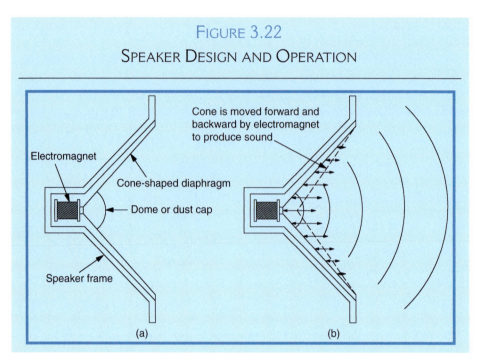

FIGURE 3.22
SPEAKER DESIGN AND OPERATION

Cone is moved forward and backward by electromagnet to produce sound

Electromagnet

Cone-shaped diaphragm

Dome or dust cap

Speaker frame

(a)　　　　(b)

Courtesy: Doug Matthews

making speakers that combine the middle and high range of frequencies into ones that cover about 80 or 90 Hz to 20 kHz. These are referred to either as *mid-high* or *full-range* speakers. Only the very low frequencies below about 80 Hz occasionally need reinforcement in event situations, especially for concerts or musical acts, and these speakers are called *subs* or *sub-woofers*, although most manufacturers' speakers in this category cover a range from about 20 or 30 Hz to about 220 or 250 Hz.

Most low-frequency speakers are of a cone-type design while the mid- and high-range speakers incorporate both a unique horn design called a *pressure driver* that uses a thin metal diaphragm, and a *horn* that helps to direct the sound in a particular direction and pattern because of its unique shape.

Speaker cabinets are also designed to enhance the specific frequencies of the speakers they house. For example, bass speakers may incorporate sound-absorbing material to reduce reflections within the cabinet since the low frequencies tend to radiate in all directions. In general, cabinets help to reinforce the low frequencies and to smooth out the quality of the bass response. Mid and high frequencies radiate outwards at about 180 degrees or less, so less cabinet design is required, although most speakers for these ranges have their backs covered with thin material to avoid interference from the vibrations of lower frequencies. See Figure 3.23 for examples of full-range and sub-woofer speaker designs (Turbosound TA-890H full range on the left; JBL JRX118S sub on the right).

FIGURE 3.23

EXAMPLES OF SPEAKERS (NOT TO SCALE)

Courtesy: Turbosound Ltd., www.turbosound.com and JBL Professional, www.jblpro.com

3.3.3.5.2 Placement

Speaker placement can be critical and depends on the type of event, whether there will be only speeches or mainly musical entertainment, the size of the audience, and the size and construction of the venue or event space. Placement **must** be made with at least a general understanding of the acoustics of the space.

In the case of an event in which there are only speeches, there are several options for speaker placement. The one that achieves best consistent sound quality throughout the event space is a distributed system. This system uses a number of full-range speakers on tripod stands placed around the space so that full coverage is obtained. For a richer sound as previously described, it may also include small sub-woofer speakers beside or under the stage (for frequencies below 80 Hz.). It is good for a relatively small space and audience (see Figure 3.24). Note that this is a side view of the space and shows only one row of speakers down one side of a wall in a 100 ft long room. This arrangement would be duplicated down the near wall with perhaps one or two speakers across the back wall as well.

Figure 3.25 is a second option for speaker placement. It uses a flown system from a ceiling-mounted truss that points a cluster of full-range speakers at the audience so that all seats are covered by the dispersion of the sound. Additionally, sub-woofers are generally placed under or beside the stage. In most situations, there would be two or more sets of speakers mounted on the same truss over the stage so that equal coverage could be maintained **across** the space.

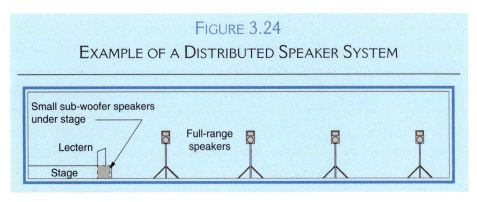

FIGURE 3.24

EXAMPLE OF A DISTRIBUTED SPEAKER SYSTEM

Courtesy: Doug Matthews

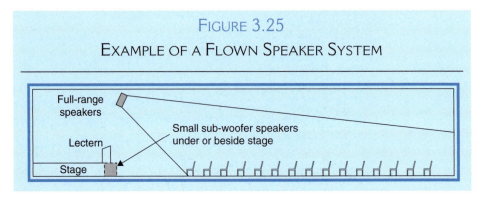

FIGURE 3.25

EXAMPLE OF A FLOWN SPEAKER SYSTEM

Courtesy: Doug Matthews

Occasionally a situation will arise that requires audience seating closer to the stage, usually because event managers want to seat the maximum number of persons in the room. If the sound system is flown, this requires that an additional set of flown speakers be aimed at the front few rows of seats as in Figure 3.26. An optional way to achieve the same thing is to either place one or two sets of the same full-range speakers on stands at the front of the room to cover this part of the audience, or place even smaller fill speakers (such as monitors) on the downstage edge of the stage pointing at the front rows of the audience.

If the event space is large and extends back from the stage more than 80–100 ft (24–30 m), there is usually the need to provide what are known as *delay speakers*. These are exactly the same types of full-range speakers except that there is a programmed delay to the sound that emanates from them in the order of milliseconds. This delay compensates for the sound coming from the speakers **nearest** to the stage and reaching the audience's ears at a time **after** it would reach them if a delay were **not** built in. Thus all sound reaches audience members farther from the stage at exactly the same time. These delay speakers also compensate for sound degradation at

FIGURE 3.26

EXAMPLE OF A FLOWN SPEAKER SYSTEM WITH FRONT FILL SPEAKERS

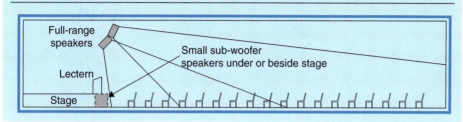

Courtesy: Doug Matthews

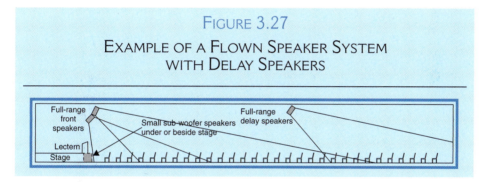

FIGURE 3.27

EXAMPLE OF A FLOWN SPEAKER SYSTEM WITH DELAY SPEAKERS

Courtesy: Doug Matthews

distant points in the event space caused by reverberation, points at which the level of reverberation and the direct sound level (i.e. the sound coming directly from the speakers versus reflected sound) are approximately equal. Farther back in the room from this point the sound quality will be poor and speech especially becomes less intelligible. Figure 3.27 illustrates the installation of such delay speakers in a long room.

In the case of entertainment, as mentioned in Section 3.2.2, the range of frequencies is much more than for ordinary speech. Because of this, large sub-woofers are demanded. These are typically placed near the stage and immediately to either side. They do not normally have to be flown because, as explained in the section on acoustic theory, low frequencies tend to bend around obstacles and therefore can cover an entire room with objects such as people in the way. Figure 3.28 illustrates how a typical event dinner might look from a side view showing such speaker placement.

One final concern in speaker placement is lateral coverage. Yes, the above placements can cover short and long rooms, but what if the room or event space is very wide? This is usually solved by arraying several speakers on the same horizontal plane but facing different directions in order to obtain coverage across the room. The exact amount and quality of coverage will depend in the end on speaker design and angle of speaker placement. Figure 3.29 illustrates this type of placement from a top view of the same event situation as in Figure 3.28.

The last point for discussion on speaker placement for special events concerns larger indoor or outdoor events, mainly concerts with large

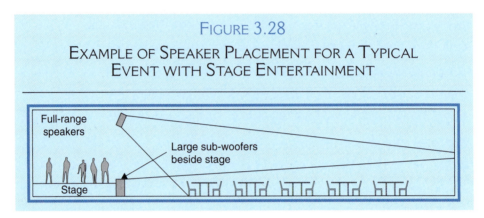

FIGURE 3.28

EXAMPLE OF SPEAKER PLACEMENT FOR A TYPICAL EVENT WITH STAGE ENTERTAINMENT

Courtesy: Doug Matthews

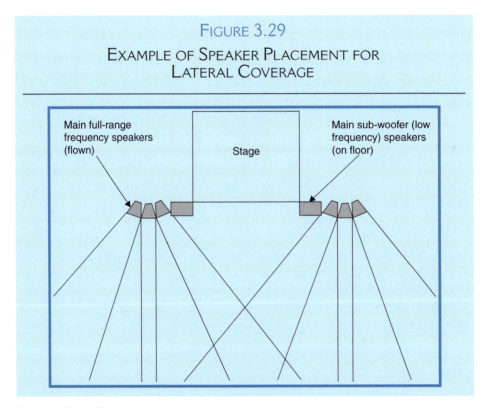

FIGURE 3.29

EXAMPLE OF SPEAKER PLACEMENT FOR LATERAL COVERAGE

Courtesy: Doug Matthews

audiences. The term 'array' has already been mentioned above in explaining the use of multiple similar speakers placed in a horizontal plane in order to achieve horizontal coverage. An array of speakers is also used to cover large distances and large audiences in the vertical plane. This is known as a *line array*. A line array is a set of identical speakers arrayed in the vertical plane to create what appears as a straight line when viewed from the front; however, it is in fact curved slightly to give greater vertical coverage. For example, a line array can be used to cover the entire vertical plane within a stadium from roof to floor. The majority of systems used in vertical line arrays are specially designed for that use alone. The individual speakers generally cover a wider frequency range than other types, usually from about 30 Hz to 18 or 20 kHz. Usually, subs are added for events involving entertainment in order to cover the very low frequencies below 30 Hz. These may be mounted on the ground or flown with the line array. Line array speakers are also designed for wider horizontal coverage, with some speakers covering as wide an angle as 120 degrees in the horizontal plane. The decision on number of speakers, curvature of the speaker array, and type of speakers is determined based on the size of the venue or event space, the audience size, the extent of coverage needed, manufacturer's specifications, and other variables. One benefit of a line array design is that special mounting and flying bracketry comes with the speakers, making setup much more efficient. Figure 3.30 illustrates a line array setup in side and plan views.

3.3.3.6   *Monitor System*

The main purpose of monitors is to allow performers onstage to hear what all the other performers are singing, what other instruments are playing, or what backup music is being played to accompany a performance or program. If an event is held in a small room with very few people in the audience, there is probably no need for any stage monitors since anyone onstage will be able to hear what is going on directly from the main speakers. However, when an event gets to any significant size in terms of audience, or the event space or venue itself becomes large, there will be a need for monitors to allow onstage performers to hear everything else that is happening on the stage. Often for many special events the audio system is quite modest, even with multiple performances onstage in a large venue. Perhaps there is a choreographed dance show, or perhaps a few speeches followed by a four- or five-piece combo for dancing, or perhaps a multimedia show with PowerPoint slides accompanied by a choir. In all these cases, there is probably no need for more than two to four monitors onstage at any time.

In these cases, monitors and their mixes can be controlled entirely from the main house mixer. For example, the Mackie CFX 20 mixer as described earlier has two auxiliary sends located on each input channel. This means that the signal from that channel can be sent to one of the

Vertical line array of speakers (flown)

Vertical coverage area of speakers

Stage

Vertical line array of speakers (flown stage left)

Horizontal coverage area of speakers

Stage

Vertical line array of speakers (flown stage right)

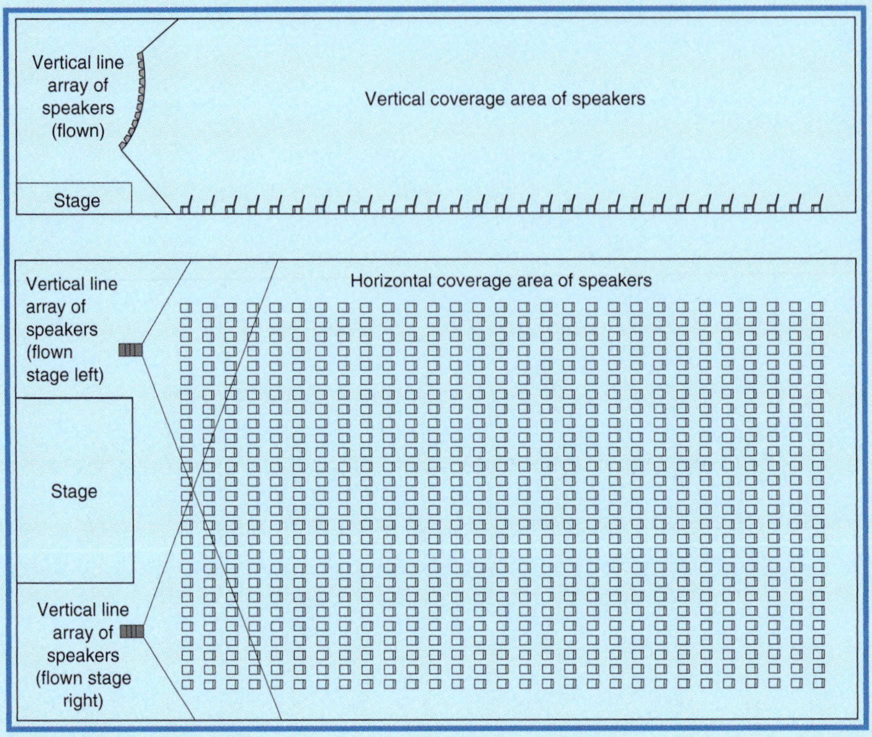

Courtesy: Doug Matthews

two auxiliary output channels on the mixer, thereby creating two separate mixes for onstage monitors that are sent back through the snake to the stage. Unfortunately, the number of different mixes is limited by the number of auxiliary output channels on the mixer. Once the number of mixes required exceeds the number of auxiliary output channels, a separate monitor mixer is needed. For example, if there is a large band playing with several instruments, lead vocals, and backup vocals, there may be quite a large number of separate mixes desired by the band. The lead vocalist, for example, may want to hear only the keyboard and bass players with a little bit of the backup vocals, the drummer may only want to hear the bass, guitars, and keyboard, the keyboardist may only want to hear the lead vocalist, guitars and drummer, etc. In this type of situation, with complex monitor mix requirements, the monitor mix must be located beside the stage. See Figure 3.31 for an example of a typical band's 'stage plot' for exactly this type of situation. It should be noted that many

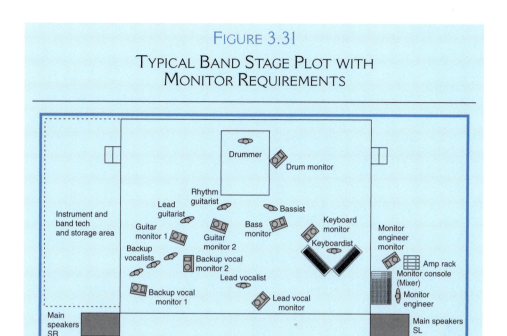

Courtesy: Doug Matthews

musical groups now prefer to work with *in-ear monitors* that are simply one-way ear bud speakers much like those available with portable MP3 players. These allow for much less equipment clutter onstage because all the larger monitors are eliminated, and for easier individual customization of mixes.

How then, is this separate monitor mix accomplished? By what is known as a *multi-input, transformer-isolated splitter*. The splitter is a device – actually a variation of the snake – that takes input signals such as a microphone or DI, and 'splits' them into two or more (usually no more than four) separate paths. There are two main types of splitters: passive (no power required) and active (power required). Passive splitters are normally used when the signal only needs to be split into two or at most three different paths. Active ones are used for four or more paths. A transformer-isolated splitter (or split snake) basically allows an audio signal (e.g. microphone) to be sent directly through it to the main mixer, while the second split goes to a monitor mixer as an identical signal. The splitter is located on or near the stage, while the monitor mixer is usually at the side of the stage. In this way, the monitors can be mixed entirely separately from the main house mix. This monitor mix and the associated equipment are essentially identical to the main mixer and its related equipment, except that the output ends up at a number of different monitors onstage instead of the main house speakers. Because the same principles apply as for the main audio system, the monitor system will not be explained in detail.

3.4   SIGNAL PATH AND EQUIPMENT LOCATIONS IN THE EVENT SPACE

Now that we have examined in detail all the main groups that comprise the audio system, let us go back and review exactly how the audio signal flows and follow it from beginning to end in a diagram.

3.4.1   Signal Path

Using the example of the nine-piece band given in Figure 3.31, we will follow the actual signal path with assistance from a more comprehensive diagram, Figure 3.32, in which the input group, the signal processing and routing group, and the output group are each outlined by dashed lines.

To review, the audio signal:

- Begins onstage with the input group, through microphones where it is converted from a sound wave into an electrical audio signal, instrument DIs, guitar effects rack, or keyboard mixer;
- Goes into a transformer-isolated split snake that sends one set of signals to the main mixer and one to the monitor mixer;
- Is processed in the signal processing and routing group, by the main house (FOH) mixer where it is raised in strength, and has various effects added in the house effects racks, then is looped back to the main mixer;
- Goes from the mixer into the output group, in which a house equalizer adjusts frequencies, a house limiter controls maximum strength, house crossovers split it into different frequency bands, power amplifiers boost its strength, and finally the house speakers which convert it back into sound waves.

The signal going to the monitor mixer is handled in almost exactly the same way as the signal going to the main house mixer, with identical components.

3.4.2   Equipment Locations

In the same way, let us review exactly where in the event space all the audio equipment is located.

- *Input group*: In special event applications, almost all the input group of equipment is located entirely onstage. This includes vocal and instrument microphones, instrument DIs, keyboard mixers, and occasionally onstage CD/DVD players or tape decks that are controlled by performers (this could also include laptop computers with CD/DVD players).

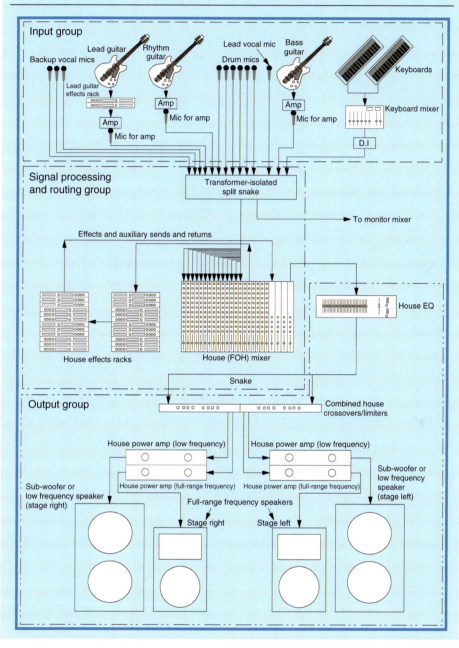

Figure 3.32
Signal Path for Typical Event Audio System

Input group

Backup vocal mics

Lead guitar

Rhythm guitar

Lead guitar effects rack

Amp

Mic for amp

Amp

Mic for amp

Lead vocal mic

Drum mics

Bass guitar

Amp

Mic for amp

Keyboards

Keyboard mixer

D.I

Signal processing and routing group

Transformer-isolated split snake

To monitor mixer

Effects and auxiliary sends and returns

House effects racks

House (FOH) mixer

House EQ

Snake

Output group

Combined house crossovers/limiters

House power amp (low frequency)

House power amp (low frequency)

Sub-woofer or low frequency speaker (stage right)

House power amp (full-range frequency)

House power amp (full-range frequency)

Sub-woofer or low frequency speaker (stage left)

Full-range frequency speakers

Stage right

Stage left

Courtesy: Doug Matthews

Other components of the input group are found usually at the house mixer location. These include CD/DVD, DAT, mini-disk or tape players, computer audio output signals (used in multimedia presentations), videotape audio outputs, receivers for onstage wireless microphones, and voiceover microphones for Masters of Ceremonies.

- *Signal processing and routing group*: This equipment, including the main house mixer and effects rack, is located at the FOH position which, particularly in the case of special events with complex entertainment and musical stage shows, should be at least 30–100 ft (9–30 m) directly across the room or event space from the stage. The general rule of thumb as suggested by Davis and Jones (1990; pp. 190–191) is that the console should not be closer to any of the main speakers than the distance between the two mains (left and right), and no farther than twice the distance between the two mains. It is not absolutely necessary to have the console at the same height as the stage. In fact, it may be preferable to have it on the floor to avoid the amplification of low frequencies by the riser structure, which would be required if it were raised. Often, due to the restrictions of space and the room layout, it is not possible to have the FOH location in front of the stage at all, but rather at the side of the room somewhere. This is not ideal and means that the audio engineer must continually monitor the sound by walking to the center of the room to listen for proper balance. Unfortunately, this is one of the negatives of the event business.

  The third member of this group, the snake, is what connects the input group to the signal processing group. There are several options for locating it. The ideal one strictly from an audio standpoint, is in a straight line on the floor between the stage and FOH. If the event is a dinner or standup reception of some sort, however, this can make it a serious trip hazard. It should therefore be matted if possible with a solid mat with yellow warning markings or at the very least with a rubber mat, again with yellow or caution cross taping. Otherwise, the safer route is also in a straight line but across or through the ceiling, which negates any matting and avoids trip hazards, but increases setup time. The third option is to route the snake around the perimeter of the room. This means that it must either go over doorways, or across the floor in the doorways. The better choice is over the doors but if it must go across the floor, again it must be matted with either a solid cable mat (best) or a large rubber mat.

- *Output group*: The components of this group have several different locations which are usually as follows:
  - *House equalizer and limiter*: These are always located near the FOH console position.
  - *Crossovers and power amplifiers*: These are usually located on or near the stage and, if there is a monitor engineer, close to him, although the crossovers can be placed at the FOH position so that fewer channels of return snake are used.

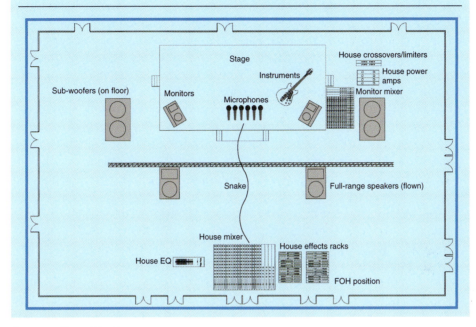

Courtesy: Doug Matthews

- *Main speakers*: The locations of these can vary depending on the type of event, the size of the audience, and so on, as explained in the section on speaker placement. However, there will always be a set of speakers near the main stage, usually at the outside edges.
- *Monitor system*: In a simple event, monitors will be controlled from the FOH position. In a complex event, the entire monitor system will be located on either stage right or left and there will be a separate *monitor engineer* assigned to control it full-time.

Figure 3.33 illustrates a room with all components placed approximately where they would be found. It is not to scale but should permit an easy understanding.

3.5   PRE-EVENT SOUND CHECK AND SYSTEM OPERATION DURING THE EVENT

In this section we examine what the audio engineer does during sound check and during the actual event.

3.5.1 Pre-Event Sound Check

Most audio systems, no matter what the size, are run in essentially the same way. Whether it is a small meeting with simple speeches and an audience of 100, or a stadium rock and roll concert, the operating principles of the audio system are similar. Once the basic components of microphones, snake, mixer, effects, equalizer, amplifiers, and speakers are set up, then it is necessary to carry out a sound check and proceed with system operation.

What is the purpose of the sound check and why does it take so long? This is perhaps one of the most misunderstood – but absolutely necessary – tasks that must be carried out for a special event to run without technical glitches, especially one with a large audience and complicated audio requirements. Event producers must understand that sufficient time has to be allotted to accomplish it. One to two hours – or more – are not unusual for a complete check.

A thorough sound check is done for several reasons:

- *Testing the system*: Because of the number of components in most systems, initial testing must be done slowly and in the right order so no damage is done to components, mainly speakers. Before the system is turned on at all, the crossover points (i.e. specific frequencies) must be set for all the speakers so that signal power is not too great for the speakers. After this, the system components are turned on in the general order of effects, EQ, mixer, and amplifiers. This is done with all volume and gain controls set to zero and most other knobs at a neutral position on the mixer. Following this, the individual speakers (mid/high then low) are tested to ensure that only the correct frequencies are coming through them.

- *Setting EQ*: The main reasons for using EQ (specific frequency adjustment) in an audio system are to prevent feedback and to help create a desired sound. Of these, feedback is of the most concern and the one annoying problem that can keep cropping up throughout an event if this procedure is not done properly. The procedure is done in exactly the same way for main speakers and for monitors. The preferred method now is to use an analyzer system that compares the output of the console with what is heard coming out the main speakers via calibrated microphones in the audience. After going to all this trouble, there may still be a problem with feedback due to the different acoustics in the venue once all the event attendees are present, so EQ usually needs to be monitored continuously during the event.

- *Adjusting individual channel signals*: From this point on during the sound check, the band or performers should be present so they can provide information to the audio engineer as to the acceptability of their sound. For this exercise, individual channel signal inputs are tested separately. For example, the lead vocalist's microphone is tested by first turning the gain control on that channel up until *clipping* or signal cutoff is shown by a light on the mixer channel. The gain is then turned down just below this level and remains there with no further adjustment during the event. From then on, the only adjustment is to the individual channel faders. The purpose of doing this is to get the maximum possible clear signal from each input source. Once this is accomplished for all channels, then the main mixer faders can be turned up and the individual channel faders adjusted to obtain a suitable overall mix coming out of the main speakers. Most audio engineers will assign a name to each channel at this time on a piece of tape and sometimes will set a preliminary level indication as well for each channel. This entire process can take quite a long time with a large band, so that time must be built into the event schedule.

As a quick review, here is the relationship amongst the different volume controls on the mixer:

- The gain control adjusts individual signals as they come into the mixer.
- The channel fader adjusts the signal level as it leaves the individual channel on its way to the main fader.
- The main fader adjusts the entire level of all signals as they leave the mixer on their way to the amps and main speakers.

■ *Setting monitor mixes*: This is a procedure that in theory is very simple. The musicians onstage decide who wants to hear which of the other performers (either instruments or vocals or both) and then those specific channels are combined in the monitor mixer to create a specific mix that is sent to that person's individual monitor. If there are only one or two mixes required as with a small band, then this mix procedure can be handled by the main mixer using the auxiliary send channels. If there are too many mixes for the main mixer, then, as described earlier, a separate monitor mixer must be set up beside the stage and an audio technician assigned to mix the monitors full-time during the event. Of course, every musical group has different requirements so there is no set mix that can be described. What should be remembered, however, is that although the procedure is simple in theory, in practice it can be the most time-consuming part of the sound check. Event producers should keep this in mind.

In the case of musical groups, Tim Lewis of Proshow Audiovisual-Broadcast in Vancouver, Canada, states how important it is to have a band that is organized for the sound check and especially for setting mixes. He cites one group that uses a method of going through the monitor mix procedure one musician at a time by having that musician play while all others raise their hands until their individual mix is perfect. This saves considerable time overall and is one of the best ways to accomplish the procedure if in-ear monitors are used (Tim Lewis, Personal Communication, September 18, 2006).

■ *Setting up effects*: This is usually the last part of the sound check and is done to enhance or improve overall sound quality rather than to cover up mistakes or poor musicianship. If you recall those effects racks and all the possible effects such as reverb, chorus, flanging, and such, this is the time that they are brought into play. The procedure is really just a balancing act in obtaining a nice sound using a combination of the individual channel effects send knob and the master effects send knob (both on the main mixer), plus the effects mixture controls and the effects level knob (both on the individual effect units).

Now that the sound check is complete, it's time to open the doors and start the event (after crew dinner break, of course)!

3.5.2   System Operation during the Event

If the sound check has been done properly, there is not too much to worry about for the audio engineer in terms of maintaining levels. However, if the event is complicated and will involve speeches, followed by entertainment, followed by a band, and all channels of a large mixer are being used, then he must be constantly vigilant. He will need to do some or all of the following during the event.

- Adjust individual channel faders on the mixer to minimize feedback and to isolate speeches (i.e. turn off all channels except the speech microphone).
- Adjust individual channel faders for instrumental solos, backup vocalists, or other inputs such as CD/DVD backing tracks, voiceover microphones, video, or PowerPoint feeds.
- Prevent feedback by adjusting house EQ and main mixer and individual channel faders.
- Adjust effects as needed for best sound quality.
- Maintain house volume to an acceptable level for the audience and client.
- Adjust monitor levels and fine-tune monitor mixes as requested by the performers (this task may be assigned totally to a separate monitor engineer).

This then, is the essence of special event audio systems. The technology is constantly changing and improving, particularly with the advent of digital mixers and the integration of tasks into single devices. However, the basics remain the same. Understand them and the new technology will become much easier to follow.

3.6   RISK AND SAFETY

As for most of the technical subjects covered in this book, producers must be concerned with risks involved in the operation of equipment and with the safety of their own or contracted personnel and event attendees. We begin by providing current known North American audio equipment standards, as follows:

- *UL 60065 (in the USA) and CAN/CSA-C22.2 No. 60065-03 (in Canada): Audio, Video and Similar Electronic Apparatus – Safety Requirements.*
- *ANSI (American National Standards Institute) E1.8 – 2005: Entertainment Technology – Loudspeaker Enclosures Intended for Overhead Suspension – Classification, Manufacture and Structural Testing.*

These standards apply specifically to the general design and use of this equipment in an entertainment context. Not listed here is the myriad of design standards that apply to individual pieces of equipment. However, most of these are covered within UL 60065. It should be noted that for Canada and the USA, this equipment is certified by Standards Development Organizations (SDOs) in each country (see Chapter 7 of *Special Event Production: The Process* for an explanation of these organizations). In the USA, the main SDO for audio equipment is the Underwriters Laboratories Inc. (UL) and in Canada, the Canadian Standards Association (CSA). Producers should be extremely cautious of allowing audio suppliers to use any equipment that does not bear a certification sticker with either of these marks on it. There is every chance that it may be of substandard quality or built by an individual with little knowledge of the standards required. In other words, it could be hazardous not only to health but also to the proper functioning of all other equipment to which it is connected. Indeed, as with other standards, it is advisable to mandate the use of only UL or CSA certified equipment within production supplier contracts.

In terms of personnel safety when using audio and A-V equipment, the OSHA and WCB guidelines in the USA and in Canadian provinces respectively must strictly apply. Associated with them must be strict adherence to the National Electrical Code in the USA and the Canadian Electrical Code when working with any electrical equipment in either country, which is essentially all audio and A-V equipment. Again, it is recommended that adherence to these standards be mandated in all supplier contracts.

As well, certain risk mitigation techniques that ensure flawless event execution are employed regularly by audio specialists based on their experience. Tim Lewis, the owner of Proshow Audiovisual-Broadcast in Vancouver, Canada, an audio and A-V specialist who has worked with such luminaries as the Dalai Lama, Queen Elizabeth II, George Bush Sr., Bill Clinton, Pope John Paul II, Bill Gates, Elton John, Diana Krall, and many others, offers some recommendations from his experience (Tim Lewis, Personal Communication, September 18, 2006).

- *Redundancy*: For every event on which he works, Lewis has what he calls a Catastrophic Backup Plan. He analyzes the audio requirements for the event and looks at what might cause a worst-case scenario or 'catastrophe.' By his definition, a catastrophe is having the audience leave because the event cannot continue. He then plans the amount of additional equipment required to prevent that from happening. For example, if a VIP or keynote speech is lost, the event is over. If a band cannot be heard, the show or dance is over. Depending on what that catastrophe is, the extra equipment might be a small powered house mixer, twin lectern microphones (or running an extra microphone cord to the lectern), additional lavalier microphones, obviously many extra batteries for wireless equipment, additional handheld wireless microphones, extra CD and DVD players, extra cables and power supply, and so on. The decision centers around what the event can do without and still survive. Lewis further stresses that the decision should be based on maintaining the highest level of professionalism and never on the cost.

■ *Ambient effects*: Producers need to be cognizant of what is happening in the event space and with other equipment. Lewis points out that ambient noise from other equipment can be problematic for audio quality. For example, fan noise from projectors, moving lights, and air conditioning can be quite high and can interfere with audio quality, thus squeezing the available *headroom* or amount of gain available before feedback. It is far better when it comes to ambient noise to turn the noise off rather than turning the audio system volume up, according to Lewis, even if is only for a very short period during a key moment in a speech or the event program.

■ *Technical capabilities of personnel*: In audio, there can be specialists in mixing audio for widely different types of events. For example, some audio engineers are trained and experienced in mixing rock and roll at concerts, some have only experience with corporate speeches, some have experience with theatrical presentations, and many more. According to Lewis, it is essential for producers to ensure from dialog with audio subcontractors that the experience of the engineers provided matches the audio needs of the event.

A combination of these tips, compliance with safety and design standards, and a well-thought out risk assessment for the particular event should alleviate most potential problems for producers in the audio area.

> ## PRODUCTION CHALLENGES
>
> 1. You are managing an event in a large indoor venue with all glass walls and a very high ceiling, in addition to quite a number of large structural columns. Explain generally why the acoustics are bad in this venue.
> 2. A keynote speaker has been hired for a conference opening general session. Besides speaking for 30 min, this person also plans to sing several songs to backing CD tracks as part of his presentation. Suggest three options for microphones for this person and why they may or may not work for him.
>
> *Continued*

PRODUCTION CHALLENGES (CONTD.)

3. Your client is dumbfounded by the 48-channel mixer that your audio engineer has just unloaded and set up on the venue wall opposite the main stage. She expresses concern that such a monster is needed for the 12-piece band and three vocalists backing your headline celebrity act, and the simple series of PowerPoint and video presentations that precede the show. Not wishing to appear ignorant, you try to explain its function. What will you say about the various capabilities of the mixer and why so many channels are needed?

4. An important corporate event has speeches followed by a short 20 min entertainment show to end the evening. There are 400 guests at the black tie dinner in a 150 ft long × 90 ft wide × 20 ft high (45 m × 27 m × 6 m) room. What are two types of, and possible locations for, a speaker system for this event?

5. Your client is concerned about the length of time required for a show's sound check. Explain why a proper sound check is required for a good show.

REFERENCES

Davis, G. and Jones, R. (1990). *The Yamaha Sound Reinforcement Handbook*, Second Edition. Milwaukee: Hal Leonard Corporation.

Eargle, J. (January 1999). *JBL Professional Sound System Design Reference Manual*. JBL Professional.

Gillette, J.M. (2000). *Theatrical Design and Production: An Introduction to Scene Design and Construction, Lighting, Sound, Costume, and Makeup*, Fourth Edition. New York: McGraw-Hill Higher Education.

Hysell, S. (2000). Crossovers. *Scott's PA System Tutorial: Setting It Up, Part 3*. Retrieved September 22, 2006, from http://www.geocities.com/SunsetStrip/Stage/4241/SetupIII.html.

Lyons, C., Vear, T. and Pettersen, M. (2005). *Audio Systems Guide for Meeting Facilities*. Shure Incorporated.

Patil, A., Rabbitt, J. and Waldrop, D. (August 2000). Act I: Scene II – Lighting & Sound Elements. *Seminar Workbook: Event Solutions Expo 2000*, pp. 59–93.

Sigismondi, G. (2006). *Audio Systems Guide for Music Educators*. Shure Incorporated.

Waller, R., Boudreau, J. and Vear, T. (2005). *Microphone Techniques for Live Sound Reinforcement*. Shure Incorporated.

VISUAL PRESENTATION TECHNOLOGY

4

LEARNING OUTCOMES

After reading this chapter you will be able to:

1. Understand the purpose of creating a visual presentation.
2. Describe the different visual sources used in presentations.
3. Describe the signal path and how the visual signal is manipulated as it travels from source to final projection.
4. Describe the different types of display and projection equipment.
5. Understand why and how a multimedia show is created using visual presentation technology.
6. Understand what happens during the setup and operation of visual presentation equipment at a special event.

The 'tag team' of audio and visual equipment (A-V) can sometimes be confusing because it encompasses so much technology. Because the audio needs of a complex entertainment program are very different from a meeting consisting mainly of speeches, audio has a separate chapter in this book, and only the visual component of A-V will be the subject of this chapter. (We will refer to visual presentation equipment, for purposes of simplicity, as A-V.) In truth, many companies offer both audio and visual equipment because they are both interrelated.

As with all other technologies, visual presentation equipment is advancing rapidly. It is the goal of this chapter to take a point in time and to explain the current theory of operation of this equipment and how the equipment is used in special events. We will therefore concentrate on the following topics:

- Purpose of visual presentations
- Visual sources
- Signal processing
- Projection equipment
- Display equipment
- Multimedia presentations
- Equipment setup and operation
- Risk and safety.

4.1 PURPOSE OF VISUAL PRESENTATIONS

'There is nothing worse than a brilliant image of a fuzzy concept.' So said famous photographer Ansel Adams. All the most advanced equipment and largest screens in the world will not make an event successful if the purpose of the visual presentation is not fully understood by all concerned before the event is designed. Clients, producers, and equipment suppliers must be in perfect synchronization. The choice of projection and display equipment, the location of equipment, the length of the presentation, and most importantly the content of the presentation are all impacted by the **purpose** of the presentation.

For example, one of the most common purposes is for educational meetings and conferences in which the presentation is primarily for speaker support. In this case, there are often no more than one or two supporting screens designed either as part of a stage set or off to one or both sides of a stage. Occasionally, smaller monitors may be used throughout the venue depending on the venue design and ease of actually seeing the speaker and stage. Projection equipment may consist of no more than one or two digital projectors for PowerPoint, and content may be entirely provided by the speakers.

On the other hand, if the purpose of the presentation is to augment an entertainment program, a décor design scheme, or an elaborate awards show, then the possibilities become endless, limited only by budget. Frequently now, with the advent of high-intensity projection systems, A-V is being incorporated into entertainment and décor design. Visual elements such as computer animations, slides, and video are easily projected onto fabric shapes, onto walls, and suspended from ceilings as part of an event décor design. Similarly, computers are being pre-programmed with PowerPoint presentations that incorporate slides and video in ever-changing combinations to augment stage shows of dance and music. In fact, technology is now at the point where virtually any computer-generated image can be used as either décor or in support of a multimedia presentation using a combination of intelligent lights and computers. In these specialized cases of multimedia shows, content is the key and considerable time must be devoted to programing it, either by the producer or by the A-V company.

4.2   VISUAL SOURCES

What we are going to attempt in this chapter is to translate a world of complex jargon and equipment into a logical pattern. Computer, video, projection, and display technologies are undergoing a quantum leap in capabilities. Much of the older analog technology will, within 3–4 years, be completely obsolete and all equipment will be digital. Due to this rapidly changing environment, many new inventions have entered the market with proprietary names and standards, so that it is easy to become lost in the extensive list of equipment available. Nevertheless, the basic methodologies are similar even though the operating principles may differ.

In order to make this chapter understandable, we will follow a visual presentation from start to finish, from its basic initial visual source to its final destination as an image displayed for an audience. Along the way, we will examine the most common equipment currently in use, paying particular attention to *how* this equipment transforms our initial source into a projected image.

In its simplest form, a presentation will follow a path similar to that in Figure 4.1. Although not in every case will a visual source be processed before going to projection, or will a projector necessarily be separate from a display. The differences will be clear as we proceed through the chapter, but we offer simplicity as the starting point.

To begin, we will review and explain the main sources of information for visual presentations, starting with the simplest and ending with the most complex.

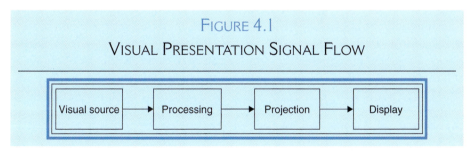

FIGURE 4.1
VISUAL PRESENTATION SIGNAL FLOW

| Visual source | → | Processing | → | Projection | → | Display |

Courtesy: Doug Matthews

4.2.1   35 mm Slides

The king of slides and slide projectors was the Kodak Company, who ceased manufacture of the venerable carousel projectors in 2004. Slides were very high-quality photos printed on photopositive slide film and inserted into cardboard or glass sleeves for projection from a carousel projector. They can/could be controlled manually or automatically from a computer. Unfortunately, for complex presentations, especially ones requiring unique graphics such as charts or logos, individual slides had to be created and individually photographed, a very time-consuming and expensive venture. There is still the occasional need for slide projection but the technology is virtually obsolete. Kodak has a web site at http://slideprojector. kodak.com/index.shtml that has been set up as an archival snapshot in time as of November 2004 to inform the public about slide projectors.

4.2.2   Overhead Slides or Objects

Still very much in use in classrooms and the occasional business meeting, is the acetate transparency. This is a page-sized sheet of acetate that can have material printed on it (e.g. a photo, typed page, chart, or logo) from a regular inkjet or other printer. It can also accept drawing on it from special pens, which makes it attractive as a live teaching tool. It must be projected onto a screen or acceptable surface using an overhead projector.

Predating the transparency/overhead projector combination was a very useful device called an *opaque projector*. This device enabled non-transparent, two- or three-dimensional objects such as books, drawings, mineral specimens, artifacts, and such to be displayed onscreen. A device called a visual presenter, which is explained in more detail in Section 4.4.3, has now replaced the opaque projector.

4.2.3   Pre-recorded Video

By definition, 'video is the technology of capturing, recording, processing, transmitting, and reconstructing moving pictures, typically using celluloid film (e.g. from movie cameras), electronic signals (e.g. from videotape), or digital media (e.g. from DVD – Digital Versatile Disk or Digital Video Disk)' (Wikipedia contributors, July 7, 2006). When we talk about video at the source, we are talking about two methods of playing it back for an audience. The first is as a stored video pre-recorded on a tape or other medium and played back later either edited or unedited. The second method is as a magnified image (*IMAG* or *image magnification*) on a screen taken directly from a camera or multiple cameras recording live action.

In order to easily follow the path of the video image from the source to the screen as in Figure 4.1, we must first fully understand how video works. Video can basically be defined by three groups of information: display standards, recording formats, and connections. Due to the fact that there are a great many different formats for both analog and digital video in existence, plus a similar number of standards and connections, it is easy to be confused.

We will try to make sense of the confusion by reviewing and explaining the different standards and formats most used in the special events industry, the reason being that videos in any of the formats could appear at an event and require viewing. Proper understanding will help in obtaining the right equipment to do the job.

4.2.3.1 Video Display Standards

Although display standards relate mostly to the way in which video images are displayed, we discuss them at this juncture because they also refer to the way in which the video material is first *encoded* on the recording medium. It defines what the video stream will look like by specifying: *frame rate, interlacing, resolution, aspect ratio*, and *color encoding*. Let us look first at what these are, and then review the different standards.

4.2.3.1.1 Frame Rate

Like movies, video takes a specific number of still pictures or *frames*, every second (i.e. *fps*, the *frame rate*). For most video, this frame rate is either 25 or 30 fps. This, of course, is how the illusion of motion is created. Video formats were designed to be used with the older style *cathode ray tube* (CRT) televisions (analog type) on which the picture is displayed by an electron beam that projects one horizontal line of information at a time. When the beam reaches the end of one line, it is signaled to return to the other side and begin a new line in a new location. Likewise, when it reaches the bottom of the display, it is signaled to return to the top to start a new series of horizontal scans.

4.2.3.1.2 Interlacing

An *interlaced* display is one in which the horizontal scans skip every second line and return to the top to fill in the missing lines. This helps to smooth out motion and flicker. A *progressive* display is one in which each frame includes all the scan lines rather than every second one. The result is a much higher perceived resolution. To summarize what this means, to be effective as a device to accurately portray the motion recorded by the video, a television display therefore has to produce at least 25 (or 30 depending on the format) full-screen pictures per second (i.e. 25 full scans) to match the 25 frames taken by the video.

4.2.3.1.3 Resolution

For analog video, resolution refers to the number of horizontal scan lines combined with the number of times per second that the entire screen is re-scanned (frame rate in hertz). For example, the National Television Standards Committee (NTSC) standard (see Section 4.2.3.1.6) calls for a resolution of 525 lines and frame rate of 60 Hz. For digital video, resolution is the number of horizontal pixels per scan line combined with the number of scan lines (i.e. vertical pixels), and the frame rate. These are expressed as combinations of three numbers and a letter indicating whether the scan is interlaced or progressive. For example, the high-definition television (HDTV) standard (see Section 4.2.3.1.6) is capable of resolutions up to 1920 × 1080p60 (i.e. 1920 pixels per scan line, with 1080 scan lines in a progressive scan at 60 fps, where the resolution of the display screen or television, is 1920 pixels wide by 1080 pixels high).

4.2.3.1.4 Aspect Ratio

Aspect ratio is the ratio of the width of a video or TV picture to the height, in other words the actual shape. Although there is no universal standard for aspect ratio, the most common ratios are 4:3 and 16:9. Traditional analog televisions and computer screens were all 4:3, but the newer HDTV models and almost all new computer screens are 16:9. These can easily be seen by the screen resolution set up on a computer in terms of horizontal and vertical pixel counts. For example, a common resolution for analog video is 1024 × 768, or 4:3 (1.33), but for digital such as the HDTV mentioned above, it is 1920 × 1080 or 16:9 (1.78). Unfortunately, when a video made on one system must be transferred to another system, there will necessarily be a loss of some of the actual picture if moving to a smaller size (e.g. HDTV to NTSC, like trying to watch a full-screen version of a wide screen movie specially formatted for an old 4:3 analog TV set), or requiring a smaller picture if moving to a larger size.

4.2.3.1.5 Color Encoding

Besides information about the size and resolution of the video picture, the video signal must also contain information about the color (known as *chrominance* in video parlance) and brightness (known as *luminance*). This is done by adding a small 'packet' of information about the color and brightness to each line scanned. The way in which the color information is stored and carried with the other information is extremely complex and differs with each of the standards. The color and brightness information are then decoded at the receiving end (e.g. television set) by built-in electronics. The differing color encoding methods are one reason why video connectors are different for different types of video.

4.2.3.1.6 The Actual Standards

In the early 1950s, the US government set up the NTSC to standardize the signal so that all TV stations and all sets would be compatible. The NTSC standard is still used in the US, Canada, Central America, South America, and Japan. The NTSC system works by painting the screen 30 times a second (actually 60 times but it is interlaced) with a frame consisting of 525 scan lines, only 480 of which are visible; the rest are used to carry synchronization and other information. The entire signal, including the audio, falls within a 6 MHz bandwidth broadcast channel. NTSC was designed as an analog standard.

According to Vrije Universiteit (2006), 'several years later, television came to Western Europe. The Europeans decided that 30 fps was overkill (Hollywood films use only 24 fps). Instead they invented a system with better spatial resolution (625 scan lines of which 576 are visible) and a lower frame rate (25 fps). When it came to the color encoding system, a split developed, with the Germans choosing the *PAL* (Phase Alternating Line) system and the French choosing the *SECAM* (SEquentiel Couleur Avec Memoire) system (like PAL, SECAM also uses 625 lines and 25 fps). The reason for the split was the desire of the French to protect their domestic television set manufacturers from foreign competition. France is the only country in Western Europe to use SECAM; the rest use PAL. Asia, Africa, and most of the rest of the world use PAL, which is technically the best of the systems. PAL and SECAM were both designed as analog standards.

Eastern Europe got television later still. The then-Communist controlled governments chose the SECAM system in order to prevent East Germans from watching West German (i.e. PAL) television. This is how television standards – much like the world – developed.'

'Several years ago, *digital video* began development and in the 1990s began to take off as an affordable replacement for analog video. Digital video is a type of video recording system that works by using a digital, rather than analog, representation of the video signal. This generic term is not to be confused with the name *DV*, which is a specific type of digital video. Digital video is most often recorded on tape, then distributed on optical disks, usually DVDs. There are exceptions, such as camcorders that record directly to DVDs, and Digital8 camcorders which encode digital video on conventional analog tapes' (Wikipedia contributors, July 10, 2006a).

Of course, as digital video and digital projection began to replace analog video and CRT television a few years ago, every country that had previously used the analog display standards decided to convert to new digital standards, which to be expected, were also incompatible with each other. The current new standards are:

- *Advanced Television Systems Committee (ATSC)*: This group helped to develop the new digital television (DTV) standard for the US, also adopted by Canada, Mexico, and South Korea and being considered by other countries. It is intended to replace the NTSC system and produce wide screen 16:9 images up to 1920 × 1080 pixels in size – more than six times the display resolution of the earlier standard. The ATSC system also supports a host of different display resolutions and frame rates. The formats below list frame/field rates and lines of resolution. The different resolutions can, like analog video, operate in interlaced or progressive mode.
  - *Standard-definition television (SDTV)*: This refers to television systems that have a lower resolution than HDTV systems. Resolutions are 480i60 (NTSC) and 480p24, 480p30, 576i50, 576p25 (PAL, SECAM).

- *Enhanced-definition television or extended-definition television (EDTV)*: This is a Consumer Electronics Association (CEA) marketing shorthand term for certain DTV formats. The resolutions are 480p60 and 576p50.
- *High-definition television (HDTV)*: This means broadcast of television signals with a higher resolution than traditional formats (NTSC, SECAM, PAL) allow. Except for early analog formats in Europe and Japan, HDTV is broadcast digitally, and therefore its introduction sometimes coincides with the introduction of DTV. The resolutions are 720i50, 720i60, 720p24, 720p25, 720p30, 720p50, 720p60, 1080i50, 1080i60, 1080p24, 1080p25, and 1080p30.

- *Digital video broadcasting (DVB)*: This is a suite of internationally accepted, open standards for DTV maintained by the *DVB Project*, an industry consortium with more than 270 members. The standards encompass specifics for transmission, content, encryption, software platform, and return channel information. This standard is expected to eventually completely replace the PAL and SECAM standards.
- *Integrated services digital broadcasting (ISDB)*: This is the DTV and DAB (digital audio broadcasting) format that Japan has created to allow radio and television stations there to convert to digital.

To put this section in context, there are many different standards and video may be recorded to any one of these. The recording can be done on different media or formats, some of which are the same for different standards. For event producers, this means that any video recorded to one of the standards usually requires a playback system capable of decoding the information from the recording medium. For example, a video may be recorded to PAL standards on a VHS (Video Home System) tape but cannot be played back on a *video cassette recorder* (VCR) in North America that accepts VHS tape because all the VCRs are made to accept only NTSC standard videos. The video may be converted to a compatible standard for the equipment available; however, this invariably results in a significant loss of picture quality. This is the reason why event producers should be familiar with the different standards. We will now examine the types of recording formats.

4.2.3.2   Recording Formats

To be able to play the captured memory of an event on video, the original signal must be changed into something that can be easily stored on a recording medium.

4.2.3.2.1   Analog Tape Formats

For analog video, this means a *waveform* transferred through video cable to videotape. When the waveform is subsequently recorded, there are changes made to its amplitude and frequency, which cause it to lose quality. Thus, any time an analog video is recorded or copied, there is some degradation of the signal and hence a loss of quality. That is why a VHS tape can only be copied once or twice before being virtually impossible to view. The most common formats for analog recording are:

- *VHS or SVHS (1/2 in.)*: VHS (Video Home System), first released in September 1976, is a recording and playing standard for VCRs, developed by JVC. A VHS cassette contains a 1/2 in. (12.7 mm) wide magnetic tape wound between two spools, allowing it to be slowly passed over the various playback and recording heads of the VCR. The tape speed is 3.335 cm/s for NTSC, 2.339 cm/s for PAL. A cassette holds a maximum of about 430 m of tape at the lowest acceptable tape thickness, giving a maximum playing time of about 3.5 h for NTSC and 5 h for PAL at Standard Play (SP) quality. Inexpensive and popular, it was used extensively for movies and home recording prior to DVDs.
- *Hi8 (8 mm)*: This is better quality than VHS and designed for low-cost industrial use.
- *Betacam/Betacam SP*: This is the professional standard of extremely high quality, but expensive.

4.2.3.2.2 Digital Tape Formats

For digital video, the light that enters the camera needs to be turned into analog signals, then *digital* or *binary code*. First, the incoming light makes contact with a *charge-coupled device* (CCD) which transforms the light into analog electrical signals, varying depending on the levels of light. The RGB (red, green, blue color) channels from the CCD are then sampled and quantized by an *analog-to-digital converter* (ADC) into a binary stream. The stream is then processed by a *digital signal processor* (DSP). The information is recorded and does not change its structure with any subsequent transmission, recording, or copying. Hence, the quality of digital video is consistent and repeatable. The most common digital tape formats (out of more than 18) likely to be encountered by event producers are:

- *Digital8*: The Digital8 format is a consumer digital version of Hi8. Digital8 equipment uses the same video cassette media as analog Hi8 equipment, but differs in that the audio/video signal is encoded digitally. Current Digital8 equipment can also record in Long Play (LP) mode, which increases recording time from 60 to 90 min. Hi8 metal-particle cassettes are the recommended type for Digital8 recording.
- *MiniDV*: The 'L' cassette is about $120 \times 90 \times 12$ mm and can record up to 4.6 h of video (6.9 h in EP/LP). The better known MiniDV 'S' cassettes are $65 \times 48 \times 12$ mm and hold either 60 or 90 min of video depending on whether the video is recorded at SP or Extended Play (sometimes called Long Play: EP/LP). A 60 min MiniDV tape will hold approximately 13 GB of data.
- *DVCAM*: Sony's DVCAM is a semiprofessional variant of the DV standard that uses the same cassettes as DV and MiniDV, but transports the

FIGURE 4.2
DIGITAL TAPE FORMATS: LEFT PHOTO: DVCAM, DVCPRO, AND MINIDV; RIGHT PHOTO: DIGITAL BETACAM

Courtesy: http://en.wikipedia.org/wiki/Image:DV_tape_sizes_2.jpg, July 12, 2006 and http://en.wikipedia.org/wiki/Image:Digibeta-L.jpg, July 12, 2006

tape 50 percent faster. DVCAM is now also available in high-definition (HD) mode.

- *DVCPRO*: Panasonic specifically created the DVCPRO family for *electronic newsgathering* (ENG) use, with better linear editing capabilities and robustness. It has a track width of 18 μm and uses another tape type (Metal Particle instead of Metal Evaporated).
- *Digital Betacam*: Digital Betacam (commonly abbreviated to *Digibeta* or *d-beta* or *dbc*) was launched in 1993. It supersedes both Betacam and Betacam SP, while costing significantly less and providing high quality and reliability. 'S' tapes are available with up to 40 min running time, and 'L' tapes with up to 124 min.

See Figure 4.2 for a comparison of digital tape formats.

4.2.3.2.3 Time Code

Videotapes are frequently edited down to much smaller versions for posterity, and it is here that a method of cataloguing all the footage is needed. The secret to doing this efficiently is by using a piece of technology called a *time code*. Professional cameras and video recorders are equipped with time code generators and readers. Quite simply this means they have the ability to place numbers representing time, like a stop watch, embedded in each second of videotape and play them back. These numbers appear along the bottom of the video monitor in a small window. They run chronologically in hours, minutes, seconds, and video frames. On the tape itself the time code looks like this: 01:45:10:12. The first two numbers are for hours lapsed, the second two for minutes, the third for seconds, and the final set of two numbers is reserved for video frames.

TABLE 4.1

TIME CODE EXAMPLE

Tape Number	Comment begins at	In at	Out at
1	Starts at: 'We're here to present the award for…'	01:45:07	01:46:21
2	Starts at: 'And the award goes to…'	00:23:10	00:24:01
3	Starts at: 'I'd like to thank my parents…'	00:57:29	00:59:27

Courtesy: Consumer Opinion Services, www.cosvc.com, rewritten by author.

Using *time code window dubs* (invisible embedding of the time code on the original tape), the tape can be more easily edited. Table 4.1 shows how a log of time codes could be used.

'Using this simple method the video editor can take a list and rapidly assemble the three comments from the three different tapes. Time code gives the exact place on each of the tapes where these comments are located. While the original tapes (i.e. the camera originals) remain without the time code permanently burned into the video image, the time code remains hidden on them and any copy of them gives working access to them. A request for a video shoot of an event might therefore sound like this: "I'd like an operator with a three chip professional camera, shooting on digital Betacam. Please make time code window dubs of all the originals we record"' (Consumer Opinion Services, 1998). See Section 4.2.4.1 for more explanation of video cameras.

4.2.3.2.4   Disk-Based Video Storage

At this time, there are several different disk types being used for digital video storage, some of which could be used to play back videos at a special event. However, before we explain what they are, we need to explain what *video compression* is. Because digital video takes up a staggering amount of storage space on a computer hard drive, the files need to be made smaller or compressed. Compression is the process of removing data for things that the human eye cannot perceive. For example, although there are literally billions of colors, the human eye can perceive only about 1024 shades, so not all the others have to be kept. Compression therefore makes storage of video information much easier.

The software designed to compress the information is called a *codec*, which is short for compression–decompression. It is used to first compress the video – and audio – information as it goes onto the disk and then within a computer to decompress the video information to allow it to be played on the computer's video player (e.g. Windows Media Player or QuickTime Player). These codecs are typically defined by the *bit rate*. The bit rate describes how much information there is per second in a stream of data, and is expressed in *gigabytes per second* (GBps), *megabytes per second*

(MBps), or *kilobytes per second* (Kbps), usually with different rates for audio and video streams. Each disk storage device for digital video will use a specific codec to store information. We will now review the most common storage formats and the codecs used:

- *Video CD (VCD)*: This is a CD that contains moving pictures and sound. A VCD looks exactly like a CD or CD-ROM except that it stores video/audio clips. A VCD has the capacity to hold up to 74 min of full-motion video along with quality stereo sound (this is 650 MB of data). VCD resolution is 352 × 288 for PAL and 352 × 240 for NTSC. VCDs use a codec called MPEG-1 (Moving Picture Experts Group) to store the video and audio. The bit rate of MPEG-1 is up to 1.5 MBps. The picture quality of a VCD is generally considered to be about the same as VHS tape. A VCD can be played on almost all standalone DVD players and on practically all computers with a DVD-ROM or CD-ROM drive with the help of a software-based decoder/player.
- *Digital versatile disk or Digital video disk (DVD)*: This is an optical disk storage format that can be used for data storage, including movies with high video and sound quality. DVDs resemble compact disks as their physical dimensions are the same (12 cm/4.72 in., or occasionally 8 cm/3.15 in.) in diameter but they are encoded in a different format and at a much higher density. DVDs require a DVD drive with an MPEG-2 decoder (e.g. a DVD player or a DVD computer drive with a software DVD player). Commercial DVD movies are encoded using a combination of MPEG-2 compressed video and audio of varying formats. Typical bit rates for DVD movies range from 3 to10 MBps. The video resolution on NTSC disks is 720 × 480 and on PAL disks is 720 × 576. A high number of audio tracks and/or lots of extra material on the disk will often result in a lower bit rate (and image quality) for the main feature. The maximum storage capacity of any DVD at this time is approximately 16 GB.
- *High-definition DVD (HD DVD)*: This is a digital optical media format which is being developed as one standard for HD DVD. HD DVD is similar to the competing Blu-ray Disk (see below), which also uses the same CD-size (12 cm diameter) optical data storage media and 405 nm (nanometers) wavelength blue laser. The maximum capacity at present is about 30 GB although 200 GB has been demonstrated but is not yet commercial.
- *Blu-ray disk (BD)*: This is a next-generation optical disk format meant for storage of HD video and high-density data. The Blu-ray standard was jointly developed by a group of consumer electronics and PC companies called the Blu-ray Disk Association (BDA). As compared to the HD DVD format, its main competitor, Blu-ray has more information capacity per layer (25 instead of 15 GB), but may initially be more expensive to produce. Blu-ray gets its name from the blue-violet laser it uses to read and write to the disk. A BD can store substantially more data than a DVD, because of the shorter wavelength (405 nm) of the

laser (DVDs use a 650 nm wavelength red laser). A single-layer BD can store enough for approximately 4 h of HD video with audio. A dual-layer BD can hold enough for approximately 8 h of HD video (i.e. up to 54 GB of capacity). Capacities of 100 GB and 200 GB, using four and eight layers respectively, are currently being researched. BD technology uses any of three different codecs at the present time: MPEG-2 as already discussed; MPEG-4 with a bit rate of between 5 Kbps and 1 GBps; and VC-1, a codec with a maximum bit rate of 135 MBps in the most advanced version.

- *Digital disk recorder (DDR)*: This is a video recording device that uses a portable hard disk drive or optical disk drive mechanism to directly record and read data. It captures both standard definition and HD uncompressed video content, provides real-time playback for rendered material, and offers plug-and-play operation. Advantages are that it is quicker into the edit with no need to digitize, hard disks can store more than most tapes, and tapes are not fast enough for the highest video data rates. Disadvantages are that hard disks are more expensive than tapes and hard disks fail more frequently than tapes.

4.2.3.3 Video Connections/Signal Types

With so many formats and standards, it is to be expected that connecting equipment is going to be a concern. A good A-V company will be fully stocked with all the cables needed, but it is useful to understand what may be required. Some of the possible connections that may occur in an event setup include: video camera to recorder; recorder, camera, or computer to switcher (see Section 4.3); switcher to computer, projector, or monitors; and recorder, camera, or computer to projector. Hardware manufacturers may refer to connectors as *signal types*. What follows is a brief summary of the main types of connections/signal types that are likely to be encountered, and what equipment they apply to.

4.2.3.3.1 Analog Connections

Analog connections can be composite video, BNC, S-Video, component video, RGBHV (red, green, blue, and H/V sync), or SCART.

- *Composite video*: This is the most basic and lowest-quality type of connection. It carries all the video information (color, brightness, synchronization) on a single, yellow RCA or composite cable. It is typically used to hook up a standard VCR and stereo equipment. Usually there are two other cables besides the yellow video, a red for right channel audio, and a white for left channel audio.
- *RF or BNC*: This is another form of a composite cable and can be changed to an RCA type with a simple adaptor. It is the type most often found on professional video equipment rather than RCA. The physical connection is more secure because it uses a twist lock.

- *Separate Video (S-Video)*: This type of connector splits the video signal into two separate components, luminance (brightness) and chrominance (color). It is typically found on most high-end televisions, all videodisk players, camcorders, digital cable and satellite set top boxes, and SVHS VCRs.
- *Component video*: With this type, the video signal is split into three components and three separate, color-coded cables: the Y cable (green) carrying luminance, image detail, and synchronization information; the Pb or Cb cable (blue) carrying color information; and the Pr or Cr cable (red) also carrying color. This connection gives a superior image over composite or S-video connections, and is most often found on high-end DVD players and HDTV tuners.
- *RGBHV*: 'These cables look identical to simple composite cables, but the RGBHV cable splits the video signal into five. There are three different types of RGB cables: RGBHV is a five-cable system that splits the video signal for color into red, green, and blue, and then has two more cables to carry the sync for the signal (horizontal and vertical sync); RGB H/V is a four-cable system that splits the color the same way, but has the horizontal and vertical sync on a single fourth cable; and straight RGB video cables again split the color signal in three, but carry the additional sync signal on one of the color cables, usually the green (called RGB sync on green). An RGBHV signal is the way a computer connects to a projector. Five pins on a 15-pin VGA (Video Graphics Array) cable are RGBHV. The projector recognizes the type of signal and projects accordingly. RGBHV connectors are found on most high-end professional monitors and some HDTV decoders' (The Projector People, 2006a). Cables can be either BNC or RCA.
- *SCART*: This is a common European connector that carries composite or RGB video and stereo audio signals in a single cable and 21-pin connector.

See Figure 4.3 for a comparison of the different analog video connections. Figure 4.3 illustrates the following connection types:

- *First row, left to right*: Composite cable (yellow in color); BNC connector; S-Video connector.
- *Second row, left to right*: Component video cables (RGB in color); RGBHV cable with BNC connectors (usually RGB, yellow or black, and white in color); SCART connector.

4.2.3.3.2 Digital Connections
Digital connections can be SDI, Firewire, DVI, or HDMI.

- *Serial digital interface (SDI)*: SDI is a 'broadcast quality' digital video connection, serving SDTV and HDTV (standard and HD) digital standards at 1920×1080 resolution. SDI is a high-speed connection of most commonly 270 MBps that is carried on one *coax* cable with a BNC connector (as in Figure 4.3). Higher speeds of 1.485 GBps exist for HD-SDI (HD) connections. It is good for long cable runs.

FIGURE 4.3

COMPARISON OF ANALOG VIDEO CONNECTIONS

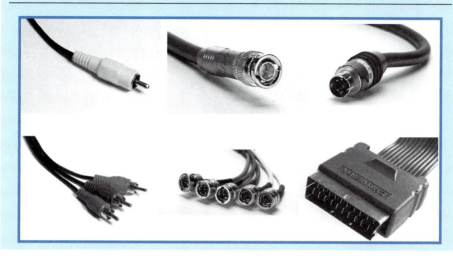

Courtesy: www.hometheatermag.com/hookmeup and www.en.wikipedia.org

- *Firewire*: Also known as *i.Link* or *IEEE 1394*, this is a high-speed connection (100–400 MBps) that is primarily used to connect data storage devices, digital video cameras, and camcorders. It comes in 4-pin and 6-pin versions. Cable length is limited to 4.5 m (15 ft) but can go higher by joining cables or by using optical connections.
- *Digital video interface (DVI)*: This is a multi-pin video connector that was designed to maximize the visual quality of digital display devices such as flat panel LCD (liquid crystal display) computer displays and digital projectors. It can transmit digital streams at speeds up to 5 GBps. Its advantage is that it does not have to convert a video signal from digital (e.g. a DVD), to analog (through the component output and cables), and back to digital again (e.g. in a TV). There are several versions in existence, all with slightly different pin configurations, that are capable of connecting analog or digital devices. They are: DVI-D for digital devices only; DVI-A for analog devices only; and DVI-I for digital and analog devices. One new version, the VESA M1, is an all-inclusive connector that supports and replaces VGA, DVI, USB, and IEEE 1394 connections. At this point, it is used primarily in projectors.
- *High-definition multimedia interface (HDMI)*: An extension of DVI, this is an uncompressed, all-digital audio and video connection system. It is the first connection to handle all audio, video, and control data. Type A is a 19-pin connector and Type B is a 29-pin connector designed to support resolutions higher than 1080p. HDMI is used with an increasing variety of digital equipment, including DVD players, A-V receivers, digital audio or video monitors, and digital TVs (e.g. plasma, LCD, etc.).

FIGURE 4.4
COMPARISON OF DIGITAL VIDEO CONNECTIONS

Courtesy: www.hometheatermag.com/hookmeup and www.en.wikipedia.org

See Figure 4.4 for a comparison of the different digital video connections. Figure 4.4 illustrates the following connection types from left to right: 4-pin (left) and 6-pin (right) Firewire connectors; DVI-D connector; and HDMI connector.

4.2.4   Live Video and IMAG

Nothing makes an audience feel closer to the action than live video. Rock concerts, award shows, meetings, and conferences use this technology extensively. IMAG is simply the projection on a large display, usually a screen, of whatever action is taking place onstage or elsewhere, and being filmed or videotaped by one or more live cameras. It applies well to events that have an audience of more than 400 or 500 persons, and in venues that are very long and narrow, placing much of the audience at a distance from the stage. A live video presentation requires the consideration of four key aspects: equipment choice, camera location(s), lighting, and personnel.

4.2.4.1   *Equipment*

The video camera is the first consideration. For purposes of this discussion, we will concentrate on only digital video cameras, among which there are vast differences. The cheapest and lowest quality are *consumer* or *prosumer* camcorders that incorporate only a single CCD. Professional cameras incorporate three CCDs, one for each of the three primary colors (RGB). The CCD is a type of sensor that converts incoming light to an electronic charge then converts the charge into a voltage. The voltage is digitized, stored in memory as an image, and then displayed on the camera LCD, on a computer, or for events, a large screen or monitor. Professional cameras also come equipped with a *camera control unit* (CCU) that allows the iris, black balance, white balance, and chroma (color) adjustments to be made remotely by another person. With these devices on a professional camera, it is possible for another person to completely control the quality of an image on a screen without the cameraperson having to worry about it.

Also necessary is a good tripod for stability, equipped with a solid *head* that allows for *pan* (movement on the horizontal axis) and *tilt* (movement on the vertical axis) functions, and a *spreader* to keep the tripod legs in position.

4.2.4.2 Locations

Prior to the event, a decision will have to be made on the number of video cameras needed to cover the action. Often, if everything is taking place only in relatively fixed positions on a stage, one camera will suffice mounted on a tripod in a fixed position. The location of this position will be critical, with a position as close to the action as possible generally being the best. However, the decision will be impacted often by audience visibility of the action, as 'close' usually means placing the camera and operator on a riser in the middle of the venue mere feet (meters) from the stage, in turn obscuring much of the audience's view and often blocking foot traffic to and from many of the seats. An option to this position is one at the rear of the venue, most likely on or near the technical riser. The disadvantage of this position is that it requires a longer lens which, coupled with the placement on a riser, can lead to shakiness of the final image caused by even the slightest movement of the riser. If possible, for optimum viewing, the height of any camera riser should take the camera on its tripod up to the eye level of any person onstage.

If there is action taking place in the audience, if there is action taking place in more than one position onstage (e.g. award winners are coming to the stage while someone is still announcing, or multiple entertainers are working at the same time), if there are multiple focal points (e.g. multiple stages), or if there is a desire to shift the focus between different points of view purely for excitement and a more professional look, then more than one camera will be required. A two camera shoot with one camera in a fixed position and one roving can often provide an adequate option with switching between the two points of view for variety. More cameras naturally provide more creative options. One big advantage of live video and particularly of using more than one camera, is that the event can be recorded for posterity for later TV viewing or even for selling or giving away copies of the event video.

The most interesting shots for live entertainment are usually from the side of the stage or from a hand-held camera onstage. An additional stationary or hand-held camera in front of the stage can take care of lead singers or shots from the audience's perspective.

For speakers or award presentations, a single camera in front of the stage either stationary or roving, can usually cover all that is required, although a second camera adds interest and can be used for over-the-shoulder shots as in interview situations. Figure 4.5 is an example of a hand-held camera near a stage.

4.2.4.3 Lighting

Correct lighting for live video is a high-priority production consideration. Because video cameras have much lower contrast or dynamic ranges

FIGURE 4.5
ROVING VIDEO CAMERA NEAR A STAGE

Courtesy: Pacific Show Productions, www.pacificshow.ca – Copyright 2006

than the human eye (e.g. 100:1 compared to 100,000:1), the lighting needs to be much brighter (i.e. higher color temperature of around 3600 K). The contrast between subjects (e.g. entertainers or speakers) and background (e.g. black stage backdrop) also must be greater in order for the video images to look realistic and not be too dark. As mentioned in Chapter 5, this is best done with a combination of unfiltered light that provides at minimum a *key light* from one side, a *fill light* from 90 degrees to the key, and a *back light* to help visually separate the background from the subject (Williams, 1999). The lighting director or supplier will need to know that live video is planned so that the correct color temperature luminaires are provided and placed in the appropriate locations for the shoot.

4.2.4.4 *Personnel*

Clifford (2005) provides a good summary of the personnel who are sometimes necessary for a professional live video presentation and IMAG. They include:

- *The director*: This is the person who calls for camera shots and communicates with the technical director who actually works the controls on the switcher (see Section 4.3). These positions are often combined. The ability to think three to five shots ahead while communicating this information to the rest of the video team is the most important quality of a director, combined with knowledge of transition and shot selection so as to enhance – not detract from – dance, drama, award presentations, or whatever is happening onstage. Directors need to specify what shot is up, what is next, and what camera those shots are coming from, starting with the camera number and then describing the shot succinctly. A common type of instruction might be, 'Standby two.' This informs the technical director and camera operators that camera two is about to be selected as the live camera. The technical director would bring this shot up in the preview monitor, and camera two's operator would make sure his shot was stable. 'Cut two' would instruct the technical director to perform a cut to that camera. 'Dissolve two' would instruct the technical director to perform a dissolve transition to camera two.

- *The camera operator(s)*: The operator (op) is the person through whose eyes the audience sees. Even given the same direction, two camera ops will see and shoot somewhat differently. A good eye and an ability to concentrate and quickly follow directions are necessary for this position.
- *The shader*: While the video director, technical director, and camera operators are all focusing on the shots and transitions between shots, another person, called a video engineer or *shader*, watches each shot as it is put on standby, and adjusts its color and brightness to match the previous shot. This is done through the CCU mentioned earlier. The shader actually changes the settings on the physical camera itself through the CCU via remote control. The shader may also be given the responsibility of operating videotape and DVD players when pre-recorded footage is to be shown.
- *A grip*: The grip makes sure camera cables don't tangle and follows the camera operators around to do this.

4.2.5   Computer-Generated Information

Effectively replacing 35 mm slides and overhead projections is computer-generated imagery. In Section 4.2.3 we discussed videos at length, and certainly much of the video imagery used in events comes from a computer and/or is digitally stored in some form. However, what we will be dealing with in this section are other kinds of digital information. We will restrict our discussion to the creation of PowerPoint presentations, primarily because that is the source of most special event computer-generated imagery. For purposes of brevity, we will assume that readers are reasonably well acquainted with the basics of PowerPoint, and will not go into detail about this. However, we will discuss storage file formats for still images and for movies, so that the resulting displayed images will be clear and readable.

4.2.5.1   *Digital Still Image Files*

Most still images that will be projected will be photographs, and the key considerations here are file format, image resolution, and image size.

- *Image size*: Most photographic or other still digital images will originate from a digital camera or a scanner, and will in all likelihood be too large or too small in size for a suitable onscreen presentation. Assuming that the intention is to fill the screen with the image, in a photo-editing program like Adobe Photoshop, the original image should be cropped to the size desired to fill the screen. In other words, if it is desired to show the entire width of the photo onscreen, then the entire width of the computer screen should be filled, so assuming the computer screen resolution is 1024 × 768 (standard), then setting the width at 1024 pixels will result in the entire width of the photo being projected and fitting perfectly onto the screen. Note that it is preferable to crop in a photo-editing program rather than in PowerPoint because PowerPoint only resizes without reducing the image file size.
- *Image resolution*: For onscreen presentations, the best resolution is 100 PPI (*pixels per inch*) and this is what should be set when cropping the photo in the photo-editing program. This allows for optimum clarity and minimum file size.
- *File format*: The enemy of effective smooth presentations is excessive file size as it slows them down. The preferred file format for projection is JPG (also called JPEG). This is a *compressed* file format, which means that it consumes less memory yet still delivers good quality. Although JPG files are the best for photos, a file format called GIF is best for images that have blocks of solid color like graphs or clip art. Like JPG, it does not take up excessive memory.
- For text and non-photographic screen presentations within PowerPoint, there is a fundamental caution that what looks good on a computer screen may not look good on a large screen. Font types and sizes should be basic (e.g. Arial or Times New Roman fonts) with a minimum of bullets on a slide, these being large bullets. Contrast is best achieved with white or yellow text on a dark background. Finally, for logos or other graphics, it is best to avoid web-sourced, low-resolution versions, and opt for an original version from the artist if possible. See the discussion above for image resolution and sizing.

4.2.5.2   Digital Movie and Video Files

Section 4.2.3 covered digital video extensively. However, it did not cover the placing of video files into PowerPoint. It also did not include some of the codecs other than MPEG-1 and MPEG-2 used for such things as streaming video that might end up in a PowerPoint presentation.

Video in PowerPoint should be used only in a support role. That means that it should be strictly of short duration to emphasize a point, no more than a minute or so in length maximum. Video clips can come in different formats. First, if they are created from an analog tape, they need to be edited into digital. Although many video-editing studios can do this, if the job is not complex, it can be done on a regular PC with a large amount of RAM. Various editing programs exist that can do this, together with a simple piece of hardware called an ADC, also called a *capture card*, which normally comes with the software. With this software, a camcorder can be plugged into the computer with the camera's connector (typically IEEE 1394 Firewire) and the tape edited using the software. The same thing can be done for digital tapes but the ADC is not required. Most of the software allows for advanced editing functions like a variety of dissolves, addition of musical backgrounds and voiceovers, titling, and such. Once the basic editing is complete, the file is still very large and must be further compressed to allow for more efficient storage and playback. To illustrate the differences in file size, an uncompressed file of a 1 min video might approach 1 GB in size, whereas the compressed version might only be 3–4 MB. The software will offer options for compression methods (i.e. codecs) and frame rates. It is useful to remember that typical professional digital video files after editing but before compression, use a resolution of 720×480 pixels, but after editing this will probably be down to 320×240 pixels or lower, a resolution that will appear very grainy on a large screen before an audience, but will appear acceptable on a small computer screen. As well, the frame rate will be lowered, which can result in a jerky quality. Therefore, unless the video is stored on a separate DVD or CD at full uncompressed file size, the quality to be expected from a PC hard drive-based file is going to be quite poor.

Other common file formats that may be encountered within a PC-based presentation are listed below, with explanations and limitations described where there may be problems in using the formats within PowerPoint.

- *Audio/Video Interleaved (AVI)*: This is a file format for Windows-based PCs. An AVI file is organized into alternating chunks of audio and video data. It is the type of file that is created when digital video clips are imported from a camcorder to a PC.
- *DivX*: As long as DivX videos end with an AVI file extension and the DivX codec is installed on the same computer, PowerPoint has no problem with DivX (Bajaj, 2004).
- *Flash*: PowerPoint, or for that matter Windows itself, does not consider Flash as a native video format. However, Flash movies can be successfully played within PowerPoint using the Shockwave Flash ActiveX control (Bajaj, 2004).
- *MPEG-1*: We have already discussed this format, which is associated with consumer digital camcorders. Resolution is usually 352×240 pixels.
- *MPEG-2*: This has also been discussed. Resolution is typically 720×480 and the file size is much larger than MPEG-1. It is associated with DVDs.
- *MPEG-4*: This newer, very flexible MPEG codec is used for both streaming and downloadable web content, and is also the video format employed by a growing number of portable video recorders. It compresses at a ratio of 10:1 or original DVD-quality size with little loss.

MPEG-7 and MPEG-10 with presumably even better resolutions and speeds are still in development.

- *QuickTime (MOV)*: Though developed and supported primarily by Apple Computer, Inc., this flexible format isn't limited to Macintosh operating systems. It is also commonly used in Windows systems and other types of computing platforms. In Windows, QuickTime files usually appear with the '.MOV' filename extension. Since the format is proprietary, the computer on which the video is running must have a QuickTime player installed. It is available from www.apple.com/quicktime. PowerPoint cannot use any videos rendered using any version of QuickTime since version 3 and the QuickTime player must be used. Prior to version 3, only QuickTime content rendered using the Cinepak codec could be played in PowerPoint (Bajaj, 2004).
- *RealMedia (RM)*: One of the most popular formats for streaming content on the Internet, RM includes the RealAudio codec for sound clips and RealVideo codec for movies. RealAudio and RealVideo files are often given the common RealMedia '.RM' file extension. RM files are often heavily compressed so they can stream over dial-up Internet connections. As with QuickTime, a RealPlayer is required to play back videos on a computer. It is available for free from www.real.com. The only way that PowerPoint and RealVideo can work together is to link a RealVideo file to a hyperlink or Action button in PowerPoint (Bajaj, 2004).
- *VCD*: VCD video files usually have the DAT extension and for all practical purposes they are MPEG-1 videos. Several tools including freeware applications can convert VCD DAT movies to MPEG files without any problem.
- *Windows media video (WMV)*: Microsoft's proprietary compression format for motion video, WMV is used for both streaming and downloading content via the Internet. Microsoft's Windows Media Player, an application bundled with Windows XP operating systems, allows playback.

Once a video is edited, it can be inserted into PowerPoint. However, as mentioned in Section 4.2.3.2.4, it must be decoded by a codec before it can be played in the presentation and this is the responsibility of the PowerPoint computer. Each Windows-based computer comes equipped with certain codecs and if one is not installed, it can usually be downloaded from a specific web site. Bajaj (2004) provides useful information on how and where to do this.

Actual insertion of the video can be done so the video plays automatically only when clicked. For unsupported formats (e.g. QuickTime and RealVideo), it can also be linked from a hyperlink or action button. A third method of playing a video is to embed a Windows Media Player object in a PowerPoint slide. Videos can be resized to fill the screen but be aware of quality loss with the lower-resolution formats as mentioned previously. An important note on playing videos within PowerPoint is that the actual video file must reside on the same computer as the PowerPoint software and presentation. Otherwise, PowerPoint will not find the link when requested. For

split it so it can feed two or more high-resolution data displays while maintaining the original quality. DAs are used in applications that require multiple projectors or monitors to display the same source's image at the same time. An example might be in a classroom setting with an instructor's computer and multiple monitors for students, or for a special event that has a number of monitors in different rooms.

4.3.2 Scalers

Scalers take one video resolution and convert it to another resolution. Scalers are typically used to match a standard-definition video signal to the *native resolution* of a digital display (i.e. the pixel count of the LCD chips in a projector – see Section 4.4.4.2.1), convert HDTV and RGB computer–video signals to a common output rate, or increase the perceived quality of a projected video image. Scalers take an analog video signal, decode it into its RGBHV components, and then use sophisticated video processing technology to scale the image to fit the native resolution of the display. Once the scaled video image has been converted to RGBHV, only a single video cable connection is needed to carry signals to the display. This greatly simplifies installation, system setup, and operation.

4.3.3 Scan Converters

Scan converters convert computer–video signals into signals that are compatible with NTSC or PAL display devices such as televisions, monitors, or projectors. When a computer-generated image needs to be displayed or recorded on an NTSC or PAL-based device, such as a monitor, a scan converter must be used. Typically, scan converters are used in applications such as computer-based video production, videotaping, videoconferencing, and event multimedia presentations.

4.3.4 Switchers

Switchers enable multiple video and audio signals to be selected and sent to one or more display devices. More sophisticated switchers, called *matrix switchers*, route multiple audio/video sources to multiple audio/video destinations. These switchers accept audio/video signals from a range of input sources – computers, cameras, DVD players, videotape recorders, etc. – and route the output to different destinations, such as projectors and monitors. They are really the heart of an event multimedia setup. Many modern switchers also incorporate scalers, DAs, and scan converters all in one unit, and can accept both analog and digital inputs. Figure 4.7 illustrates a typical matrix switcher with built-in scaler and converter.

Courtesy: http://www.extron.com/product/product.asp?id=system7sc

PRODUCTION WAR STORY

It's the middle of a serious presentation onstage to a major conference about human interaction and training. Suddenly, on the screen behind the speaker a screen wipe of a silhouetted nude dancer flicks across the screen. A collective guffaw from the audience takes the keynote speaker by surprise as the event manager literally runs across the room to the control console, a look of uncontrollable rage on her face.

What happened? The video tech, with too much time to spare waiting while the PowerPoint presentations rolled one into the other, was playing with screen wipes on his preview monitor but inadvertently flipped a switch that put one of them on the main screen. Embarrassing? You bet! Incompetent? Definitely! The event manager had every right to be angry. The damage was done and there was no turning back or saving this situation.

The restitution was an immediate substantial discount and apology from both the A-V company and from the production manager who should have been more closely monitoring the situation. This approach actually won an accolade letter from the event manager to the producer of the show because of his proactive mindset.

What were the lessons learned? The A-V company was chosen based on price rather than experience. Definitely a poor decision. The production manager also learned a valuable lesson about the need to understand the proper use of equipment and the need to more closely monitor what the technicians were doing in relation to the event's running order.

Courtesy: Doug Matthews

4.4   PROJECTION EQUIPMENT

Following our initial simple signal path illustrated in Figure 4.1, the next step after the visual source has been processed, is projection of the visual image. Projectors come in many shapes and sizes, but the three main types used for special events are slide projectors, overhead projectors (OHP), and video/data projectors.

4.4.1   Slide Projectors

Although almost completely obsolete (called *legacy technology)* and seldom used for special events, there is still a possibility that 35 mm slides and slide projectors will appear at the occasional meeting or conference or for large projection systems for décor. They are capable of projecting from front or rear, they can accept lamps with sufficient brightness to display images on screens for large audiences, and they can be controlled remotely. Most A-V companies should have at least one or two in stock.

4.4.2   Overhead Projectors

As mentioned in Section 4.2.2, OHP are used to project page-size transparencies onto a screen. There are two basic types of OHP, *transmissive* and *reflective*. Transmissive projectors have their light source in the base of the machine and project the light up through the glass *stage* upon which is placed the object to be projected, and then through a lens and onto a screen. They are bright and work well with *LCD projection panels*, which are really just thin flat panels placed on the OHP stage, that take the image from a computer and allow it to be projected using the OHP light source, but rather old technology now. Reflective projectors have their light source in the head of the projector and project it down onto a reflective stage, then back up through the lens onto a screen. They work best with transparencies.

The key considerations for choosing an OHP are lamp brightness and type of lens. Lamp brightness determines how dark a room must be and also what type of presentation will work (e.g. LCD projection panel or transparency). Current lamps can provide brightness up to 11,000 lumens (see Chapter 5 for a discussion of lumens), and are either halogen or metal halide (more reliable and expensive) types. Lens choice determines sharpness of the final image and focal length, which is further reflected in the distance between the OHP and the screen. If there is minimal distance available between OHP and screen, a shorter focal length lens will be needed.

Concerns with OHP are primarily that they are front-projection systems and as such, require placement at the front of a venue, relatively close to the screen, thus potentially blocking the view of some audience members. They

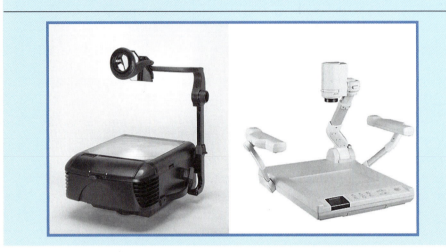

Courtesy: Left photo: 3-M, www.3mcom; Right photo: Samsung SVP-5500STP

also require the presenter or another person to be physically beside them to change transparencies. See Figure 4.8 for an example of an OHP.

4.4.3 Visual Presenters

Visual presenters are the successors to the opaque projectors of yesteryear, the large bulky devices used to view and project three-dimensional objects such as book pages, scientific specimens, and such. Today's devices incorporate a color video camera mounted on a movable arm that is positioned over a large base on which objects can be placed. The base, called the stage, usually has side and bottom lights to illuminate the objects such as books, solid objects, or transparencies. The camera has a lens that lets the user obtain an image of the entire object, or it can zoom in for close up views to see very small areas. Many digital visual presenters can plug directly into a video/data projector using the data signal port. Some digital visual presenters can be connected to a computer. Here the image obtained by the presenter is sent to the computer, processed, and appears on the computer's monitor or a laptop's LCD and, of course, can also be transmitted to a projector for display on a large screen. An advantage of the digital visual presenter is that it permits the capture of images in a computer-based digital format. A connected computer can then save a file of the subject or item placed in the viewing area (e.g. as a JPEG). The digital visual presenter is, in a sense, a scanner, since it can capture live images at high resolution to a computer file (McIntosh, 2005). Figure 4.8 illustrates a typical visual presenter.

4.4.4　Video/Data Projectors

Video/data projectors are the ones most likely to be encountered for projecting computer imagery at special events, as well as straight videos. They will be the projectors of choice for PowerPoint presentations, CADD (computer-aided design and drafting) drawings, and often CD or DVD-based movies. An A-V company may offer a choice of projectors and a producer or event manager will be more able to make the right choice knowing what each type of projector can do. In this section, we will review current projector technology, the key specifications, and other features that can improve a presentation.

4.4.4.1　*Projector Technology*

There are three types of video and data projectors currently in use: CRT, LCD, and DLP projectors. Each has advantages and disadvantages, based on the technology.

4.4.4.1.1　CRT Projector

Early color television sets and subsequently computer monitors and video/data projectors were based on CRT technology. Cathode rays are basically streams of electrons emitted by a heated electron gun (the cathode) at the back of the monitor/TV, which are attracted to the anode (screen) at the front of the monitor/TV due to a voltage difference between the cathode and anode. The screen is coated with a phosphorescent material that emits light as soon as the electrons hit it. The electron beam is steered along a predetermined path on the screen by electromagnetics. In color monitors and TVs, there are three electron guns, each corresponding to the three primary colors of light: RGB. Most modern CRT projectors are color and have three separate CRTs (instead of a single, color CRT), and their own lenses to achieve color images. The RGB portions of the incoming video signal are processed and sent to the respective CRTs whose images are focused by their lenses to achieve the overall picture on the screen.

The advantages of a CRT projector are (Wikipedia contributors, June 13, 2006):

- It has a long CRT life, typically that of a normal television picture tube.
- It can achieve good to very good color resolution, brightness, and picture size.
- Once set up, there is minimal maintenance, unlike projectors that use lamps.
- It has a superior black level (i.e. black is actually black and not dark gray).
- As with CRT monitors, the image resolution and the refresh rate are not fixed but variable within some limits. Interlaced material can be played directly, without need for imperfect de-interlacing mechanisms.

The disadvantages are:

- It tends to be bulky and heavy.
- It has low maximum brightness levels. A room has to be completely dark and the eyes of viewers coming from a daylight environment have to adapt to the darkness for a minute or two before image details can be seen.
- It suffers from uneven color mixing.
- Focusing is not even.
- It requires more time to set up and adjust for a good overall image.
- It is costlier than other types of projectors due to the complex circuitry required to control and synchronize the three CRTs to achieve optimum picture quality.

4.4.4.1.2   LCD Projector

These projectors utilize *liquid crystal display* (LCD) technology. An LCD is a thin, flat display device made up of any number of color or monochrome pixels arrayed in front of a light source or reflector. Each pixel consists of a column of electrically charged liquid crystal molecules suspended between two transparent electrodes, and two polarizing filters. The liquid crystal twists the polarization of light entering one filter to allow it to pass through the other. When an electrical charge is applied to the electrodes, the molecules of the liquid crystal align themselves parallel to the electric field, thus limiting the rotation of entering light. By controlling the twist of the liquid crystals in each pixel, light can be allowed to pass though in varying amounts, correspondingly illuminating the pixel (Wikipedia contributors; Liquid crystal display, July 10, 2006b). 'An LCD projector has three LCD prism panels that allow RGB light to pass through its pixels. These separate colors are then converged and projected. Electrical signals turn on pixels within a set based on the resolution of the unit' (The Projector People, 2006b). The best image quality can be accomplished with a blank white or gray surface to project on, and for this reason dedicated projection screens are often used.

The advantages of an LCD projector are (Silva, 2006):

- It is compact, lightweight, and easily portable because the LCD chip is very small.
- It has very high contrast and brightness.
- It has lower power consumption than other projectors.

The disadvantages are:

- It can sometimes exhibit a *screen-door effect* on a large screen caused by being able to see individual pixels due to the magnification.
- Since an LCD chip is made up of a panel of individual pixels, if one pixel burns out it displays an annoying black or white dot on the projected image. Individual pixels cannot be repaired. If one or more pixels burn out, the entire chip has to be replaced.

- It is best only at its native resolution. For many projectors this is 1024 × 768, so that any other signal it receives (e.g. an HDTV signal of 1920 × 1080) must be scaled to fit, thus causing loss of quality.
- Lamps must be replaced every 1000–2000 h and are expensive.

Also in development is a new technology based on the LCD called *liquid crystal on silicone* or LCOS. The concept of LCOS is to combine LCD panels with the low cost of a silicone backplane to achieve extremely high resolutions that are not feasible with LCD or DLP technologies. Several proprietary variants exist, such as JVC's D-ILA and Sony's XRD versions.

4.4.4.1.3   Digital Light Processing Projector

Digital light processing (DLP), a technology developed by Texas Instruments, forms the core of the last type of projector. 'In DLP projectors, the image is created by microscopically small mirrors laid out in a matrix on a semiconductor chip, known as a *Digital Micromirror Device* (DMD). Each mirror represents one pixel in the projected image. The number of mirrors corresponds to the resolution of the projected image: 800 × 600, 1024 × 768, 1280 × 720, and 1920 × 1080 (HDTV) matrices are some common DMD sizes' (Wikipedia contributors, July 8, 2006). These mirrors can be repositioned rapidly to reflect light. The rapid repositioning of the mirrors (essentially switching between 'on' and 'off') allows the DMD to vary the intensity of the light being reflected out through the lens, creating shades of gray in addition to white (mirror in 'on' position), and black (mirror in 'off' position).

There are two primary methods by which DLP projection systems create a color image, those utilized by single-chip DLP projectors, and those used by three-chip projectors. In a single-chip system, color is added as the light passes through a high-speed color wheel placed between the lamp and the DMD chips. In a three-chip system, a prism is added to divide the light into RGB and each DLP chip is then dedicated to only one of these colors and the light is then recombined and passed through the projection lens.

The advantages of DLP projectors are (Silva, 2006; Wikipedia contributors, July 8, 2006):

- Images are superior to other projectors in terms of depth, color, contrast, and smoothness.
- They have less of a screen-door effect than LCD projectors.
- There is no possibility of screen burn-in.
- Lamps are more easily replaceable than for LCD projectors.
- They are compact and have low power consumption.

The disadvantages are:

- Although a DLP projector doesn't exhibit the screen-door effect of many LCD units, a DLP projector can exhibit what is referred to as the *rainbow effect*. Basically, the rainbow effect is exhibited by a brief flash of colors (like a small rainbow) when the viewer rapidly looks from side to side on the screen or looks rapidly from the screen to the side of the room. Fortunately, this does not occur frequently and many people do not have sensitivity to this effect at all.

- There is some fan noise.
- Replacement lamps are expensive.

4.4.4.2 *Key Specifications for Video/Data Projectors*

For special events, projectors need to do many things, from projecting PowerPoint text in a small, darkened meeting room, to projecting DVD movies or live video in a convention hall or an open-air stadium for an audience of thousands. No single projector will handle all these situations and the choice will depend on the key specifications of the projector, these of course being driven by the design technology discussed above. Listed below are these key specs.

4.4.4.2.1 Resolution

Projectors use rows of pixels to make the images seen onscreen. The clarity of the image depends on how many pixels are projected and it is measured by projector resolution. The resolution that is built into the projector is dependent on the technology discussed previously and is called the projector's native resolution for digital data. For most projectors this may be *SVGA, WVGA, XGA,* or *SXGA,* all expressed as two numbers indicating the number of pixels across the screen and then down the screen. Although many projectors also accept other resolutions, for example HDTV resolutions at 1920 × 1080, the best viewing will be at the native resolution because the projector must scale up or down to be able to show other resolutions and this can result in a loss of quality. Table 4.2 summarizes the recommended projector resolution for different projection requirements.

TABLE 4.2
RECOMMENDED PROJECTOR RESOLUTIONS

Type of Presentation	Recommended Minimum Resolution	Projector Class
PowerPoint-type presentation software, clip art, or simple graphics (e.g. pie and bar charts)	800 × 600	SVGA
External data sources like VCRs and DVD players	854 × 480	WVGA
Excel-type spreadsheets and detailed graphics (e.g. architectural drawings)	1024 × 768	XGA
CADD applications or ultra high-resolution graphics	1280 × 1024	SXGA

Courtesy: 3 M Meeting Network, www.3m.com.

Also part of projector resolution is video resolution, which is expressed in lines per inch and refers to the analog video standards we have already discussed in Section 4.2.3.1.6, specifically NTSC, PAL, and SECAM. Occasionally, a client may have to decide between projecting video and PowerPoint because of the two different resolutions.

4.4.4.2.2 Brightness

Brightness of a projector is measured in *lumens*, a term discussed in Chapter 5 that indicates the intensity of a light source. In the case of a projector, this is the lamp. The venue size, audience size, and ambient light are what will determine the brightness required. Most professional projectors for business uses are in the 2000–5000 lumens range, which is good for large venues and relatively subdued ambient lighting. If the lighting approaches daylight (e.g. in an outdoor stadium or brightly lit room), a higher rating is required. For example, my company produced a daylight event in a stadium and required a 12,000-lumen projector, which was barely adequate for the ambient conditions. Some high-end professional projectors are available with over 20,000 lumens for just these conditions. Table 4.3 provides a helpful summary of recommended projector brightness levels for certain ambient conditions.

TABLE 4.3
PROJECTOR BRIGHTNESS/AMBIENT LIGHT RELATIONSHIP

Projector Brightness	Best for These Conditions
700 lumens	▪ Smaller rooms ▪ Smaller audiences ▪ Dark or dim lighting
700–1600 lumens	▪ Normal business-sized conference rooms and classrooms ▪ Medium-sized audiences ▪ Reduced lighting
1200–2000 or more lumens	▪ Large conference rooms or classrooms ▪ Normal room lighting
2500 or more lumens	▪ Large venues, including conference rooms and auditoriums ▪ Most lighting conditions

Courtesy: 3M Meeting Network, www.3m.com.

4.4.4.2.3 Contrast Ratio

This is the ratio between the brightest white and the darkest black and complements brightness. The higher the contrast ratio, the clearer the image will be. Room light impacts contrast so a higher ratio is better if the room will be well lit during projection. A contrast ratio of 1500:1 is good, but 2000:1 is considered excellent.

4.4.4.2.4 Weight and Portability

Although for special events, weight and portability are not as much of a concern as for small meetings and classrooms, it is still useful to know about size, since some projectors have to be mounted in unusual locations at special events to serve different purposes. For example, they may serve as a component of décor by projecting looping images of scenery or people onto tensile fabric décor pieces. This might entail mounting them on trussing or temporary lightweight structures. For this purpose it is better to have a light, highly portable machine. Most of the smaller units weigh in the order of 5–10 lb (2.25–4.5 kg), whereas the units like the Barco XLM HD30 pictured in Figure 4.9 weigh 400 lb (180 kg), are much larger, and are intended for more permanent installations or at least minimal moving around.

4.4.4.2.5 Available Input and Output Ports

Critical to the success of any presentation using a projector is the ability of the projector to accept the information from the source. The source may be video, data, or any combination of the analog or digital information we have already discussed. Here are the most common inputs and outputs found on projectors:

- *Video inputs*: These include composite video, S-video, component video, DVI, and especially in the higher-end projectors, HDMI and BNC. This means that the projector will accept the connectors for these types of video that we reviewed in Section 4.2.3.3.
- *Data inputs*: These include VGA and USB as discussed in Section 4.2.5.3.
- *Audio inputs and outputs*: Many low-end projectors have their own speakers and will accept audio inputs. Likewise, they have audio out and can send the audio signal to an external audio system. For most special events, for the best-quality audio it is recommended that the audio for any video or computer information be taken directly from the source

FIGURE 4.9

EXAMPLES OF VIDEO/DATA PROJECTORS (NOT TO SCALE)

Courtesy: Barco, www.barco.com and http://bssc.sel.sony.com/BroadcastandBusiness/DisplayModel?m=0&p=12&sp=98&id=80151

to the main mixer of the house audio system rather than use the lower-quality audio of the projector.

4.4.4.3   *Other Features of Video/Data Projectors*

Projectors have come a long way in a very short time and most now have the following features as part of the package. It is useful to know what they can do.

- *Zoom lens*: This is useful if the exact placement of the projector cannot be controlled. In fact, many have optional lenses with different focal lengths, allowing more flexibility in placement.
- *Keystone correction*: This corrects for rectangular distortion caused by positioning the projector away from the central axis of the screen or projection surface.
- *Remote control*: Most now have remote control capability over focus, keystone, power, page up or down, color mode, freeze, resize, menu, onscreen pointer, and other features. Many projectors are now also operated with wireless technology.
- *Front or rear projection*: Many projectors have the capability of projecting from the front or rear of screens (i.e. by reversing the image).
- *Power consumption*: The low-end, lower-brightness projectors only consume in the 300–400 W power range; however, the higher-end, brighter projectors can consume up to 8 KW of power. This is important to know when planning for power requirements for an event. Refer to Chapter 9 for more details about electrical power.

Figure 4.9 gives examples of typical video/data projectors. The projectors represented are: on the left, a large, professional, heavy-duty projector, the Barco XLM HD30; and on the right, a more portable, multi-purpose projector, the Sony VPL-PX41.

4.5   DISPLAY EQUIPMENT

The final step in the process outlined in Section 4.2 is displaying the image(s) of the visual source. There are many ways to do this and we will look at each one in order to help in making the right choice for a special event. The equipment choices for display are:

- Plain screens
- Monitors
- Video walls
- LED (light-emitting diode) screens
- Teleprompters
- Other unusual surfaces.

4.5.1 Plain Screens

Undoubtedly what comes to mind as a first choice for displaying images is a projection screen. Screens are used more than any other display medium in special events, in particular with video/data projections, IMAG, visual presenters, overheads, and even occasionally old 35 mm slides. There are several concerns that must be addressed before deciding on a particular screen.

4.5.1.1 Front or Rear Projection

This is the first decision that must be made for any event. Each type of projection has advantages and disadvantages.

- *Front projection*: This type of projection takes up far less space than rear projection, and is particularly good if the projector is truss or ceiling mounted, thus eliminating any chance of screen interference caused by people walking in front of the projector. However, there is a greater chance of light interference from other ambient sources such as stage or house lighting, and there may also be audio system interference from projector fan noise. Generally speaking, front projection is less difficult to set up.
- *Rear projection*: This type of projection eliminates chances of audience members casting shadows on the screen when walking in front of the projector and it is less prone to ambient light interference. However, it may require a large area behind the screen for projector setup and this area must often be cordoned off and even curtained off to minimize light spillage on the projector and screen from external doors. Using a mirror with the projector can decrease the area required for rear projection setup; however, the mirror must be *front-surfaced* to eliminate double images.

Note that for either front or rear projection, screens may be suspended from ceilings or trusses for better viewing. Supplemental suspended screens are frequently added in positions partway down a large venue if the viewing distance from the back of the audience is too far to the main screens(s) (Figure 4.10).

4.5.1.2 Types of Screens

There are two common types of screens that are available.

- *Tripod*: These are for front projection only. The fabric pulls up and out of a metal cradle. The base is a three-legged tripod. They are available only up to 8 ft × 8 ft (2.4 m × 2.4 m) in size and are best used for presentations in small rooms or spaces with audiences under approximately 150 people.

FIGURE 4.10
EXAMPLE OF SUPPLEMENTAL SCREENS

Courtesy: Pacific Show Productions, www.pacificshow.ca – Copyright 2006

■ *Fast-fold*: These consist of a fabric that snaps to a rigid aluminum frame. The screen may be used for front or rear projection depending on the type of fabric. Legs may be adjusted to various heights and the screens may also be flown if required. They are available in sizes up to 30 ft (9 m) in width.

4.5.1.3 *Screen Surface and Material*

'In front projection, matte white surfaces (by far the most popular) offer excellent definition for finely detailed images, such as computer text, while providing very good images from color slides and overheads. Smooth silver or white pearlescent surfaces provide particularly bright images best for video or computer projection, but are too prone to *hotspotting* for overheads. Glass beaded surfaces offer a brighter image with some sacrifice of sharpness. They are intended for general video, slide, and film projection use, but are not recommended for computer data. *Lenticular* surfaces are designed for video and slide projection (not for overheads) and for rooms with sidelight from windows. They work by focusing projected light that would otherwise be disbursed on the vertical axis onto the horizontal where it can be viewed. In the same way, ambient sidelight that would otherwise mix with the projected image is reflected away.

In rear projection situations, there are several coatings and screen materials designed for specific situations. Most standard surfaces are best for rooms with a relatively narrow seating cone and good lighting control, with specialty surfaces available when viewing angles will be wide or lighting high' (United Visual Inc., 2006). Rear screen fabrics are translucent and allow the image to pass through from behind. They attach only to fast-fold frames.

4.5.1.4   Other Features and Concerns

Understanding several other features of screens may improve the viewing experience.

- *Gain*: This is 'the ability of a screen to gather light from a projector and direct it to a certain location. A high gain screen can be important in situations where room lights must remain high for note-taking or discussion, particularly if those lights wash onto the screen surface. Gain varies with screen surface. . . . Most matte white screens are rated at a gain of about 1.0, and most glass beaded screens provide a gain of about 2.5. Lenticular surfaces are rated from 1.5 up to about 3.0, and rear screens offer gains up to 5.0' (United Visual Inc., 2006).
- *Viewing angles*: 'No matter what a screen's stated viewing angle, seating an audience outside a 90 degree cone has inherent problems that no screen will overcome. At angles greater than 45 degrees from a line perpendicular to the center of the screen, images appear distorted, with objects looking taller and thinner than they should. Thus, most screens are designed to focus projected light back to an audience within that 90 degree cone, and images viewed from beyond that will appear quite dim' (United Visual Inc., 2006).
- *Screen dressing*: By *dressing* we mean finishing off the screen installation with defining borders, usually black drape. These give it a professional appearance, mask the support framing, assist in giving the perception of a brighter image, and help to mask any setup behind the screen, especially for rear projection. Most professional screens come with black borders anyway, but the addition of short drapery sections along the top and bottom of the screen plus full-screen height drape on either side finishes the setup properly. Obviously, the side draping can extend as far as required in any direction by adding panels.

4.5.1.5   Determining Screen Size

Correct screen size is determined be using a general formula. Find the distance to the last row of seats and divide by **eight** to determine the screen height, then apply the aspect ratio of the media you will be using to arrive at the screen width. Usually this is 4:3 for computer or video images, but may be 16:9 for HDTV formats. For example, using Imperial units, if the last row of seats is 70 ft from the screen, then the height should be approximately 8.75 ft (i.e. 70/8 = 8.75), or for the closest screen size, 9 ft. Using the 4:3 ratio will then give a screen width of 12 ft (i.e. 9 × 4/3 = 12). Note that the first number in screen sizing is the screen height and the second is the width. One caveat that goes with the above formula for determining screen size is that if the images are finer in detail than simple graphics, the guiding number of eight changes to six for reading spreadsheets or text, and to four for detailed drawings like CADD. Finally, the minimum distance from the screen to the first row of seating should be at least two times the width of the image on the screen, and the bottom of the screen should be at least 40–48 in. above the floor.

4.5.2 Monitors

Monitors can be thought of as combinations of projectors and screens. For special events they are often used in small venues and as supplementary displays to larger screens to cover sections of audience that the screens cannot cover in large venues (e.g. at the front of an audience not within the viewing angle of the main screens). In terms of appearance, the monitors used for events are no different than consumer monitors.

Monitor technology is changing rapidly. Presently, there are four technologies in common use: CRT, LCD, DLP, and plasma. We have already discussed how the first three work, but have not mentioned plasma.

Plasma monitors are flat, lightweight surfaces covered with millions of tiny glass bubbles. 'Each bubble contains a gas-like substance, the plasma, and has a phosphor coating. The bubbles can be considered as the pixels, each pixel bubble having three sub-pixels: one red, one green, and one blue. When it is time to display an image signal (RGB or video), a digitally controlled electric current flows through the flat screen, causing the plasma inside designated bubbles to give off ultraviolet rays. This light in turn causes the phosphor coatings to glow the appropriate color' (Plasma People, 2006).

In terms of advantages and disadvantages of each type of display, they all now give excellent quality. CRT monitors tend to be bulky and are not used much anymore in special events. LCD, DLP, and plasma are lightweight, flat, thin displays, with plasma still having a slight advantage in clarity and a wider viewing angle.

Current maximum known diagonal screen sizes for these types of monitors are: 73 in. (29 cm) for CRT, 103 in. (40 cm) for plasma, 65 in. (25 cm) for LCD, and 73 in. (29 cm) for DLP (Wikipedia contributors, May 12, 2006). It is interesting to note, however, that small and even miniature versions of monitors are seeing some use in special events. Notable new versions include miniature, desk, or table-mounted monitors, and small monitors as portable, human-mounted advertising devices.

Just as we thought monitor technology was stabilizing, however, on the very near horizon are three exciting new ones, which will probably all be competing for business within the next 5 years or less. They are as follows:

- *Surface-conduction electron-emitter display (SED)*: This is a flat panel display technology that is basically a 'squashed' CRT. The CRT uses the properties of a self-luminous display to ensure a high luminance, clear colors, and wide viewing angle. 'When this technology is applied to a large screen display, however, the television becomes excessively heavy and requires a much deeper unit. The SED solves these problems using a glass substrate with electron emitters, equivalent to the electron gun in the CRT, arranged to correspond to the number of pixels, and a second glass substrate coated with a fluorescent substance. These two glass substrates are brought close together, and the space between them is vacuum sealed. This allows for a thin construction that does not require the conventional electron beam deflection required in the CRT, while still allowing for crisp, clean color, and movement display using a light emission principle similar to the CRT' (Toshiba Corporation, 2006).

- *Field emission display (FED)*: 'The front panel of an FED is essentially the same as a flatscreen CRT: a glass sheet. But in place of a cathode "gun" that sprays electrons through a bulky vacuum tube and onto a phosphor-coated screen, FEDs use millions of microscopic electron emitters (actually carbon nanotubes, the most efficient emitters known), which are arranged in a grid about 0.08 in. behind the phosphor. . . . The end result is a monitor that produces more accurate color, truer black, and smoother motion tracking than plasma and LCD models' (Captain, 2006).

- *Organic light-emitting diode (OLED)*: This is a thin-film LED (see Section 4.5.4 and Chapter 5) technology in which the emissive layer is an organic compound, sandwiched between two thin-film conductive electrodes. In essence, it is a screen and projector all in one piece of extremely thin, flexible material. This technology lends itself to the actual printing of the light-emitting screen using ink-jet printers, a fact that renders it cheaper to manufacture than any other existing technology. OLEDs and their newer versions polymer OLEDs (PLED), phosphorescent OLEDs (PHOLED), top-emitting OLEDs (TOLED), and flexible OLEDs (FOLED) all have a greater range of brightness, colors, and viewing angles (e.g. approaching 180 degrees) than any other technology. This means they will be able to be used in such things as clothing and portable displays. They are already evident in cell phones, PDAs, digital cameras, military head-up displays, and car stereos.

4.5.3 Video walls

Video walls are high-end image display systems consisting of multiple monitors (*cubes*) placed in various configurations such as 2 × 2 (e.g. 4 monitors with an overall aspect ratio of approximately 4:3), 3 × 4 (e.g. 12 monitors with an overall aspect ratio of 16:9 or HDTV size), and almost any other combination desired. The monitors are especially constructed for this type of display, typically vary from 2 to 4 or 5 ft (0.6 to 1.2 or 1.5 m) in depth, and are designed to be stacked together. The monitors use the same technology as found in other projection systems (e.g. CRT, LCD, or DLP).

FIGURE 4.11

Courtesy: http://www.electrosonic.com/view_profile.asp?id=191#

The technology basically takes video, digital data, and/or computer graphics input and feeds it into a processor that manipulates and splits the signal to allow it to go to one or more monitors. Almost limitless possibilities are available for uniquely displaying the image or combinations of images. The advantages of a video wall include constant resolution and brightness no matter to what size the image grows. Figure 4.11 gives an example of a large video wall installation in China that measures 20 ft high by 98 ft (6 m × 29 m) wide. Multiple video/data projectors are now replacing video walls in some situations but they too must still be programmed and require a dedicated content person to operate them.

4.5.4 LED Screens

In its most simple form, an LED is a *light-emitting diode*, which is a semiconductor device that emits light when electricity is passed through it. This effect is a form of electroluminescence. The color of the emitted light depends on the chemical composition of the semiconducting material used. LEDs are also explained in Chapter 5.

In a traditional LED screen, the screen corresponds to the computer screen driving it. Each pixel corresponding to a computer pixel consists of three LEDs: RGB. This has made for resolution that is better viewed from a distance. The latest innovation in LED technology is popularly called *virtual pixel* or *V-tech* technology. The virtual pixel is a multiplexed pixel that allows a tighter screen resolution by using pixel-sharing techniques, essentially making one pixel correspond to one LED. LED screens are now ubiquitous, and one finds them everywhere as signs of varying sizes. Use in the special event business is increasing, particularly in the celebrity concert side.

4.5.5 Teleprompters

A teleprompter is the modern version of the old theatrical cue cards used to help with the speech of someone onstage. A modern teleprompter is a display device that prompts the person speaking with an electronic visual text of a speech or script, by sending the script to a flat panel that is projected up to one-way mirror glass that in turn reflects the writing directly at the eye level of the presenter. A teleprompter system usually requires three or four components to function: a dedicated host computer and operator; prompting software that can reverse and variably scroll the text; a scan converter to convert computer output to NTSC or PAL composite video signals if using a video monitor; and a teleprompter display device with mirror hood. Teleprompters come in several different versions: a hooded version that can be placed directly onto the front of a camera for TV or onscreen personalities so that it appears they are speaking directly to the camera; a floor-mounted panel with eye-level prompter glass used for executive presentations from a stage; and a stage-mounted prompter that looks much like an audio monitor that can be used for singer lyrics. An alternative method that serves the same purpose is to place a small flat-panel monitor on a stand just below the top level of a lectern and it in turn can act like an onstage laptop computer to project PowerPoint slides. This is called a *confidence monitor*.

For special events, the executive-type teleprompter is most often used. With such a teleprompter, from the perspective of the audience, it appears as though the speaker is speaking extemporaneously with only preplanned glances to the notes on the lectern. The eye contact with the audience assists the speaker to connect in a relaxed demeanor and with confidence.

4.5.6 Other Unusual Surfaces

There is probably no industry more ready to push the boundaries of display technology than special events. The industry regularly projects images and movies onto such surfaces as the sides of entire large buildings, tensile fabrics, and water screens. Actually, there is nothing new in the display technology itself, rather a more creative approach to the use of existing projectors. This often requires challenges with lenses and mounting locations but standard projectors are used. Figure 4.12 illustrates the use of projection on a water screen. See also Chapter 6 and the discussion of water screens as special effects.

Courtesy: Laservision Pty. Ltd. A.B.N., www.laservision.com.au, © Copyright Laservision. 2007

4.6   MULTIMEDIA PRESENTATIONS

The expectations associated with the term *multimedia presentation* are diverse and often end up not being met in special events. That is probably because of a lack of understanding of the term. We feel it is of such importance in today's special events that it is worthy of a dedicated section in this chapter, devoted to not only the understanding of what it is but rather to what it has the potential to do, largely due to the part played by visual presentation technology.

What, then, is a multimedia presentation? According to one definition, 'multimedia is the use of several different media (e.g. text, audio, graphics, animation, video, and interactivity) to convey information. Multimedia also refers to the use of computer technology to create, store, and experience multimedia content' (Wikipedia contributors, July 11, 2006). Herein lies the problem. On one hand, the expectations of those more attuned to working with computers, such as A-V companies and anyone under the age of 50 years, are for a multimedia show to incorporate mainly computer technology and video. On the other hand, those of a generation able to remember the 1960s, associate multimedia with the influential work of Andy Warhol in his groundbreaking, 1966 performance 'Exploding. Plastic. Inevitable,' which was then termed 'multimedia' and combined the rock music of the Velvet Underground with cinema and performance art.

Arguably, this was the true beginning of not only the visual aspects of the psychedelic phenomenon, but also of adding visual content in the form of lighting effects, video, and IMAG to concert performances.

To be sure, multimedia can encompass all these influences, but to get it right, the producer has to have very clear goals at the outset of the project in order to meet the expectations of the client and audience. To do this, let us consider – as did Mulhall (2005) – that there are two types of multimedia presentations: traditional and non-traditional. The traditional, contrary to the influences explained above, includes only the simplest of presentation content and equipment, such as basic video, still images, PowerPoint on a screen, and a live presenter, but with minimal interaction between the audience and speaker or audience and the visuals themselves. Only the speaker interacts with the visuals (e.g. by changing slides). The non-traditional presentation may include not only video and PowerPoint, but also newer technology (e.g. water screens, tensile fabric screens, theatrical scrims, Catalyst software and DL2 lights, or special effects) along with live performances and possibly audience interaction.

It is this second form of multimedia presentation, like the one originating with Warhol, that we are concerned with in this section. As Warhol said at the time of his 1966 presentation, 'We all knew something revolutionary was happening. We just felt it. Things could not look this strange and new without some barrier being broken.' Of course, what everyone had experienced was the emotional power of combining visuals and performance. That is the secret to getting a message across with multimedia, the power of emotion. Here are some tips on doing it right.

4.6.1 Setting Goals and Content for the Show

To start with, multimedia can be expensive. There is always a temptation that 'more is going to make it better.' That is why it is necessary to understand and discuss with all concerned what the exact goal of the presentation is before the project is launched. There may not be a reason for using three live video cameras if two will do. Perhaps the show is not complicated enough to warrant prerecording and synchronizing everything to tape. As with entertainment and décor, the sensory experience is being heightened through the addition of more exciting visual stimuli and audio effects, so these stimuli had better get the point across in the most efficient manner possible. This means a close examination of the goals. Some of the more common goals of a multimedia presentation include the following:

- Improving the understanding of a particular message, such as corporate goals.
- Motivating sales forces.
- Evoking emotions in order to more easily sell a service or product, or motivate to take some action.
- Educating in a cultural or spiritual context.

Once the goal has been determined, then it requires creative sessions with the producer and A-V supplier to decide what sort of show content should be developed. The combinations are almost endless, but here is some food for thought based on the above generic types of goals.

- If there is to be a specific message such as a corporate sales goal, will the company president be part of the show and will he or she be able to, or want to, deliver the message without help from additional images or video? Will signage suffice for a message or must extra pizzazz be added? Will he or she need to use PowerPoint with perhaps a laptop computer near or on the stage?
- If the goal is motivational, how is it best delivered? This is where the list of possibilities is long. Cheerleaders, motivational keynote speakers, upbeat dance routines, celebrity acts, magicians, cirque shows, and many others have been used as live entertainment together with moti-vating slides, videos, special effects, and automated lighting. Who will write the script and direct the show?
- Does the show require an emotional appeal or impact and how will that best be achieved? This can sometimes be done by using a pre-recorded video clip with good scripting, videography, editing, and perhaps suitable emotional background music. On the other hand, it might be better achieved more dramatically with a live performance, especially if the performers are good at bringing out emotion from audiences (e.g. the drama of a Shakespearean actor, the flawless performance of a professional ballerina, the power of a 100-voice choir, etc.), which in turn can be augmented with other visuals such as still images or short video clips.
- If the goal is to tell a story or educate, what length is the show to be (shorter is always better, in the order of 5–10 min or so)? Is it too cere-bral to be effective as a multimedia presentation (most presentations work best if the message is fairly straightforward)? Will it need exten-sive scripting and rehearsing? All these can take extra time and money. Often, telling a story requires intensive research for, and editing of, still and video images in order to make them suitably relevant to the subject, in order to achieve the emotional impact sought, and in order to make them clear and of high enough resolution to be effective.
- In any of the scenarios, will there be live video and how many cameras will be needed?

4.6.2 Choosing Equipment and Personnel

Once content has been determined, then equipment and personnel must be planned. The options once again are almost limitless, but usually end up being restricted by budget. Here are some points to consider.

4.6.2.1 Screens and Projection Surfaces

If there is only one stage and all the presentations are intended to be from there, is there any sense to have auxiliary screens or monitors elsewhere in the venue or is the audience small enough that they will be fully engaged with a large screen or projections surfaces at or near the stage? Typical screen setups for large, seated audiences include: a large stage backdrop screen(s) with occasional smaller screens as part of the larger one(s); corner screens set diagonally across the front corners of the venue, usually flanking the stage; and supplementary screens for large audiences sometimes flown on trussing partway down a long venue. Not used too often are side screens. If the screens are close to the stage and there will be performances, their visibility will be influenced by any light spillage from stage lighting, so the entire show will also have to be reviewed with the lighting designer. As well, any stage performances may have to be restricted to only the downstage area if there is front projection, due to the possibility of shadows falling on the screen surface from the performers.

Sheila Stack, the award-winning President of Impact Productions in Denver, Colorado, finds it useful to split a large main screen in order to gain better control of her shows. This allows her to determine at her discretion when to go to a live camera and when to go to another source such as PowerPoint if a critical point is being made by a speaker that must pre-empt the live shot. The split allows her to use both shots at the same time, thus avoiding missing anything. She is also an advocate of placing a confidence monitor at or near the base of a lectern in order to give instructions to a speaker such as when to stop and get off stage, when to lengthen, and such. It is less visible and obtrusive than an IFB monitor (see Chapter 3), and separate from a teleprompter. For this monitor, as with a teleprompter, a dedicated computer operator is required (Sheila Stack, Personal Communication, April 5, 2006).

4.6.2.2 Projectors

The main concern for projectors is whether they are used for front or rear projection and what brightness is needed, depending on the ambient light. Also required is the distance to the screens or projection surfaces and the material of the surfaces. The show does not necessarily have to be on only screens. It can be partly on other surfaces like water screens, fabric, walls, and décor components as mentioned earlier. Lens focal length is also critical, and is influenced by the final decision on projector placement. Front projection in a large venue, for example, may very well be from a projector suspended from a lighting truss. The truss location is decided based mainly on lighting concerns and so the projector lens has to be chosen to ensure optimum projection from this location.

In order to achieve better brightness and to add a redundancy safety factor, Studley and Monner (2004) recommend *hot stacking* projectors on a main screen. This means overlaying two projector signals onto the screen rather than just using one. They like to work with two identical projector models to do this.

4.6.2.3   Video Cameras

Section 4.2.4 dealt at length with IMAG and the use of video cameras. Suffice it to say that prior to embarking on a multimedia show, the number of cameras and the exact locations of the cameras must be determined. Usually, for best results and to enable a creative variety of shots, at least two cameras, one stationary, and one roving, are required. The standard camera used for events is a digital Betacam.

4.6.2.4   Personnel

Personnel are chosen based on the complexity of the show. They may include:

- Technical director to call the camera shots and video switches from a central location, usually front-of-house.
- Camera operator for each camera plus a grip for each roving camera.
- Shader or switcher operator to operate the signal processing, switching equipment, and videotape recorders at the front-of-house position. This position will also typically have one *preview monitor* per camera, and one preview monitor for the final signal before it goes to projection equipment, so the operator can ensure what will be viewed on the final display has the correct color balance, resolution, and size.
- One or more computer operators depending on the number of computers and the complexity of software and digital images used as part of the show. Each computer will have a monitor for previewing images before sending them to the switching hardware. The location is usually backstage with the rest of the A-V equipment for the show.
- Possibly an extra technician to assist with complex tasks and equipment problems.

4.6.3   Putting it Together

Putting a multimedia show together means more than just showing up with a collection of tapes, PowerPoint computer, and video cameras. A good multimedia show is a full-blown work of art, much like a musical composition or a stage play. It requires a story line, a script, performers who are professional, good production support, and extensive rehearsals. Inevitably, the job of writing and scripting a story line falls to the show producer who must interpret the goals of the show set by the client and deliver a stunning multimedia performance that gets the point across. This may be, in its simplest form, just a series of PowerPoint slides interspersed with video clips or guest speakers, but put together in a logically flowing format. On the other hand, it may be an actual story written from scratch that is used as an analogy to deliver a message. This might involve actual scripting. It might involve researching for, selecting, and editing still images. It might involve auditioning and contracting appropriate live entertainment to supplement and emphasize the message. It might be very short or it might extend over an entire event.

Whatever the case, it is helpful to treat visual sources such as live or recorded video and still images as another form of performer, albeit with some limitations but many capabilities. In this way, the technology can be fit into the story line whenever it will improve the delivery of the message, particularly the emotional side. This means that the show must be built as any entertainment program, with a logical flow to a climax, using all the disparate elements. Chapter 1 of this book and Chapter 8 of *Special Event Production: The Process* discuss the creation and execution of such a show in detail.

My company created many multimedia shows, but one sticks in my memory as a fine example of the intricate mixture of such disparate elements. The concept was to use an original Native American legend as an analogy to the historic rise and success of the client company. My task was to write the story, find the performers, choose the background music and much of the imagery, and rehearse the show with my A-V colleagues who also assisted with video selection, still image and video editing, and putting it all together with the appropriate equipment. We ended up with a complete three-act play that was performed on three different stages throughout dinner, each stage with a separate large screen as a backdrop. The play was narrated by an old chief whose scripted lines we had to prerecord in a studio and whom we placed behind a scrim where he sat by a campfire 'telling' the story. The logistics were complex to say the least, and the timing of the entire visual component with live dancers, rhythmic gymnasts, giant puppets, stiltwalkers, and backing imagery was a challenge. It called for an experienced show-caller (see Chapter 8 of *Special Event Production: The Process*), a well-written script broken down into logical segments with accompanying cues for music and visuals down to the second, and edited video clips that were accurately time coded.

Sheila Stack of Impact Productions, also echoes my own personal experience when she states that 'a good multimedia show needs: pre-determined exact camera locations for live shots, strict scripting, extensive rehearsing, and pre-production that matches imagery to music to provide emotional impact.' She has provided a sample in Figure 4.13 of one of her award shows that used two main screens primarily for IMAG, with four smaller screens for award winners and other related interest-generating imagery. According to her, the show had many rapid cues and all images had to be of perfect quality and in perfect order on all the computers feeding the screens.

FIGURE 4.13
TYPICAL MULTIMEDIA SETUP IN A BALLROOM

Courtesy: Steve Crecelius/WonderWorks Studios and Impact Productions, www. impactprods.com

4.7   EQUIPMENT SETUP AND OPERATION

Once the use and format of the presentation is determined, the producer and A-V supplier must decide on the optimum equipment for the job, using combinations of the available projection and display options, and then proceed to setup and operation.

4.7.1   Setup

Like lighting, visual presentation equipment can involve a time-consuming setup due to the requirements to occasionally fly projectors and screens, the need for dark time to check colors and alignment, and especially due to the need for rehearsing complex cues and switching. In order to ensure the right equipment and locations are chosen, here are the most important questions a producer must ask an event manager.

- How many attendees are there and what is the room layout? If this is a classroom setting, then more people can be accommodated within the space and there will likely be no obstructions to sight lines. This means that screens can probably go only at the front of the room. If a dining setup, then attendees will be facing all different directions and projection to different locations in the room may have to be considered. If the event is in multiple rooms simultaneously, then smaller TV monitors in each room might be appropriate.

- What size of projection system is needed? If there is a large spread-out audience, that means a larger screen size. The formula for screen size given in Section 4.5.1.5 may be used.
- Is projection to be rear or front? As explained in Section 4.5.1.1, each of these types has advantages and disadvantages.
- Are sight lines to the screens clear or is there a possibility of any obstruction caused by people walking in front of a projector or of table centers or architectural elements (e.g. columns) being in the projection path? If so, then a decision must be made to change either the projection system or the event design.
- Do presenters need computer support in the form of remote mouse control or cabling for laptop computers near the stage?
- Is a teleprompter required for speaker or MC (Master of Ceremonies) scripts and, if so, is there sufficient unobstructed space for it near the stage?
- If a video wall is being used, is there sufficient space to allow for a large enough wall for easy viewing and where exactly is the optimum location?
- If IMAG is being used, where will the camera(s) be placed in order to obtain a good picture yet cause minimal obstruction to audience sight lines?
- Is there appropriate technical support at the venue in the form of electrical power, ceiling hanging points with an acceptable load rating, and easy and early room access?
- Is the budget sufficient to do the job?

Once the answers are known and equipment chosen, the setup can proceed. It involves the following tasks:

- Preparation of all equipment takes place in the shop. If there is a multimedia show, some pre-programing may be required, as may be the loading of special software on a computer.
- Equipment is delivered and loaded in.
- Screens or A-V-related display equipment, such as monitors or video walls, are positioned and set up, either flown or floor mounted. They are then dressed with drapery material. Display equipment requiring it is connected to electrical power.
- Switching hardware, preview monitors, show control computers, and VCRs are set up backstage and connected as required. This equipment is tied into electrical power and Internet if required. Audio from the switching hardware is tied into the main audio mixer in and out. Intercom is set up between the switcher position, all camera operators, and any additional technical personnel controlling equipment. Internet connections are tested.

- Projectors are positioned and set up, either on projector carts or ceiling mounted from trussing or other supports. Correct cabling is then run from the projectors to the switching position. Electrical power is connected to projectors.
- Speaker support equipment, such as teleprompters, confidence monitors, onstage computers, and/or remote control devices, is set up, connected, and tested.
- Video cameras, if used, are positioned, electrical power is connected, if possible, for all stationary cameras, and cabling is run from the cameras to the switching position.
- Cameras are tested and balanced for color, projector alignment is finalized, video walls are aligned and color-corrected, VCR recording and tapes are checked, switching between sources is checked, preview monitors are checked, and all audio feeds in and out of the switching hardware are checked for levels.
- An event and/or show talk-through or rehearsal normally takes place after all this has been done in order to ensure all cues are correct. This is especially important if the show involves a combination of verbal and tape cues, as with a multimedia show that might include live performers and lighting or special effects.

Figure 4.14 outlines the general layout of visual presentation equipment at an event, and the routing of signals from their sources to their final display.

4.7.2 Operation During the Event

Operation of visual presentation equipment during an event can be complex and stressful. It requires an intimate knowledge of the equipment and its capabilities as well as a thorough understanding of the event and show running order with all the cues involved. Assuming a complex show environment, the following represent the most important tasks of the A-V team:

- Providing live camera coverage of the event according to the cues and shots called by the technical director.
- Adjusting the color, resolution, and format of all live and precorded video before screening.
- Adjusting and correcting all still images before screening.
- Previewing and switching all visual presentation sources before screening according to cues given by the technical director.
- Adjusting audio levels going to and returning from the main house audio mixer.
- Running videotape recorders.
- Communicating with lighting and audio engineers to ensure levels of audio and lighting work smoothly with the visual presentation.

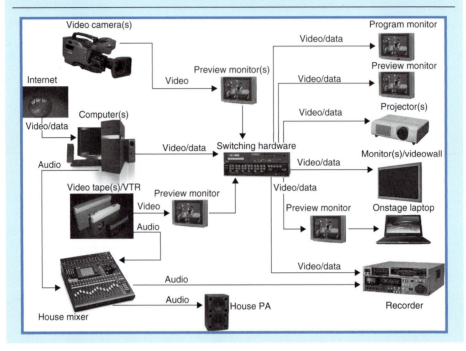

Courtesy: Doug Matthews

As with décor and lighting, a plan for equipment strike after the event is over must be coordinated with the other suppliers (partly because A-V equipment is often part of the trussing used for lighting and audio), the event manager, and venue personnel to ensure conflicting tasks are minimized.

4.8   RISK AND SAFETY

Visual presentation equipment is highly complex and evolving rapidly, yet standards still apply to its safe design and use. The current known North American visual presentation equipment standards are as follows and should be adhered to by contractors:

- *UL 60065* (in the USA) and *CAN/CSA-C22.2 NO. 60065-03* (in Canada): *Audio, Video and Similar Electronic Apparatus – Safety Requirements.*
- *IEC (International Electrotechnical Commission) 60574-7 Ed. 1.0 b:1987: Audiovisual, Video and Television Equipment and Systems. Part 7: Safe Handling and Operation of Audiovisual Equipment.*

In addition, all personnel safety guidelines of the Occupational Health and Safety Administration (OSHA) and Workers' Compensation Board (WCB) in the USA and Canada must apply, as must adherence to the electrical codes of both countries.

Again, as with audio, risk mitigation techniques that ensure safe and professional event execution are employed by knowledgable visual presentation specialists. Tim Lewis of Proshow Audiovisual-Broadcast in Vancouver, Canada, again offers the benefit of his extensive experience (Tim Lewis, Personal Communication, September 18, 2006):

- *Redundancy*: This is as critical for A-V equipment as it is for audio equipment. There is a significant failure rate of CDs and DVDs provided by suppliers (e.g. performers) and presenters, especially when trying to play them in different recorders. Lewis usually dubs a CD or DVD brought to him onto a trusted format (e.g. Beta SP, DVCAM) and plays it in his own fully checked-out machine. He may also bring a second brand of recorder if there is any doubt that there may be trouble playing CDs or DVDs, especially if the requirement is very high profile, as when it is part of a VIP presentation. For PowerPoint presentations, he is insistent on redundancy and always provides a minimum of two computers onsite at the A-V console position, and all presentations are loaded onto the two computers. Each computer is equipped with a CD/DVD burner for quick copying when necessary.

  He also provides at least one additional projector that can be quickly hooked up and used with front projection off a cart in case a flown or floor-supported show projector goes down. He stocks a wide variety of lenses with differing focal lengths for all projectors in order to work in event situations that may not allow sufficient space either behind or in front of screens. In this way, there are far fewer restrictions on space placed on the venue and the client.

- *Equipment quality*: Lewis is especially cognizant of problems that can occur with personal laptop computers provided by presenters. He does not allow presenters to use their own computers onstage or even at the console position, instead preferring to load presentations onto his own pristine computers that are equipped with the latest version of all software (e.g. PowerPoint and Windows). To alleviate presenter stress, he provides top-of-the-line remote cueing hardware that uses RF signals and has built-in laser pointers. As well, he provides a confidence monitor near the lectern for the presenter. He notes that his preference is a small monitor attached to a microphone stand that sits just below the lectern top out of audience sight lines, making it less obvious than a presentation teleprompter.

  For video, Lewis refuses to use less than professional, TV quality equipment, notably cameras. He insists on using only highly skilled video camera operators, preferably with a lot of television experience, as well as a good video director with similar training. As he says, 'Bad camera operation can destroy an IMAG presentation.'

- *Effects of other equipment*: Similar to the ambient noise effects mentioned in Chapter 3, other equipment might interfere with visual presentations. For example, automated lights should never be mounted on the same truss as projectors because motion is transferred to the projectors with obvious consequences.
- *Professionalism*: Personnel make all the difference. Lewis insists on only providing highly trained technicians with a professional approach to the event (as with the camera ops). He recommends that all personnel be briefed before any event that such things as idle chatter and improper comments should never be part of the show, especially on intercom. Focus must be maintained at all times.

Similar to audio, these tips plus compliance with safety and design standards and a thorough analysis and documentation of the specific event's risks should minimize most potential problems.

PRODUCTION CHALLENGES

1. A client company wishes to project images and videos during an event that celebrates the company's 50-year history. Included are old photographs, 16 mm film, VHS videos, and one of the original telephones they used. What would have to be done to this archival material to make it presentable on a screen and what equipment could be used to project it?
2. You have been given videotapes from clients in Eastern Europe and Britain and must project them at a conference. Explain what must be done to make them presentable and include a short explanatory background of the different tape format standards.
3. Explain frame rate, interlacing, resolution, and aspect ratio as they pertain to video.
4. An opening ceremony for a major 5000-person conference is taking place in a football stadium. You need to cover the event with IMAG and the screen will be the stage backdrop. The rear-most seating is 300 ft (90 m) away. The largest screen obtainable to you is 20 ft (6 m) in width. Suggest solutions so that the entire audience will be able to see the proceedings and explain how to calculate the screen sizes to be used.
5. For the kickoff to a theme event, you have been asked to recreate the inside of a 1960s era nightclub, complete with psychedelic images, music, and lighting as a 5 min multimedia presentation. Suggest some visual sources to do this and possible ways that it could be accomplished including equipment or surfaces to be used for projection and display.

REFERENCES

Bajaj, G. (June 18, 2004). PowerPoint and Video. *Indezine*. Retrieved March 27, 2006, from http://www.indezine.com/products/powerpoint/ppvideo.html.

Captain, S. (2006). The Next Must-See TV. *Wired Magazine*. Retrieved April 3, 2006, from http://www.wired.com/wired/archive/13.12/start.html?pg=19.

Clifford, P. (January/February 2005). Live Video Equipment and Personnel. *Church Production Magazine*. Retrieved March 26, 2006, from http://www.churchproduction.com/article.php?issue_path=issue_37_01-05&article_num=677.

Consumer Opinion Services (1998). *How to Use Video for Focus Groups*. Retrieved March 27, 2006, from http://www.cosvc.com/vidconprimfg.html.

Extron Electronics (2006). *Products*. Retrieved April 7, 2006, from http://www.extron.com/product/index.asp.

McIntosh, B. (Spring 2005). Choosing a Visual Presenter. *South Carolina Technology News*. Retrieved March 31, 2006, from http://www.myscschools.com/features/sctn/tips/vp.htm.

Mulhall, J. (August 22–25 2005). Raising the Bar Using Multimedia. *Seminar Workbook: 9th Annual Event Solutions Idea Factory*, pp. 93–98.

Plasma People (2006). *How Plasma Works*. Retrieved April 3, 2006, from http://www.plasmapeople.com/how-plasma-works.asp.

Sauer, J. (2006). Using Video in PowerPoint. *Creation*. Retrieved March 27, 2006, from http://www.presentations.com/presentations/creation/article_display.jsp?vnu_content_id=1258067.

Silva, R. (2006). *The LCD Video Projector – What You Need to Know*. Retrieved March 29, 2006, from http://hometheater.about.com/cs/television/a/aavprojectora_3.htm.

Studley, J. and Monner, J. (August 28–31, 2004). Managing Multimedia: A Behind the Scenes Look at Working Smartly. *Seminar Workbook: 8th Annual Event Solutions Idea Factory*, pp. 246–256.

The Projector People (2006a). *Deciphering Cables and Connections*. Retrieved March 24, 2006, from http://www.projectorpeople.com/tutorials/dec-cable.asp.

The Projector People (2006b). *Display Definitions*. Retrieved March 29, 2006, from http://www.projectorpeople.com/tutorials/display-def.asp.

Toshiba Corporation (2006). *What is the SED?* Retrieved April 3, 2006, from http://www3.toshiba.co.jp/sed/eng/about/index.htm.

United Visual Inc. (2006). *How to Choose a Projection Screen*. Retrieved March 31, 2006, from http://www.unitedvisual.com/2tips/2tscr101.asp.

Vrije Universiteit Amsterdam (2006). *Video Technology*. Retrieved March 23, 2006, from http://www.few.vu.nl/video/video-technology.html.

Wikipedia contributors (May 12, 2006). Comparison of Display Technology. In *Wikipedia, The Free Encyclopedia*. Retrieved 18:46, July 12, 2006, from http://en.wikipedia.org/w/index.php?title=Comparison_of_display_technology&oldid=52822349.

Wikipedia contributors (June 13, 2006). CRT Projector. In *Wikipedia, The Free Encyclopedia*. Retrieved 18:28, July 12, 2006, from http://en.wikipedia.org/w/index.php?title=CRT_projector&oldid=58450868.

Wikipedia contributors (July 7, 2006). Video. In *Wikipedia, The Free Encyclopedia*. Retrieved 18:01, July 12, 2006, from http://en.wikipedia.org/w/index.php?title=Video&oldid=62639597.

Wikipedia contributors (July 8, 2006). DLP. In *Wikipedia, The Free Encyclopedia*. Retrieved 18:40, July 12, 2006, from http://en.wikipedia.org/w/index.php?title=DLP&oldid=62740763.

Wikipedia contributors (July 10, 2006a). Digital Video. In *Wikipedia, The Free Encyclopedia*. Retrieved 18:10, July 12, 2006, from http://en.wikipedia.org/w/index.php?title=Digital_video&oldid=63111942.

Wikipedia contributors (July 10, 2006b). Liquid Crystal Display. In *Wikipedia, The Free Encyclopedia*. Retrieved 18:35, July 12, 2006, from http://en.wikipedia.org/w/index.php?title=Liquid_crystal_display&oldid=63057498.

Wikipedia contributors (July 11, 2006). Multimedia. In *Wikipedia, The Free Encyclopedia*. Retrieved 18:51, July 12, 2006, from http://en.wikipedia.org/w/index.php?title=Multimedia&oldid=63183908.

Williams, B. (1999). *Stage Lighting Design 101*, Second Edition. Retrieved January 2006, from www.mts.net/williams5/sld.

LIGHTING SYSTEMS

LEARNING OUTCOMES

After reading this chapter you will be able to:

1. Explain the objectives of event lighting.
2. Understand the qualities of light and how they can be manipulated for specific purposes in a special event.
3. Describe the basic capabilities of the main types of lighting instruments used for special events.
4. Understand how effective event lighting is achieved through proper design.
5. Understand how event lighting is controlled.
6. Explain the requirements for an efficient event lighting setup.
7. Understand and explain what a lighting operator does during an event.

Lighting is one of the fastest growing – and changing – technical fields in special events. Used for meetings, rock and roll concerts, outdoor architectural highlights, and every type of special event, lighting can be costly, frustrating, and power-hungry, yet still provide an amazing component to an event. It is one of the primary ways to achieve emotional impact, especially if done by an experienced professional lighting designer (LD).

For special events, good lighting design should enhance the event experience without drawing too much attention to itself as a separate entity. This is accomplished by understanding from the outset exactly for what purpose the lighting will be used, what types of lights will be used to achieve this purpose, and how the design will be carried out. Although most producers subcontract to a lighting company, they should ideally understand what equipment is available and how it works, in order to provide the best lighting design for the available budget. In this regard, this chapter will discuss and illustrate the following topics:

- Objectives of event lighting
- Qualities of light
- Lighting instruments
- Event lighting design
- Between concept and execution
- Lighting control, setup, and operation
- Risk and safety.

5.1 OBJECTIVES OF EVENT LIGHTING

When people enter a special event, they are entering a new environment, an environment that has been purposefully transformed into one that is different from their normal one. This new environment can be as simple as a darkened room with a single spotlight on a keynote speaker onstage, to a room that has been changed into an undersea wonderland. In both cases, lighting plays an influential role in the success of the transformation. It is in this transformation that the objectives of event lighting lie. These objectives include:

- Visibility
- Relevance
- Composition
- Mood.

We will examine each one to see how it can influence the transformation of an event space.

5.1.1 Visibility

Considered the most fundamental function of event lighting, visibility simply means that for an event audience to clearly understand what is going on within the event space, they must be able to see the action or the appropriate décor. Although this may seem obvious, it is amazing how many producers fail to understand the importance of *selective visibility*. By selective, we mean that 'well lit' does not translate into turning all the house lights up full and leaving them there for the duration of an event. Selective means lighting only what an audience **needs** to see **when** they need to see it.

For example, if the only activity happening on a large stage is a keynote speaker at a lectern, then there is no need to light the entire stage, but rather just the speaker himself. In this way, the focus of the moment is on the speaker, and the audience is not distracted by anything else onstage. Likewise, if a 40 ft wide, decorative painted mural is placed against a wall, it should be fully lit in order to be seen and to be an effective component of the themed décor; however, if it only covers half the wall, there is no reason to light the other half.

Although visibility presumes that certain objects or people will be lit, its effectiveness is not solely dependent on the intensity of the lighting. It is also affected by contrast, size, color, and movement of the object(s) being illuminated, as well as the distance of the light source from the object and the condition of the eyes of the observer.

5.1.2 Relevance

Stage lighting specialists sometimes refer to this objective as naturalism, style, or even structure. According to Williams (1999), this means that the lighting design should provide a sense of time and place through the use of such items as simulated sunlight or moonlight. In event lighting, it really is more than this because a special event often comprises more than what is happening onstage.

For example, in a large special event that has different eras themed in different rooms, relevance might mean: strobe lights, lasers, and smoke in a futuristic setting; simulated gas lamps in a Victorian setting; lots of colored neon in a 50s setting; and simulated fire in a prehistoric setting, all of which could be used to light décor or simply to add to the relevance of the theme by using these means to actually light just the room itself.

At the same time, if there is action taking place within those settings, perhaps in the form of themed entertainment, that action might also have to be lit in a way that is relevant to the dynamics of the action within the theme. For example, a futuristic dance troupe might be accompanied by high-energy automated lighting moving in time with the music, a Victorian singer might be lit by old-time stage footlights, a 50s diner scene with characters from Happy Days might have a mirror ball, and a prehistoric cave campfire scene with actors might use low light level amber tones to illuminate the scene with moving fire images on the cave wall.

5.1.3 Composition

Composition refers to how effective the LD has been in helping to create an overall event environment. The lighting should take into account the same design elements and design principles that a decorator would use and, in fact, should be designed in conjunction with the décor design. For example, here are possible considerations within each of these groups.

5.1.3.1   Design Elements

As with décor, the design elements are:

- *Space*: Are all three dimensions effectively illuminated? (e.g. Does lighting cover walls and ceilings – and even floors?) Is lighting used to actually 'fill' the space by using smoke or haze that will reflect the light beams?
- *Form*: Does the lighting design enhance the form of objects? (e.g. Are they made to look attractive? Do they become focal points? Are they more three dimensional as a result of using proper lighting to create depth?)
- *Line*: Are the lines of objects made to be part of the whole design? (e.g. Does rear lighting effectively separate a dark-suited speaker from a black velour stage backdrop?)
- *Texture and ornament*: Does the lighting bring out the texture in objects?
- *Light*: Is the light intensity too high or too low?
- *Color*: Does the lighting design complement the event's overall color scheme?

5.1.3.2   Design Principles

Similarly, the design principles are:

- *Proportion*: Is the lighting of different event components in proportion to each other? (e.g. Is a large décor vignette lit by big lights and another lit by small lights?)
- *Balance*: Is the lighting design symmetrical or asymmetrical? This applies especially for stage lighting.
- *Rhythm*: Is there a repetitive pattern in the lighting or are there smooth transitions between colors?
- *Emphasis*: Is there a lighting focal point or is lighting used to illuminate a decorative focal point?
- *Harmony*: Does the overall lighting design create a comforting, or harmonious feeling, particularly in conjunction with other décor?

5.1.4   Mood

Mood refers to how lighting affects the psychological reactions of the audience at an event and how it reinforces the emotional tone of a themed venue or of a stage performance. This is often done by using an appropriate color – or changes of color – to elicit an emotional reaction, as outlined in Section 2.1.1.6.1 of Chapter 2. However, it can also be accomplished by other means, such as using automated lights for excitement or combining lighting with various special effects to strengthen the effects and add to the emotion. We will discuss this in more detail in Section 5.4.

5.2   QUALITIES OF LIGHT

Before committing to a design of any sort, the LD must first understand the actual qualities of light itself. In other words, how can this 'raw material' in the form of a light beam emanating from a fixture be manipulated to achieve the desired look? The qualities of light that the designer is able to manipulate are:

- Intensity
- Distribution
- Color
- Direction
- Movement.

We will discuss each of these in turn.

5.2.1   Intensity

In simplest terms, this refers to the strength of a light source. However, there are some other relative measurements that are also associated with a light source and what happens when the light is projected over a distance and strikes an object.

Intensity is the strength of a light source (e.g. the actual lamp inside the light fixture), or the light output. It is measured in lumens or candles. *Illuminance* is the light level actually falling **on** the surface of an object being lit. It is measured in lux (metric) or foot-candles (Imperial) where 1 ft-cd = 10.76 lx. *Brightness* is the effect of light leaving the surface of an object being illuminated. It is what the human eye actually sees. It is affected by the intensity of the light source, the distance from the source to the object, and the properties of the object (e.g. color and texture). It is measured in foot-lamberts. These three measurements are related mathematically by the *inverse-square law*, $E = I/D^2$, where E is the illuminance in foot-candles, I is the intensity in lumens, and D is the distance in feet between the source and the point of calculation on the surface.

Generally speaking, objects that appear bright draw more attention to themselves. Because of this, it is the job of the LD to ensure that those objects needing attention, whether they be performers or decorative, are appropriately bright.

5.2.2 Distribution

Distribution refers to the manner in which light strikes a surface and reveals an object.

It can be applied to how objects appear, in that they might be softly lit as part of a larger scene with light that has no sharp edges. On the other hand, they may be individually lit with a small, sharply defined, single light beam.

On another level, distribution can be applied to the appearance of light that uses an image projector of some sort, such as a *gobo* in front of an *ellipsoidal* fixture (to be discussed in more detail later in this chapter) or an actual projector. These in turn produce certain desired images on a surface such as a wall or scrim.

On a third level, distribution can be applied to the shape of a light beam itself when viewed through smoke or haze effects.

5.2.3 Color

As with the design tools of event décor, color is the most noticeable and strongest quality of light. Indeed, all light is colored, and white light is simply a mixture of all visible wavelengths (colors) between infrared and ultraviolet (UV) radiation on the electromagnetic spectrum. One of the keys to good lighting design is a thorough understanding of color. We begin with some definitions.

Hue is the pure form of a color with no white, black, or gray added. *Tint* is the mixture of a hue with white. *Shade* is the mixture of a hue with black. *Tone* is the mixture of a hue with black **and** white (gray). It is sometimes also called *value* (see Chapter 2). *Saturation* refers to the amount of hue in a color mixture. For example, a pure red color (like fire-engine red) would be said to have a high saturation of red.

In the world of lighting, the color wheel takes on a slightly different appearance from the color wheel associated with décor, which uses pigments. For light, the primary colors are red, blue, and green. The secondary colors are yellow (mixture of red and green), cyan (mixture of green and blue), and magenta (mixture of red and blue). Figure 5.1 illustrates a lighting color wheel, also called a *visual* or *RGB color wheel*.

The two differing color wheels, the one for pigment as described in Chapter 2, and the one for light, are often confusing since they do not make logical sense when mixing colors. Technically, as pointed out by Fitt and Thornley (2002), 'the lessons learned from mixing the colors of paint are somewhat different to those for mixing the colors of light. It has to be realized that light is the source of all color, but pigments in paint (or in dyed fabrics – author) are simply reflections or absorbers of parts of the light that illuminates them. If a beam of red light and a beam of green light are superimposed the result is yellow. On the other hand, if we mix red and green paint, we get rather a nasty looking "brown black" color. When using light, all spectral colors can be created by adding various component parts of red, green, and blue light and

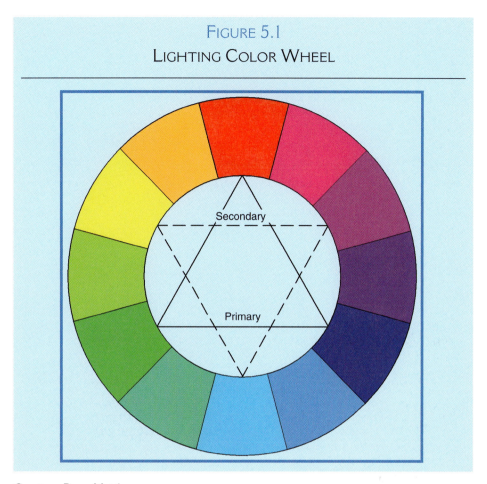

FIGURE 5.1

LIGHTING COLOR WHEEL

Secondary

Primary

Courtesy: Doug Matthews

the system used is called "addition," ultimately creating white. Pigments derive their colors by **subtracting** parts of the spectrum, therefore the system with pigments is called "subtraction" and ultimately creates black.'

For special events, the LD is frequently called upon to not only light stage performances, but also decorative elements. These are particularly sensitive to the interaction between the hues of light and pigment hues, since most décor is pigment based (e.g. fabrics, painted surfaces, costumes). Table 5.1 illustrates the interaction between the two types of color, and can serve as a guide for what a decorative element or person looks like when subjected to a certain color of light (Fuchs, 1929).

To add to the confusion, additive and subtractive color mixing are also found in the lighting world alone. Additive color mixing refers to the combining of two or more colors to form a new color. As illustrated in Figure 5.2, the combining of red and blue light sources, for example, will produce a new color, magenta. Subtractive color mixing refers to the filtering of light. When light passes through a single colored *gel* or filter, only the wave length corresponding to the color of the filter will pass through it, also as in Figure 5.2.

TABLE 5.1

INTERACTION OF COLORED LIGHT WITH COLORED PIGMENT

Color of Pigment	Color of Light							
	Violet	**Blue**	**Blue-Green**	**Green**	**Yellow**	**Orange**	**Red**	**Purple**
Violet	Deep violet	Dark violet	Dark violet	Violet	Dark brown	Dark brown	Dark gray	Dark violet
Blue	Light blue	Deep blue	Light bluish gray	Light blue	Dark bluish gray	Black	Gray	Blue
Blue-Green	Dark blue	Very dark blue	Dark bluish gray	Dark green	Greenish blue	Dark greenish brown	Black	Dark blue
Green	Bluish brown	Light olive green	Light greenish gray	Intense green	Bright green	Dark green	Dark gray	Dark greenish brown
Yellow	Scarlet	Greenish yellow	Greenish yellow	Greenish yellow	Intense yellow	Yellow orange	Red	Orange
Orange	Scarlet	Light brown	Light brown	Light brown	Orange	Intense orange	Intense orange red	Scarlet
Red	Scarlet	Purplish black	Dark maroon	Maroon	Bright red	Orange red	Intense red	Red
Purple	Reddish purple	Dark violet	Maroon	Purplish violet	Light brown	Maroon	Reddish brown	Deep purple

Courtesy: http://www.rosco.com/canada/technotes/filters/technote_1.asp

The last important concept of color in lighting design is the meaning of color. As outlined in Chapter 2 when we discussed décor, every color has certain emotions attached to it. It is these emotions that the LD tries to enhance in order to make his design more effective.

5.2.4 Direction

For special event lighting, there are three areas of concern with respect to lighting direction: stage and entertainment lighting, décor and theme lighting, and ambient lighting. In all cases, the effect of directional lighting is similar, but the desired outcome may be different. Let us examine the different directions that may be used to light people or objects and then see what the differences may be, using Figure 5.3 as a guide. Figure 5.3 illustrates the following:

- *First row, left to right*: Front lighting; top lighting; rear lighting.
- *Second row, left to right*: Side lighting; up lighting.

FIGURE 5.2

ILLUSTRATION OF ADDITIVE (LEFT) AND SUBTRACTIVE (RIGHT) COLOR MIXING IN LIGHT

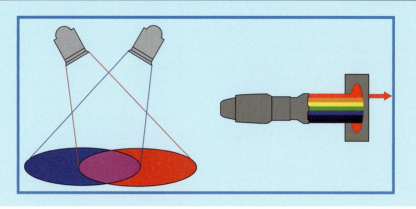

Courtesy: Gillette, 2000

FIGURE 5.3

DIRECTION IN LIGHTING

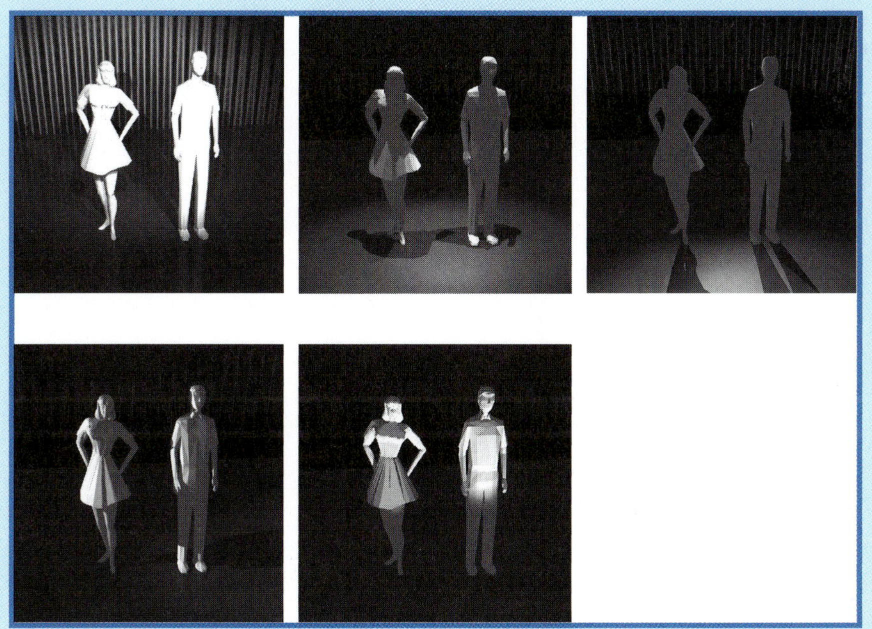

Courtesy: Doug Matthews

We begin with front lighting. Although this direction gives the best visibility, it also tends to make objects and people appear 'flat.' For lighting people and stage shows, this is one direction that is absolutely necessary so the audience can see what is happening onstage. Generally speaking, in almost every instance of special event entertainment, some component of continuous front lighting will be needed, even if it is not fully bright or not white. On the other hand, for ambient lighting and theme décor lighting, front lighting is not always desirable. If lighting walls, for instance, to achieve a general mood, direct lighting is less desirable than up lighting as it tends to highlight the flaws in the wall. However, if a large painted mural is part of the décor, front lighting may be the right choice in order to give the best visibility and render the mural scene more realistic. The same would apply if the front lighting is a gobo and a clear, proportionally correct pattern is required to be seen on the wall.

The next direction, top lighting, on people adds shadows to faces but also adds nice highlights to hair and shoulders, which onstage can help to separate people from backgrounds. For décor purposes, top lighting is often used to light table centers with pin spots or automated fixtures, to give crisp, undistorted beams of light throughout the event space. It is also used for highlighting décor vignettes and for floor lighting.

Rear lighting, the next direction, is very useful for adding dimension to persons or objects onstage and for separating them from the background. Similarly, for décor it can help to add a third dimension and make a display seem more 'alive.'

Side lighting is highly desirable in some form when lighting people onstage as it also adds dimension and makes the body shape more obvious. In the same way, it can add shape and emphasize texture in décor. However, when lighting flat décor as in the case of murals, it tends to highlight flaws in the surface and is not recommended.

The final direction for lighting is under or up lighting. When used to light people, this is associated with a ghoulish, macabre effect as seen in movies and is not desirable unless it is being used for a special effect. However, for décor, especially for ambient lighting, it is one of the most effective directions, particularly for up lighting walls, ceilings, and backdrops.

5.2.5 Movement

A related aspect of direction is *movement*. Movement indicates any change in lighting that gives life to the lighting and brings it closer to the natural world. It is usually of timed duration and can include:

- a change in direction;
- a change in color;
- a change in intensity;
- a change in distribution, such as the appearance of different gobos from the same fixture;

- the movement of an offstage light such as a followspot or automated fixture.

According to Williams (1999), 'movement may be rapid or very subtle, slow, and imperceptible. Such may be the case of a designer that provides a slow shift in sunlight from one side of the stage to the other throughout the duration of a play. The audience may not notice the shift; however, they often may "feel" the result of the change emotionally. . . . Up until recently, movement was probably the least utilized quality of light by the stage LD. This all changed in the 1980s when the automated lighting fixture was born. The modern automated fixture can now move physically – directing its beam from one part of the stage to another (or any other area within the event space – author). In addition, the automated fixture can "move" from one color or effect to another, at any speed. The changes and combinations of intensity, form, distribution, color, and movement are endless.' There will be more on automated lights in the next section.

5.3   LIGHTING INSTRUMENTS

Depending on where one works, lighting terminology differs. In North America, a lighting instrument is also called a *fixture* or *unit*. In Britain, it is known as a *light fitting* or *lantern*. In the engineering and architectural communities and the rest of the world, it is known as a *luminaire*. This will be our common term for the remainder of this chapter.

In this section, we will be discussing the basic construction of luminaires, the different types, and what each is used for in special event lighting.

5.3.1   Construction of Luminaires

All the terms defining a lighting instrument mentioned above, refer to a 'package' which, for every type of luminaire, is comprised of the following components.

5.3.1.1   *Outer Housing*

This is a metal or plastic, specially shaped container that houses the whole instrument and prevents light from spilling to undesired locations.

5.3.1.2   *Lamp*

This is the source of the light. Similar to an everyday household light bulb, lamps for event lighting are normally made up of a glass or quartz envelope, a base, and a filament (usually made of tungsten and powered by electricity) surrounded by a gas (called a *gas discharge lamp*). Depending primarily on the gas used within the bulb, the light produced may vary slightly in its 'whiteness.' This variation is an indication of different color *temperatures*. The only real significance of different color temperatures is that if luminaires with different temperatures are being used for lighting a specific scene, then different gels will probably need to be used to achieve the same apparent color. We will discuss gels in more detail shortly.

5.3.1.3 *Lens*

This is a curved, glass 'plate' that is positioned at the front of the luminaire to give the light beam emanating from a luminaire its characteristic shape. Most lenses used in event lighting are curved a certain way to make the beam either narrow or widely dispersed, and with 'hard' or 'soft' edges for effect. Two common types are the *Fresnel lens* and the *plano-convex lens*. Generally speaking, the greater the curvature of the lens and the smaller the focal length (distance from light source to lens), the greater will be the dispersion of light. This wide angle of the beam is known as the *beam angle*, defined as the point in the cone of light emitted by the luminaire where the light level is diminished by 50 percent when compared with the level in the center of the beam. A related term is the *field angle*, which is defined as the cone of light where the level diminishes to 10 percent of the level in the beam's center. Figures 5.4 and 5.5 illustrate focal length and beam angles.

What this means in simple terms, is that a luminaire with a short focal length and/or a thick lens, will have a greater field angle and beam angle than another luminaire with the same diameter but longer focal length and/or thin lens. Using a luminaire called an ellipsoidal reflector spotlight or ERS as an example, if there are two such luminaires, each with a diameter of 6 in., but one has a focal length of 9 in. (known as a 6 × 9) and the other has a focal length of 12 in. (known as a 6 × 12), the luminaire with the longer focal length (6 × 12) will have a narrower beam of light at the same distance in front of the lens. However, an additional important fact is that it will also be able to throw its light farther. A 6 × 9, for example, might have an effective range or throw distance of about 35 ft (10.5 m) while a 6 × 12 might have an effective throw distance of about 50 ft (15 m). Knowing how a luminaire is constructed and what the focal length of the lens is becomes very important for the LD when he must prepare his gear for lighting a stage, lighting a wall with gobos, or effectively using luminaires for any component of a special event, since the distance from the luminaire to the object being lit must be known in order for him to choose the correctly focusable luminaire.

5.3.1.4 *Reflector*

Inside the luminaire, the lamp produces light that emanates in all directions, including to the rear of the luminaire. In order to make the luminaire efficient, a curved reflector is placed at the rear of the luminaire that takes the excess light and redirects it toward the lens. There are various reflector

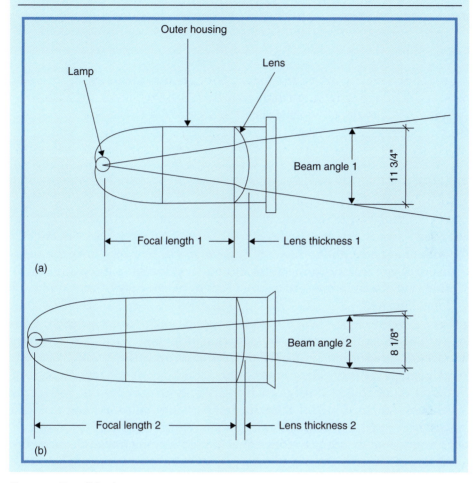

FIGURE 5.4

FOCAL LENGTH/LENS CURVATURE/BEAM ANGLE RELATIONSHIP

Courtesy: Doug Matthews

designs for each of the different types of luminaire and they play an important part in the intensity and shape of the light coming from the luminaire.

5.3.1.5 *Accessories*

In addition to the four main components of construction, most luminaires also come with accessories that improve their performance. They generally include some or all of the following:

- *Lamp socket*: This is a socket designed to accept the specific lamp.
- *Electrical cord and connector*: These tie into the lighting circuitry.

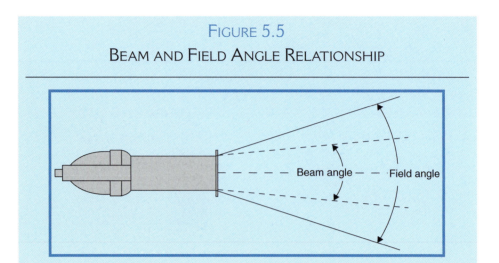

FIGURE 5.5

BEAM AND FIELD ANGLE RELATIONSHIP

Beam angle — — Field angle

Courtesy: Doug Matthews

- *Mounting yoke with a pipe or 'C' clamp*: The mount allows the luminaire to *pan* (rotate horizontally 360 degrees) and *tilt* (move vertically up and down), then to be securely locked into place on an overhead truss or pipe support.
- *Color frame clips*: These metal clips accept a lightweight metal or heat-resistant fiber holder (color frame) for *colored gels (filters), donuts, barn doors*, or *gobos* (image projection) (see Figure 5.6).
  A colored gel is typically made of plastic or glass and comes in a large selection of colors. A gel normally serves three purposes: to correct for the color temperature of a specific lamp, thereby allowing uniform light all over a surface; to provide drama and effect in lighting décor or performers; and to diffuse or soften light (e.g. up lighting walls). Occasionally, *dichroic* filters are used as gels to change the light's color. These are made by vacuum depositing thin films onto heat resistant glass and are much cooler. They reflect rather than absorb unwanted wavelengths. Because they are expensive, they tend to be used mainly in automated fixtures. See Figure 5.6, top row, left (color frame with gel).

  - A donut is a metal plate used to increase the clarity of patterns in an *ERS* by reducing halation and sharpening the image (Figure 5.6, top row, right).
  - A barn door is a metal apparatus with independently adjustable flaps, or that are used to control light spill (Figure 5.6, bottom row, left).
  - A gobo stands for *go-between* and refers to a small metal cutout incorporating a pattern that can be projected onto any surface. This enables the luminaire (typically an ERS, to be explained later), to act as an image projector. Gobos come as stock patterns from a number of manufacturers or they can be customized into names, company logos,

FIGURE 5.6
LIGHTING ACCESSORIES (NOT TO SCALE)

Courtesy: Doug Matthews and Q1 Production Technologies, www.q1pt.com

black and white or color photographs and graphics, and almost any pattern desirable. They are used extensively in the special events industry as décor and for messaging within an event space. Figure 5.6, bottom row, right, illustrates a gobo holder and a city skyline with clouds gobo.

5.3.2 Types and Uses of Luminaires

Being highly competitive, the lighting industry has produced a plethora of luminaires with various trade names, many with the same capabilities. Additionally, there is interaction among the TV, movie, theater, and special events industries, each with their own preferences for certain luminaire types, which contributes to the confusion. We will attempt to cut through this confusion by categorizing and explaining the most common types of luminaires used in the special events industry. Some of the lesser-used ones will be omitted in the interest of keeping to the point. The main categories of luminaires are:

- Spotlights
- Floodlights
- Projectors
- Automated fixtures
- Specialty lighting.

5.3.2.1 *Spotlights*

Spotlights are designed to provide narrow and controlled beams of light to localized areas of a stage, a performer, a decorative element, or other event focal point. In an event, they are typically used for area and wash applications such as highlighting a décor vignette in a corner of a room, accenting a table center, highlighting a speaker at a lectern, following roving performers, or washing an area of a performance stage with colored light. Their throw distances vary between 15 to over 100 ft (4.5–30 m) and their projected lighting area can vary from a few feet to 20 ft (6 m) in diameter. Figure 5.7 illustrates these main types of luminaires. The types of luminaires include:

- *Top row, left to right*: ERS (Courtesy Leviton Manufacturing, Inc., www.leviton.com); Fresnel spotlight (Courtesy Doug Matthews and Q1 Production Technologies, www.q1pt.com); PAR64 spotlight (Courtesy http://www.55.sk/images/webpage/30425.jpg).
- *Bottom row, left to right*: Pin spotlight (Courtesy http://northernlightfx. com/ebay%20stuff/pinspot.jpg); followspot spotlight (Courtesy Lycian Stage Lighting, www.lycian.com); box flood (Strand).

5.3.2.1.1 Ellipsoidal Reflector Spotlight

One of the true workhorses of the lighting industry, the ERS also goes by the names *Source Four* (as marketed by ETC – Electronic Theater Controls), *Leko* (as marketed by Strand Lighting), and *profile*, a term in common use in the UK. It is the most sophisticated of conventional instruments. Its beam shape is round and uniform with a hard edge, and various lenses inside the changeable barrels control the size of the beam. Some units are focusable so that an image can be projected, and *framing shutters* allow the beam to be shaped to eliminate light spill onto projection screens, the audience's eyes, and such. The *lens trains* available provide beam angles ranging from very wide (50 degrees) to very small (5 degrees), an important consideration when choosing the right one for gobo projections at various distances. Options include *irises* to further reduce the beam spread, rotating pattern holders to make the projected images spin, and others. This is the best instrument to use with gobo patterns. Power requirements vary from 500 to 1000 W and throw distances from 10 to 100 ft (3–30 m). Besides its use with gobos, it is

FIGURE 5.7

EXAMPLES OF SPOTLIGHT AND FLOODLIGHT LUMINAIRES
(NOT TO SCALE)

a popular luminaire for isolating key areas and people onstage, such as a speaker at a lectern. Figure 5.7 illustrates a typical ERS, and Figure 5.8 shows what a snowflake gobo would look like when used in an ERS and focused on a wall.

5.3.2.1.2   Fresnel Spotlight

This is one of the standard stage lighting instruments. The Fresnel produces a characteristically intense, soft edged beam created by the pebbled surface on the back of the Fresnel lens, named for its French inventor. It provides lighting for theaters, clubs, and TV. For special events, it is typically used to provide large color wash areas onstage, and its soft beam edge easily permits blending of multiple beams and colors. Beam spread can be modified from spot to flood (about 15–70 degrees). Power requirements vary from 150 to 5000 W with throw distances of 10–40 ft (3–12 m) (see Figure 5.7).

5.3.2.1.3   PAR Can Spotlight

A PAR can is comprised of a PAR (parabolic aluminized reflector) sealed beam lamp and a mounting fixture and base (the can). It produces a high intensity narrow beam of light and is available in many different sizes and powers.

FIGURE 5.8

SNOWFLAKE PATTERN GOBOS PROJECTED ON A WALL
USING AN ERS

Courtesy: Pacific Show Productions, www.pacificshow.ca – Copyright 2006

The bigger the number with a PAR can, the bigger its size. Electric lamps used in PAR cans are sized by multiples of 1/8 in. (0.3 cm). To convert the PAR number to inches, divide the lamp number by 8. Therefore, a PAR64 is 8 in. in diameter. A PAR64 is the most used such luminaire, especially for stage washes when flare and a very soft beam edge are not a problem. It is also commonly used as an inexpensive alternative for up lighting walls. Its power requirements are 500 or 1000 W. PAR cans also come in a variety of smaller sizes which are used more for display, décor, and architectural lighting purposes. Some of these sizes and their power requirements include PAR36 (100 W), PAR38 (60–300 W), PAR46 (200 W), and PAR56 (300 and 500 W). They often come with aluminized outer housings as an option (Figure 5.7).

5.3.2.1.4   PAR Pin Spotlight

Pin spots are very narrow angle PAR lamps in a basic can-type housing. Beam spreads are very narrow and range from approximately 5 to 10 degrees. Pin spots come in power ranges of 75–1000 W, and have a throw of 5–50 ft (1.5–15 m). They are sometimes referred to as 'rain lights.' All PAR lamps for pin spots are low voltage and require transformers to transform the mains voltage (120 or 240 V AC) to the proper lamp operating voltage. Usually, the transformer is incorporated into the rear of the fixture (Williams, 1999).

FIGURE 5.9

EXAMPLE OF PIN SPOTLIGHTS HIGHLIGHTING
TABLE CENTERS

Courtesy: Nat Raider Productions, www.natraider.com.

Pin spots are useful for providing accents, highlights and specials, and are particularly effective when all general lighting is dimmed down, allowing the pin spot(s) to highlight or draw attention to something (e.g. table centers in a dark ballroom). Most pin spots can be dimmed. They are controllable only by aiming them where wanted (see Figures 5.7 and 5.9).

5.3.2.1.5 Followspot Spotlight

This is a manually operated luminaire designed for following performers as they move about a stage or a venue. Modern followspot fixtures consist of a cylindrical housing 4–6 ft in length, mounted on a telescopic stand with castered legs. They are usually fitted with a manual iris and a color filter changer. A followspot is designed to provide a hard beam edge. Controls often exist to soften the beam edge when required. Followspots are traditionally mounted as high as possible at the rear of an event space, in order to *front light* the performers if they are on a stage. The size of the room and the distance to be projected are the factors that determine the size and intensity of the unit to be used. Usually, they are 250–3000 W in power, and throw 50–200 ft (15–60 m) (see Figure 5.7).

5.3.2.2 *Floodlights*

Floodlight fixtures (*floods*) consist simply of an enclosed light source in a box with one open side. Floods are designed to provide a wide, even distribution of light over a large area. Typical beam angles range from 70 to 150 degrees. Most units come with a fixed beam angle, although a few units are adjustable between flood and wide flood. Typical wattages range from 500 to 1500 W. Floodlights do not use lenses but some may have a clear protective safety glass. A *scoop* is really just a streamlined *box flood*, usually with similar lighting characteristics. The design of the box floodlight has changed little over the years; however, the modern box flood now uses an internal reflector, for greater efficiency. Floodlight fixtures are particularly well suited for lighting backdrops and sky cloths. Typically, a continuous row of floodlights is arranged above and parallel to the backdrop, at a distance of 3–10 ft (0.9–3 m) away. For additional interest and impact, a row of fixtures may be used to up light the backdrop, from the floor, although front lighting is best if it is a scenic backdrop. Floodlights are also sometimes used for the lighting of scenery, to provide large area washes, and as work lights. Individual fixtures are commonly available in both scoop (round, open front) and box flood (square or rectangular, open front) designs (Williams, 1999) (see Figure 5.7).

5.3.2.3   Projectors

Some form of scenic projection has existed in the theater world for hundreds of years, with the earliest models constructed without a lens (some of which are still in use today). At the present time, however, the systems have become very sophisticated, and digital technology is merging with lighting. We discuss this more in the sections on automated lighting fixtures and in Chapter 4. Suffice it to say that projectors in use today for special events are capable of projecting multiple images produced from slides, photographs, paintings, computer graphics, and other media. They are focusable and often can be combined with other projectors to form continuous, high-resolution images on very large surfaces, such as walls or buildings.

5.3.2.4   Automated Fixtures

In the history of the lighting industry, there is no invention that has revolutionized it more than the automated fixture. 'Although automated fixtures (also called *moving lights, intelligent lights,* or *kinetic instruments*) have only been used in the special events industry since the late 1980s, the concept has been around since an original US patent was issued to Herbert F. King of Newtonville, Massachusetts in 1928, for an "automatic spotlight"' (Cadena, 2005). Real development, however, did not take place until the late 1980s and accelerated in the 1990s to the point where today, almost all special events, concerts, and stage performances with even modest budgets use them.

What are automated fixtures? Quite simply, they are the fusion of all the static luminaires that we have discussed into a single unit that can be remotely controlled. 'The common feature of automated fixtures is movement, often very rapid: light beams pan the stage and event space, zoom in and out, change shape and color, diffuse and sharpen; gobos materialize, spin around, change pattern, then disappear' (Gillette, 2000; p. 353). Most such luminaires include a number of internal features, which can create almost endless combinations of effects.

- *Color wheels* with dichroic lenses used to change the color of the beam (like having a variety of colored gels available).
- *Pattern wheels* with gobos used to change the shape of the beam (like having many different gobo patterns to choose from).
- Shutters used to *dim* or *strobe* the output (like using a strobe light or dimming the light).
- Automated lens trains used to focus the beam (like a Fresnel lens).
- Irises used to change the size of the beam.
- *Gate shutters* to *square off* the beam (like using a highly focusable light with barn doors for a small or large area).
- *Prisms* used for splitting the beam into three or five images, which can then be rotated.

5.3.2.4.1 Regular Automated Fixtures

As expected, these luminaires are complex in their design. Power requirements are typically 1000–1200 W and they operate on two main principles, *moving yoke* or *moving mirror*. The moving yoke principle achieves beam movement by using very precise electric *step motors* to control movement of the entire yoke and body of the fixture. The moving mirror principle achieves beam movement by reflecting the beam off a step motor-controlled mirror mounted on the body of the fixture. See Figure 5.10, which illustrates, from left to right: a moving yoke automated fixture (Vari-Lite VL3000 Wash) (Photo Courtesy Lewis Lee); a moving mirror automated fixture (Cyberlight Turbo) (Courtesy High End Systems Inc., www.highend.com); and a digital light (DL2) (Courtesy High End Systems Inc., www.highend.com).

FIGURE 5.10

EXAMPLES OF AUTOMATED FIXTURES

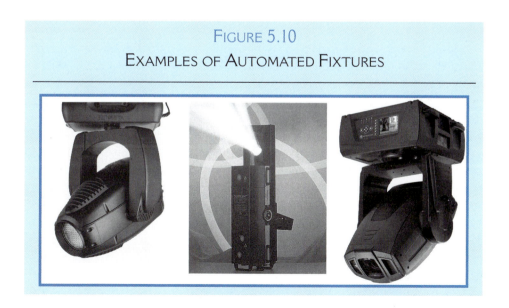

There are also numerous models of automated fixtures known as Disco Lights that utilize the same basic designs but come in various forms and shapes that create differing effects. They are typically cheaper and less capable overall than the more sophisticated designs.

5.3.2.4.2   Digital Lighting

A recent development that has burst onto the lighting scene is the merging of digital projection technology with automated lighting technology. This has produced products that provide the entire gamut of automated lighting features **plus** the ability to project literally any type of digital graphic images, including digital photographs, computer graphics, and digital video from one fixture onto any surface in a three-dimensional space. This almost certainly means the eventual demise – or certainly reduced use – of static projectors, since a digital projector can be installed almost anywhere and has the capability to manipulate the projected image in many more ways than a conventional projector. The latest models also incorporate their own digital video cameras within the unit, thus providing yet another function that previously required a separate piece of equipment, and enabling very efficient switching between different media inputs and special effects.

The current models operate using the same *DMX512 digital protocol* that operates other automated fixtures. See Section 5.6.1.3 for an explanation of this control method. However, this technology requires separate, dedicated computer software to run it. Some models come with a built-in computer and some require a separate computer. See Figure 5.10 for an example of the latest equipment (the DL2).

5.3.2.5   *Specialty Lighting*

Within the lighting industry, there are a number of specialized lights that are used frequently for events that do not fall exactly into the categories we have already discussed.

5.3.2.5.1   General Specialty and Decorative Lighting

These include:

- *Aircraft landing light (ACL)*: This is a high intensity, tight beam PAR lamp that derives its name from its use as an actual bright light mounted on aircraft. The true ACL is 28 V and 250 W, although there are many variations. It is often used to add dramatic effect to stage shows, especially concerts.
- *Blacklight*: This light, a *UV* light source used to create special lighting effects with fluorescent materials, works best on light-colored material at low ambient light levels.
- *Chaser lights*: These are miniature lamps connected together on an electrical cord and/or encased in plastic tubing (also known as *rope lights*) that

may be controlled to go on and off (*chase*) in patterns such as forward, reverse, alternating, or random blinking.

- *LASER*: Actually an acronym for *Light Amplification by Stimulated Emission of Radiation*, this word has become synonymous with a device that produces pencil-thin beams of coherent monochromatic light. It is used primarily for special effects and is discussed in more detail in Chapter 6.

- *Strobe light*: A *strobe* is a device that gives multiple rapid bursts of high intensity light. Strobe lighting is almost always produced by a compact xenon strobe lamp activated by a power supply and timing circuitry. Strobe lights can be simple low-power devices with fixed flash rates, or sophisticated devices triggered by a lighting control console at specific intervals. It should be noted that strobe lights set at certain frequencies might trigger epileptic seizures.

- *Searchlight*: Manufactured in the Second World War to detect enemy aircraft at night, searchlights are still in use today for special events. Using a carbon arc light source, they are capable of projecting a wide, intense beam of light into the sky at night.

- *Neon*: Neon is a type of discharge lighting generated by a high voltage across two oppositely charged electrodes at opposite ends of a long, thin glass tube filled with neon gas. As the electrical charge flows between the electrodes, electrons collide with neon atoms causing them to give off energy in the form of visible light. Different colors can be obtained by mixing other gases, or by using fluorescent coatings. For special events and advertising, the glass tube is customizable and may be bent to form letters and different shapes. Small, battery-powered neon designs are popular as table centerpieces.

- *Fiber optics*: Optical fibers are long, thin strands of flexible glass approximately the width of a human hair. They transmit light through a thin glass central core which is covered with an optical cladding material that reflects the light back inside the core whenever the fibers bend. This in turn is protected by an outer plastic buffer coating. These fibers are used in special event applications as battery-powered, light-emitting bundles for centerpieces or small 'sculptures,' and as the main light source for star drops (see also Chapter 2 on Décor).

- *Pin lights*: Also known as *miniature lights* or *fairy lights*, these are the typical low-voltage Christmas lights that now come in strings of 50, 100, and 150. They can be plain white or colored and can also be set up to twinkle randomly. The latest strings come in various shapes such as swags, tree wraps, netting, icicles, and curtains. For events, they work very well in large quantities used in foliage, trees, and florals, or with sheer draping.

- *Mirror ball*: A lighting effect popular in discos and ballrooms and in use since as early as 1897, this is a large plastic ball covered with small mirror pieces and motorized to rotate. When a spotlight (usually a pin spot) is focused onto the ball, specks of light are thrown around the room.

5.3.2.5.2　Light-Emitting Diodes

According to UK lighting firm Enlightenment, 'most people will be aware of light-emitting diodes (LEDs) as the small indicators typically used in clock displays and electronic equipment standby lights. The *LED* has been around for many years, but it is only recently that the necessary light output and range of colors has become available for use in the entertainment industries. Considerable research has gone into improving the basic design of the LED, with the introduction of really bright devices in the 1980s, and the long-awaited arrival of the blue LED in the 1990s. Recently, the process has culminated in the introduction of a white LED' (Evans, 2006). This technology has provided the potential for LEDs to be used in a number of special event applications, including large-format video screens, foldable fabric screens with LEDs embedded in them (see Chapter 2), novelty items such as under-lit dance floors, tables (Figure 5.11), and stages and now as replacements for many of the conventional luminaires that we have already described. In most of these new applications, the LEDs are controllable with DMX (digital multiplex) protocol (see Section 5.6.1.3 for an explanation) via a computer, which means they can be programmed to display graphics (e.g. names, logos, messages, photos) on surfaces.

'LED technology provides important advantages over conventional incandescent sources: they are cool running, enabling silent operation with no fans; the color temperature and color rendering does not alter over the exceptionally long life of the device; they have flicker-free operation, ideal

FIGURE 5.11
UNDERLIT LED TABLES

Courtesy: Ice Magic, www.icemagic.biz

for film and video work. In addition, the LED is a directional light source, meaning that no additional reflector or lenses are required. LEDs are impervious to heat, cold, shock, and vibration, have no breakable glass parts, and can be easily waterproofed. Using LEDs instead of the traditional incandescent lamp source provides an unsurpassed silent, non-mechanical, additive color mixing system, and the fixtures can produce stunning and instant effects, from the subtlest of dissolves to the fastest of high impact stroboscopic color sequences' (Evans, 2006). Benefits to the end user include the following, according to Evans (2006):

- Reduced air conditioning costs in installation and maintenance.
- Reduced electrical running cost, typically up to 85 percent.
- No lamp failure as maintenance costs are reduced in terms of both consumables and manpower.
- No color filters because dirt build-up and filter degradation are eliminated.
- Ability to change color from the lighting console with momentary action eliminating mechanical color-changing sluggishness, using DMX512 control protocol.
- Additive color mixing is a non-wasteful process: standard color filters absorb white light to produce the color required.
- No dimmer circuits are required, so individual circuits to lights are also eliminated.
- Infrastructure reduction reduces touring/trucking and rigging problems.

LED luminaires are rapidly coming into the market, accompanied by additional capabilities, not the least of which is remote focusing and onboard color changers and effects, all of which are time savers and cost savers when power consumption and lamp life are considered. This is expected to be one of the biggest areas of growth in special event lighting over the next 10 years.

5.4   EVENT LIGHTING DESIGN

Williams (1999), in his extensive online explanation of stage lighting, states that a 'lighting designer must be an artist. He must understand style, composition, balance, esthetics, and human emotion. He must also understand the science of light, optics, vision, the psychology of perception, and lighting technology.' Williams wrote this with reference to lighting for the theater. Although the description of the LD is true, in the special event environment the luxury of a week or more to design and install a lighting configuration for a stage performance as in a theater is not an option. Designers in events have only one chance and often no more than a cursory preliminary visit to the event venue before actual installation. Often, the design has to be completed in a rush, sometimes only a matter of days or even hours before installation. Besides this minimal time frame for design, the installation must frequently be completed the day of, or at best the day before, the event itself. Focusing of luminaires and programming of automated fixtures is often accomplished literally moments before the doors to the event open. The event LD must therefore be able to design with the same artistic flare as the theater LD but must add an equal capability to be organized and to work under extreme pressure.

Steve Matthews, a Production Manager with Q1 Production Technologies, one of Canada's foremost event lighting companies, considers a complete understanding of the following topics to be critical for successful event lighting design (Steve Matthews, Personal Communication, March 2003):

- Conceptual design
- Practical design
- Physical design
- Between concept and execution
- Lighting setup, control, and operation.

5.4.1   Conceptual Design

Before beginning the design, the LD needs to know the purpose of the event and exactly what the goals for the lighting are in the mind of the event producer. The design will ultimately fail if both LD and event producer do not agree on these. For example, is the event's purpose to be an award show with a few simple presentations, or does the event producer expect a show with enough lighting pizzazz and excitement to rival the Academy Awards? Other key questions center around what is being lit, what concept the event producer has in mind, and whether only an ambience is needed or something specific must actually be illuminated. The categories of conceptual design include theme, ambience, and practical illumination.

- *Theme*: This refers to the enhancement of a specific event theme, usually decorative, through the use of lighting. It can vary from complementing a theme's colors, to lighting props, tables, walls, floors, and ceiling.
- *Ambience*: When we think of ambience, we often imagine a quiet restaurant with soft music in the background and candlelit tables. What is trying to be done when one talks about ambience is to set a *mood* for an event, something that makes the attendees feel a certain way. For the special event LD, ambience is not quite so restrictive as creating that intimate restaurant mood. The event might not be a simple dinner. It might be a rock concert requiring high-energy, automated lights for a 20-something crowd, or it might be a dinner and awards show for a 50-something group of academics. Obviously, the ambience required will be vastly different for these two extremes.
- *Practical illumination*: This refers to more of the plain, less creative use of lighting for such mundane items as stage backdrops, lecterns,

IMAG (image magnification) and video, and guest speakers. The practicality concern goes back to our statement at the beginning of this chapter about selective visibility, in that an audience must be able to see only what they **need** to see **when** they need to see it.

5.4.2 Practical Design

Keeping the three categories of conceptual design in mind, the LD moves on to practical design. Practical design forces the LD to consider how all the design elements and design principles that we discussed in Section 5.1 will be used to accomplish the goals set out by the event producer. Let us examine the practical applications of this theory.

5.4.2.1 *Lighting for Themes*

Décor and event theming using light is a vast field with perhaps only a handful of truly gifted LDs in North America. When it is done well, it is usually the single event component that causes gasps from guests as they enter the event space. Some practical considerations that have proven effective for designers include:

- Using complimentary colors for props, such as greens to enhance trees, and reds or ambers to enhance wood.
- Choosing the event colors at the outset with the event producer and trying to keep the lighting in those color families.
- Using lighting in conjunction with special effects, each to enhance the other. Examples include lighting along a path at floor level under fog, rapid automated light movement to enhance indoor pyro and confetti cannons, or lighting effects and gobo patterns on a water scrim.
- Using all the dimensions and surfaces within the event space. They can all be used for lighting: ceilings for cloud patterns or changing colors; walls for theme gobos or up lighting; floors for gobos, color washes, and wild movement.
- Striving for the unusual, such as: lighting under tables; unique lighting of table centers (not necessarily pin spots but battery-powered electrical colored wiring or mini lights); reverse lighting of the audience instead of the event space and walls; and lighting of different event elements and theme prop vignettes at different times as the event progresses.
- Flying luminaires as much as possible in order to minimize clutter and distraction. For example, pin spotting table centers from above is effective and classy.
- Keeping instruments hidden from view and out of people's eyes.

Figure 5.12 is an excellent example of theming using lighting under bars and on walls.

FIGURE 5.12

EXAMPLE OF THEMED LIGHTING

Courtesy: Hollywood Lighting Services – Portland/Seattle, www.hollywoodlighting.biz

5.4.2.2   Lighting for Ambience

If this can be done very subtly, the effect is better and often can affect the 'mood' of the event and of the guests. Some considerations that help to achieve the right mood, be it low key or highly exciting, include the following:

- Using indirect lighting for such things as walls, ceilings, pillars, and tables.
- Using the psychology of color. This means that colors used for lighting must be flattering to the attendees (staying away from cool colors that do not flatter the skin), yet must create a dramatic and desirable environment to be in. Refer to Section 5.2.3 for more information.
- Using color-changing instruments that can be programmed to change slowly over time and thus give a continuously 'new' look and feel to the event every few minutes.
- Minimizing jolting contrast changes, such as a quick movement from purple to orange or yellow, or from red to blue, rather making it a more gradual, subtle movement through several colors.
- Generally keeping brightness levels low.
- Trying to avoid light spillage on unwanted or extraneous objects.

Figure 5.13 shows the difference in ambience before and after good lighting design is applied to a room.

Courtesy: Q1 Production Technologies, www.q1pt.com

5.4.2.3   *Lighting for Practical Purposes*

Most events have some element of the more mundane such as the need to light the company president giving his annual address or the award recipients as they come onstage. Often, the mundane must be mixed with the need for ambience and theming, and it is necessary to plan for this well ahead of time since many luminaires can serve double duty, especially automated fixtures. Some of the considerations for practical lighting include the following.

5.4.2.3.1   Lighting for Live Entertainment

Using front lighting is best to illuminate performers for visibility, but back lighting to create energy and to set the mood for the performance. The inclusion of automated fixtures on a back line is common in many high-energy performances. If a single performer or small group of performers is onstage, or especially going to be roving throughout the audience, one or more followspots is recommended. Depending on the type of performance (e.g. themed cirque-type show, comedy, dance, or music), a variety of front color washes is probably required so that the entire stage will be covered with even light, but also so that different onstage moods can be created for different segments of the performance. Typically, single luminaires (e.g. ERS or Fresnel) are used to isolate and focus on individual performers who may be important within a group, such as soloists in a band. The best way to provide for all contingencies in lighting a stage performance is to discuss in as much detail as possible, the needs of individual acts and performers, and then ensure that the LD is able to provide for those needs with a sufficient variety and number of luminaires.

5.4.2.3.2　Lighting for the Camera (Still or Video)

Using colored filters is not recommended, as the cameras require a common light color among all fixtures as well as a consistent temperature. Filters should only be used to correct for color temperature. Normally, lighting for the camera is bright and white. Cameras are less forgiving of color variations than is the human eye. Backlight is also essential to create a visual separation between the subject and the background.

5.4.2.3.3　Lighting for People Other than Entertainers

Front light coming from two sides helps to eliminate shadows. Complimentary colored filters help to enhance the appearance of good health. Warm colors (pinks and ambers) improve the apparent health of the subject and cool colors (blues and lavenders) enhance the colors in clothing and sets. Backlighting is also recommended, although not always necessary, again to separate the subject from the background.

5.4.2.3.4　Lighting for Attention

Attention generally refers to the use of flashy effects and new concepts in order to grab the attention of the audience, often in preparation for an important presentation or stage performance segment. Considerations include the following:

- Projecting a logo as a gobo design is simple, inexpensive, and rewarding. Everyone likes to see their name in lights, and they can be projected on walls, ceilings, floors, screens, or any other reflective surface.
- Automated lighting is an excellent way to add professional pizzazz and high-energy flash to an award show or gala event. Using the new automated fixtures described earlier, such as the DL2 digital fixture, allows unlimited combinations of graphics, gobos, lighting effects, and computer images to be used throughout a three-dimensional space.

Of course, most large rock concerts now incorporate many automated fixtures. Figure 5.14 shows lighting for attention in just this setting, and the same sort of design – albeit probably on a more limited budget – can be created for any special event.

5.4.3　Physical Design

The physical design of the event lighting refers to how it will be accomplished. This is when the designer brings out his toolbox and puts the right luminaires in the right number in the right location and makes the magic happen. Primary considerations include the design of the venue itself, where and how the luminaires will be mounted, the number and variety of luminaires, and where and how lighting will be controlled.

FIGURE 5.14

LIGHTING FOR ATTENTION: TRANS SIBERIAN ORCHESTRA IN CONCERT

Courtesy: Lewis Lee, Bryan Hartley, and Q1 Production Technologies, www.q1pt.com.

5.4.3.1   *Venue Physical Characteristics*

Every event space is different and an early site visit prior to designing the event lighting is essential. This enables the LD to mold the space with light. It also helps to establish the optimum number and types of luminaires to be used. The purpose of the site visit is to help the LD understand the following, especially if the event is to be held in an indoor venue:

- *Shape of the room*: Is it open, square, and does it contain obstructive columns?
- *Ceiling height and design*: If the ceiling is too high or too low, lighting will be impacted and the effects either heightened or lessened, requiring either more or fewer luminaires. If large chandeliers or complex recesses form large parts of the ceiling, extra luminaires may be needed or a different approach taken. For example, lighting can be reflected off large crystal chandeliers **without** the chandeliers being turned on, to create spectacular colored ambient effects on the ceiling (see Figure 5.13).
- *Control of existing house and ambient lighting*: Will daylight through windows or translucent ceiling material such as tenting be a factor in lighting design? Where and how is house lighting controlled and can a remote controller be used at a lighting control console position in order to save time and effort in turning house lights on and off?

■ *Stage position*: Where will the stage or stages be positioned and how large will they be? Will there be one main stage and/or several satellite stages that need separate lighting or could one or two followspots be sufficient to light the satellite stages? Will there be a backstage area that requires work lights for performers or other technical personnel? Will there be elements of a stage set that require lighting? Often, these questions will require input from the event producer as well as the venue manager.

5.4.3.2 Lighting Support

Luminaires must be mounted on something and in a location that provides optimum illumination to achieve the goals of the lighting design. Even though it could be directly on the floor or other surface (e.g. table, stage, or décor), the exact location, method of mounting and support, and tentative setup time required have to be determined well before the event takes place. The site visit is vital to establishing this.

5.4.3.2.1 Location of Lighting Support

The LD will be asking a number of key questions during the site visit to best determine where the lights will be positioned.

■ Will lighting be flown (rigged from the ceiling) or ground supported on lighting trees or lifts? If flown, the designer must know the exact location of ceiling hanging points, how many there are, and what their load rating is. Flying lighting or audio is normally a much more expensive proposition than ground supporting it due to the additional work and time required, sometimes including the use of qualified union labor, extra time to rig the ceiling points, and time delay for other installation components such as décor and dining tables.

■ If trees or lifts are used, prime locations must be chosen to permit optimum lighting of stages and sets without blocking sight lines, without creating hazards to foot traffic, by eliminating lights in guests' eyes, and by minimizing cable runs.

■ Are there permanent obstructions in the venue? If there are pillars in the room or sets and other décor elements that might block the path of light from any luminaires, then the design must be changed or a new support method devised.

■ If followspots are to be used, where is the optimum location for them and will risers be required to elevate them to the required height?

5.4.3.2.2 Lighting Suspension Systems

For special events, there are two general methods of mounting luminaires: ground supported and flown or ceiling mounted. These break down into further categories.

5.4.3.2.2.1 *Ground-supported systems*

Ground support can be simple or complex. We will examine the possibilities in ascending order of complexity.

- *Placement on a surface*: The simple version can mean actually placing the luminaires on the ground, floor, or other surface, such as a stage, table, audio speaker, or décor piece. In this situation, the luminaire is simply plugged into either a separate electrical circuit or into a dimmer circuit, focused, and controlled from the lighting console.
- *Lighting trees*: A second type of ground support uses *lighting trees*. These are simple aluminum structures comprising: a horizontal bar to which the luminaires are clamped; usually from four to six fixtures such as Fresnels or PARs; and a vertical, adjustable, aluminum support pole with a tripod base. Trees are a good solution for lighting a simple and low-budget stage performance, and they also are good if setup time is minimal. The setup normally incorporates one tree on each side of the stage with luminaires from each tree cross-focused to light the entire stage in a wash.
- *Genie lift-supported truss or lift*: Continuing upward in complexity, the next form of ground-supported system incorporates a special heavy-duty support machine called a *Genie Super Tower*, manufactured by Genie Industries. This machine is wheeled and vertically extendable, capable of supporting up to 800 lb (363 kg) of weight, making it excellent for supporting a long *truss* line with many luminaires.

  A note should be made here about truss. Trussing is the hardware universally employed to support lighting. Luminaires are individually clamped to the truss, which is then raised to the proper *trim* height for lighting a stage or other event components. Trussing is made of heavy-duty aluminum or aluminum alloy tubing and comes in a variety of sizes and shapes. The most common shapes in cross-section are box, rectangular, and triangular, varying from 12 in. (0.1 m) square to more than 20 in. (58 cm) × 38 in. (95 cm) in rectangular cross-section. Section lengths vary from about 2.5 ft (0.75 m) to more than 118 ft (36 m), with tubing diameters of 1 in. (2.5 cm) to 3 in. (7.5 cm). Generally, different manufacturers make different sizes within these extremes. Lengths can be joined together to make longer, continuous truss lines. Trussing also comes in curved sections and, depending on the manufacturer, a variety of colors, thus enabling a limitless range of shapes and looks. More discussion on the installation, loading, and safety of trussing can be found in Section 9.2.
- *Ground-supported tower systems*: At the next level of ground support are towers. These are further divided into three more designs:
  - *Rigging tower*: This is basically a vertical or near-vertical section of truss with base plates or removable outriggers at the bases. A V-shaped base supports a mast that can be erected by means of an erection system which also acts as a stabilizer once the mast is in place. The tower may be used to support lighting and audio (see Figure 5.15).

FIGURE 5.15

EXAMPLE OF RIGGING TOWERS

Courtesy: Domenico Nicolamarino and Ital Stage, Italy, and Prolyte Products Group, www.prolyte.com

- *Ground-support tower*: This tower is designed to support a grid without the need for suspension points. It is typically set up in a box-like design of four vertical towers, each with outrigger feet for stability. Each vertical tower can support upward of 2–4 tons (4000–8000 lb) of horizontal truss. The horizontal truss sections are raised and lowered by means of an electric motor and chains built into the tower. Towers are especially useful in large indoor venues when ceiling hanging points are too high, unreachable, or unable to support sufficient weight for the planned lighting.
- *Roof systems*: These are essentially the ground-supported tower system (e.g. four vertical truss sections with horizontal cross members for hanging lighting and audio) with the addition of a roof whose shape is determined by extra truss sections attached to the top of the tower system. This roof structure is then covered with fire-retardant polyvinyl chloride (PVC). The entire roof is raised with the remainder of the horizontal truss. Roof systems are used extensively for outdoor events for weather protection. Heights are variable, typically up to 30 ft (10 m) or so.

5.4.3.2.2.2 *Flown systems*

A flown system is one in which lighting trussing is attached to *hanging points* (mounting hooks or bolts stressed to carry a certain load) in a ceiling of a venue, usually by means of heavy-duty chains and pulleys or chains and motors. Flown systems may also support audio speakers and audio-visual projectors on the same truss as the lighting. Black masking drape is often used to hide the truss structure from the audience once the system is in place. More is discussed on this subject in Section 9.2.

5.4.3.3 *Types of Luminaires*

Deciding on the number and type of luminaires to use is what makes a good LD and can make or break the effectiveness of the lighting design. Of all the instruments available from the lighting toolbox, the designer must choose the ones that will best achieve the event goals, including budgetary goals. In making this decision, the LD must review the following:

- *Required intensity*: How bright must each luminaire be to give the effect desired? Most lights come in multiples of 100 W power.
- *Required color*: What is being lit and how will it be affected by different colors? Are colors required to enhance the effect? What gels or gobos to use will be determined by the answer to this question.
- *Required coverage*: How big an area must each luminaire cover? Will the budget allow for only eight luminaires to illuminate a 32 ft wide × 24 ft deep (9.6 m × 7.2 m) stage, or can more luminaires be added? The answers will determine the number and type of luminaires to be used.
- *Required functionality*: Is some high-energy pizzazz needed or just static lighting for a speech? Will the person or thing being lit be in motion? The more pizzazz, the more costly because automated fixtures will probably be used.
- *Power*: What will the total power consumption be? See Section 9.1 for more detail on power calculations.
- *Cost*: What is the budget for lighting?

5.4.3.4 *Lighting Console Position*

Most events require a location for the lighting operator and the lighting console(s). The last concern on the site visit is to determine where control will be and if technicians will be required to operate the lights during the event. Usually, the best location for controlling lighting is in the middle of the venue at the back of the event space, ideally directly opposite any performance stage (i.e. at the *front-of-house* or *FOH* position near the audio console); however, reality does not always allow this. The designer must know the exact location in relation to power supplied in order to determine the length and routing of cable runs. In addition, the designer must know if the lit objects or people will be easily viewable, if there will be a raised platform for the control area, and if a remote house light control will be available at the console position.

5.5   BETWEEN CONCEPT AND EXECUTION

What we have been doing up to this point in our discussion of lighting design, is to follow a typical LD through the necessary steps and thought processes required to arrive at a tentative design for the special event. This design might include lighting for entertainment, for décor, or for architecture, and it might be either indoors or outdoors. Having now asked all the right questions and determined the type of lighting that is needed, the LD will return to his shop and take several more steps in preparation for setting up the event.

First, if the event is relatively complex, meaning that there will be a large number of different luminaires used, possibly mounted on a large truss structure, or in several different locations, the LD will choose the required luminaires and determine where they will be mounted based on an analysis of the answers to the questions asked previously. These choices will then be laid out on a *lighting plot* or *lighting plan*. This is simply a hand or *CADD* (computer-aided design and drafting) drawing of all the specific fixtures in their exact locations, drawn to scale, and in relation to what they are lighting (e.g. stage or décor element). The drawing also indicates for each fixture, its dimmer and channel assignments, the fixture number and type, and any and all accessories such as color filters required. See Figure 5.16 for a simple example of a two-dimensional lighting plot drawn in CADD. For some events, an LD will draw a three-dimensional rendering of the lighting plan in CADD, which gives a very accurate visualization of the exact lighting effects, since the latest CADD software takes into account the types of lights and the amount of light, the various surfaces in the space including their reflectivity, and integrates it all into an accurate picture. Some of the more common programs now used for such three-dimensional representations are WYSIWYG and Vivien from Cast Group and Vectorworks from Nemetschek. CADD is also discussed in detail in Chapter 8 of *Special Event Production: The Process*.

Second, and now with the lighting plot in hand, the LD will prepare a crew and installation schedule, along with power requirements, which will be passed to the producer, and thence to the venue. In considering the crew required, often for complex events, the LD will not be the person present but instead the lighting crew will consist of one main operator (crew chief), possibly one programmer for automated fixtures, and one or more followspot operators. In addition, the LD – or the setup crew chief – will prepare all the necessary control and dimming equipment, the mounting and

FIGURE 5.16

EXAMPLE OF A COMPUTERIZED SPECIAL EVENT LIGHTING PLOT

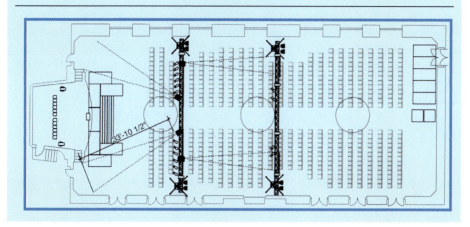

Courtesy: Q1 Production Technologies, www.q1pt.com.

support hardware for the complete lighting installation, and load calculations for the rigging company if lighting is to be mounted on trussing.

5.6   LIGHTING CONTROL, SETUP, AND OPERATION

A basic special event conventional lighting system is actually comprised of three main components: the luminaires themselves, a dimming system, and a control console (also called a *lighting desk* or a *lighting board*). These components must all be hooked up in the proper sequence and tested before the event can proceed. We have already explained how the different types of luminaires are used. Let us now examine how the dimming system and control console work in order to create that unique event environment. From there, we will review what happens during an event lighting setup and what exactly the lighting operator does during an event.

5.6.1   Lighting Control

The control system allows each luminaire to be controlled (e.g. dimmed, faded in and out, shut on or off, color changed, movement changed, gobo patterns changed, etc.) from a central location where the lighting console is positioned, ideally at the FOH position opposite the stage. It includes the dimming system, the lighting control console, and a control protocol that enables communication between the luminaires, the dimmers, and the console.

5.6.1.1 Dimming System

In most event lighting situations, luminaires are not used constantly at full power but must occasionally be faded or turned off. This is accomplished by using dimmers. Each dimmer regulates one lighting circuit, or channel, allowing the attached luminaire's intensity to vary by varying the electrical supply sent to the luminaire. Each dimmer is designed to work to a maximum electrical load. For example, a 2000 W dimmer might be loaded with two 1000 W ERS spotlights or up to four 500 W luminaires (such as four PAR64s). This is an important point to remember. If one dimmer channel is assigned to one luminaire, only that luminaire will dim when the channel is used; however, if the dimmer channel is assigned to four luminaires, all four luminaires will dim at once when the channel is used. The LD will determine the best combinations of luminaires and dimmer channels in his concept and lighting plot.

A typical dimmer pack comprises several dimmer modules, all housed together. They may even be conveniently mounted on rolling racks, enabling the control of many lighting circuits. The dimmer packs are usually physically located in the event space close to the stage, or as close as possible to electrical power and ideally the luminaires as well.

5.6.1.2 Control Console

This is the front end of the lighting control system. It is the equivalent in lighting to what the mixer is in audio. Simple stage lighting can be controlled using a manual control console. This has a single level control or *fader* for each dimmer channel. It might also provide for two faders per channel, allowing the operator to set up two separate *scenes* (combinations of lights) and *cross-fade* (fade one scene in at the same time the other is fading out) between them.

More complex event lighting requirements will be handled by a digital memory control console. Most of these consoles are capable of storing dozens – or hundreds – of different scenes, allowing for countless different 'looks' to be created and programmed ahead of the event. For example, a low light level, cool-colored background for a musical ballad might be followed immediately by a high-energy rock dance routine requiring moving lights and warm colors, a change that is easily accomplished with preset scenes and fade times. Modern consoles also allow for *soft-patching*, or the assignment of more than one individual dimmer channel to a console channel. This allows more luminaires to be controlled as a logical unit than a single dimmer channel allows. Many of the higher-end consoles have more than one *DMX universe*, which simply means that it can handle 512 more separate channels for each DMX universe. In other words, such a console can handle literally thousands of fixtures and lighting cues. See the explanation of DMX control in the next section.

Mention should be made about the use of automated fixtures and control consoles. Each function of an automated fixture requires a single console channel. For example, if an automated fixture offers a color wheel and a spinning gobo, these features will take up to two channels on the console. Most state-of-the-art lighting control consoles have fully automated fixture control built into them, including some form of *joystick* or moving control wheel. In fact, some are now at the point of being able to duplicate the linear movements of a followspot, with minimal programming, one of the previously impossible tasks for automated fixtures. With the multiple DMX universes available, the many channels needed no longer pose a major problem.

5.6.1.3 Control Protocol

Control protocol refers to the language used to communicate between the luminaires, dimmers, and control console. Traditionally, lighting control used an analog system in which there was one wire per channel. In other words, the control console sent an electrical signal (1–10 V) through a wire to the dimmer, which in turn sent the signal through a wire to the luminaire. This system had two big disadvantages. First, one console channel could only control one luminaire and second, the system required extensive wiring between the dimmers and the console, two components usually separated by large distances in a special event.

In 1986, a new digital standard was created for the lighting industry called *DMX*, with today's version being DMX512. The notation refers to the number of channels that this new system can handle (512). It is now the industry standard for controlling all lighting fixtures, including automated fixtures, and such accessories as smoke machines. In theory, it works quite simply. The console sends a separate signal of a unique numerical value (*base address*) destined for a particular dimmer and luminaire (or combination of luminaires) into a built-in *multiplex* unit which takes the individual channel data and encodes them into a format suitable for sending down the DMX cable with all the other channels' data. This single cable replaces the many cables of the analog system. At the dimmer end of the cable, the data are fed into a *demultiplexer* (demux), which in turn splits the signal back into the individual channels of the dimmers. The demux unit is now normally built into the dimmers. DMX cabling (i.e. from the console to the dimmers) for lighting is called *5-pin XLR*.

Once the signal is received by the dimmers near the stage, it is sent further down another *multicore* cable (often called *Socapex* after the manufacturer) which carries the signals of up to six luminaires closer to the actual fixtures, and then once again split into individual bundles of 15 A cables directed to each separate luminaire. Figure 5.17 illustrates this signal path and the location of all components in a typical special event lighting control setup.

5.6.2 Lighting Setup

Lighting often requires considerable time for setup due to several factors that render it different from other technical equipment. It is a labor and time-intensive series of tasks that need to be done correctly or not only will

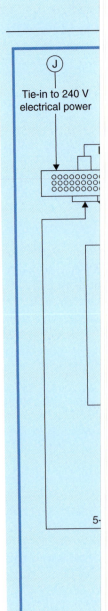

Tie-in to 240 V
electrical power

Cadena

Evans,
    fram

Fitt, B.
    Thea

Fuchs,
    from

Gillette
    and (
    McG
Willian
    from

5-

Courtesy: Doug Ma

the show be pc
physical injury

In all but the
on support trus

6.1   WHAT ARE SPECIAL EFFECTS?

The term 'special effects' has taken on several connotations in today's world. For most people, what immediately comes to mind and what seems to have become the default definition, is movie special effects: computer-generated outer space travel (Star Wars); giant beasts (King Kong); impossible movement (The Matrix Series and Crouching Tiger, Hidden Dragon); simulated disasters (Poseidon Adventure); and cartoon animation. Most of these, while possible in limited situations, are not what we use in special events. What then, do we use, and what is different about what we use compared to movie special effects?

Put simply, special effects used in special events are unusual and creative technological surprises timed to emphasize an event element. The main difference between our (special events industry) special effects and those of the movies is the fact that we use them for emphasis at strategic moments during the event. For the most part, they are not intended as the only entertainment, with notable exceptions such as a community fireworks show.

Admittedly, we borrow heavily not only from the movie industry in effects (e.g. artificial snow, wind, rain, and, on rare occasions, prosthetics, blood, and stunts) but also from some of the more ancient theatrical effects (e.g. fireworks, magic, and illusions), from computers (e.g. talking heads, video effects, catalyst system), from science (e.g. lasers, UV and blacklighting, robotics, light-emitting diodes or LEDs), and from older technology (e.g. balloon effects, streamers, confetti, bubbles). The influences are definitely varied and numerous. We often adapt these effects for our own use. Sometimes, they actually further evolve into other more fascinating inventions and effects (e.g. LED dance floors).

What about the actual presentation? According to Jaworski (2003), for a successful special effect presentation, one must consider four essential elements: surprise, whether the effects are remarkable, timing, and taste. The element of surprise is crucial, and effects must not be 'telegraphed.' The surprise extends also to the type of feeling that needs to be elicited from the audience. For example, they can be alarmed and startled by fireworks, happy and uplifted by confetti and streamers, or energetic and excited by a combination of upbeat music and pyrotechnics.

Remarkable means that the effects stretch the imagination from the 'usual.' They go beyond what an audience has seen to something they have not. Often this is through a combination of effects or a combination of entertainment and effects. For example, a regular show might simply use a stage presentation of entertainment and pyrotechnics. A better show might bring together a water curtain, pyrotechnics, lasers, and the stage presentation. However, by adding choreography to time the effects to music and then bringing all the elements in one at a time so that the show builds to a climax, the presentation rises to another level.

Timing the placement of effects tends to be intuitive. It is money wasted to place them at an inappropriate time during the event. It is also a waste of money to use them just for the sake of doing something different. They must be timed to coincide with a key moment in the event: the announcement of a location for the next year's event; the end of a song; the end or beginning of the event or show; the presentation of an award; and so on. It is usually the producer, in conjunction with the special effects expert, who decides the timing of the presentation.

Taste is mostly a matter of matching the client's vision with the producer's. It means that there must be a mutual understanding of what will work for both the audience and the producer and what show will incorporate the best effects based on the knowledge of what is available to match those tastes.

6.2 TYPES OF SPECIAL EFFECTS

The list of special effects grows every year, with more colorful, bigger, noisier, higher, wider, denser, longer, and safer being some of the adjectives describing the never-ending innovations that cause hearts to skip beats. Although identifying the latest and greatest is a rapidly moving target, we will attempt to review and explain what the main ones are and how they are used. Some may seem obvious by their omission; however, that is either because they are very simple to use (e.g. bubble machines), or because we have reviewed them as part of other resources (e.g. automated lighting, mirror balls, balloon drops and walls, video effects).

6.2.1 Streamers and Confetti

The term 'confetti' refers to small pieces of paper in large quantities that are thrown by hand, launched by a special device, or dropped from a height. The term 'streamers' refers to long pieces of paper spread in the same manner. The confetti and streamers used for events come in a multitude of colors, sizes, shapes, and paper types. The traditional and most common paper type is tissue paper which, being lightweight, is able to travel farther and dwell for longer in the air. It also comes in shiny Mylar in different colors, but is difficult to clean up and does not travel as far as regular confetti. In terms of shapes and sizes, confetti is now available from ¼ in. (0.6 cm) diameter round shapes (seldom used) to 3 in. (7.5 cm) × 4 in. (10 cm) rectangular strips, plus triangles and other custom shapes, including play money. Standard confetti is not colorfast, so should not be used over diners or outside when it is raining or there is wet ground.

Streamers are available in lengths ranging from 12 ft (0.36 m) to 50 ft (15 m), and widths ranging from ³⁄₁₆ in. (0.5 cm) to ½ in. (1.3 cm), all in multiple colors. Like confetti, they also come in Mylar. The larger streamers are best used either outdoors or indoors when ceilings are very high. Both confetti and streamers can be made flame resistant. Confetti and streamers may be customized with logos and graphic messages, as well as special shapes.

Confetti and streamer cannons consist of long plastic tubes or barrels that are filled with the densely packaged streamers or confetti and launched using a compressed carbon dioxide (CO_2), air, or nitrogen cartridge or cylinder. These cannons come in various sizes from about a 1 in. (2.5 cm) to a 4 in. (10 cm) diameter barrel that can be up to 40 in. (100 cm) long, and even larger. They are capable of launching confetti and streamers anywhere from 30 ft (9 m) to 250 ft (75 m). All are reusable in that they only require new charges of streamers and confetti and new compressed gas cartridges (usually CO_2). Cannons come as handheld models as well as remotely triggered models via wireless or DMX protocol. They can be mounted on floors, overhead trussing, stages, and almost any surface. Some manufacturers have also developed a portable backpack version that carries extra charges. For truly large events when massive amounts of confetti in a continuous flow are required, a *confetti blaster* is used. The blaster provides a continuous feed of confetti that is combined with air and compressed CO_2 in a venturi tube that shoots the confetti outward for a total time of up to a minute. The difference between the blaster and confetti cannon is that the blaster is a continuous feed, whereas the cannon is a single rapid shot. The blaster is hand controlled and must have an operator while the cannon can be operated remotely.

At present, there are no safety or other standards for confetti, streamers, or cannons and launchers, and no permit is required. The main caution is obvious and that is to not point them directly toward people.

6.2.2   Fog, Smoke, and Haze

To create 'other-worldly' and dreamy looks, nothing beats fog, and to make light and laser beams sparkle and dance in the air, smoke, and/or haze are a must. There are three main types of machines used to generate these effects.

6.2.2.1   Fog

The older and most common fog machine uses *dry ice*. 'These machines produce a low lying, rolling fog effect by dropping solid CO_2 (dry ice) into boiling water. Dry ice is very cold (-70 degrees Celsius) and will lose about 30 percent of its volume every day as the CO_2 sublimes back to a gas. The solid CO_2 is available in pellet or block form from industrial gas suppliers and can be stored in an insulated polystyrene container. The visible "fog" effect is actually water vapor. The CO_2 gas is invisible' (ELH Communications Ltd., 2004). Dry ice fog gives the 'walking on clouds' effect. Figure 6.1 depicts a reception area with low-lying dry ice fog.

FIGURE 6.1

DRY ICE FOG EFFECT

Courtesy: Wayne Chose Photography and Pacific Show Productions, www.pacificshow. ca – Copyright 2006

There are some contradictory problems with dry ice fog. The first is that it is most effective when air circulation is bad in that it remains close to the ground and does not dissipate quickly, making the effect more impressive. Contradicting this is the need, for health reasons, to disperse the fog through room ventilation so that concentrations do not get high enough to cause breathing problems. Fortunately, this is a small problem as most of the dry ice fog is water vapor and CO_2 does not reach toxic levels very quickly. However, it is a good idea to maintain ventilation and use the fog away from areas with high air flow such as entrance doors in order to avoid too rapid dispersion. Dry ice, due to its extremely cold temperature, must also be handled and stored safely. This includes the wearing of gloves when handling it and the use of heavily insulated containers for storing it. Dry ice machines also require a full-time operator to monitor the flow and to constantly feed the dry ice into the machine.

6.2.2.2 Smoke

To generate smoke, 'a glycol/water mixture is vaporized by heating under compression. Nearly all smoke machines work this way. Glycol or mineral oil *smoke guns* all work on the same principle although their size, precise method of operation and the chemical used do vary. The basic principle is that a mineral oil or glycol-based substance is heated, atomizing the substance.

This is then forced out of the machine under pressure' (ELH Communications Ltd., 2004). This produces a familiar 'white cloud' effect, which rises and spreads throughout the air. Thicker smoke is produced by increasing the length of the smoke burst. As opposed to fog, smoke rises in the air and can obscure viewing depending on its density. To confuse matters, commercial smoke machines are often called fog machines or foggers.

It is also possible to use *heavy smoke* or *low smoke* as an alternative to fog. A low smoke machine or *LSG* (low smoke generator) uses a standard smoke machine connected to a chiller unit. This makes the smoke colder than the surrounding air, causing it to fall to the floor in a similar manner to dry ice fog. An LSG uses liquid CO_2 to chill the smoke fluid. The advantages of this type of machine, according to Mike Kaerne of Holly North Production Supplies Ltd. in Vancouver, BC, are that the fog can actually be pushed **up** as high as 16 ft (4.8 m) and **outward** as far as 20 ft (6 m). There are also no toxicity problems and the machine can be controlled by DMX (Mike Kaerne, Personal Communication, July 5, 2006).

Another spectacular fog/smoke effect is created by pushing liquid CO_2 through nozzles at high pressure in devices called *cryojets*. They are used to generate fog bursts, which shoot dense white fog straight up into the air (Figure 6.2). They can be ganged together and controlled remotely but only work with regular 110 V switches. The CO_2 is pumped to each jet via a common line, much like a hose.

FIGURE 6.2
CRYOJETS AT A FOOTBALL GAME

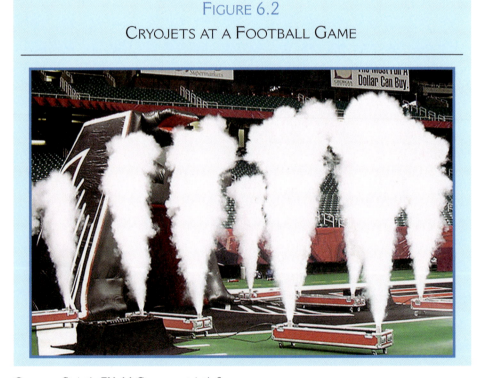

Courtesy: Strictly FX, LLC, www.strictlyfx.com

6.2.2.3 Haze

For haze, 'a very fine mist is produced which is used for enhancing light beams in the air. This is either produced by vaporizing oil (an *oil cracker*) or by dispersing a glycol fog using a fan. Cheaper haze machines use a low-output glycol fog machine with a fan to disperse the output. More expensive machines use different vaporization techniques to produce a very fine and regular haze output' (ELH Communications Ltd., 2004). From a safety point of view, on glycol-based machines the nozzle of the machine may be hot. The haze may condense in and on nearby equipment.

Like confetti and streamer cannons, smoke machines, foggers, and hazers can be set off remotely using DMX controllers, similar to those used in lighting.

6.2.2.4 Safety of Fog, Smoke, and Haze

Smoke machine(s) and hazer(s) should be tested in the event venue prior to the event. If there are smoke detectors, then there is a very distinct possibility that a smoke machine might set them off. There are many venues where smoke machines cannot be used because of the fire alarm systems installed. In fact, these devices are now banned in many venues, or the fire department must stand by onsite for a large fee. If possible, smoke detectors should be disabled during – and only during – the effect. Again, however, the venue may charge for this service. If this is not possible, a test run is advisable. If in doubt, smoke should not be used because evacuation of the venue during the show is not the effect sought.

'In relative terms, the ingredients used in smoke and haze fluid are quite safe, but there is an ongoing debate in the entertainment industry about whether the output of a smoke machine is safe or not. When exposed to strong concentrations of the fog many people tend to get watery eyes and dry throats and noses. Persons suffering from asthma or allergic sensitivity may experience irritation, discomfort, or allergic symptoms when exposed to heated fog effects. It's a good policy to ensure that where smoke is being used in the vicinity of performers it is kept to the minimum required to achieve the desired effect and to post warnings. Other safety hazards include: the condensation of smoke back to fluid near the nozzle of the machine, causing a slipping hazard; the nozzle of the machine, which is very hot, causing burns; and large amounts of smoke causing panic and disorientation in an audience' (ELH Communications Ltd., 2004). Current safety standards for smoke and fog machines are listed below:

- *BSR E1.23: Entertainment Technology: Design and Execution of Theatrical Fog Effects.*
- *BSR E1.29: Product Safety Standard for Theatrical Fog Generators that Create Aerosols of Water, Aqueous Solutions of Glycol or Glycerin, or Aerosols of Highly Refined Alkane Mineral Oil.*

Both these standards are put out by the Entertainment Services and Technology Association (ESTA) and applicable to North America.

6.2.3 Lasers

As the International Laser Display Association states, 'There's no light like it: the most vivid, saturated color palette available; a contrast ratio unsurpassed by the best film and video technologies; the ability to reach out in three dimensions and shower an audience with cascades of beams or embrace them in waves of moving light. It's about enchanting an audience with dreamlike visions. It's about exciting crowds with visual effects that move faster than any other light-form' (ILDA, 2006a). Lasers for special events consist of three main components: a light source (the laser itself), a projector, and software. We will examine these and then briefly discuss safety.

6.2.3.1 *The Light Source (LASER)*

The word LASER is an acronym. It stands for *Light Amplification by the Stimulated Emission of Radiation*. By 'radiation', however, the acronym refers to a radiant vibration, not an emission of radioactive particles. In other words, the emissions of lasers are in the form of light. The lasers typically employed in events are called *ion gas lasers*, due to the fact that they utilize a gas or a mixture of gases as the lasing medium. The stimulation comes in the form of electricity, which excites the atoms of the gas: as the electrons in these atoms are given more energy, they tend to jump to a higher orbit. These unnaturally high orbits, however, don't last long, and the electrons fall back to their proper orbital shells, to be once again excited by the influx of electricity. It is this process of the electrons returning to their original orbits that creates the laser light we see' (Mueller, 2005). The three general types of light show graphics lasers are low-power helium/neon (red), medium- and high-power argon (green-blue), and mixed gas argon/krypton (red-yellow-green-blue).

6.2.3.2 *The Projector*

The laser projector is the heart of the graphics system. 'Using tiny moving mirrors, a single beam of laser light can be moved so fast the human eye no longer sees the individual beam. Instead, the audience sees fans, cones, tunnels, or cascades of beams that fill the air. Specialized optics (*diffraction gratings*) can create sheets of light by splitting one beam into hundreds of individual shafts of light. Bounce mirrors can ricochet beams throughout a venue. Realistic wire-frame images can be projected onto walls, buildings, and even mountains to advertise products or tell a dramatic story. Wispy, cloud-like graphics called *lumia* can fill ceilings, and psychedelic abstract graphics can be created with eye-popping colors and contrast' (ILDA, 2006b).

6.2.3.3 The Software

Laser show software is available for almost every personal computer, and there are even programs with their own custom computers. It is the software that creates the two main types of laser effects: aerials (also called *atmospherics*) and animation projection. The laser effect that most causes audiences to gasp with wonder and delight is the experience of seeing laser beams move through open air. Walsh (2005) describes how it is done. 'These effects are called "atmospheric" because they rely upon beams sculpting the atmosphere of the venue, with no projection screen involved. To help make the beams visible indoors, laserists often introduce particles into the air, usually using theatrical fog machines. If a laser beam is coming toward the viewer, the apparent brightness of the beam is increased. Beams that are perpendicular to the viewer are perceived as much less bright. Those going away from the viewer vary in apparent brightness depending upon the ambient light in the background. For creating successful beam shows, it is wise to plan the display as coming toward the audience' (see Figure 6.3).

Dryer (2005) aptly describes animation projection created by *laser scanning*. 'Animated neon That's an approximate description of laser scanning: the richly colored line-drawing quality of a neon sign set in motion with equal contrast and even greater color saturation. It's a medium that makes any message special. Laser scanners can project names, logos, and animated imagery onto almost any surface including the side of a mountain, the curved dome of a planetarium, even a sheet of pulsating water. To do this, a laser produces a tiny linear beam of intense light that appears as a small dot when it strikes a surface. To make it move you have to "scan" it by wiggling one or more mirrored surfaces. Once the dot of light moves fast enough,

---

FIGURE 6.3

LEFT PHOTO: LASER AERIALS; RIGHT PHOTO: LASER GRAPHICS

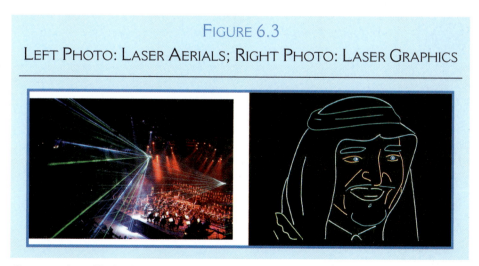

Courtesy: http://upload.wikimedia.org/wikipedia/commons/f/f7/Laser_effects03.jpg, July 12, 2006 (left); http://www.hw-laser.de/ueberuns/000000961b0e2f431/index.html (right)

a phenomenon called *persistence of vision* causes your eye to perceive the movements of the dot as solid lines of light.' This movement is achieved through a combination of the laser projector's hardware and special software (see Figure 6.3).

6.2.3.4 *Laser Safety*

According to Plaser Spectacles, Inc. (2003), 'The hidden danger of lasers is to the eyes. A laser beam containing only a small fraction of the power contained in a medium power laser (as little as 5/1000th of a watt) can burn a spot in the retina when focused through the eye's natural lens. With laser light shows, a problem exists between the necessity to view the laser beams in the show and yet not damage the audience's eyes from laser exposure. In many parts of the world, lasers used in laser shows are scanned directly into the audience and over their eyes (called *audience scanning*). If the laser beam is being scanned quickly enough, there will be no damage to the eyes, because the beam never settles in one spot for long enough to burn. However, if failure in the scanning apparatus occurs, the beam will stop moving, and there is great potential for damage to be done if anyone is in the way of the beam. The primary means of laser light show safety in the USA is provided simply by keeping the beam away from the audience. There are two rules for doing this: the "3 m (10 ft) vertical clearance" rule, and the "2.5 m (8.3 ft) horizontal clearance" rule. If there is an audience standing or seated in a given area, the laser beams used in a show must not drop lower than 3 m measured vertically above the surface that the audience is upon. Measured horizontally, the beams must not come any closer than 2.5 m to any place that the audience can reach. Audience barriers are required to ensure that the audience stays within this "safe zone," and danger/warning signs are required to be posted to inform people of the fact that laser radiation is present.' The best way producers can ensure laser safety is to require laser companies to adhere to current international and North American standards and regulations on the use of lasers, as listed below:

- *IEC 60825-1:2001: Safety of laser products Part 1: Equipment classification, requirements and user's guide* (international standard).
- *Code of Federal Regulations CFR 1040.10: Laser Product Regulation 21* (US regulation).
- *US Food and Drug Administration (FDA): FDA Laser Notice 50.*

6.2.4 Fireworks and Pyrotechnics

Fireworks are the earliest use of explosives known to man, invented in China in the 9th century. Such important events and festivities as New Year's and the Mid-Autumn Moon Festival were and still are times when fireworks are guaranteed sights in that country. Nowadays, they can be seen around the world at festivals and regular celebrations, whether public or private. Chemically, they are classed as low explosive pyrotechnic devices in contrast to the infinitely more powerful high explosives such as TNT and the dynamites.

There has always been some confusion about the difference between fireworks and pyrotechnics. The pyrotechnics industry (APA, 2004) uses the following definitions:

- 'Fireworks: Any composition or device for the purpose of producing a visible or an audible effect by combustion, deflagration, or detonation, and that meets the definition of consumer fireworks or display fireworks.
- Pyrotechnics: Controlled exothermic chemical reactions that are timed to create the effects of heat, gas, sound, dispersion of aerosols, emission of visible electromagnetic radiation, or a combination of these effects to provide the maximum effect from the least volume.
- Theatrical pyrotechnics: Pyrotechnic devices for professional use in the entertainment industry. Similar to consumer fireworks in chemical composition and construction but not intended for consumer use.'

For definition in the special events industry, there is now fairly common usage that interprets pyrotechnics as indoor, close proximity, smaller devices that create effects of relatively short duration (i.e. theatrical or *proximate pyrotechnics* as above), and fireworks as outdoor, distant, larger devices that create effects of relatively long duration (i.e. *display fireworks*).

In terms of regulations, there are very distinct differences. The US and Canadian governments have classified fireworks and pyrotechnics according to their potential hazards. The US government now classifies them according to their shipping hazards only, compared to the old system that classified based on shipping and use. The new US system categorizes them as follows:

- Display fireworks (i.e. outdoor). Class 1.3G, with United Nations shipping category UN0335. These were the old Class 'B' fireworks.
- Proximate pyrotechnics (i.e. indoor, theatrical). Class 1.4G and 1.4S, with United Nations shipping categories UN0431 and UN0432, respectively. These were the old Class 'C' fireworks. Some may also fall under other classes, so all details of each class should be thoroughly understood.

The Canadian government's classifications are based on composition and roughly parallel the US categories. Class 7.2.2 represents display fireworks and Class 7.2.5 represents theatrical pyrotechnics. However, the United Nations shipping regulations for fireworks and pyrotechnics also apply in Canada.

6.2.4.1   Display Fireworks (Outdoor)

Display fireworks make the wonderful outdoor shows we have come to love and of which we never seem to tire. They are often the climax of special events, whether they are public festivals for 100,000 persons or private corporate events with 100 VIPs. The two most important aspects of their use are how they work and safety.

6.2.4.1.1 What Are Display Fireworks?

There are three kinds of display fireworks: high level, low level, and ground level.

6.2.4.1.1.1 *High level*

The most impressive and well-known type of display fireworks are *aerial* or high-level fireworks. A single typical display or aerial firework is formed into a *shell* consisting of four components (Brain, 2006).

- 'Container: This is usually pasted paper and string formed into a cylinder.
- Stars: These are spheres, cubes, or cylinders of a sparkler-like composition. The stars are the key ingredients that produce the intense light and color of the firework. Stars in turn are composed of: a fuel which allows the star to burn; an oxidizer which produces oxygen to support the combustion of the fuel; color-producing chemicals (Helmenstine, 2006 gives a good explanation of how the color is achieved); and a binder which holds the pellet together.
- Bursting charge: This is a packed, black powder charge at the center of the shell that is also sprinkled between the stars to help ignite them.
- Fuse: The fuse provides a time delay so the shell explodes at the right altitude. When the fuse burns into the shell, it ignites the bursting charge, causing the shell to explode. The explosion ignites the outside of the stars, which begin to burn with bright showers of sparks. Since the explosion throws the stars in all directions, a huge sphere of sparkling light is created that is so familiar at fireworks displays.'

The shell is usually launched from a *mortar*. Mortars are generally made of *FRE* (fiber-reinforced epoxy) or *HDPE* (high-density polyethylene). Some older mortars are made of sheet steel, but have been banned by most countries due to the problem of shrapnel produced during a misfire. The mortar also contains a lifting charge of black powder that explodes to launch the shell. When the lifting charge fires to launch the shell, it lights the shell's fuse. The shell's fuse burns while the shell rises to its correct altitude and then ignites the bursting charge so it explodes. These mortars are clearly seen in the show preparation of Figure 6.4. Mortars range in size from 2 in. (5 cm) to 12 in. (30 cm) diameter but do come in diameters up to 16 in. (40 cm), the use of which requires special permission.

There are also complicated shells that burst in two or three phases, called *multi-break shells*. They may contain stars of different colors and compositions to create softer or brighter light, and more or fewer sparks. Some shells contain explosives designed to crackle in the sky, or whistles that explode outward with the stars. Multi-break shells sometimes incorporate a shell filled with other shells, or they may have multiple sections without

FIGURE 6.4

PREPARATION FOR AN OUTDOOR FIREWORKS DISPLAY

Courtesy: http://upload.wikimedia.org/wikipedia/commons/c/ca/Preparing_Firework.jpg, July 12, 2006

using additional shells. The sections of a multi-break shell are ignited by different fuses. The bursting of one section ignites the next. The shells must be assembled in such a way that each section explodes in sequence to produce a distinct separate effect. The explosives that break the sections apart are called *break charges*, and the *pattern* that an aerial shell paints in the sky depends on the arrangement of star pellets inside each shell. Both Brain (2006) and Wikipedia contributors (July 2, 2006) provide good descriptions and illustrations of some of the more common patterns.

Occasionally, shells are launched into the air using *rockets*. A rocket can be considered a 'shell on a stick,' which, instead of being fired into the air from a mortar tube, is mounted onto a rocket motor to which a stick is attached. Cylindrical in shape, the rocket has a cone-shaped head filled with stars. Upon ignition, the gases from the propellant erupt out of the bottom of the cylinder and the rocket rises high into the air.

6.2.4.1.1.2   *Low level*

Besides high-level fireworks, display fireworks are actually divided into two other categories. The first is low-level or *ground-to-air fireworks* that either perform below approximately 200 ft (60 m) or begin their display at ground level and rise to complete their effect. Some examples of low-level fireworks are:

- *Candles or Roman candles*: A candle is a cardboard tube which contains alternating layers of compacted black powder and single stars. When lighted, candles eject a series of colored stars one by one into the air and often emit a shower of glowing sparks between each shot.
- *Cakes*: A cake is a device consisting of a number of individual tubes of effects (e.g. comets, mines, etc.) set up together but not stacked as in a candle.
- *Comets*: This is an effect. A special composition pellet is propelled from a mortar or shell and produces a long-tailed effect. Large comets are constructed much like aerial display shells, with attached lift charge ready for loading into mortars.
- *Mines*: This is a tubular device, comprised of a plastic bag containing a black powder lifting charge and a number of colored shells, balanced by a wooden or plastic base. The mine is designed to propel any number of items aloft such as stars, whistles, and floating fireworks.

6.2.4.1.1.3   *Ground level*

The last category is ground-level fireworks that function on the ground. Some examples of ground-level fireworks are:

- *Fountains*: Fountains are designed to project brilliant jets of sparks into the air much like a water fountain. Shaped like a cone or cylinder, the fountain's pyrotechnic composition is pressed into the case in the same way as for a rocket motor, but on a short rather than a long central cavity. Both gold and silver are common in colored fountains.
- *Wheels and drivers*: These are revolving pieces turned by drivers mounted radially on spokes. Various effects can be attached to the wheel, such as colored lights and fountains. 'Catherine' or 'pin' wheels are small wheels spinning on a pole.
- *Gerbs*: A gerb is a cylindrical preload intended to produce a controlled spray of sparks with a reproducible and predictable duration, height, and diameter. The pattern looks like a sheaf of wheat.
- *Lances and lancework set pieces*: Lances are small flares used in the makeup of portraits, flags, and mottos known as lancework set pieces. The outline is constructed on a wood lattice and a design picked out in appropriate colors of lances.
- *Waterfalls*: Waterfalls are a series of gerbs (without nozzles) suspended fuse side down from a wire or rope strung between two points. The gerbs are all ignited simultaneously and produce a curtain of sparks.

Figure 6.5 illustrates a typical outdoor public fireworks display showing a clear distinction among high-level, low-level, and ground-level effects.

FIGURE 6.5

OUTDOOR FIREWORKS DISPLAY

Courtesy: HSBC Celebration of Light, www.hsbccelebrationoflight.com

6.2.4.1.2   Display Fireworks Safety

Fireworks safety is extremely important. The USA and Canada have set up stringent regulations that govern the permit requirements, setup, placement, loading, safe distances of crowds, cleanup, storage, and transportation of commercial display fireworks. In the USA, the most important documents are the *National Fire Protection Association standard NFPA 1123: Fireworks Display (2006 Edition)* and *NFPA 1124: Code for the Manufacturing, Transportation, Storage and Retail Sale of Fireworks and Pyrotechnic Articles (2006 Edition)*. In Canada, the comparable governing document is the *Display Fireworks Manual*, put out by the Explosives Regulatory Division (ERD) of Natural Resources Canada. Any event producers contemplating using display fireworks should obtain a current copy of the applicable federal documents, as well as local state, provincial, or municipal regulations which may differ throughout each country. Generally speaking, any event producer who wishes to hold an outdoor fireworks display must have the following in their possession, either personally or through the official fireworks contractor.

- License or certification to work with display fireworks. This could be either a state requirement (if in the USA), and requirements may differ throughout the country, or a federal requirement (if in Canada). In Canada, certification is the law and is set to federal standards by the ERD. Anyone who handles display fireworks must be at least an Apprentice. Certification is divided into the following classes (ERD, 2006).
  - '*Apprentice*: An Apprentice (a prerequisite to becoming a Fireworks Supervisor) may, under the direct supervision of a Fireworks Supervisor, perform the same duties that his/her supervisor is allowed to perform on the display site.
  - *Fireworks Supervisor, Level 1*: This person must have met the current Apprenticeship certification requirements. The scope of duties, limitations, and certification requirements applicable to Fireworks Supervisor, Level 1 are extensive and can be found on the ERD web site at http://www.nrcan.gc.ca/mms/explosif/edu/edu_displayB_e.htm.
  - *Fireworks Supervisor, Level 2.* Fireworks Supervisors, Level 1, who have gained experience under the supervision of experienced Fireworks Supervisors, Level 2, and assisted in displays where shells over 155 mm (6 in.) have been fired (or who have attended advanced training in the field of fireworks) can apply for a Level 2 certificate.
  - *Visiting Fireworks Supervisor*: Out-of-Country Fireworks Supervisors may assist a certified Canadian Supervisor who assumes all responsibilities for the display setup. Out-of-Country Fireworks Supervisors can obtain a Visitor Card (issued on a yearly basis, plus pay required fees) upon submission of proof of competence.'

  Any producers who are planning display fireworks shows should always insist that the fireworks contractor be fully certified.
- Approval to purchase display fireworks (usually federal and/or state).
- Permit to hold a fireworks display (usually the AHJ or *authority having jurisdiction*, such as local municipal fire, parks, or police department). Occasionally, the permit and approval to purchase are the same, depending on the jurisdiction.
- Permission of landowner, lessee, or agent to hold a fireworks display.
- Insurance of a minimum amount and type as specified by contract (i.e. the client/producer contract) and local regulations (usually the same organization that grants the permit). The most common minimum amount now required is $5 million liability.
- A site plan with complete details of crowd and fireworks locations, emergency access, water locations, etc. (usually a requirement of the AHJ).

Setup of fireworks involves: the placement and securing of mortars on wooden or wire racks; loading of the shells; and if electronically firing, wiring and testing. Safe distances from crowds are critical. For example, setup of mortars in Canada requires a minimum angle of 10–15 degrees down range with a safety distance of at least 200 m (220 yard or yd) down range and 100 m (110 yd) surrounding the mortars.

Loading of shells is a delicate process, and must be done with caution. Loaders must not only ensure that the mortar is clean, but must also make sure that no part of their body is directly over the mortar in case of a premature fire. Wiring the shells is a painstaking process, whether the shells are being fired manually or electronically. For any *chain fusing* or wiring of electrical igniters, care must be taken to prevent the fuse (an *electrical match*, often incorrectly called a *squib*) from igniting. If the setup is wired electrically, the electrical matches are usually plugged into a *firing rail* or *breakout box* which runs back to the main firing board; from there, the firing board is simply hooked up to a car battery, and the show can be fired when ready. Fireworks specialists always advise that any electronic firing device must have a removable key for safety purposes. Since commercial-grade fireworks are so large and powerful, setup and firing crews are always under great pressure to ensure that they safely set up, fire, and clean up after a show. Occasionally, if safe distances and proper setup are not possible on dry land, and an event is near water, a barge may be used for setup and firing of the show.

6.2.4.2 Proximate or Theatrical Pyrotechnics (Indoor)

The use of explosions, flashes, smoke, or flames onstage is known as proximate pyrotechnics. Generally, pyrotechnics can be divided into categories based on the device's main effects, among them bangs, flashes, flames, or smoke. A basic proximate pyrotechnic device generally consists of a container to hold the materials (of an obviously hazardous nature), a fuel, and an oxidizer, as well as additives to increase the strength of the bang or the flash.

6.2.4.2.1 Types of Proximate Pyrotechnics

The most well-known categories of proximate pyrotechnics are:

- *Flash powders*: Of all the effects used on stage, the flash effect is probably the most common. Most flash effects are created by igniting a fine-grained powder contained within a steel mortar. The resulting effect is a bright flash whose duration and color can be changed with various additives. The device in which the powder is typically used is called a *flash pot*. It should be noted that *flash paper*, unlike flash powder, is a form of *nitrocellulose* that burns quickly and completely with a bright flame, no smoke, and no ash. It is safe to use in handheld devices.
- *Noise effects*: A noise effect is often used in conjunction with either smoke or flash. It is created by igniting a suitable compound within a confined area.

- *Smoke effects*: A smoke effect is created by heating a suitable dye or other agent to just below its flashpoint to create an aerosol. Smoke is available in different colors and volumetric outputs.
- *Airburst effects*: These effects are intended to simulate outdoor aerial fireworks shells without hazardous debris. Airbursts are designed to be suspended in a lighting truss that is at least 6 (small airburst) to 8 (large airburst) meters (20–27 ft) above the ground. They produce a ball-shaped flash that is cool before reaching the lower levels or stage floor. There is very little smoke. An airburst that produces a flash of light and projects stars in all directions is called a *starburst*.
- *Gerb effects*: This effect is the same as the ground-level gerb. Gerb effects are widely variable, with plumes of usually silver or gold, durations of half a second to 30 seconds, and heights of up to 30 ft (9 m). Accompanying whistling and crackling sounds can be created as well. Waterfalls (upside-down gerbs without nozzles) are used extensively in proximate pyro.
- *Line rockets*: Also known as *grid rockets*, these are small whistling rockets that run along a steel cable. The cable must be securely fastened at each end, and is usually up to 50 m (167 ft) in length. The line rocket is attached to the line by a plastic tube and takes between 2 and 4 s to travel the 50 m.
- *Fire*: Live fire and flames are always an impressive effect no matter how they are used. *Flame cannons* shoot gigantic fireballs up to 35 ft (10.5 m) in the air. *Flame bars* can be used to emit flames from various shapes, whether it is a flat bar, arch, or a custom shape. *Flame projectors* create a small tower of fire from a fixed point. Flames can also be colored. Live fire in other forms (e.g. torches, wands, finger tips with special gloves) is sometimes used to create uniquely choreographed entertainment. Figure 6.6 illustrates fire being used at an indoor event.

6.2.4.2.2 Proximate Pyrotechnics Safety

In the wake of the disastrous fire at a Rhode Island nightclub in 2003 caused by the improper use of proximate pyrotechnics, the special events industry has been under constant pressure to demonstrate the safe use of indoor pyrotechnics. As with display fireworks, both the USA and Canada have regulations that govern the use of proximate pyrotechnics. In the USA, the most important document is the *National Fire Protection Association standard NFPA 1126: Standard for the Use of Pyrotechnics before a Proximate Audience (2006 Edition)*. Also related to this in the USA are *NFPA 1124: Code for the Manufacturing, Transportation, Storage and Retail Sale of Fireworks and Pyrotechnic Articles (2006 Edition)* and *NFPA 160: Standard for the Flame Effects before an Audience (2006 Edition)*. In Canada, the comparable governing document is the *Pyrotechnics Special Effects Manual*, put out by the ERD of Natural Resources Canada. Again, any event producers contemplating using indoor pyrotechnics should obtain a current copy of, and be fully conversant with, the applicable federal documents, as well as

FIGURE 6.6
LIVE FIRE CHOREOGRAPHY

Courtesy: Wayne Chose Photography and Pacific Show Productions, www.pacificshow. ca – Copyright 2006

local state, provincial, or municipal regulations which may differ throughout each country. To ensure proper risk management, event producers who wish to use indoor pyrotechnics must understand the following:

- *Transportation*: This is normally a federal regulation and producers should ensure that the pyrotechnics contractor is familiar with all requirements for the safe transportation of pyrotechnics products. In the USA, due to the new classification system, not all products may have the same regulations for transportation. In the USA, the applicable department is the Department of Transportation (DOT) and in Canada, the ERD, with requirements as laid out in the *Pyrotechnics Special Effects Manual*. Both countries must adhere to United Nations regulations for transportation.
- *Possession and storage*: In the USA, this is regulated by the Bureau of Alcohol, Tobacco and Firearms (BATF), and in Canada by the ERD. Particularly in the USA, because of the different new classes, possession and storage requirements are not common for all proximate pyrotechnics.
- *Licensing*: In the USA, licensing to use proximate pyrotechnics is usually a state responsibility, although sometimes a city one, with standards possibly differing throughout the country. In Canada, certification is the law and is set to federal standards by the ERD. The following are the different

types of certification for pyrotechnics special effects in Canada, obtained by taking the appropriate courses from the ERD (ERD, 2006).

- *Theatrical user*: This is an unsupervised person using basic pyrotechnics.
- *Assistant*: This is an unsupervised person using basic pyrotechnics, and all other authorized articles and powders if supervised.
- *Pyrotechnician or special effects pyrotechnician*: This certification requires extensive experience within the pyrotechnics industry. The pyrotechnician can use all authorized articles and powders.
- *Out-of-country technician*: If a technician is based outside Canada and is participating in the production of a pyrotechnics special effects event in Canada, that person must:
  - employ a certified Canadian technician of the applicable class and obtain a Visitor Card (issued on a yearly basis, plus pay required fees) upon submission of proof of competence, or
  - obtain Canadian certification through the Canadian process for qualifying technicians.

  Any producers who are planning shows with proximate pyrotechnics should always insist that the pyro contractor be fully certified.

- *Permits*: In addition to proper licensing or certification, a permit to hold the proximate pyrotechnics show on a specific date in a specific location is often required. Permit issuance is normally the responsibility of the *AHJ* which is typically the local fire department. Like licensing, permitting regulations vary greatly, from none to stringent requirements that include licensing, insurance, pre-performance testing, and the hiring of a fire watch (generally a fireman who stands by during the performance to ensure that all necessary safety precautions are followed). Permits are frequently obtained by the contracted pyrotechnics company rather than the event producer. For cases in which actual fire and open flames are used, AHJ regulations vary widely and may be governed by the type of fuel used, such as gas or propane.

As with display fireworks, there are other safety items that should be addressed when a proximate pyrotechnics show is planned.

- *Insurance*: The insurance industry is very concerned about, and may not fully understand, the scope and importance of proximate pyrotechnics in special events. It has proven to be difficult for producers to obtain sufficient – or even any – insurance for events that incorporate pyrotechnics, yet all local regulations and universally most contracts require insurance (the standard being $5 million liability), with all parties being co-insured with each other. When it is available, it is often extremely expensive. The apparent overreaction of the insurance industry to the Rhode Island disaster of 2003 indicates a need for continued vigilance on the part of producers and the demonstration of a solid understanding of what is required for the safe conduct of a proximate pyrotechnics show. This goes as far as understanding the subtle differences between classes of pyrotechnics (e.g.

between flash paper and flash powder) and the relative hazards of each – or lack thereof – so that they may be explained to insurance companies and permit-granting authorities to minimize the potential for having a permit rejected or for having overly costly insurance demanded. It certainly behooves all producers and pyrotechnics companies to document and have readily available: all necessary licenses, permits, purchase approvals, site and venue plans; production schedules and details of how the pyro will be used; emergency procedures; permissions from venues and proof of compliance with their requirements; and a complete listing of all pyrotechnics to be used, including their accompanying *Material Safety Data Sheets* (MSDS) and *Product Safety Data Sheets* (PSDS). Professional pyro companies should understand this and should be prepared.

- *Venue concerns*: Indoor venues are also very worried about the disaster potential of indoor pyrotechnics. The venue must be given all the necessary information about the show, and producers must ensure that any décor or stage set pieces and any flammable parts of the venue or the venue décor (e.g. drapes) are completely flame treated or the performance moved to safe distances.

For producers, the key to the safe conduct of a pyrotechnics show is to completely understand and follow all federal, state/provincial, and municipal regulations, to be prepared with necessary documentation, and to cooperate fully with the appropriate authorities.

PRODUCTION WAR STORY: THREE PRETTY VOCALISTS AND SOME VERY SCARY PYRO

We were to culminate the formal segment of our railroad-themed dinner event with a pyrotechnic segue into an entertainment program beginning with three beautiful female vocalists. The segue was to begin with a historical character in costume striking a giant gold spike, a symbolic representation of both the past and the driving of the last spike. From the spike, a single line rocket would travel to the venue ceiling where it would hit a modern satellite, symbolizing the future, from which three more line rockets would travel down to the stage, ending up at the top of each of three magic reveal doors. From the doors would emerge the three vocalists through the smoke created by three flashpots, to begin their show, fittingly with the song, 'Fire.'

This all happened exactly as planned and was greeted by enthusiastic applause from the audience. However, there was a noticeable momentary uncertainty and slight staggering on the part of the vocalists, as they emerged in their glamour through the smoke and began their first song somewhat hesitatingly, which was unusual as they had always been extremely professional on stage.

Continued

6.2.5 Atmospherics

This is the name applied to artificial snow, wind, and rain. Companies who deal in atmospherics, usually movie special effects firms, supply specialized machinery to create these natural elements. Although not used extensively in special events, there are occasions for atmospherics when they can add an element of realism to theme events. The two most common atmospherics used in events are snow and water effects.

6.2.5.1 *Snow*

Artificial snow can be an impressive special effect as a static part of set dressing or as a dynamic effect when falling from above. Thanks to the movie industry, there are now a number of different but highly effective ways to achieve these effects (over 140, according to Mike Kaerne of Holly North, a special effects company in Vancouver, BC). The ones most commonly used for special events are the following:

- *Falling snow that remains on the ground*: The old way to achieve this effect was plastic snow. Unfortunately, it was not fire resistant and the dust from it could cause breathing difficulties, a big problem when it required blowing with a fan. New technology has produced products that are composed of rice and wheat derivatives, making them biodegradable, non-toxic, non-slippery, and fire retardant. This snow is blown out of snow machines that incorporate internal fans and super-quiet operation. It can also be blown farther using additional fans.

- *Falling snow that evaporates*: Also blown out of snow machines with fans, the secret to this product is in the composition of the fluid that turns into 'snow.' According to Kaerne, the snow is really soap bubbles that are created when the snow fluid is blown through a modulator inside the snow machine. With the new machines, the size of the flakes and the fall time can be controlled by varying an onboard switch and adding an external fan respectively. These machines can be *daisy-chained* (linked together) and controlled using DMX. One machine typically covers an area of 10 ft × 20 ft (3 m × 6 m). The choice of fluid affects the dryness of the flakes and hence the length of time before complete evaporation. The snow produced is biodegradable, non-toxic, and flame retardant.
- *Static snow*. For permanent snow cover on sets, stage, floor, or ground, the most realistic is a 'snow blanket.' This material is 1½ in. (3.8 cm) thick, and comes in rolls 5 ft (1.5 m) wide and approximately 100 ft (30 m) long. It helps to dress background or distant areas needing large coverage. Foreground areas can be dressed with different paper snow that looks extremely realistic, but which must be treated with fire retardant.

In addition to snow, there are new products that mimic ice and icicles that can be used to form ice walls, ice slush, and ice carvings with a more realistic appearance than simple Plexiglas.

6.2.5.2   Water Effects

When one mentions water effects, for many people what immediately comes to mind is either the old dancing water fountains of the 1950s or rain effects used in movies. The technology of today, however, has moved water to an entertainment genre almost in itself. Advances in nozzle and pump systems, which now allow water to be distributed in very small jets at high pressure, have enabled larger and more sophisticated devices. These advances have manifested themselves in several impressive ways.

6.2.5.2.1   Water Curtains

Water curtains (or *water scrims*) are created by very narrow streams of water falling from distribution piping. The water is caught in a trough and recirculated using pumps, back through the upper distribution piping. The distribution piping requires a truss to be set up for support. The curtain is then used as a projection medium for lighting, video, cinema, still, or laser images, although the projection is best from the rear due to the physics of projecting through water droplets. Water curtains have many different applications: back drops or sets for stages; corridor water walkways; part of exhibition stands; and as part of reveal sequences in which it is possible to turn off individual sections of the water instantaneously, allowing cars, people, or any type of product to be uniquely revealed. See Figure 6.7 for an example of a water curtain stage backdrop. Water curtains are sometimes called *rain curtains*, although these tend to be smaller with fewer nozzles and used primarily as architectural enhancements.

FIGURE 6.7

EXAMPLE OF A WATER CURTAIN

Courtesy: Mirage Water Works, www.miragewaterworks.com

6.2.5.2.2 Water Screens

Also known as *aquascreens*, water screens, unlike water curtains, are used only outdoors. They work basically like upside-down water curtains and can be set at heights ranging up to 30 m (100 ft) and widths up to about 100 m (330 ft). A translucent screen composed of tiny jets of water is produced by a pressurized, recirculating, submerged system of semi-circular nozzles which can be installed on a barge, on a lake, or in the sea either in a tank already in place or as a custom installation. Many systems are temporary. The screen is invisible when not in use, appearing and vanishing at will. Another attraction is the relief effect of the images, which the eye perceives in three dimensions. A dark background is normally required and all images, including computer graphics, still images, video, movies, automated lighting, and lasers, can be projected. The downfall of outdoor water screens is their susceptibility to wind.

6.2.5.2.3 Fountains

Using new and improved technology, fountains have also made a comeback. With finer jets and computerized control, they can now be designed to augment other effects such as the water screens, lasers, pyrotechnics, and automated lighting, and even live entertainment, indoors or out. They can be customized for any particular show. Fountains can range in heights up to about 30 m (100 ft) and can be choreographed to live or recorded music. For indoor use, a portable tank must be used.

6.2.5.2.4 Other Water Effects

Some of the older standbys from movie special effects are now regularly used in special events, according to Mike Kaerne of Vancouver special effects company Holly North.

- *Indoor rain*: The effect of real rain is achieved with similar but simpler technology than a water curtain. Water flows through a metal piping grid system suspended on trussing, but under lower pressure than with a water curtain. The grid is designed with random holes so that the flow produced becomes droplets rather than streams of water, thus resembling rain. The water can be either recirculated (more expensive), drained through venue floor drains using a garden hose, or pumped out. The main difficulty with rain is that it requires twice the catchment area than throw area due to dispersion as the water falls.
- *Jungle mist*: This is a simple and inexpensive effect with high impact that creates the impression of a steamy jungle or rain forest. It is simply a fine spray that spreads over a stage or other area yet leaves little moisture buildup.
- *Custom water effects*: Custom fountains, jets of water, and water labyrinths are just some of many different applications for water effects. An example of this customization has been created by the Living Garden in which a live statue becomes a decorative fountain with water streams emanating from her fingers and head.

At present, there are no known safety regulations or standards for the atmospherics described; however, possible risks might be water damage to materials or décor as a result of overspray or leaks.

PRODUCTION CHALLENGES

1. Explain to your clients why you do not recommend repeating a streamer cannon effect at the end of their presentation after doing it at the beginning.
2. You are planning to begin a stage show with thick fog rolling over the stage and disappearing over the downstage edge into the front rows of the audience. Describe two different methods of achieving this effect.
3. Describe in general terms how a show laser works.
4. The local fire department demands that you obtain a permit for a large outdoor fireworks show that your client wants as a farewell for 5000 convention attendees. It is to be held in one of the city's parks. The fire chief wishes to meet with you as this is the first time you have ever done such a show. List in detail all the applicable documents that should be included in your presentation and what you should know to convince him that you are aware of the regulations and risks involved.
5. You are planning a grand entrance to a winter-themed event and want guests to walk through a forest of snow-covered live evergreen trees with snow drifts all around, in the middle of a heavy snowstorm. Explain how you would achieve this effect.

REFERENCES

American Pyrotechnics Association (APA) (2004). *Glossary of Pyrotechnic Terms*. Retrieved July 3, 2006, from http://www.americanpyro.com/Safety%20Info/glossary.html.

Brain, M. (2006). *How Fireworks Work*. Retrieved July 3, 2006, from http://people.howstuffworks.com/fireworks.htm.

Dryer, I. (October–December 2005). Show Basics: Small Beam of Light Leads to Dazzling Images. *The Laserist*, *16*(3). Retrieved June 30, 2006, from http://www.laserist.org/Laserist/showbasics_2.html.

ELH Communications Ltd. (2004). Foggers and Smoke Machines. *Epanorama.net*. Retrieved June 29, 2006, from http://www.epanorama.net/links/lights.html#fogger.

Explosives Regulatory Division (ERD), National Resources Canada (2006). *Education*. Retrieved July 5, 2006, from http://www.nrcan.gc.ca/mms/explosif/edu/edu_e.htm.

Helmenstine, A.M. (2006). Chemistry of Firework Colors: A Marriage of Art and Science. *Chemistry*. Retrieved July 3, 2006, from http://chemistry.about.com/library/weekly/aa062701a.htm?once=true&.

International Laser Display Association (ILDA) (2006a). *Discover Lasers: Why Lasers?* Retrieved June 30, 2006, from http://www.laserist.org/discover_lasers.htm.

International Laser Display Association (ILDA) (2006b). *Technology: How We Do It*. Retrieved June 30, 2006, from http://www.laserist.org/technology.htm.

Jaworski, J. (2003). *The Secret to Creating Real 'WOW' Power at Your Events*. Source and exact date unknown.

Mueller, B. (October–December 2005). Show Basics: Making Light. *The Laserist*, *16*(3). Retrieved June 30, 2006, from http://www.laserist.org/Laserist/showbasics_4.html.

Plaser Spectacles, Inc. (2003). *Factors in Designing Safe and Legal Laser Light Shows*. Retrieved June 30, 2006, from http://www.laserspectacles.com/pages/safety.htm.

Walsh, T. (October–December 2005). Show Basics: Atmospheric Effects Are True Show-stoppers, Indoors Or Out. *The Laserist*, *16*(3). Retrieved June 30, 2006, from http://www.laserist.org/Laserist/showbasics_1.html.

Wikipedia contributors (July 2, 2006). Firework. In *Wikipedia, The Free Encyclopedia*. Retrieved July 3, 2006, from http://en.wikipedia.org/w/index.php?title=Firework&oldid=61631557.

STAGING

LEARNING OUTCOMES

After reading this chapter, you will be able to:

1. Understand the language that is shared between theater and special events.
2. Describe the three main types of special events stages and how they are constructed.
3. Describe the options and accessories available for stages.
4. Explain how to determine the correct size of a stage for a given purpose.
5. Describe the different types of stage curtains.
6. Understand how stage sets are designed and how they can be used to enhance a special event.

What is it about a stage that can cause exhilaration one minute and terror the next? Why is it that by physically raising a person or group of persons above the level of other people, the perception of that person or group by the other people instantly changes? Quite simply, over the centuries, we as human beings have come to subconsciously equate positions of power and higher social status than ourselves with a physical difference in height. Most political and religious leaders have always spoken publicly from raised positions or platforms, and hence we consider anyone who speaks or performs from such a position as special in our eyes. We attribute more credibility and importance to their utterances, whether those utterances are serious or humorous, true or false.

In this chapter, we examine not the psychology of being on a stage, but the humble construction of that structure that has been so supportive of human social and theatrical drama since ancient times. In so doing, we cover the following topics:

- Language of the stage
- Types and construction of stages
- Placement and sizing of stages
- Stage draping
- Stage sets
- Risk and safety.

7.1   THE LANGUAGE OF THE STAGE

In special events, nowhere is our shared heritage with the world of theater more obvious than in staging, and we have borrowed extensively from theater terminology. The first instance of this is the style of stages, which go all the way back to the Greeks. The second important instance is in the directions for performers and those using the stage.

7.1.1   Styles of Stages

There are three main styles of stages that are used in theater with accompanying similar, but modified, types in special events. It is useful to know what these are and how they are constructed:

- *Thrust stage*: The stage projects into, and is surrounded on three sides by, the audience. The fourth side contains the scenery or backdrop. Entrances to the stage may be made from backstage or through the audience and up onto the front of the stage (Figure 7.1). This type of stage most closely resembles the ones commonly used for special events, although the backstage entrances are sometimes not used as there is no backstage area available, and usually the audience only surrounds the stage on one side (the front), unless space is in short supply.
- *Proscenium stage*: In this configuration, the audience watches the action through a rectangular opening (the *proscenium arch*) that resembles a picture frame. Scenery or a backdrop typically fills the space behind and upstage of, the actors or performers. Entrances to the performing space are made from backstage (Figure 7.2). This type of stage is most often found in modern theaters, but occasionally a reasonable facsimile is constructed for special events by using curtains to mask the backstage area that extend outward to venue side walls from the fronts or near fronts of the stage. The proscenium arch per se, however, is non-existent.

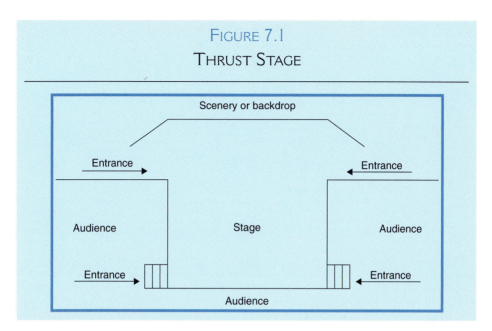

FIGURE 7.1
THRUST STAGE

Scenery or backdrop

Entrance

Entrance

Audience

Stage

Audience

Entrance

Entrance

Audience

Courtesy: Doug Matthews

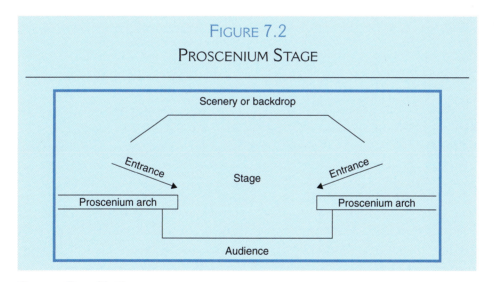

FIGURE 7.2
PROSCENIUM STAGE

Scenery or backdrop

Entrance

Stage

Entrance

Proscenium arch

Proscenium arch

Audience

Courtesy: Doug Matthews

■ *Arena stage*: This type of stage – sometimes called a *theater-in-the-round* –
is completely surrounded by the audience and any entrances must be
made through the audience to the stage (Figure 7.3). Stairs to the stage
may be placed in the center of each side, on corners, or any other location desired. In special events, this type of stage is most often found in
concert settings; however, even there, the stage more often resembles a
thrust stage configuration. Occasionally, an arena-type stage will be
constructed for other special events, but audio, lighting, and sight-line

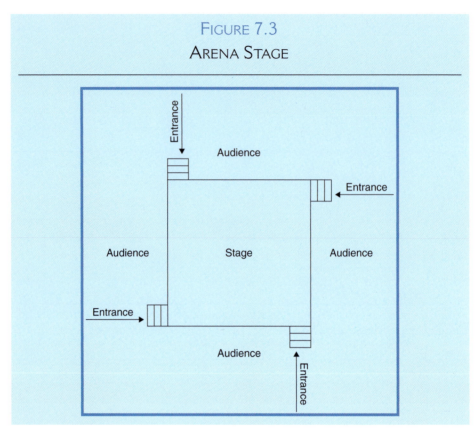

Figure 7.3
Arena Stage

Entrance

Audience

Entrance

Audience   Stage   Audience

Entrance

Entrance

Audience

Courtesy: Doug Matthews

challenges can pose problems. There are usually no scenic elements on this type of stage.

7.1.2   Stage Directions

The second area of theater language that we share is stage directions. Production of an event with entertainment and action on a stage involves constant references to specific locations on the stage. To properly direct the action, whether it is the simple movement of lights, re-locating a microphone, or movement of people, all participants must understand the directions. It has become standard custom to give stage directions as if one is on the stage looking at the audience. Hence, stage left is to the left and stage right is to the right, downstage is in front, and upstage is behind a person on the stage. These same directions provide the reference if one is off the stage as well. The terms *upstage* and *downstage* probably evolved in the 16th or 17th century during the era of *raked* stages which were purposely sloped stages built that way to create the illusion of depth. Figure 7.4 shows these directions.

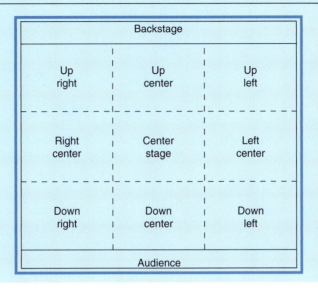

FIGURE 7.4
STAGE DIRECTIONS

	Backstage	
Up right	Up center	Up left
Right center	Center stage	Left center
Down right	Down center	Down left
	Audience	

Courtesy: Doug Matthews

7.2   TYPES AND CONSTRUCTION OF STAGES

Temporary staging has come a long way from the rickety pageant wagons of medieval England and the makeshift platforms of itinerant Commedia Dell'arte players in Renaissance Italy. Most staging used for special events today is one of three types: manufactured decks and support systems, custom stages, or mobile stages. We will examine each of these types and their construction, and then review common accessories for stages and other optional indoor structures.

7.2.1   Manufactured Decks and Support Systems

This type of stage comes in standard sizes of *decks* (sometimes called *risers* or *platforms*) that connect with each other to form larger surfaces (stages). Depending on the specific manufacturer and the design, they may have legs as an integral part of them or separate legs that attach to them. Typical rectangular deck sizes are 8 ft × 4 ft (244 cm × 122 cm), 4 ft × 4 ft (122 cm × 122 cm), or 8 ft × 6 ft (244 cm × 183 cm). Not all manufacturers make all the different sizes and, due to proprietary designs, decks from one manufacturer are usually not compatible with decks from a different manufacturer. This means that it is unlikely that a large stage could be built using decking from two different manufacturers. Some manufacturers have begun to make decks in unusual shapes that allow for a larger variety of overall stage shapes than traditional rectangles. Notably, for example, the Prolyte Products Group in the Netherlands, now makes trapezoidal, triangular, quarter-circle, and curved sectional 'donut' riser shapes that enable the construction of static round stages, oblong stages, triangular stages, and almost any other configuration desired.

Manufactured decks typically consist of an extruded aluminum frame into which is fitted thick plywood sheeting, or a sandwich construction of cellulose honeycomb between thin sheets of plywood. Total thicknesses vary between about 3 and 4 in. (7.5 and 10 cm). Manufacturers usually offer optional surface treatment for the decks in the form of carpeting, varnished or unfinished wood, slip-resistant polypropylene, or fiberglass sheeting. Modern decking also has fixed holes in the top corners that will accept proprietary safety railings, as well as proprietary fittings on the underside for legs and supporting frames. Some decks are even reversible.

Supporting legs and frames for staging are as different as the riser surface shapes. Again, depending on the manufacturer, the legs may be fixed in height or have variable height settings. There are two reasonably standard height systems in use, one that works with 6 in. increments (e.g. standard leg heights of 6, 12, 18, 24, 30, 36, 42, 48 in.) and one that works with 8 in. increments (e.g. standard leg heights of 8, 16, 24, 32, 40, 48 in.), with comparable metric sizes in 15 and 20 cm increments. Legs can be the only means of support, with a single leg supporting each corner, or they can be part of a larger frame system that incorporates horizontal and diagonal cross bracing. Many legs come with height-adjustable feet as well as more continuously variable height adjustments using cotter pins or special screws with indents at 2 in. (50 mm) increments. Legs and frames are usually constructed of extruded aluminum. Some of the frames telescope and rotate for easier storage and some, besides telescoping, are permanently attached to stage decks for more efficient setup. Hotels and conference centers often purchase manufactured staging for use in special events, but event managers are usually charged for their setup and use.

These types of manufactured stages are often used for purposes other than entertainment or ceremonial. Thanks to the variety of leg lengths, they can be perfect for temporary tiered flooring for seating or dining to afford audiences or guests better visibility for action taking place on other surfaces. Figure 7.5 illustrates such use.

Temporary circular stages are sometimes mounted on tracks and bearing assemblies and connected to motors that allow them to rotate. This is often seen in trade show situations to demonstrate products. It can also be very effective for entertainment presentations to achieve quick changes of stage sets; however, it is costly and for large stages must be strictly designed to permit sufficient loading and to determine the correct motor size.

FIGURE 7.5

EXAMPLE OF STAGING USED FOR TIERED
DINING AT AN ICE SHOW

Courtesy: Lighting by Q1 Production Technologies; event produced by Pacific Destinations Inc.

7.2.2   Custom Stages

The ingenuity of event producers and expectations of clients will always maintain a demand for customized staging, for shapes and sizes that are not achievable with manufactured systems. In this particular genre of staging, specialized staging companies come into their own. There are numerous companies in the industry that build stages out of wood and customize them with paint or other finishes and surface materials. Often these companies also provide complete set-building capabilities as well, which we will discuss in Section 7.5. The advantage of custom staging is that it can be built to fit into any space, of any size or shape, and of any theme or material. Some examples of situations where customized staging may be used are:

- For covering of awkwardly shaped or dangerous surfaces. This might be ground with rocks, gardens, or other obstructions that cannot be covered easily by manufactured staging, or that is at too great a slope. It might also include water such as swimming pools or lakes.
- To accomplish a unique design for an event. This is most often used in concert situations and for major award ceremonies where the set and stage design must be original and attention grabbing.

- For large stages in situations where there is insufficient manufactured staging available or for which the rental of such staging would be excessively expensive. This might occur again in a concert setting or in a convention facility that does not own sufficient staging.
- To replace manufactured staging which may not be strong enough in a certain situation. For example, this might be to support heavy cars or trucks at a product launch.
- To fit a stage into an awkward space. If an event is being held in an unusual venue with architecture that does not lend itself to the standard rectangular staging, custom-fitted staging may be necessary.
- To extend an existing stage over existing seating in a theater or arena. This might entail constructing additional oddly shaped decking to butt against an existing stage, or to fit over seating that does not allow the regular spacing or fitting of support frames and legs of manufactured staging.
- To create a unique themed stage. A stage may need to be constructed that does not even resemble a traditional stage in order to fit into a particular event theme. See for example, Figure 7.6, a stage that was especially constructed for a jungle-themed Bar Mitzvah, and built to resemble the

FIGURE 7.6
EXAMPLE OF A THEMED STAGE

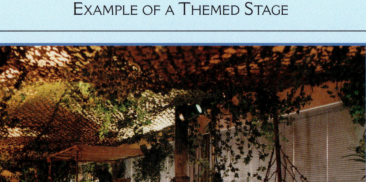

Courtesy: Alan Gough, www.visionmasters.net, and Pacific Show Productions, www.pacific show.ca – Copyright 2006

African Queen riverboat from the Humphrey Bogart movie of the same name. This stage was used for presentations and for a DJ.

7.2.3 Mobile Stages

Mobile staging has come a long way from medieval pageant wagons. Typically used for outdoor events, although also viable indoors, an entire series of easily erectable mobile stages is now available from several manufacturers in stage surface sizes ranging from about 24 ft × 20 ft (7.3 m × 6.1 m) to about 50 ft × 40 ft (15.3 m × 12.2 m). These stages are designed to fit entirely into and as part of a towable trailer. An onboard hydraulic system is used to literally fold the stage surface and roof into the trailer. These systems come equipped with trussing stressed to support full lighting and audio systems. With most, there is a variety of accessories and options available, such as stage extensions, roof canopy extensions to cover equipment (e.g. lights on the trussing), stairs, ramps, safety rails, fire-retardant wind walls, vertical and horizontal banner supports, A-V screen support, generator, and heating and air conditioning. These mobile systems have greatly increased the efficiency of technical setups. One such system is illustrated in Figure 7.7 which shows the stage being transported (left photo) and then in side view at an event (right photo). Note some of the included accessories: stairs, stage extension, roof extension to support the line array speakers, and a fire-retardant wind wall to cover the back.

FIGURE 7.7
MOBILE STAGE SETUP

Courtesy: Briere Production Group Inc., www.bpg-inc.ca and http://www.flickr.com/photo_zoom.gne?id=303152310&size=o

7.2.4 Accessories for Stages and Other Optional Structures

Staging for special events is more than just decks and legs. Particularly with safety in mind, there are accessories that make for safer work on stages and easier access to them, specifically stairs, ramps, safety railing, and deck covering. As well, there are other indoor temporary structures that fit easier classification under staging options, namely dance floors and choral/band risers.

7.2.4.1   Stairs

All stage manufacturers provide stairs that match their decking and leg heights in design and size. Some are equipped with wheels or casters that tilt out of the way when the stairs are in use. Most stairs have holes or attachment points to accept safety railing. For safety, the edges of stairs and stages are often marked with bright masking tape for better visibility.

7.2.4.2   Ramps

Some manufacturers provide optional ramps for wheelchair and disabled access. Occasionally, custom ramps need to be built to provide this access. In the US, all such ramps must conform to *ADA* (Americans with Disabilities Act) *Standards for Accessible Design, Section 4.8*, which specifies slope, width, landing, and handrail requirements.

7.2.4.3   Safety Railing

In the interest of good risk management, it is becoming increasingly necessary to provide safety railing (also called *guardrails*) on access stairs, ramps, and the backs and sides of stages themselves. Most safety railing is constructed of tubular steel and comes in heights of 39 in. (1000 mm) to 42 in., depending on whether it is manufactured to metric or Imperial standards, the lower height being the metric version. Railing comes in fixed or adjustable lengths, depending on the manufacturer. Most railing attaches to the stage surface in one of two ways: by fitting *spigots* into pre-drilled holes on the stage corners then placing the railing posts over the spigots; or by attaching a clamp or gripper-type adaptor with a spigot built onto it, to the stage surface that then accepts the railing post. Different railing designs have different load ratings and these should be checked before installation to ensure they are adequate for anticipated use. For example, one manufacturer (Prolyte) has two versions, one that is light duty and can resist only 30 kg/m (20 lb/ft) of horizontal loading, and one heavy-duty version that can resist 100–200 kg/m (67–134 lb/ft) of horizontal loading. Any event in a public area should have only heavy-duty railing with a high load rating installed.

7.2.4.4   Deck Surface Covers

Besides the finishes already discussed for stage surfaces, occasionally performers may demand that certain surfaces be provided for them. Dancers, especially ballet and contemporary, fall into this category. They require a surface that is forgiving yet is not too slippery and they may request a surface material generically known as a *Marley* carpet or flooring. This type of flooring is composed of a layer of mineral fiber interply sandwiched between two layers of thin PVC (polyvinyl chloride) with a smooth finish. The flooring comes in rolls of 98 ft (30 m), widths of 78.5 in. (2 m), and a thickness of 0.08 in. (2 mm). It must be rolled out on top of an existing stage (hard surfaced, not carpeted) and taped together. The name comes from the company that originally manufactured it, but it is now sold by Harlequin Floors (www.harlequinfloors.com) under several different brand names. If dancers must dance on an existing stage, their preference is normally a smooth wooden surface with no uneven joints. This may mean that joints between deck sections must be taped to cover irregularities.

7.2.4.5 Dance Floors

Dancers may also request a hard surface for tap dancing that can often be provided simply by placing sections of wooden dance flooring on top of existing carpeted staging. Standard dance floors typically come in 3 ft × 3 ft (910 mm × 910 mm in Europe), 2 ft × 4 ft, 3 ft × 4 ft, or 4 ft × 4 ft (1220 mm × 1220 mm in Europe) sections (depending on the manufacturer) and interlock via tongue and groove aluminum edges on each section, sometimes with additional screws for extra safety. They also have interlocking beveled edges that eliminate the possibility of tripping. Finishes are usually smooth varnished wood or painted. Some have vinyl surfaces with simulated wood grain. Plexiglas surfaces and underlit LED (light-emitting diode) floors are also available, as mentioned in Chapter 5. Custom floors, like stages, can be made to almost any size and finish. There are a few manufacturers that make 'sprung dance floors' which are really just shock absorbing, closed cell foam blocks that suspend the wooden floor above an existing, hard uncompromising surface.

If a dance floor is actually being used for dancing for guests, the correct size must be determined. One starts by using the educated assumption that only about 30–50 percent of the guests will be dancing at any given time. Next, the average area occupied by a single dancer (e.g. 2–3 ft² per person or 0.2–0.3 m² per person) is multiplied by the number of people. Let us assume for example, using Imperial measurements, that the total number of persons attending an event is 500 and that it is a crowd that enjoys dancing so we can use the high figure of 50 percent of them being on the dance floor at any given time. This means the dance floor area required will be between 500 and 750 ft² (depending on whether we use the 2 or 3 ft² per person assumption). Using another assumption that the dance floor available is comprised of 3 ft × 3 ft sections (9 ft² per section), then the total number of sections of dance floor required will be 55–84 (i.e. 500/9 at the lower end of size, to 750/9 at the upper end of size). If we wanted to make a square dance floor using the larger size for safety, then each side would be nine sections long or 81 ft, for an actual total area of 729 ft². How did we arrive at this number? First, we calculated the square root of the maximum number of sections we need since we want a square dance floor (i.e. $\sqrt{84} = 9.17$), and the closest whole number to this is 9 so we will use 9 sections per side.

Instead of opting for a square dance floor, if we want to match the width of the dance floor to the width of the stage and the stage is 24 ft across, then the width of the dance floor will be eight sections (24/3) since each section is 3 ft wide. Thus the length of the other side of the dance floor will be 10 sections or 30 ft (i.e. 84 sections/8 sections = 10.5 or 750 ft²/24 ft = approximately 31.25 ft or 10 sections of 3 ft wide flooring). Note that the numbers are rounded to obtain the closest number of sections.

7.2.4.6 Choral and Band Risers

Frequently, events utilize large choirs or choral groups, concert bands, and symphony orchestras as part of their entertainment programs. These large musical groups usually require specially designed risers for their members in order for them to easily see their director/conductor, and for the audience to see all of them. These risers are positioned on top of the event staging, but occasionally may be placed directly on the floor. Although the risers may be custom-made, they are more often manufactured in standard sizes. These types of risers are constructed similarly to stage decks in that they have separate decks that are attached to legs (primarily steel) and support frames (steel or aluminum). They can be configured in rectangular or curved shapes using pie-shaped sections of decking. Usually, the deck rise is 7 or 8 in. (18 or 20 cm) and there are three or four decks in total, giving a total rise of between 21 and 32 in. (53–80 cm). Deck widths are usually 16–18 in. (40–45 cm) for choral risers and 36–48 in. (90–120 cm) for band risers. Deck surfaces are often reversible with one side being non-slip textured polypropylene and the other carpeted. Decks themselves are usually laminated honeycomb. The entire assemblies fold up or dismantle into individual sections and are portable. Some are equipped with their own wheels.

7.3 PLACEMENT AND SIZING OF STAGES

In Chapter 1 we discussed placement of stages with respect to the effective presentation of entertainment. The same options hold true for all other types of presentations, namely against a wall, in corners, or in the center of a venue. For that matter, a stage or stages can be placed anywhere in a venue that is convenient for those using it and those viewing the onstage activities. What is a little more complicated is determining the correct size for the stage.

7.3.1 Horizontal Size

Determining the correct area of a stage is sometimes more art than science. Unfortunately, event planners and managers often do not give it enough consideration. The horizontal area must accommodate any and all activities that will take place on it. Even though speeches may occupy 3 h and 55 min out of a 4 h program with only one speaker appearing at a time, but there is a finale with a 12-member dance ensemble, the stage has to be big enough from the outset to accommodate the dance ensemble. In other words, it must be large enough to allow for the activity that will require the most space, no matter how important or how long that activity is in relation to the rest of the staged program.

For most activities, there are no golden rules. Every performing group usually has a minimum size of stage that will accommodate their performance and they should be consulted prior to event setup to ensure that the properly sized stage is ordered. Generally, for speakers at a lectern, a minimum of 15–20 ft^2 (1.4–1.8 m^2) is required. Unfortunately, if the event consists of only speeches by one or two persons at a time such as an awards ceremony, having a small stage might not automatically be the correct choice. The stage size in relation to the size of the venue and also in relation to the size of the stage set and any additional décor or audio-visual equipment must be taken into consideration. For example, if an awards ceremony is to take place with a stage set up in the middle of a 150 ft (45 m) long wall, and two large A-V screens with surrounding drape are to extend to the side walls on either side of the stage, it does not make good design sense to have a stage that is only 8 or 12 ft (2.4 or 3.6 m) wide as it is completely out of proportion to the remainder of the room's décor and the scale of the entire venue. The stage must reflect the correct proportion, and should be more in the order of about one-third of the total width of the venue or 50ft (15 m) wide, in spite of the small number of persons occupying it at any given time. Part of the extra space may also be taken up purposely with a well-designed stage set.

In the case of musical groups, it is better to compute an accurate size of stage based on fairly static area requirements for individual musicians. As outlined in Chapter 8 on Tenting, the following guidelines are repeated here for calculating stage sizes for musical groups:

- *Electronic rhythm instruments*: 25–30 ft^2 (2.5 m^2) per musician (e.g. guitar, bass, keyboards) including amplifiers and equipment.
- *Acoustic instruments*: 10–15 ft^2 (1.3 m^2) per musician (e.g. brass, woodwinds, strings) including chairs and music stands.
- *Drummer*: 50–70 ft^2 (6 m^2), including all equipment. Drummers are often elevated on a small riser, usually 8 ft × 8 ft × 6 to 12 in. high (244 cm × 244 cm × 30 cm), for better visualization.
- *Spinet piano*: 30 ft^2 (2.5 m^2).
- *Full grand piano*: 100 ft^2 (9 m^2).
- *Vocalists*: 10 ft^2 (1 m^2) per vocalist if backup and not moving too much; 30–50 ft^2 (4–5 m^2) per vocalist for a lead vocalist, and possibly more if part of a show band.

As an example using Imperial units, a five-piece regular dance band with a single lead singer, a drummer, a keyboard player, a bass player, and a guitarist, would require approximately 155–210 ft^2 of space using the variable area extremes from the above list. This would equate to a stage with horizontal dimensions of 16 ft × 12 ft for the absolute minimum-sized stage, and at least three choices for the stage that would accommodate the band in a roomier manner. These possibilities would be 16 ft × 16 ft, 20 ft × 12 ft, or 20 ft × 16 ft, all assuming single riser dimensions of 8 ft × 4 ft. Since most musicians do not like to play beside a drummer but rather in front, and since a drum kit is approximately 8 ft deep, this means that the drummer occupies essentially the back or upstage 8 ft of the stage alone. Thus, there must still be at least 105 ft² of stage area remaining (155 ft² minimum less 50 ft² minimum for the drummer). If the stage size is 20 ft × 12 ft, that means there is only the front or upstage 4 ft remaining for the rest of the band to play on, a total of only 80 ft² of space (i.e. 20 ft wide × 4 ft deep, after subtracting the upstage 8 ft occupied by the drummer), which is inadequate. Therefore, the correct stage size should be 20 ft wide × 16 ft deep, which would leave an ample 160 ft² (i.e. 20 ft wide × 8 ft deep, after subtracting the upstage 8 ft occupied by the drummer) for the rest of the band. Although this sounds complicated, it is an exercise that a producer must go through if an adequately sized stage is to be provided for the entertainment planned.

In addition to drum risers for dance or show groups, larger musical ensembles such as symphony orchestras or big bands often specify tiered riser sections on top of the regular stage for the different orchestra sections, such as percussion, strings, brass, or woodwinds. The height and horizontal size of these risers is usually determined by the orchestra leader, and specified in their contract rider.

7.3.2   Vertical Size

The first assumption in determining the height of a stage is that the special event is not being held in a venue with a permanent stage such as a theater. Otherwise, the height is dependent on the size of the audience, whether they will be sitting or standing, and whether the ground or floor is level. We will assume in this section that the surface is level. Standing audiences can occur for concerts, receptions, dances, trade shows, product launches, and others. Seated audiences can occur at dining events, award ceremonies, opening and closing ceremonies, meetings, and numerous others. We will deal with each of these.

7.3.2.1   Standing Audience

In order to make an educated determination of the correct height for a standing audience, we must make some assumptions of human characteristic body dimensions and typical spacing between persons in a standing crowd. Using Imperial units and for purposes of this exercise only, let us assume that the average person is conservatively 5 ft 11 in. tall and that in a standing crowd, people will tend to space themselves no closer than 2 ft apart. Also, we must assume that persons in the crowd are able to maneuver themselves sufficiently to see over the heads of other persons two rows ahead of them (i.e. about 4 ft in front of them). If we further assume that at minimum any persons in the audience must see at least the top part of the head of an average person standing on and near the front of the stage, then we can draw some sight lines to assist us with calculating the correct stage height that will relate directly to the size of the crowd. Figure 7.8 does just this. Note that at 25 ft away from the stage, a person is able to see the top part of the head of someone onstage if the stage is 3 ft in height. Likewise, at 50 ft from the stage, the height must be raised to 4 ft to achieve similar visibility and at 100 ft away from the stage, the height must be at least 8 ft for the same visibility. It is clear from this explanation that given a specific audience size and venue size, a stage should be constructed of sufficient height to enable the entire audience to view the stage in the worst case scenario. For example, even in the case of a standup reception at which there will be stage entertainment, the assumption must be made that during the entertainment, attendees will crowd the stage to the extent that they will be about 2 ft apart, even though when the entertainment is **not** on, this may not be true.

This is dramatically illustrated in Figure 7.9 with the eye-level view from a person standing approximately nine rows back from a 3-foot high stage during a dance. The visible portion of the persons onstage is approximately only from the waist up, which equates almost perfectly to the calculated sight lines of Figure 7.8. As a matter of interest, it is usually better to have band stages – or at least the lead vocalists – a little lower (e.g. 24–36 in. or 60–90 cm high) than might be optimum for visibility, as it adds to the intimacy between the band and dancers.

7.3.2.2 Seated Audience

For a seated audience, the height is also determined by the ability to see over the head of a person sitting directly across a table (if dining) or directly in front by two rows (if seated). We will illustrate the principle by using a dining situation in which diners are seated at 72 in. diameter round tables, separated by 10 ft. Exactly the same principle applies as for the

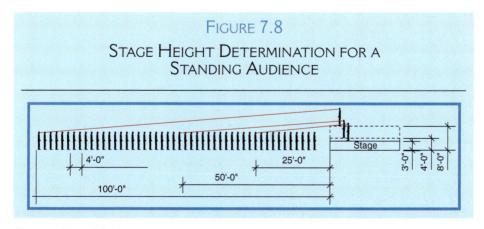

FIGURE 7.8

STAGE HEIGHT DETERMINATION FOR A
STANDING AUDIENCE

Courtesy: Doug Matthews

FIGURE 7.9
SIGHT LINES TO A STAGE IN A STANDING CROWD

Courtesy: Pacific Show Productions, www.pacificshow.ca – Copyright 2006

FIGURE 7.10
STAGE HEIGHT DETERMINATION FOR A SEATED AUDIENCE

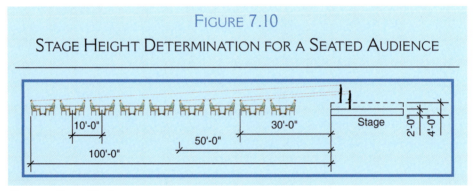

Courtesy: Doug Matthews

standing scenario, except that, because the distance from the observer to the person opposite is much greater than the critical distance in a standing crowd, the angle is lower and so the stage can be that much lower in height. Figure 7.10 illustrates the angles and can be used to calculate approximate stage heights. Once again, the worst case scenario must be assumed and if the tables are less than 72 in. in diameter (e.g. 60 in. rounds) then the calculation must be rechecked. Note also that because of the low angle, a constant stage height may be used for the nearest 50 ft to the stage before the stage height really needs to be increased, unlike the standing situation.

It should be kept in mind that the variables in determining stage height are many (e.g. slope of ground, closeness of audience to each other, whether the performers stay on mainly the downstage portion of the stage), so the above analysis is only intended to be a general guideline and not a hard rule. Each situation will be different and in some cases, a lower stage might be adequate.

PRODUCTION WAR STORY:
ONE SMALL DETAIL. . .

As part of a final night celebration for a large insurance convention, we were asked to produce a custom entertainment show in conjunction with the Sheraton San Diego. A professional, well-established technical production and staging company was also brought on board. This being the case, I felt that we would be in good hands.

As the Sheraton wanted this show to be completely custom, the technical production and staging company began developing a total custom stage for the performance and we were brought in early so that our performance needs would be considered in the development of the stage. Conversations during the planning and construction of the stage included our requests for concealed stage entrances on stage left, stage right, and center stage, as well as reminders that the floor of the stage must be constructed using wood, and then covered in Marley or some such surface to ensure safety for the show's dancers. We also took great care to indicate the kind of stairs to be used to ensure performer safety with their elaborate costumes.

Months were spent developing the show creative, building the costumes, producing the orchestral tracks, casting, and rehearsing the show. We maintained contact throughout this period with the technical producer, including a check of stage drawings.

On show day, we moved into the venue expecting the day to run smoothly. We had been rehearsing offsite, and had taken great care to ensure that the costuming would work despite the choreography and show staging. We were ready. The stage too seemed ready when we entered the ballroom. Everything we talked about seemed to be included, except the most important element of all . . . the wooden floor with a Marley surface atop. To save money, and unbeknownst to us, the technical producer had changed his mind due to cost and used a low-pile carpet as a stage surface instead of what we had requested.

Horrified due to the intricacy of the choreography and the safety of the performers, we immediately showed our concern, which was met in a most disagreeable manner by the technical producer. Clearly in the wrong, he began to shout at us, insisting that the carpet would be fine, and that we were simply too demanding. He just did not agree that there was a problem other than the one we were creating.

Given that we had no more time to change the flooring and still be able to rehearse on the set, we determined that we would do the best we could under the circumstances, and dance on the carpet. We spent our onsite rehearsal time changing the choreography to work on carpet. This naturally only served to confuse the performers, who had spent weeks rehearsing.

What should have been a smooth, well-rehearsed performance ended up looking somewhat reckless and **unrehearsed**. We had spent tens of thousands of dollars and months preparing for this opportunity to wow our audience, and came up short thanks to a lack of communication on the part of the technical producer.

Courtesy: Anthony Bollotta, Bollotta Entertainment, San Diego, USA

7.4   STAGE DRAPING

Stages do not look good all alone. Because they are very short in stature when in a room full of people, they require higher embellishments to let people know where they are. For special events, this embellishment often takes the form of either draping or creative stage sets. In this section we will discuss the different types of stage draping.

7.4.1   Backdrops

Drapes used for stage backdrops are usually constructed out of cotton or poly-ester *velour*, or *commando cloth*. Velour is a rich fabric with a thick, light-absorbing pile. It is the most desirable fabric for stage curtains as it hangs beautifully with-out wrinkles, and is opaque. Most of the new polyester fabrics are inherently flame resistant whereas the older cotton material must be treated for flame resist-ance. Although available in a variety of colors, velour is most often black for spe-cial events. Commando cloth is an inexpensive, 100 percent cotton fabric that does not have the rich look or feel of velour but is an excellent and economical alternative. It also comes in a variety of colors but black is the most common one for special events. These fabrics usually come in 54 in. (136 cm) wide rolls of up to 100 yd (90 m) in length and must be custom-made for drapes. Generally, most lighting and audio-visual companies stock custom drapes.

Drapes can be safely suspended on freestanding supports, typically what is known as *pipe and drape hardware* for up to 16 ft (4.8 m) in height. Pipe and drape hardware consists of vertical, variable extendable, aluminum poles placed onto a solid steel base plate which are weighted down for safety. The drapes are attached by pushing an extendable horizontal aluminum pole through the upper sleeve in the drape and attaching the horizontal pole to the vertical poles. For heights greater than 16 ft, stronger vertical supports such as Genie lifts or truss towers with solid anchoring feet are recommended.

As we mentioned in Chapter 2 on Décor, stages may also have decorative murals as backdrops rather than plain drapes.

7.4.2   Masking Curtains

The same drapery material is also used for *masking curtains* to hide parts of the stage and equipment. Masking curtains can be flat or pleated with fullness. Their size is usually determined by sight lines to minimize or elim-inate any view to the backstage area. They are usually black as they are meant to become 'invisible' when the lights are dimmed. The following are explanations of the different types of masking curtains:

- *Borders* hide lights and other equipment mounted above the stage. They are finished with fabric ties at the top and hang from the same trussing used for mounting the lights, on the audience side of the truss.

- *Legs* hide offstage areas (*wings*) used for entrances, change and preparation areas, and sidelights. Their size and location is usually determined by keeping sight lines in mind. They are typically mounted on freestanding pipe and drape hardware as described.
- *Mid-stage travelers* or *rear travelers* are used as stage dividers to create a smaller space or to hide equipment or backdrops near the back wall. They may consist of two panels with a center overlap and open to the sides, or, depending on the available space, a traveler may be one panel and travel offstage on a curved track to one side. Travelers are usually mounted on a special drapery track (like household drapes) in turn mounted to trussing that allows them to be opened with rope pulls. Both travelers and wings often have extensions that go from the edge of the stage to side walls or that form part of A-V screen dressing as discussed in Chapter 4.

Figure 7.11 illustrates these different masking curtains: borders (left); legs (center); and mid-stage travelers (right). Drapery backdrops and legs can be further enhanced with lighting or decorations that can be hung from them or over them, such as signs, A-V screens, and other material, fabrics, and objects.

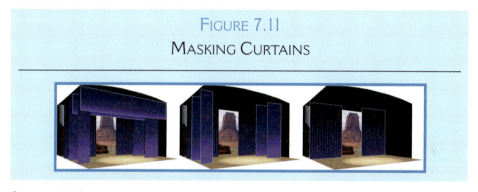

FIGURE 7.11
MASKING CURTAINS

Courtesy: I. Weiss, www.iweiss.com

7.4.3　Stage Skirting

One other type of stage draping is skirting for stages. Although most staging manufacturers sell matching skirting that is clipped onto the stage surface or attached by Velcro, some designers choose to match other décor by customizing skirting in a specific color or style. For this, they will generally use lightweight material and clip it or staple it onto the stage. Stage skirting is a must for a professional finish to the stage.

7.4.4　Front Curtains

In theatrical terminology, the main drape across the front of the stage goes by several names: *grand drape, proscenium curtain, main curtain, act curtain*, *house curtain*, or *front curtain*. Front curtains in theaters can be of several styles, each referring to the style of opening:

- *Draw* or *pleated curtain*: 'The draw curtain is composed of two sections of curtain suspended from a traveler track, allowing the curtain to part in the middle and pull offstage into the wings. . . . Where the drapes meet in the center there must be an overlap of at least 12 in. to block any light leak' (Sew What? Inc., 2006) (Figure 7.12: top row, left).
- *Tableau curtain*: 'The tableau curtain is made in two halves much like the draw curtain. However, by means of lines and rings sewn diagonally to the drapes on the back side, each half of the drape can be raised diagonally creating a draped opening. The shape of the draping and the width to which it opens revealing the stage is determined largely by the position and angle of the lines and rings' (Sew What? Inc., 2006) (Figure 7.12: top row, right).
- *Venetian* or *contour curtain*: 'The Venetian curtain is designed to be gathered vertically when raised by a counter weight system in order to expose, or close, the stage. . . . When raised simultaneously the drape will lift and fall with the bottom edge parallel to the stage floor. When the lines are manipulated individually however, arched openings of various shapes can be created' (Sew What? Inc., 2006) (Figure 7.12: bottom row, left).

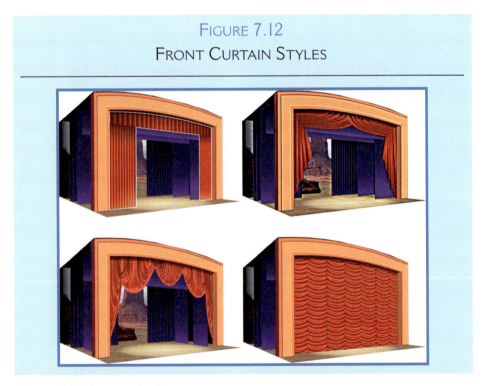

FIGURE 7.12

FRONT CURTAIN STYLES

Courtesy: I. Weiss, www.iweiss.com

- *Austrian* or *puff curtain*: 'The Austrian curtain is manufactured similarly to the contour but has only 50 percent fullness horizontally. The 'puffs' or 'smiles' of the Austrian curtain are created by adding 100 percent sewn-in vertical fullness. These sewn scenarios require that the lines be raised simultaneously, and the drape will always lift and fall with the bottom edge parallel to the stage floor' (Sew What? Inc., 2006) (Figure 7.12: bottom row, right).

In special events, due to the temporary nature of the installation and to the fact that front drapes are traditionally very heavy and cumbersome to maneuver and install, they have hitherto not been used unless the event was being held in a theater. Now, however, some companies are making portable, multi-contour front drape systems that can be installed in temporary situations but that resemble full theater draping. The Sico Insta-Theater, for example, is actually a complete portable stage setup incorporating staging, lighting and support trussing, drape backdrop, wings, front truss border, and draw-style front curtain. Another company, All Staging Unlimited, offers a 'contour curtain system' which comes as a motorized combination Austrian/Venetian curtain hung from a truss line. It can be brought into an event and mounted in front of the stage. As well, they offer a 'kabuki' system that works in reverse and drops to open. It is expected that the industry will see more of these offerings in the near future.

7.5   STAGE SETS

In Chapter 2 on Décor we briefly discussed the use of sets as part of themed décor in a venue, which may have been stand-alone large set pieces or pieces used on a stage. These would not have been custom-designed for the event but would have been existing set pieces available for rental from a prop house or décor provider. In this chapter, we deal with the use of stage sets custom-designed specifically for a given event. Typical events at which these are used are product launches, sales meetings, incentive meetings, award ceremonies, concerts, and association meeting general sessions. In these types of events, the stage and the set are the main and probably only, focal point in the venue. Often the set and the stage are left in place for the duration of a meeting which could be up to a week or more. Thus, they have to be attractive, durable, and versatile enough to be easily changed in a small way to create a new 'look' for different sessions. Let us now examine the key considerations in achieving effective set design.

7.5.1   Design Procedure and Criteria

The design process typically begins with meetings among the client, set designer, and event producer to lay out the general goals of the design. Unlike a theater set design for which the goals are to establish a time and place, as well as the mood and spirit of a play, the goals of a corporate set design are invariably to reinforce the goals of the event itself and to deliver or emphasize a message. For example, it may require a futuristic design to reinforce a sales meeting's theme of 'Selling Effectively in the 21st Century.' It may require a giant three-dimensional representation of a company logo in the corporate colors to help motivate a group of employees on an incentive trip. It may require a series of framed screens that allow for the playback of movie clips at an award show. Whatever the client's goal, the set designer must have a clear understanding of it before proceeding.

In addition to establishing the goals of the design, these meetings should also determine what will be happening onstage (e.g. who will be part of the onstage activities and what their movements on- and offstage will be), the exact location of the event (e.g. what room in what venue), how long the setup time will be, and what the budget will be. With this, the designer can further proceed to the initial design phase. In this phase, the designer will:

- Establish the size and shape of the set in relation to the stage size and to the location of the stage in the venue (often requiring one or more visits to the venue to take measurements).
- Locate entrances and exits to the stage, such as doors, ramps, stairs, or arches.
- Create a color and texture for the general background.
- Add logos, graphics, or openings for visual presentations to the set.
- Determine the number and location of scenic pieces or additional props if needed.
- Develop a colored rendering by hand or using CADD (computer-aided design and drafting).
- Draft a *ground plan* (top view), *front elevation* (front view), plus possibly an *end or side elevation* (from the side of the stage) of the set either by hand or by CADD.

At some point in this process, the designer will probably consult with the lighting company to ensure that appropriate colors and luminaires will be used to correctly light the set. Occasionally, the designer may build a miniature three-dimensional model, although this tends to happen more in theater than in special events where time and budget are very limited. With possibly some iterations following until the exact design is found, the next step is for construction of the set, for which the set designer has the responsibility to supervise.

7.5.2 Construction and Installation of the Set

The set designer may or may not be the same person or the same company as the set builder. However, once the design is approved, the set must be built.

Unlike theater, corporate event sets are usually stationary and are built of any one or more of the following structural components:

- *Flats*: Flats are lightweight frames made of wood or steel tubing and are used to make two-dimensional, painted scenery. They are normally covered with Muslin, plywood, door skin (⅛ in. thick wood paneling), paper, Masonite, velour, or other fabrics and materials. They vary in size from about 2 to 6 ft (0.6–2 m) in width, and 8 to 16 ft (2–5 m) in height. The frames are normally constructed of 1 in. × 3 in. (2.5 cm × 7.5 cm) wooden sections. For large sets, flats are screwed or hinged together. Often they are painted in perspective or with other trompe l'oeil to give the impression of three-dimensional objects. They are often anchored to the stage floor with wooden braces, held up with a combination of braces and weights such as sandbags, or braced with small L-shaped metal feet (brackets) on each side to make them freestanding.
- *Cutouts*: A cutout is a piece of thin wood or other firm material that is cut to represent an exterior outline of an object. It may be used on its own or attached to a flat. For example, a flat representing the edge of a forest might have a straight edge (the flat) along a tree trunk and then a cutout representing leaves higher up where the foliage begins.
- *Platforms*: These are used to add levels to stages, whether a few steps up or a higher level representing a different location and are made out of wood with construction that is similar to, but sturdier than, flats.
- *Murals, scrims, and cycloramas*: These are discussed in Chapter 2. They are more often used to augment a theme when onstage rather than convey a corporate message.
- *Projections*: Projections have been used increasingly through the 20th century as integral parts of set designs. For corporate sets, projections might be still images, like PowerPoint, or moving images shot on video or film. They are typically projected onto a screen surface designed and built into the set. They are discussed in Chapter 4.

Before installation, each flat or individual section of the set is constructed first. The set is then brought in section by section and screwed together. Final paint touchups may be required after construction and often time must be allowed for final painting to dry.

Figure 7.13 illustrates two finished but totally different stage sets. Of interest in Figure 7.13 (left) are the cutout colored shapes, the yellow stairs used for entrances from backstage, and the locations of two A-V screens strategically positioned as part of the set. In Figure 7.13 (right), several items are noteworthy. The stage surface itself is completely coordinated with the stage set in color and texture. The lectern position has been considered in the construction of the set to permit optimum visibility and also to not intrude on sight lines to screens. Two large A-V screens have been built into the set itself on each side of the stage to afford the audience a better view of IMAG projections. The set has been designed specifically for the venue out of primarily flats, so that it fits comfortably and covers the floor to ceiling area. The finish and color of the set is neutral so that lighting reflects well from it. Lastly, upstage and downstage entrances and exits have been designed into the set.

FIGURE 7.13
EXAMPLES OF CORPORATE EVENT STAGE SETS

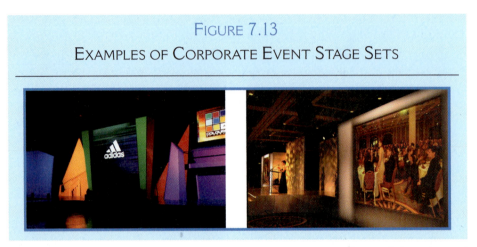

Courtesy: Hollywood Lighting Services – Portland/Seattle, www.hollywoodlighting.biz and Pacific Show Productions, www.pacificshow.ca – Copyright 2006

7.6   RISK AND SAFETY

Because staging supports people – and sometimes automobiles and other heavy inanimate objects – of critical importance is the safe allowable loading for a given stage. Too many event producers and event managers are unaware of the fact that there are currently no North American standards for allowable loading. Why is this important? Consider the fact that, since 2003, at least nine temporary stages have collapsed at special events in various countries around the world. In many of these incidents, people were injured. Event producers must be aware of the allowable loading for any given stage design, and since there are no standards, it makes this point even more important because, as part of proper risk management, the stage provider, whether it is a hotel or a subcontracted staging company, should be able to provide producers with the deck manufacturer's figures for safe loading limits. In the case of customized staging, the builder should have made proper calculations or should provide proper calculations from a certified structural engineer to prove that the staging will be adequate for the loads anticipated. These limits should state allowable loads of several types:

- *Uniformly distributed loads (UDL)*: This means how much weight the entire deck can support overall. This value decreases as stage height increases.
- *Point load*: This refers to the maximum weight that a single small point on the deck can support (e.g. a car wheel or a truss tower beam). This is often

where problems occur. Typical regulations specify a point loading of 7 kN (kiloNewtons) for a 'point' measuring 50 mm × 50 mm (i.e. 2 in. × 2 in.). In North American engineering terms, this load translates into just over 400 psi (pounds per square inch). Of course, the upper limit to a point load will be the UDL if the area of loading is greater than 4 in^2 (2500 mm^2). Note that point loads are different and usually less over the center portion of a deck than over the edge or corners where there are supporting beams.

- *Lateral forces*: These forces occur due to movement on the stage such as dancing people and moving set pieces, and also by force applied to protective handrails (e.g. someone falling against it). Regulations usually require a deck to be able to absorb 10 percent of the vertical loading on the horizontal plane. In other words, if the deck is stressed to support 4000 lb UDL, then the allowable lateral force should be 400 lb. Put another way, if there are four supporting legs and the deck is stressed to 4000 lb, each leg supports 1000 lb of vertical force and must also support 10 percent of that or 100 lb in lateral force before collapsing.

The only known standards for recommended allowable stage loading (including guardrails) are in Europe where *DIN 4112: Temporary Structures: Code of Practice for Design and Construction*, in Germany, and *Temporary Demountable Structures: Guidance on Procurement, Design and Use*, in the UK, provide good guidelines. In terms of the railings and other options for stages, once again only Europe (Germany) has provided structural and safety standards for the construction of these additions to staging in the form of *DIN 15920-11: Stage and Studio Set Up; Safety Regulations for Practicals, Ramps, Steps, Stairs and Stage Balustrades*. The result of not having standards is that staging is not manufactured to consistent load ratings, which means that one manufacturer's staging may not be as strong as another's. This may lead producers to make erroneous assumptions about the strength of a stage and/or its options (e.g. guardrails).

Otherwise, for North America, the safety standards that pertain to workers using or building staging are encompassed by the OSHA (Occupational Safety and Health administration) and WCB (Workers' Compensation Board) standards in the US and Canada respectively, copies of which should be in the possession of all producers.

Production Challenges

1. Explain to your new employee what the different styles of stages are that have been inherited from the theater, and also what the different stage directions are.
2. A rich client wants to hold a dinner party and dance in his garden, with the band stage placed over top of a sloping rock garden. Explain to him why a manufactured stage cannot be used and also the circumstances when a custom stage must be used for a special event.

Continued

3. You want to place a large Hummer vehicle on four sections of staging with one wheel on each deck as part of a product launch. The Hummer weighs 8000 lb and each deck has an allowable UDL of 4000 lb, with an allowable point load of 400 psi where each of the Hummer wheels will be placed. The Hummer's wheel footprint is 36 in^2 and each wheel supports 25 percent of the Hummer's weight. Will the staging support the Hummer?

4. A client wants to hire a 10-piece show band that includes three lead vocalists, a drummer, a guitarist, a bass player (both electric), a pianist using a full grand piano, two saxophone players, and a trumpeter. Using 4 ft × 8 ft sections of staging, what is the minimum size of stage that is required for this group? Assume that the stage height is 2 ft and that all musicians will be playing downstage of the drummer.

5. You have been asked to create a stage set design for an awards ceremony that will honor pioneers in the logging industry. The set must incorporate a natural look as if it is in the forest with mountains behind. You are not allowed to use live trees and must construct the set out of regular theatrical material, allowing for two backstage entrances and two A-V screens on either side of the stage. Describe possible structural components that could be used in the construction and what the final set might look like.

REFERENCE

Sew What? Inc. (2006). *Grand Drape*. Retrieved June 20, 2006, from http://www.sewwhatinc.com/ tage_grand_drape.php#granddrape.

TENTING

Ever since humans developed to the point where they were able to construct their own shelters, they have sought to tame nature. Nomadic peoples were undoubtedly the first to realize that it would be more efficient to create a portable house that required less construction than a permanent one every time they decided to stop on their journeys. Their crude attempts at such shelters were the first known predecessors of today's spectacular tented environments. Over the intervening millennia, tents have appeared in every conceivable situation, and today they enable special events to take place in locations that would have previously been inaccessible.

In this chapter, we will explore the use of tents in special events, starting with why and how they are used today. We will then explain and illustrate the different types of modern tents used in events, including fabrics and accessories, followed by a review of setup considerations, then a look at where tent technology is today and where it might go in the next few years, and finally end with a review of risk and safety as it pertains to tenting.

8.1   WHY USE A TENT FOR A SPECIAL EVENT?

In Chapter 1 of *Special Event Production: The Process*, we examined the underlying reasons why special events are held: political, religious, educational, social, and commercial. These, however, are not necessarily the same reasons why one would choose to use a tent for a special event in today's world. In essence, a tent is an alternative venue, nothing more, nothing less, but one with very special characteristics that sometimes make it more attractive than a traditional venue such as a conference center, a hotel, or another permanent structure. According to John Schluetter, President of Karl's Event Rental, a major supplier of event tenting in Milwaukee, Wisconsin (Schluetter, 2004), a tent provides an interesting venue, it creates additional space, and it can be personalized in that it represents a blank artistic canvas. Because so many of today's special event attendees have used traditional venues on a regular basis, they are looking to escape from hotels and convention centers in favor of a unique venue that takes advantage of the geography of the local area. Tents afford them the opportunity to do this, often enabling an event to take place in a locale where no buildings exist but that is an attractive setting in itself. Additionally, some destinations do not have facilities of sufficient size to accommodate larger groups and a tent may provide the only alternative for an event. In forming additional space, a tent can be placed closer to key activities that require support structures to enable them to take place at all. Examples are the large temporary tented corporate pavilions at air shows (e.g. Paris and Farnborough Air Shows) and automobile races.

As a blank canvas, a tent starts with plain bare walls, ceiling, and floor. It therefore permits designers to transform it into a unique environment with décor and lighting, and even to design complete interiors as full working offices, restaurants, clubs, warehouses, and other unique uses such as prisons. The other primary advantage of tents is that they can expand or contract to the required area relatively rapidly and relatively cheaply when compared with more permanent structures.

8.2   TYPES AND STYLES OF TENTS

The Tent Rental Division of the Industrial Fabrics Association International (IFAI) defines a tent as 'a structure composed of a covering made of pliable material or fabric that is supported by mechanical means such as poles, metal frames, beams, columns, arches, ropes, and/or cables.' The word 'tent' is sometimes used interchangeably with 'pavilion' and 'canopy,' though a 'canopy' can also refer to a tent without sidewalls, a small tent, or even an awning-like structure. In the UK and Australia, the 'marquee' is synonymous with 'tent.' A 'marquee' in the US, however, is defined as either 'a canopy projecting over an entrance or doorway' or 'a connecting canopy between two tents.' The explanations of the following four Tent Rental Division categories are provided by the IFAI (2002), and are used with permission. They are generic in nature and do not constitute an endorsement of a particular tent type, brand, or company. Figure 8.1 illustrates these generic tent design types.

The types of tents illustrated in Figure 8.1 are:

- *First row, left to right*: Pole tent; pipe frame-supported tent.
- *Second row, left to right*: Box-beam, frame-supported (clearspan) tent; tensile fabric structure.

8.2.1   Pole Tent

This is a tent that features a set of individual poles arranged beneath the fabric roof to support and define the shape of the structure. The fabric roof is tensioned over the poles and attached to ropes and/or cables at designated spots around the fabric's edges. The ropes or cables are anchored to the ground using stakes, augers, or weights around the perimeter of the tent. Pole-supported tents are the grandfather of the tent industry, and were once

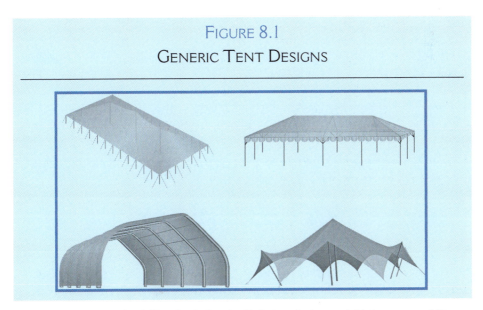

FIGURE 8.1

GENERIC TENT DESIGNS

Courtesy: IFAI Procedural Handbook for the Safe Installation and Maintenance of Tentage Copyright 2002 © Industrial Fabrics Association International, Roseville, MN. Used with permission

the only type of tent available. Though they have lost ground to newer designs, pole-supported tents remain popular in the US and are still considered an important part of most tent rental inventories. They are also referred to as 'push-pole tents.' Traditional pole tents require center poles; however, newer versions have center poles supported by cabling in the roof, thereby eliminating the interior pole going to the ground. Because of the tensioned roof structure, these newer versions have a more contoured look. Pole tent sizes range from about 10 ft (3 m) × 10 ft (3 m) to 60 ft (18 m) × 300 ft (90 m) (see Figure 8.1).

8.2.2 Pipe Frame-Supported Tent

This is a tent with an assembled framework made of aluminum or steel pipes that supports the fabric roof and defines the shape of the structure. The rigid framework allows the tent to be freestanding without additional support, but requires the same rope or cable anchoring system as a pole-supported tent to hold it in place, as specified by applicable fire or building codes. Pipe frame-supported tents are popular for events that require smaller tents. Most manufacturers make units as small as 10 ft (3 m) × 10 ft (3 m) that are easy to set up and tear down. They are also suitable for smaller events that require few, if any, interior obstructions since the frame system makes interior supports unnecessary. Pipe frame-supported tents are available in a wide variety of styles and sizes up to widths of 40 ft (12 m). These tents are often not as wind resistant as other types (see Figure 8.1).

8.2.3 Box-Beam, Frame-Supported (Clearspan) Tent

This is a type of tent that features an assembled framework of box-beam, I-beams, or truss arches that support the fabric roof and define the shape of the structure. The stronger construction of the aluminum or steel box-beam frame makes these tents more suitable for larger or longer-term applications than other types of tents. The box-beam framework also allows for large areas of unobstructed 'clearspan' space beneath the fabric roof. The larger structures require heavy equipment because of the size and weight of their parts. These tents come in widths ('spans') ranging from about 30 ft (9 m) to almost 300 ft (90 m) and can withstand higher wind loads than other tent types. They are also referred to as 'free-span tents' (see Figure 8.1).

8.2.4 Tensile Tent or Structure

This is a type of tent that shares some characteristics with the pole-supported tent, but relies more on the tensioning of the fabric roof for its structural integrity and shape. The use of tensioned fabric to resist applied loads and shape the fabric membrane means less of a traditional support structure is needed to maintain it. Tensioned fabric structures are now common architectural features the world over. These permanent structures, which are manufactured to last for years after their installation, are referred to as tension structures, tensile structures, or membrane structures (see Figure 8.1).

8.2.5   Inflatable Tent

Not part of the IFAI's definitions, but new on the horizon, is a variety of large inflatable tents. These seem to be almost exclusively manufactured in China, and are adaptable to most of the same uses as regular tents. However, they must be connected to a constant flow of air by means of a fan. These inflatables offer several advantages, including easy erection and dismantling, the fact that they are all clearspan, and their low cost. They also lend themselves to easy customization with color and graphics. Stability under wind loads, fire-retardant capabilities, air fan/pump requirements, and anchoring methods for these tents are as yet untested and unknown. Figure 8.2 shows one such tent with a length of 16 m or approximately 50 ft, a width of 10 m or approximately 33 ft, and height of 6.5 m or 20 ft. It is made of polyvinyl chloride (PVC) tarpaulin material and comes in a variety of sizes.

FIGURE 8.2

EXAMPLE OF INFLATABLE TENT

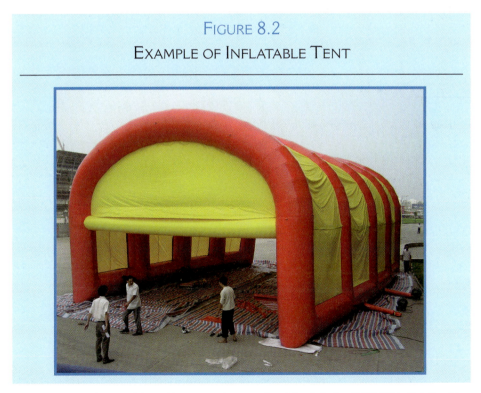

Courtesy: Jessie Lee and http://www.ecplaza.net/tradeleads/seller/2951412/sell_inflatable_tent.html#none

8.2.6 Fabrics

The primary fabric for tents is a vinyl-laminated polyester, but a small percentage of use is still seen for canvas. The newer polyester fabrics are more durable and resistant to weather effects, including water and sunlight damage. All fabrics are treated with flame retardants.

Most tent sidewalls (pieces of fabric generally attached to the roof structure and used to enclose the sides of tents) are made of lighter weight vinyl-laminated polyester. They – and the roof structure – can be designed with clear vinyl as windows and be as large as the entire tent if desired, although with less strength and durability.

8.2.7 Determining the Correct Tent Size

Tented events have to be comfortable, and overcrowding is one of the serious errors that a producer can commit. Depending on the type of event, what follows are some general guidelines and area allowances for determining the size of tent required. These are also useful for planning indoor events.

- *Stand-up reception or cocktail party*: 6 ft^2 (0.5 m^2) per person.
- *Sit-down dinner*: 10–12 ft^2 (0.9–1.1 m^2) per person, depending on whether the tables seat 10 or 8 persons respectively.
- *Buffet table or bar*: 100 ft^2 (9 m^2) per 8 ft long table/bar.
- *Auditorium or theater-style seating*: 6 ft^2 (0.5 m^2) per person plus 4–6 ft (1.2–1.8 m) width for aisles.
- *Dance floor*: 2–3 ft^2 (0.2–0.3m^2) per person, assuming 50 percent of guests are dancing at any given time.
- *Speaker stage or platform*: 10 ft^2 (0.9 m^2) per person.
- *Bandstand*: As given in Chapter 7, 25–30 ft^2 (2.5 m^2) per musician for electronic rhythm instruments (e.g. guitar, bass, keyboards), including amplifiers and equipment; 10–15 ft^2 (1.3 m^2) per musician for acoustic instruments (e.g. brass, woodwinds, strings), including chairs and music stands; 50–70 ft^2 (6 m^2) for a drummer; 30 ft^2 (2.5 m^2) for a spinet piano; 100 ft^2 (9 m^2) for full grand piano; 10 ft^2 (0.9 m^2) per vocalist if backup and not moving too much; 30–50 ft^2 (4–5 m^2) per vocalist for a lead vocalist, and possibly more if part of a show band.

Obviously, for more complicated events such as trade shows, more specific measurements would have to be made.

8.3   TENT ACCESSORIES AND OPTIONS

In keeping with the requirement for a tented environment to be as comfortable as possible, today's tents offer options for styles and accessories that will make a tented event equivalent to a classy hotel ballroom.

8.3.1 Tops

Although traditional white is still the norm for most tent tops, various colors and stripes are now making their way into the market in all tent sizes. For all sizes of tents, particularly clearspan, a clear top is now an option almost universally. Because of the vinyl used, clear tops are not as strong as regular material. Figure 8.3 illustrates a tent with a clear top.

FIGURE 8.3
EXAMPLE OF A CLEARSPAN TENT WITH A CLEAR TOP

Courtesy: Tents Unlimited, Inc., www.tentsunlimited.com

8.3.2 Sidewalls

Most tents come with optional sidewalls, which can be installed for weather protection. These can be plain white fabric (or any color nowadays), clear vinyl, clear French windows, screen, mesh, real glass, or rigid PVC (Figure 8.4). The degree of elegance, fire resistance, or security, is up to the user. Manufacturers have their own methods of fastening fabric walls to frames, but most involve some sort of strap system. However, a relatively new method of attachment of walls and ceilings to tent frames is known as a *keder* system. In essence, this system allows walls and ceiling components to slide into frame rails rather than lacing up, thus saving considerable setup time and improving tent stability. For hard walls, some manufacturers offer complete interchangeability amongst hard walls, glass walls, and doors.

FIGURE 8.4

EXAMPLE OF SIDEWALLS WITH WINDOWS

Courtesy: Karl's Event Rental, www.karls.com

8.3.3 Gutters

Most tents have optional gutter systems to prevent rain damage. Depending on the tent design, these come in vinyl and lace to the tent frame or even hard plastic complete with plastic downspouts.

8.3.4 Doors

As with walls, fitted doors can be provided to have a finished look that works with the remainder of the tent, or they can be customized. Doors can be single or double, and they can have panic hardware installed. All doors should conform to the code standards for tents, including tempered glass inserts or French panes that may be placed in them. Smoked glass and sliding doors are also available options from some rental companies.

8.3.5 Lighting

Standard tent lighting is usually achieved with bowl or globe lights made of PVC resin. They come as single units or as multiples in the form of simple chandeliers, and are used mostly for social events. Other industrial style lights that use mercury vapor or halogen technology and are very bright are used more for tradeshows and general lighting of larger areas. Generally, all styles are able to be mounted from tent frame components and also come as freestanding units. More elaborate chandeliers are available from some rental companies as well as string lights. Theatrical lighting is used extensively for tented events (see Chapter 5), but is normally designed and installed by a lighting company.

Not to be forgotten is site lighting. Tents are often set up in unlit locations and if the event will extend past sunset, it will be necessary to light all access walkways, washroom areas, and paths connecting tents. As with the inside of tents, industrial-type lights can be used on poles and connected to portable power generators, or lighted helium globes can be used. These are large tethered helium balloons with lights inside that float high over a site thus covering a large area.

8.3.6 Liners

According to Tracey (2005; pp. 33–34), 'liners beautify tent interiors and mask a multitude of sins, including tent mechanics, wiring, outdated lighting, and soiled tent tops. The tent liner, in effect, acts as a drop ceiling. . . . Leg drapes can be added to the tent in blouse or tailored styles to match the look of the ceiling liner. . . . Liners offer other practical benefits. They help mitigate outdoor temperature fluctuations, so less power is needed to heat or cool the structure. The liner provides a sandwich of air between it and the tent that acts as a blanket of insulation. . . . Liners are offered in pleated and smooth styles. Commonly used materials include taffeta polyester, muslin, duvateen, or any flameproof fabric.' Liners also come in white, black, and up to 50 or more other colors. Most liners are installed and hoisted to the ceiling using a rope and pulley system, then affixed to the tent frame using hooks and tabs. Some are both functional and highly decorative.

8.3.7 Flooring

Today's tent flooring comes in a multitude of options. For most special event applications, if there is any doubt whatsoever about weather conditions of if the event is being held on anything but the very firmest and flattest of surfaces, proper flooring should be a consideration. The use of flooring has the advantage of preventing water from accumulating on top of the walking surface by providing a path for drainage underneath it. As well, it provides a level, obstacle-free, and thus safer, surface. The two general categories of flooring are *lay down* and *rollout*. Lay down floors can be either *stick-built* or paneled. 'Stick-built' refers to the now almost obsolete method of building a wooden floor using custom lumber construction to a specified height and over any obstacles. It has been replaced by plywood panel systems combined with adjustable aluminum legs that enable large areas to be covered even when the ground is uneven, thanks to the vertical adjustability of the legs. Some companies even have flooring systems that connect directly onto integrated base plates (e.g. Roder HTS), ensuring extra stability. A number of manufacturers also provide flat, interlocking plastic panels that are best used directly over paved or cement surfaces. These panels can be installed at roughly half the cost of plywood panels and much faster. Built into them are drainage channels and their modularity permits installation around trees, obstacles, or existing structures. They come in several colors. Most are extremely durable and strong enough for vehicular traffic.

Similar to rigid plastic paneling is the first of the 'rollout' options, hinged plastic panels. They literally come in rolls and roll out directly onto the ground, eliminating the intermediate step of physically having to interlock individual panels. The last type of flooring, and one that needs a dry flat surface to begin with, is carpeting. This is normally placed on top of pre-built flooring such as wooden or plastic paneling, or directly on top of pavement or concrete as long as wet weather is not anticipated, to give a more elegant and finished appearance.

8.3.8   Heating, Ventilation, and Air Conditioning

Numerous options exist for heating and cooling tents, depending on the time of year and the weather conditions. For heating, there are mainly two options, the first being an electric resistive heater, which comes either as a small radiant heater that can be mounted on the ceiling or on a pole, and covers about a 150 ft^2 (14 m^2) area, or as a larger unit that heats a wider area, but requires 240 or 480 V three-phase electrical power to operate. Many local fire departments now prohibit the small, mushroom-shaped localized propane heaters and any other types that have the fuel source located within the tent, for safety reasons.

For larger tented events, the second option, an all-season unit that combines heating and air-conditioning, must be used. Typically, the unit can distribute cool- or warm-treated air via a white Dacron duct hung in the ceiling of the tent, or in the side walls. The machine can be positioned directly in the tent wall, or just outside (Figure 8.5). The direct method of airflow in either the heating or the cooling mode works most efficiently because it reconditions the air within the tent. The filtered air is then returned to the tent, which lowers the humidity. A typical all-season unit delivers 20 tons of air conditioning (8000 ft^3 or about 220 m^3 per minute of air). It also can incorporate a 45 kW heater. These units need 480 V and

FIGURE 8.5

TYPICAL ALL-SEASON HEATING AND
AIR CONDITIONING UNIT

Courtesy: Marquee Tent Productions, www.marqueetents.com

three-phase power to operate. In addition, there are air conditioning only units which range from 20 tons up to 60 tons of cooling per machine. They are ideal when heat is not necessary. The cost is less to rent than the all-season machines and can be used where space is not a factor. These units also operate on 480 V and three-phase power. When power is required, a portable generator must be brought into the tent site (Doran, 1994). It should be noted that the air conditioning load (in tons) or heating load (usually in British Thermal Units or BTUs per cubic foot) prediction is not a simple calculation but is based on several factors, including tent size (volume), number of persons in the tent, and the temperature difference between the desired internal tent temperature and the outside ambient temperature. The results will determine the number of units required to meet the desired inside temperature for the entire tent. Most rental companies will have software or charts that accurately predict the load based on these known parameters.

8.3.9 Branding and Marketing

As Schluetter (2004) pointed out, tents provide a blank canvas. Indeed, what better canvas for branding a corporate image than a huge blank white

FIGURE 8.6

EXAMPLE OF BRANDING SIGNAGE
ATTACHED TO A TENT

Courtesy: Karl's Event Rental, www.karls.com

surface in often highly visible locations? Many companies have realized the possible marketing opportunities this presents and are attaching signage to the sides, ends, and tops of tent structures. Figure 8.6 illustrates an event in which the sponsor has taken advantage of the visible location to add corporate signage to the tents. It can also be used purely as decorative accessory if desired, as can be seen in this figure where the large, colored end piece is more decoration than advertising.

According to Knight (2005), graphics are also being printed right onto tent fabrics, thanks to wide format digital printers. 'Graphics do not stop on the outside of the tent either. Interiors utilize extensive graphic merchandising displays, colorful murals, and pop-up displays to reinforce brand awareness. . . . For special events on a smaller budget, mass-produced graphic backdrops can be affixed onto tent sidewalls.'

Other accessories that may be required for a tented event such as fencing, portable washrooms, and temporary power are dealt with in more general terms in Chapter 9, since they also pertain to other areas of events besides just tenting.

8.4   SETUP CONSIDERATIONS

Planning for an efficient, safe, and accessible tent setup begins long before the event. The main considerations include the site itself and conducting a site survey, the weather and time of day of the event, accessibility and safety concerns and the associated permits, and finally, the plan for installation.

8.4.1 Site and Site Survey

Assuming that there is an optimum amount of time before the tented event, the tent rental company should be brought into the initial planning stage about 6 months prior to the event or sooner. In conjunction with the producer and/or event manager, they will conduct a site survey to determine:

- If the site is large enough to hold the tents and all the activities planned, including stages, tables, chairs, bars, dance floor, catering preparation tent(s), and washrooms.
- The location of fire hydrants, fire and emergency vehicle access routes, access routes for supplier vehicles, existing washroom facilities, and existing power and its specifications. Fire trucks require a minimum of a 10 ft (3 m) wide access road throughout the site. At this time, tentative plans may also be made to augment any emergency services required such as planning for St. John's Ambulance attendants to be onsite, and where they will be located.
- The tentative location and orientation of all tents, any security fencing or barriers needed, entrances and exits to the site, temporary power setup, bus or vehicle drop-off points, and parking.
- If the ground surface is one into which tent anchors can be safely placed. Many companies will test the soil to determine the type of staking required. If the surface is asphalt, gravel, concrete, or wood, special anchoring may be needed in the form of weighted blocks of some sort. Occasionally, the owners of asphalt surfaces may allow temporary holes as long as they are properly patched after the event.
- If tent anchoring will disrupt unseen underground infrastructure such as telephone, gas, water, sewer, and hydro, or if overhead infrastructure will be too close to tents. Any tenting or anchoring must generally be at least 18 in. (45 cm) away from marked utility lines, and at least 10 ft (3 m) away from overhead power lines. Utility companies should be contacted at least 2 weeks before the event to mark underground lines. Property owners should also be asked to mark private underground lines such as sprinklers.
- If the surface is level and will not present a problem for catering and seating. An uneven surface may require proper leveling and flooring.
- If ground obstructions (e.g. shrubbery, fountains, pavement, trees, buildings, etc.) will get in the way of planned tent locations.

Based on the results of the site survey, a tentative schematic site plan will be drawn up by the tent rental company or the producer. See Figure 8.7 for an example of an actual tent site plan that joins together a large tent with five

FIGURE 8.7

EXAMPLE OF A SCALED CADD TENT SITE PLAN

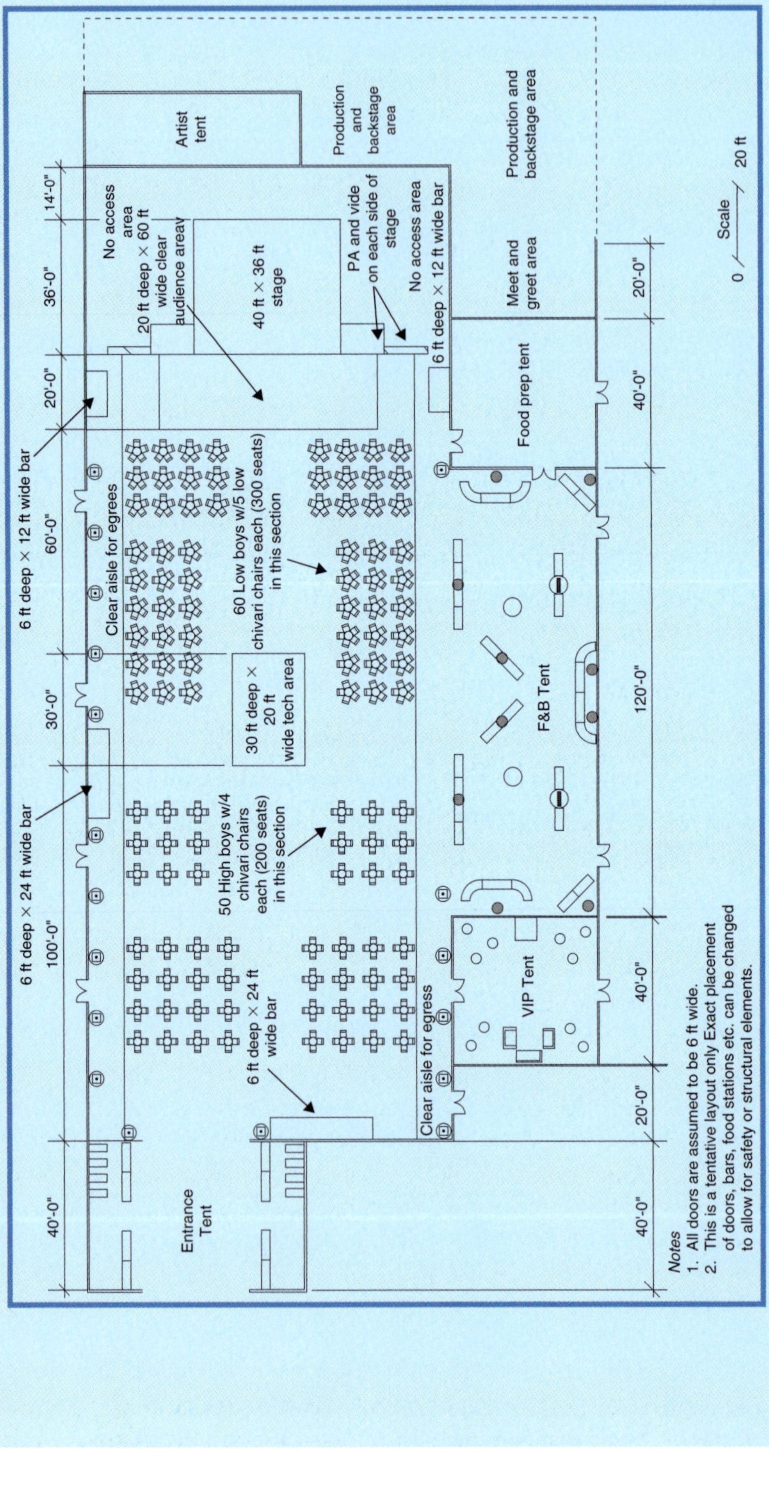

Courtesy: Doug Matthews

other smaller tents around it used for the entrance, VIPs, food and beverage, food preparation, and performer green room.

8.4.2 Weather and Time of Day

The actual date of the event could have an effect on setup. Some climates are prone to rain, some locales are very dry and hot, some are windy, and some combine all of the above, not to mention varying lengths of daylight at different times of the year. As a result, the producer should know clearly what the likelihood is for any of these conditions to exist during the event and also how much daylight will be available without supplementing lighting. Here are the main areas of concern:

- *Rain*: In any potentially wet climate, there must be an allowance made for proper drainage, either by the use of a certain type of tent (some provide better runoff than others), installing sidewalls and gutters, or providing portable flooring.
- *Wind*: Pole and frame tents can generally withstand winds of up to 30–35 mph (50–55 km/hr or kph), whereas clearspan tents are generally safe in winds up to 70 mph (115 kph). If high winds are a possibility during the event, the choice of tent may have to be changed. Note that in many municipal jurisdictions, the special event department, if there is one, will, by law, require a qualified structural engineer to inspect and certify that the tent setup is structurally sound. This may be required in order to obtain final approval for the event and may not happen until after all tents are set up, so the correct choice of tent is critical ahead of time.
- *Heat* or *cold*: This is always a 'what if' scenario, like rain. If any doubt exists at all, one should be prepared for the worst in terms of temperature extremes. If the event will go on after sunset, there is a good chance the temperature may also go down and the tent will need heat. If it is during a hot summer day, it will undoubtedly need air conditioning. As described earlier, all-season heating and cooling units may be the answer to wide temperature fluctuations.
- *Darkness*: Since planning often begins six or more months before an event, the amount of ambient light available for the event may be much more or less than it is during initial planning. As well, sun direction may impact the amount of light and heat in a different way than it does at the time of the initial site survey. Therefore, light for the event should be anticipated ahead of time and the necessary interior tent and exterior site lighting planned using the options mentioned in Section 8.3.5.

8.4.3 Installation

Once permits have been approved and site plans drawn up, the critical step of tent delivery and installation takes place. Installation must be done correctly from an engineering point of view or the tent may be unsafe. The Tent Rental Division of the IFAI has created a manual just for this purpose, based on significant research, entitled the *IFAI Procedural Handbook for the Safe Installation and Maintenance of Tentage* (IFAI, 2002). It can be obtained from their web site at http://www.bookstore.ifai.com. Essentially, a correct and safe installation involves proper layout and squaring, staking or anchoring, and erection and tightening of *guy wires*. For anything except the very smallest and simplest of tents, installation is normally the responsibility of the tent rental company. For general knowledge only, what follows are some of the methods used for installation. For purposes of this explanation, we will assume that a traditional rectangular pole tent is being used.

8.4.3.1   *Layout and Squaring*

A properly squared tent is aesthetically pleasing and is more structurally sound. We will look at three methods of laying out and squaring a tent, as described in IFAI (2002).

- *Traditional method*: The purpose of the layout is to make the perimeter of the tent taut and the corners squared. There will always be excess fabric in the interior portion of the tent due to the amount of material needed to make up the pitch of the tent. Groundcover should be used to protect the fabric during installation. The basic steps are as follows:
  - Place one end of the tent where desired and drive a small stake through each of the corner poll side grommets on that end.
  - Proceed down the length of the tent, pulling every other rope out from the center and away from the end. It is important to work opposite someone and to pull each opposing rope simultaneously, so the tent is not pulled out of square while it is being stretched.
  - Once this is accomplished, the tent is ready to be staked. Starting with each corner, measure out in both directions a distance equal to the heights of the side pole or slightly less. Refer to the tent manufacturer's instructions to determine the exact distances.
  - When all corners have been staked, run a string line from corner stake to corner stake, then place a stake opposite each side pole grommet along the straight line.
- *Pre-staking method*: In certain instances where there are objects present that would preclude the possibility of fully stretching and squaring the tent, or if the tent is too large to be stretched, it may be necessary to pre-stake the area. This method measures the diagonals to square the perimeter of the tent. The tent is first laid out and the four corners located. The staking charts provided by the tent manufacturer should be used to get the proper dimensions for the tent being installed. The Pythagorean Theorem is used to calculate the diagonal, where 'A' is the length of the stake line, 'B' is the width of the stake line, and 'C' is the diagonal. $A^2 + B^2 = C^2$, where C = the square root of C^2 (Figure 8.8). Once the first diagonal has been

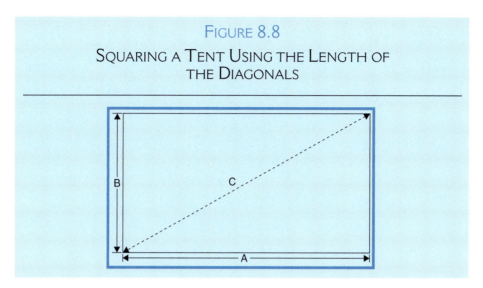

measured, the second one should also be measured and then the two compared. If they are not equal, then the corners of the tent should be moved
until the two diagonals are of equal length.

- *3–4–5 method*: This method is used when a tent is too long to make measuring of the entire tent practical, or there is some obstacle to prevent measuring the diagonal. It uses the same triangulation method but on a smaller
scale. The procedure is as follows. Using a 40 ft × 80 ft (12 m × 24 m) tent
as an example, the first two corners are laid out along the 40 ft width. This
becomes the 'four' side. Next, measure down the length to 30 ft, which
becomes the 'three' side. The distance from this point back to the first corner should be 50 ft (15 m) ('five' side). It may be necessary to move one or
two of the points in order to achieve an accurate 3-4-5 triangle. Once the
entire tent is marked out, it is advisable to check at least one other corner to
be certain that the tent is square (Figure 8.9).

8.4.3.2 *Staking*

According to IFAI (2002), 'proper staking is a prerequisite for a safe tent
event. Stake failure occurs primarily in two ways. The first is in tension, in
which the resisting frictional forces between the soil and the stake are insufficient to keep the stake from yielding to pullout forces along its axis. The
second results when the sideways force imposed by the stake against the
surrounding soil is greater than the soil can push back, so the soil yields
by bulging above the surface. Consequently, the stake pushes the uncon-
fined soil out of its path.' Thanks to an IFAI initiative, recent research has
confirmed what most tent rental companies already knew. The larger the
stake diameter is, the greater is the holding power, and the deeper a stake
can be driven into the soil, the stronger will be the anchoring power.

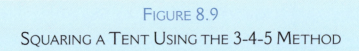

FIGURE 8.9

SQUARING A TENT USING THE 3-4-5 METHOD

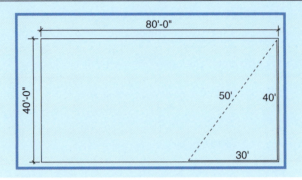

Courtesy: IFAI Procedural Handbook for the Safe Installation and Maintenance of Tentage, Copyright 2002 ©

Most good tent rental companies take the time to ensure that they are providing more than adequate anchorage for a tent, by comparing the required anchor pounds with the total anchor pounds of the specific stakes they are using. The IFAI Procedural Handbook (2002) provides a formula for the total anchor pounds required for a specific tent:

$$APR = W \times L \times PSF \times SF$$

where anchor pounds required (APR) = width of tent (W in ft) × length of tent (L in ft) × pounds per square foot (PSF) × safety factor (SF). For this calculation, PSF is an industry standard of 15, and SF is also an industry standard of 1.50.

Every stake should have a pull rating in pounds. With this information, the total actual number of stakes used for the tent is multiplied by the pound rating of the stake system to arrive at the total *holding power* of the entire stake system. This number should be equal to, or greater than, the number calculated by the total APR formula. If it is not, the number or size of stakes should be increased.

8.4.3.3   *Erection and Guy Wire Tightening*

Once stakes are in place (with guy wires relatively loose), the tent must be physically erected. Traditionally – and still today – smaller tents are erected by using sheer 'muscle power.' A crew lifts poles and frames into position manually and then tightens guy wires. However, for large tents, many companies are now using winches to replace muscle power to lift tent panels into place. After the tent has been erected, traditional rope guy wires must be manually pulled and tightened. Once again, however, the tent industry has advanced and is now using ratchet-style tent straps in place of ropes. This makes it much easier and faster to tighten guy wires.

PRODUCTION WAR STORY:
IT JUST KEPT COMING!

The tented event was being held for 400 of a university's top donors. With one eye on the weather (a rain storm was predicted), we proceeded to install all the elements necessary for a first-class event, including a fireworks finale!

Due to the extreme heat that day, the decision had been made to increase the air conditioning. Our logistics manager notified us only a few hours before the event that the main generator had failed, and it was necessary to bring in a replacement. Before the failed generator could be removed, smoke started pouring out of it. The smoke quickly turned to fire. Within seconds, our logistics manager was on the phone to 911. The production assistants evacuated the tents. Our executive producer called the client to inform her of the situation. A call was then placed from our office to the communications department. Because of the high-profile nature of this event, the press would most likely be on their way! Our office got in contact immediately with the client's press office to strategize. The technical director and stage managers were sent to another space for script read-throughs. It was vital to maintain focus on the production aspects of the event scheduled to kick off only 3 h later!

Within 8 min, the fire department and police were on the scene. Within 20 min, the fire was largely put out and the immediate danger was over. Unfortunately, a new wrinkle appeared. A diesel fuel leak was discovered to be pouring into the ground underneath the catering tent. HAZMAT technicians took toxicity readings and concluded that the catering tent must be shut down. Hearing this, the president of the university determined that the event should be cancelled. We asked for a little more time to come up with a solution. With our rain plan in place, we had already erected a marquee tent for guest coverage as they walked to the main tent from the valet area. We enlisted the help of a 15-man crew to lift and carry it to the opposite side of the main tent onto a patio overlooking the campus fountain. Our original plan called for a fireworks finale to be staged there. However, with the diesel leak, that part of the program was cancelled for safety reasons and catering was able to move to the newly established location. At 4:20 p.m., with 75 min until show time, the main tent was given a clean bill of health, catering and technical staff were brought back to complete the set up, the new generator had arrived and all technical equipment was back online.

At 4:45 p.m., the storm, our original worry, hit with a vengeance. Severe thunder, lightning, and a heavy downpour lasted for nearly 20 min. All workers were told once again to evacuate the tent. At 5:05 p.m., the storm cleared. Those who had evacuated returned. At 5:30 p.m., the first guest arrived and cocktails were served as we wrapped up rehearsals in the main tent. The event was a grand success. Our entire production team, led by the executive producer, maintained their focus and pulled off the show beautifully (minus the fireworks). The caterer was able to serve from the new location and the press stories were controlled.

We credit this success to several things: keeping your cool no matter what; keeping the safety of others first; respecting the authority of safety organizations and working with them as partners; and ultimately, being confident that there is always a solution!

Courtesy: Sarah Hyrb Winkler, P.W. Feats, Baltimore, USA; www.pwfeats.com

8.5 TENT TECHNOLOGY TODAY AND IN THE FUTURE

Thanks to advances in materials technology and a demand for architecturally unique and environmentally friendly structures, tent technology is in a rapidly evolving transitional period. The boundaries between tensile fabric structures and tents are becoming blurred as designers seek to combine practicality with esthetics. In the same manner, tents are becoming more like semi-permanent buildings. Here are some specific examples of today's tent technology and where it might lead in the very near future.

8.5.1 Size and Shape

It seems that everywhere one looks, clearspan tents are becoming a dominant feature of events, and they are getting much larger. Widths ('spans') of up to 90 m (almost 300 ft) are now available with heights of over 12 m (almost 40 ft) at the apex, and unlimited lengths. Indeed, even the simple pole tent has expanded considerably. For example, the enormous New Galaxy tent from De Boer Vinings is 26 m (almost 85 ft) high and its base is 60 m (195 ft) wide by 107 m (almost 350 ft) long, dimensions that make it as big as a football field. This is enough space to accommodate 4000–10,000 guests.

Not only are the structures expanding in the two horizontal dimensions, they are also expanding upwards. Tents are now available in multiple levels. Two storey tents are used frequently at large sporting events and trade shows. Features and options include stairways, various configurations of covered and uncovered terraces and balconies, picket fencing, railings, doors, and others. Expect big tents to be here to stay.

Tents are becoming shapelier as well as larger. We have already seen the results of hybrid technology in the simple pole tent in which the ground-to-roof supporting pole has been replaced almost universally by a pole supported by the roof frame or tension cables, thereby creating a much more attractive roof line and a completely clear, useable tent area. Now, beginning to appear are larger curved tents (Figure 8.10) that will undoubtedly evolve into a variety of shapes that serve clients' desired functions.

8.5.2 Modularity and Portability

Interestingly, the ancient nomads of central Asia often carried their *yurts* (unique round Asian tents dating back centuries) with them on oxen-driven wagons, negating the need to dismantle them in their entirety prior to moving. Although that wasn't exactly modularity, the principle is similar. A segment of today's tented structures has 'evolved' to the point that they are designed to be transported and erected in 'modules' rather than

FIGURE 8.10

EXAMPLE OF A CURVED TENT

Courtesy: Universal Fabric Structures, Inc., www.ufsinc.com

completely dismantling and erecting them from the ground up. Specialist Structures Ltd, Wiltshire, UK, is an example of a company that has designed a unique multistorey integrated building and exhibition system called the Space Building System. This modular 'construction kit' structure can be built, moved, and reassembled in any number of different configurations and locations. Mezzanines, staircases, lifts, bridges, integrated utilities, balconies, and walkways are built into the Space System, together with a number of patented technological innovations, not least of all that the system locks together without the use of nuts and bolts. Their proprietary system uses rigid walls, an integrated load bearing floor, and a variety of roof options. In effect, the building carries its own foundation, so there is no need to attach it to the ground. See Figure 8.11 for an example of this system.

Another example of an easily demountable tent comes from FTL Design Engineering Studio, who created the 2002 Harley Davidson Machine Tent as part of a world tour. This vast circular tent is dominated by a large central mast which bears most of the weight. The circular configuration is broken down into six segments, which allows for quick fabrication and installation. Each of the tent's six segments is supported by a secondary mast, and for ease of erection, internal motors hoist the masts, and the six pieces of exterior fabric are easy to handle (Bahamon, 2004).

FIGURE 8.11

EXAMPLE OF MODULAR TENT STRUCTURE
WITH GLASS WALLS

Courtesy: Specialist Structures, www.fast-architecture.com

8.5.3 Cross-Cultural Influences

In North America, we sometimes tend to think that we adapt and use inventions in the most practical and esthetically pleasing way. In the case of tents, other cultures have proven us wrong. The extremely practical central Asian yurt and the flowing, 'organic-like' Bedouin tent are but two examples of alternate tent concepts that have been successful in other cultures over an extended period of time. Some companies are capitalizing on these designs in everyday life and in special events.

Several companies in North America have already realized the all-season advantages of yurts and have been manufacturing them for consumer, commercial, and governmental use for several years, although large versions on the scale of some larger tents are yet to appear. Most uses to date are for camping and as alternative cold weather climate habitation. The disadvantage of yurt design is primarily the relative lack of portability; however, this may be outweighed by their practicality in terms of being very wind and weather resistant. It is only a matter of time before portability is simplified and we see yurts as viable alternatives for special events, if not in total design, at least in shape.

F3 Freeform Bedouin Tents, a division of Unit Solutions International in South Africa, has developed a freeform tent based on the Bedouin style that permits tents to be completely flexible in their setup. Larger tents with

Courtesy: F3™ form Instant stressed membranes, www.bedouintents.co.za

canopies of up to 10,000 m² (over 100,000 ft²) can be erected with sides up or down or a combination thereof. Poles can be moved around to accommodate varying numbers of guests and to create different shapes. Canopies can be wrapped around trees, rocks, and walls and erected with or without poles. These tents have already been successfully used for special events in South Africa (Figure 8.12).

Additionally, tensile architecture from other cultures is having an influence on tent design with highly artistic results. For example, Russian architect Anwar Khairoylline has exhibited colorfully painted tensile fabrics as building covers and as individual tents. His unique high-peaked and strikingly colored designs are reminiscent of classic Russian church roof architecture. They are distinctly eastern, Cossack-like in concept, yet warm and welcoming at the same time (Figure 8.13 left). As well, Khairoylline has designed specifically shaped tents for mass manufacture but with proprietary cultural designs appliquéd to the walls and roofs of individual tents, thereby enabling very different and eye-catching structures (Figure 8.13 right) (Anwar Khairoylline, Personal Communication, July 25, 2006). These types of design concepts may soon become apparent to Western tent manufacturers and desired by the special event industry.

8.5.4   Materials Technology

As in almost every industry, advances in materials technology are making a profound impact on tents. Composites and materials that combine high

FIGURE 8.13

EXAMPLES OF CULTURAL INFLUENCES ON TENT DESIGN:
A TENT IN A MARKET IN NIZHNEKAMSK,
RUSSIA (LEFT); INDIVIDUAL TENT DESIGN FOR A
MASS MARKET TENT (RIGHT)

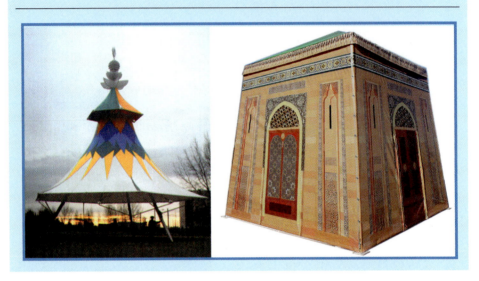

Courtesy: Anwar Khairoylline, www.mi.ru/~anwar-da

strength with light weight have been popular in the automobile and aviation industries for over 20 years. They are now about to enter the tent world in the form of frames that are much stronger and lighter than traditional aluminum. These same composites will also see use as tent walls for semi-permanent buildings such as prisons, hotels, and other structures that require high security. De Boer Vinings, for example, has already used their PVC hard walls for temporary tented prisons.

In another up and coming technology, solar power, Iowa Thin Film Technologies Inc., has developed a new series of tents that incorporate tissue-paper thin film *photo-voltaic* (PV) panels in cooperation with FTL Design Engineering Studio. Anderson (2004) states, 'When integrated into tent fabric, it makes a lightweight, durable source of field power. The power that's generated is stored in batteries and can be used for a variety of purposes such as lighting, ventilation, field communications, global positioning systems (GPS), satellite phones, and laptop computers.' The product can be used as a mesh covering over existing tents or alone (Figure 8.14). Power output for the tents ranges from 200 W to 2 kW. Several tents can be joined together to increase power flow. What this means for special event tenting is that quite possibly in the very near future, tents may serve as their own power source, especially if this technology is integrated into large clearspan tents.

FIGURE 8.14

TENT MESH COVERING INCORPORATING SOLAR PANELS

Courtesy: PowerFilm Inc., www.powerfilmsolar.com

Natural disasters and environmental sustainability have also had an effect on tent design. From the need for instant, strong, and inexpensive shelter coupled with the need for recyclable products, has come the concept of tent covers and structural supports made out of material other than fabric or metal. Of interest are developments utilizing cardboard and cement. One Japanese architect, Shigeru Ban, has been developing 'paper tube' structures for several years, using rolled cardboard tubes as supporting structural members for walls and roofs. A recent design resembling a tent, with cardboard-tube-supported walls and a transparent membrane as a roof, is being used as a boathouse in an interpretation center in Pouilly-en-Auxois, France.

In a related invention, Australian architects Stutchbury and Pape, working in association with the Ian Buchan Fell Housing Research Unit at the University of Sydney, have developed a 100 percent recyclable house that is fully transportable and can be assembled by two people in 6 h (Sydney Olympic Park, 2005). The roof covering is a lightweight material that is as transportable as the structure. Similar to a tent fly, the roof fabric assists in holding down the building, providing a diffuse light in the day and a glowing box at night. This structure is a viable option for temporary housing and might even loosely fit the definition of a tent.

A final novel development is a structure whose intended purpose is to improve upon two current methods of providing emergency shelter: tents, which provide only poor protection, and prefabricated, portable buildings that are expensive and difficult to transport. Dubbed the Concrete Canvas, the shelter, according to Hooper (2005), incorporates the best aspects of both forms. It is almost as easy to transport as a tent, but is as durable and secure as a portable building. The brainchild of engineers William Crawford and Peter Brewin at the Royal College of Art in London, it is essentially a 'building in a bag,' a sack of cement-impregnated fabric. To erect the structure, water is added to the bag and then it is all inflated with air. Twelve hours later the Nissen-shaped shelter is dried out and ready for use.

8.6   RISK AND SAFETY

There are extensive safety regulations in effect in most municipal jurisdictions that must be met before an occupancy permit will be issued to hold a tented event. Occupancy permits should be sought no later than about 1 month before the event. These regulations pertain exclusively to the tents themselves and the interior of the tents.

Kucik (2004) provides an excellent checklist for producers and event managers who are seeking permits for tent installations. Some of the key questions included are the following, the answers to which producers would do well to have available for any tent permit requests.

- Will there be flammable or combustible materials within 10 ft (3 m) of the structure?
- Will fire extinguishers be in clear view and accessible?
- Will the exits, exit aisles, and exit discharge be clear and unobstructed?
- Will there be a fire alarm system, public address system, or alternate method of occupant notification provided for occupant loads exceeding 300?
- Is all tent fabric fire retardant and does it meet the requirements of *NFPA 701, Standard Methods of Fire Tests for Flame-Resistant Textiles and Films* (a US standard)?
- Are all tents/membrane structures provided with a minimum of 20 ft (6 m) perimeter space for emergency egress by the occupants and with a minimum 20 ft roadway for access by emergency personnel?
- Are the tops of tent stakes blunt or covered so as to prevent injury?
- Are there a minimum of two separate exits from any point in the structure where the occupant load is less than 500 persons; three exits for occupant loads between 500 and 999 persons; or four exits for occupant loads exceeding 1000 persons?
- Are changes of elevations at exits, exit access, or exit discharge in compliance with code?
- Is panic hardware or an approved equivalent provided on all exit doors that are lockable?
- Will exits remain accessible and unobstructed while the tent is occupied?
- Are exits designed and arranged to be clearly recognizable and distinctly marked as a means of egress?

- Are directional exit signs provided if exits are not readily visible from all points in the structure?
- Is emergency lighting provided in the tent to illuminate the exit access ways?
- Is the occupant load posted?
- Do electrical installations comply with *NFPA 70, National Electrical Code*?
- Are crowd managers being provided, with a means of emergency forces notification, at a ratio of 1 to 250 people when occupant loads exceed 1000 individuals?
- Are cooking and/or open flames being proposed in the structure? If yes, explain.
- Are pyrotechnics being used in the structure? If yes, explain.
- Are decorative or acoustical materials such as hay, straw, and wood chips being used in the structure? If so, explain.
- Are there motorized vehicles being brought into the structure? If yes, explain.
- Is seating for assembly use accommodating more than 200 persons fastened together in groups of not less than three and not more than seven?
- Are distances between tables and chairs in accordance with local standards?

As well, in 2004, the Orange County Fire Rescue Department in Orlando, Florida created an extensive set of guidelines for tent permit submittals that makes the criteria for safe tent installation very clear. It is one of the most stringent such guidelines known. It is extremely thorough and, for further reference, may be found at http://www.orangecountyfl.net/cmsdocs/dept/ocfrd/ofm/standard6000tents2006.pdf.

Otherwise, in the United States the main safety standards of concern for tenting are produced by the National Fire Protection Association (NFPA) and include:

- *NFPA 70, the National Electrical Code*, pertinent to any electrical installations within tents.
- *NFPA 101, the Life Safety Code*, applicable to the egress of people from tents.
- *NFPA 102, the Standard for Grandstands, Folding and Telescopic Seating, Tents, and Membrane Structures, 2006 Edition*, that covers the construction, location, protection, and maintenance of tents and air-supported structures.
- *NFPA 701, Standard Methods of Fire Tests for Flame-Resistant Textiles and Film*.

In Canada, the equivalent information is covered in the *National Fire Code* and the *National Building Code*, both 2005 editions, published by the National Research Council Canada, and the *National Electrical Code* published by the Canadian Standards Association.

Humanity's love affair with tents extends back to prehistoric times, yet even though most cultures are well past a nomadic lifestyle, it continues unabated today as a means of remaining close to nature. Now, though, it is for more social and commercial reasons and in more comfortable surroundings. Survival is no longer the driving force for 'pitching a tent.' Thanks to our inherent ingenuity, the venerable tent is not just getting old, it truly is getting better.

PRODUCTION CHALLENGES

1. Why are tents used for special events?
2. A large stand-up reception with heavy hors d'oeuvres is planned for a hot summer evening for 3000 corporate VIPs and you are producing the event, which is to be in a tent near a local lake. Explain to your client five possible types and sizes of tents that you might be able to use, including at least one advantage and disadvantage for each type.
3. The weather for the event in question three is predicted to be hot with the possibility of wind and thundershowers. The event will last past sunset. List the possible accessories that will be necessary for this event and why. Keep in mind that the ground surface is a lawn sloping gently down to the lake and that the guests wish to have a good view of the lake throughout the event.
4. Again for the event in question three, outline 10 safety and accessibility considerations that you will have to discuss with your client and your tent rental supplier.
5. Explain some of the new technological developments in tents and consider some ways that they may be incorporated for use in special events.

REFERENCES

Anderson, B. (July 7, 2004). Solar Power Tent Wins Company Award. *The Tribune Online*. Retrieved June 2, 2006, from http://www.powerfilmsolar.com/news/webpages/tribne04.htm.

Bahamon, A. (2004). *The Magic of Tents: Transforming Space*. New York: Harper Design International and LOFT Publications.

Doran, B. (December 1994). Don't Be Left Out in the Cold. *Tents*. pp. 10–13.

Hooper, R. (March 15, 2005). Need a Building? Just Add Water. *Wired News*. Retrieved June 5, 2005, from http://www.wired.com/news/technology/0,1282,66872,00.html.

Industrial Fabrics Association International (IFAI) (Copyright 2002 ©). *IFAI Procedural Handbook for the Safe Installation and Maintenance of Tentage*. Roseville, MN: Industrial Fabrics Association International.

Knight, Ed. (August 2005). Tents Today, Tents Tomorrow: Trends & Options for Experienced Tent Professionals. *Seminar Workbook: 9th Annual Event Solutions Idea Factory*, pp. 173–177.

Kucik, D. (2004). Working with Code Officials: A True Story. *Tent School 2005 Handouts: IFAI Tent Expo*. Roseville: Tent Rental Division, pp. 29–30.

Schluetter, J. (August 2004). Planning the Perfect Tented Event. *Seminar Workbook: 8th Annual Event Solutions Idea Factory*, pp. 139–141.

Sydney Olympic Park (2005). Houses of the Future. Retrieved June 5, 2006, from http://www.housesofthefuture.com.au/hof_houses04.html.

Tracey, F. (2005). Making Your Tent Install Be the Best! *Tent School 2005 Handouts: IFAI Tent Expo*. Roseville: Tent Rental Division, pp. 33–34.

MISCELLANEOUS TECHNICAL RESOURCES

9

Sometimes neglected in the rush to produce an event are critical resources and technicians that work behind the scenes to make everything else function smoothly. This chapter is devoted to these resources, which include electrical power, rigging, and temporary structures. If not dealt with knowledgeably, these resources may cause other event elements to fail. We therefore want to ensure that producers have as complete an understanding as possible of them.

9.1   ELECTRICAL POWER

Virtually everything at a special event nowadays requires electricity, from audio and lighting systems to catering hot plates. Ensuring that adequate power is available for the event is usually one of the duties of the producer. Although calculating the exact power required for all suppliers is not part of these duties, the producer should understand generally how to calculate the electrical power required and what the consequences may be if it is not available. In this section, we will therefore examine how to calculate electrical service requirements, how electrical distribution works, when portable power must be used, and finally safety considerations for working with electrical power.

9.1.1   Determining Electrical Service Requirements

Determining correct electrical service requires matching the power draws of the special event equipment (e.g. lighting, audio, A-V) with the power available in a given venue or at an event site. Power is distributed to large venues such as hotels, arenas, and convention centers in what is commonly referred to as *single-phase* or *three-phase alternating current* (*AC*). This power is usually available from venues in several optional 'packages.' Each of these packages is defined by the voltage or *electromotive force* (E), the amperage or *electrical current* (I), and the *power* (P). Note that 'P' can refer to either the power available from the venue or the power consumed by equipment. The key is to match the two and allow for a safety factor. The relationship amongst these variables is given by a derivative of Ohm's law for AC, namely:

$$I = \frac{P}{E \times PF}$$

if a calculation for the amperage is sought, or alternatively,

$$P = I \times E \times PF$$

if a calculation for power draw in watts is sought, where PF is the *power factor*. This is a number less than one that defines, in an AC circuit, the *real power* compared to the *apparent power*. Simply put, it reflects the fact that due to the way that AC works, the power that a device sees is less than the power that comes into the circuit, and it is device dependent. Typically, for devices such as lights, this factor is in the order of 0.80 and this is a commonly used number. For purposes of simplicity only, this may be considered our safety factor. The above formula works for single-phase power, and here we need to explain the differences between single- and three-phase power. From this point on, we will be referring to the various electrical terms by their units of measurement: voltage in volts (V), amperage in amps (A), and power in watts (W) or kilowatts (kW).

In North America, most power connection points are 120 V, and are frequently referred to as 120/208 V three phase, or 120/240 V single phase. Single-phase power can be either 120 or 120/240 V. In 120 V single-phase service, there is only one *leg* of power feeding the service. In this case, the 120 V is known as the *line-to-neutral voltage* and it is found in single wall outlet receptacles in event venues and most North American homes. Since power is also defined by amperage, most common wall outlets deliver 15 A of electrical current and 120 V, thus allowing up to 1440 W to be drawn safely using the above formula (e.g. the equivalent of a good hair dryer); however, this is insufficient for most special event applications and higher amperage connections must be used to provide enough power.

In a 120/240 V single-phase service, there are two legs of power feeding the service: two wires each carrying 120 V. Because of the way AC works, the V in each of these legs is always 180 degrees out of phase with the other leg, making the available voltage appear as 240 V when the two legs are connected together, which is known as a *line-to-line voltage*.

In a 120/208 V three-phase system, there are three legs of power – or three separate wires – each carrying 120 V. A 120/208 V three-phase power connection actually requires five wires: three *hot* (live) lines each carrying 120 V and a variable number of amps, one neutral wire, and one ground wire. In this system, the three legs are 120 degrees out of phase and the actual available voltage is equivalent to $\sqrt{3}$ or 173% of the single-phase voltage (i.e. 120 V × 173% = 208 V). To account for this, the single-phase formula must be further modified for all calculations involving three-phase power to the following:

$$I = \frac{P}{1.73 \times E \times PF}$$

Now, let us look at how this is all applied for an event. As an example, let us consider that a venue offers the following electrical service packages, in ascending order of cost:

- 20 A, 120 V single phase;
- 30 A, 120/240 V single phase;
- 30 A, 120/208 V three phase;
- 60 A, 120/208 V three phase;
- 100 A, 120/208 V three phase;
- 200 A, 120/208 V three phase.

For this example, let us assume two possible scenarios using lighting. The first one is for eight PAR64, 500 W luminaires for a small stage show. To determine total power, in simple terms, it is a matter of adding up all the luminaires' total wattage, assuming that we might want to connect them all together on a single dimmer system. For example, eight PAR64 stage luminaires each drawing 500 W will require 4000 W, or in another term for the same thing, 4 kW (i.e. 4000 W/1000 W/kilowatt) of power. Using the above formulas the lighting designer (LD) will now calculate what electrical service package is required. The first assumption will be the use of the cheapest package, that of 20 A, 120 V single phase. Knowing the total power draw of the lights, the required amperage can be calculated as follows:

$$I = \frac{4000}{120 \times .80} = 42 \text{ A}$$

Obviously, the package offered is inadequate since it is only 20 A. The LD will now try the next feasible power package of 30 A, 240 V single phase. The calculation is:

$$I = \frac{4000}{240 \times .80} = 21 \text{ A}$$

This package will be safe for the intended lighting as the required amperage (21) is less than the amperage provided (30). Of course, another option is also the 60 A, three-phase service, but that is more expensive and is overkill.

Now let us consider a second scenario, more of a concert-type show, with 40, 1000 W PAR64 luminaires. The total power draw will be 40,000 W (i.e. 40 kW). The LD might begin by calculating the current required using a single phase, 240 V service, as follows:

$$I = \frac{40,000}{240 \times .80} = 208 \text{ A}$$

Again, this is a higher required amperage than any of the options offered, so three-phase service must be considered. The lowest possible option that may provide sufficient power is 200 A, 208 V, three-phase service. The calculation is now done using the three-phase formula:

$$I = \frac{40,000}{1.73 \times 208 \times .80} = 139 \text{ A}$$

This option will therefore provide sufficient power for the lighting since the required amperage of 139 is less than the provided amperage of 200.

Also a consideration for the LD is the voltage drop over their own cables between the lights and the dimmers and the console, but they will already have this calculated and have it built into their power requirements. The same holds true for other suppliers such as audio and A-V. For more discussion and theory pertaining to AC and power distribution, Bloomfield (2006), Wikipedia contributors (2006), Candela (2006), Brain (2006), and Electricians' Toolbox (1997) make good reading.

9.1.2   Electrical Distribution

Now that the amount of electrical power available is known, all that is needed is to connect to the power outlet in the venue using a matching connector and then distribute the necessary power to all equipment. We begin with connection and then move to actual distribution.

9.1.2.1   *Accessing Venue Power*

Depending on the amount of power required as calculated above, the decision will have to be made by the equipment supplier (e.g. lighting, audio, A-V) whether single phase will suffice or whether the load is going to be so great and/or the devices so many that three phase will be needed. Let us first look at single phase.

9.1.2.1.1   Single-Phase Connections

The most common connections for taking single-phase power from the venue are:

- *NEMA 5 (National Electrical Manufacturers Association)*: This is also referred to as a Type B, North American 3-pin, and sometimes just a 'wall plug,' or 'Edison.' All NEMA 5 devices are three-wire grounding devices rated for 125 V maximum, coming in 5-15, 5-20, and 5-30 versions (the second number refers to the amperage of the circuit). The 5-15 is by far the most common electrical outlet in North America. The Type B plug is used in events only with 120 V single phase and therefore small electrical loads (see Figure 9.1).
- *NEMA 14*: 'The NEMA 14 devices are four-wire grounding devices available in ratings from 15 to 60 A. Of the straight-blade NEMA 14 devices, only the 14-30 and 14-50 are common. The 14-30 is used for electric clothes dryers and the 14-50 for electric cooking ranges. For events, the most common is the 14-50, often referred to as a *range plug*. It is used mainly for small audio and lighting systems. The voltage rating is a design maximum of 125/250 V. All NEMA 14 devices offer two *hots*, a neutral and a ground, allowing for both 120 and 240 single-phase use. They differ in rating and shape of the neutral pin. The 14-30 has a rating of 30 A and an L-shaped neutral pin. The 14-50 has a rating of 50 A and a straight neutral pin sized so that it will not fit in the slot of a 14-30' (Wikipedia contributors, August 10, 2006) (see Figure 9.1).
- *NEMA twist-lock*: 'Twist-locking connectors were first invented by Harvey Hubbell III in 1938 and "twist-lock" remains a registered trademark of Hubbell Incorporated to this day, although the term tends to be used generically to refer to NEMA twist-locking connectors manufactured by any company. Unlike non-locking connectors, twist-locking connectors all use curved blades that have shapes that conform to portions of the circumference of a circle. Once pushed into the receptacle, the plug is twisted and its now-rotated prongs latch into the receptacle. To unlatch the plug, the rotation is reversed. The locking coupling makes for a very reliable connection in commercial and industrial settings. Like non-locking connectors, these come in a variety of standardized

configurations and follow the same general naming scheme except that they all begin with an "L" for "locking." The L5-20 (20 A) is the most common. Once again, the connector families are designed so that 120 V connectors, 208/240 V connectors, and various other, higher-voltage connectors cannot be accidentally intermated' (Wikipedia contributors, August 10, 2006) (see Figure 9.1 for an example). For special events, twist-lock connectors are used only for single-phase applications, typically in theaters, arenas, and occasionally in hotels and convention centers for relatively small lighting requirements. Twist-lock connectors are more common in Canada than the comparable stage pin connectors (SPC) in the USA.

- *SPC*: An SPC is a standard for theatrical lighting, although occasionally they can be used with something else. They are usually rated for 15–20 A at 110–120 V, single-phase stage lighting applications, primarily in the USA and not in Canada. See Figure 9.1 for an example from Entertainment Power Systems, the SP-20 SPC, male and female. Both the SPC and the twist-lock connector would typically be plugged into dimmer packs for lighting.

FIGURE 9.1
SINGLE-PHASE ELECTRICAL CONNECTIONS

The connections represented in Figure 9.1 are:

- *Top row, left*: Type B, NEMA 5–15 electrical plug (courtesy http://en.wikipedia.org/wiki/Image:Domestic_AC_Type_B_US.jpg).
- *Top row, right*: NEMA 14–50 socket design (courtesy http://www.levitonproducts.com/catalog/model_279.htm?sid=A84FEBB977668939D5EDCB7F86FD66E8&pid=1208).
- *Bottom row, left*: NEMA twist-lock connector (courtesy http://en.wikipedia.org/wiki/Image:L21-30plug_proc_small.jpg).
- *Bottom row, right*: Male and female SPC (courtesy Entertainment Power Systems, www.entertainmentpowersystems.com, U.S. Pat. No. Des. 502,919).

9.1.2.1.2 Three-Phase Connections

Once it is determined that the power requirements are very large, suppliers will request hookup to three-phase power at the venue. This can come in one of two ways:

- *Pin and sleeve*: Pin and sleeve circular male connectors mate directly with female receptacles that are often present in major hotels and convention centers for high-power applications. Depending on the venue, current ratings vary up to about 400 A and voltage ratings vary up to about 600 V AC. Contact arrangements are from three to five pins. The contacts in the plug are pins and those in the receptacle are simple cylinders (sleeves). These connectors are often referred to as 'Blue Hubbell' after a manufacturer, although they come in different colors and configurations. The object of this connection is to take the house power and output it to compatible five-wire *Cam lock connectors* (see Section 9.1.2.2). It is typically the lighting company that will bring the male pin and sleeve connector to the venue and tie it into the female receptacle. In essence, the pin and sleeve connector is really no more than an adaptor. Figure 9.2 (left top) shows a typical three-phase tie-in consisting of a five-pin Blue Hubbell pin and sleeve connector at one end of the tie-in and five different colored Cam lock connectors at the other end.
- *Wall box*: This situation also occurs in many venues. The three-phase power comes into the venue and is distributed to wall boxes that have five terminal lugs inside instead of a female pin and sleeve connection. For this type of tie-in, a qualified electrician is required (usually from the venue), who connects the lugs with the bare wire ends of female Cam lock connectors for the lighting or audio techs to use. Sometimes, the Cam lock connection has already been made in the venue. With a wall box situation, it is important to ensure that the correct voltage and amperage are present, and that all safety precautions are followed due to the high risk of serious injury or death. Nobody but a qualified electrician should be allowed to make these connections.

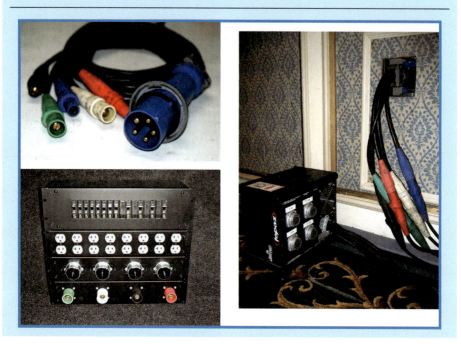

Courtesy: Doug Matthews and Q1 Production Technologies, www.q1pt.com, and Pro Stage
and Audio, www.prostageandstudio.com

9.1.2.2   *Distributing Three-Phase Power*

Once the tie-in has been made to the house three-phase power, connections must be made to *distribution panels* or *boxes*, sometimes also referred to as *distro boxes*, or in many cases, directly into a lighting dimmer pack.

The primary connector for accomplishing this is the Cam lock connector. Cam lock connectors are attached to the ends of the pin and sleeve wiring or the direct wall box wiring. Amundson (2006) states, 'Cam lock connectors come in three sizes (1015, 1016, and 1017). The 1016 size is the most common with a maximum rating of 400 A. Most Cam locks are weatherproof, with their colored rubber boots protecting innocent fingers when open and forming a watertight connection when connected.' The colors correspond to the different functions of the line, and are not arbitrary, as follows: green (ground), white (neutral), black (phase one), blue (phase two), red (phase three). See Figure 9.2 (right) for an example of Cam lock connectors used to connect hotel house power to a lighting dimmer pack. Note the colored connectors as described. Also note the blue male Hubbell (pin and sleeve) connector (provided by the lighting company) inside the wall which would have been attached to a female pin and sleeve connection provide by this hotel.

With the house power now going into a distribution panel (or dimmer pack as illustrated), this power must now be broken down into smaller 50 A circuits of single-phase power for use with the various lighting, audio, or A-V components (and sometimes musical equipment). That is the purpose of the distribution panel (or dimmer pack when specifically for lighting), which will usually contain a number of different connection options (as described in Section 9.1.2.1.1) as well as individual circuit breakers for each circuit. See Figure 9.2 (left bottom), a typical distro panel that has the color-coded Camlock inputs (green, white, black, red), four twist-lock output connections, 16 NEMA 5 output connections (actually eight *duplex* NEMA 5 connections), as well as 20 circuit breakers for each of the 20 total single-phase circuits.

9.1.3 Portable Power

Whenever an event is held away from one of the standard event venues such as hotels, arenas, or convention centers, and particularly outdoors, there is a high probability that electrical service will not be readily available. In these cases, portable generating units must be brought in. These units are typically trailer towed and take the place of the house power that would be found indoors, and most come with at least some power distribution breakout. They come from various manufacturers and in various sizes that provide power up to 400 V AC and amperages from 250 to 2400 (Garber, October, 2002). Most run on diesel fuel and nowadays, thanks to technological advances driven by the movie industry, are extremely quiet, allowing them to be placed fairly close to event guests – but hidden – without fear of too much noise interference. Two points bear mentioning in the use of portable generators. The first is that fuel levels must be monitored constantly to ensure that fuel does not run out. As noted by Garber (2006), some rental companies actually have global positioning systems (GPS) that enable them to monitor their rental units to check the fuel status. The second point is that for large events, a backup unit can act as insurance in case the first one goes down, and also to spread the electrical load more evenly.

9.1.4 Electrical Safety Considerations

For personnel safety, the appropriate organizations in the USA are the Occupational Safety and Health Administration (OSHA) and the National Fire Protection Association (NFPA), as well as individual states. The NFPA has a safety standard (*NFPA 70E: Electrical Safety in the Workplace, 2004 Edition*) that is the document to which the OSHA adheres. Installation and general design standards for electrical equipment are covered in detail in *NFPA 70: National Electrical Code (NEC)*, and although it is not law, most jurisdictions require compliance with the NEC. Additionally, specific design standards come from NEMA and they 'define a product, process, or procedure with reference to one or more of the following: nomenclature, composition, construction, dimensions, tolerances, safety, operating char-acteristics, performance, rating, testing, and the service for which it is designed' (NEMA, 2006). These are numerous and event producers should ensure that suppliers use equipment that meets these standards whenever there is a standard.

In Canada, responsibility for the electrical safety of personnel rests with the provinces and territories. Every province and territory adopts and enforces the same installation code, promulgated by the Canadian Standards Association (CSA), *C22.1-07: Canadian Electrical Code, Part I (20th Edition), Safety Standard for Electrical Installations*. The electrical codes are eventu-ally incorporated into each jurisdiction's regulations for enforcement. With respect to equipment design standards, these requirements are set through *CSA C22.2: Canadian Electrical Code, Part II*. Again, they are adopted (with or without modifications) and enforced by the provincial and territo-rial electrical safety authorities. This ensures that equipment installed in conjunction with the CEC will be compatible and safe to use under the installation rules. CEC Part II contains a myriad of individual equipment standards, and event producers should ensure that the equipment from their suppliers meets the standards wherever applicable. Many are compatible with US standards.

Useful guidelines for general personnel electrical safety that pertain to the event environment can also be found at the Electricians' Toolbox web site (www.elec-toolbox.com) and at the Canadian Centre for Occupational Health and Safety web site (http://www.ccohs.ca/oshanswers/safety_haz/electrical.html); however, the applicable standards for each state/province should be understood completely by event producers. Van Beek (2004) also provides some useful explanations about circuitry and safety, although ori-ented to Europe.

9.2   RIGGING AND TRUSSING

In special events, there are frequent occasions when décor pieces, lighting equipment, audio speakers, visual presentation equipment, and even people must be suspended or *flown* over a stage and/or an audience. To safely rig and fly equipment, a thorough knowledge of rigging hardware and methodology is necessary. If items are improperly rigged and flown, people can be killed! The intent of this section is to present a general overview of rigging, an expla-nation of some of the equipment that is commonly used in the special event environment, and a brief review of safety.

9.2.1   Overview

Rigging involves raising equipment and people to a height above the ground. In so doing, the *rigger* or qualified technician must attach support cable and occasionally hoisting equipment to *hanging points* in the ceiling of a venue. These are specially strengthened structural locations in the building that permit the hanging of heavy objects up to certain load limits. Usually, the ceiling of a venue is equipped at these locations with bracketry or bolts for this purpose. Riggers need to know the proper methods of securing items like cable (wire rope) to this bracketry and then to other objects (e.g. trussing for lighting) without the possibility of slippage or cable or bolt breakage. 'Overloading a line poses a serious threat to the safety of personnel, not to mention the heavy losses likely to result through damage to material. To avoid overloading, the rigger must know the strength of the rigging system and components used in it. This involves three factors: *breaking strength*, *safe working load (SWL)*, and *safety factor*. Breaking strength refers to the tension at which a line (e.g. cable) will part when a load is applied. Breaking strength has been determined through tests made by cable manufacturers, and tables have been set up to provide this information. The SWL of a line is the load that can be applied without causing any kind of damage to the line. A wide margin of difference between breaking strength and SWL is necessary to allow for such factors as additional strain imposed on the line by jerky movements in hoisting or bending over sheaves in a pulley block' (ePanorama.net, 2006). The safety factor of a line is the ratio between the breaking strength and the SWL. Safety factors will vary, depending on such things as the condition of the line and the circumstances under which it is to be used. The safety factor is usually four to ten.

Rick Smith, the president of Riggit Services Inc. in Vancouver, Canada, a certified rigger with over 20 years of experience in event rigging, notes that before rigging begins, the load rating of the venue hanging points has to be in writing from either the venue or from an engineer. He cautions that too often the somewhat hazy corporate memory of either venue staff or older technicians is the source of a load rating, and that is neither professional nor safe (Rick Smith, Personal Communication, September 7, 2006).

9.2.2   Rigging Equipment

Rigging and its ancestry derive from the theater world and go as far back as the ancient Greeks, with a myriad of ropes, cables, pulleys, and lifting equipment designed for that environment. For simplicity of understanding, we will restrict our discussion to basic attachment hardware, flying methods, and trussing.

9.2.2.1   *Basic Attachment Hardware*

The most common hardware used for events includes:

- *Wire rope*: 'Often called cable, this is the most common method of attaching gear to ceilings. Wire rope is a material made of several strands of thin steel wire groups. Different types of wire rope exist, the main differences being the arrangement of the wires, and the type of steel used. One type of wire rope used frequently is called *hoisting cable*, and is typically 6 × 19 in construction. This means that there are 6 larger strands of 19 wires each. Hoisting cable is often used in fly systems, as it is strong and flexible. *Aircraft cable* is another type of wire rope that is used often in theater applications. It is usually 7 × 19 in construction, and is more flexible and stronger than hoisting cable. Aircraft cable is made out of specially processed steel that has a very high tensile strength' (Richardson, 2000).

- *Thimbles, wire rope clips, and swages*: 'Any time the wire rope needs to be attached to a hang point that would cause the cable to sharply bend, a device called a *thimble* must be used. Thimbles simply guide the cable into a natural curve shape and offer a degree of protection to the cable in the loop. To secure the end of the rope, wire rope *U-clips* are used. These clips provide an effective means for terminating cables. Another method for securing the ends of wire rope is through the use of *swages*, or *nico-press sleeves*. Small metal sleeves are pressed on to the wire rope with a special tool. These sleeves are permanent, but act much in the same way that clips do. When properly applied, swages can hold the full rated working load of the cable they are attached to' (Richardson, 2000).

- *Shackles, turnbuckles, and hooks*: 'A wide variety of additional rigging hardware exists for various tasks. *Turnbuckles* are used in situations where small adjustments need to be made in the length of a cable. Usually turnbuckles are not used to bear load, but rather in tensioning guy wires. *Shackles* are often used with locking *hooks* to connect between wire rope and nylon harnesses or rope' (Richardson, 2000).

- *Chain*: Chain is typically used in conjunction with *pulleys* or *chain motors* to raise trussing on which luminaires and audio speakers may be clamped. It is important to note that only welded-link steel chain should be used to bear loads, and the load capacity of the chain should be verified to ensure it can carry the anticipated load.

- *Slings*: 'One of the most common ways to hang truss for flying is through the use of slings made of a synthetic material such as polyester. A modern sling consists of a synthetic fiber core encased in a woven synthetic casing. Slings of this nature tend to be very strong and quite durable, and by nature conform to the shape of the load they are carrying. There are many acceptable methods for attaching slings to the truss to fly it. The most common involves the use of four slings. When the truss is flown point down, a choker scheme is used, whereby the sling wraps through itself and around the truss' (Richardson, 2000).

Figure 9.3 (left) illustrates a combination of the hardware discussed above. Note the black sling supporting the truss, the wire rope acting as an additional safety cable, the thimbles and swages on the rope ends, and the chain fall and red hook that are used in conjunction with a pulley system to hand raise the truss into position. The large black bag is used to contain the excess chain once the truss has been raised.

FIGURE 9.3
RIGGING HARDWARE

Courtesy: Doug Matthews and Q1 Production Technologies, www.q1pt.com (left photo), and Prolyte Products Group, www.prolyte.com (right photo).

9.2.2.2 *Flying Methods*

There are generally two main methods used to fly equipment or people in special events:

■ *Chain and pulleys*: In certain situations with relatively light loads, a pulley system is attached to the ceiling hanging point and a heavy-duty chain as described above is run through the pulleys. There are usually at least two pulleys on a length of truss or more if the length is a long one. The pulley system is mechanically advantaged which means that when it is pulled by hand to raise the trussing, the actual weight pulled is much less than the weight of the truss.

■ *Chain motor*: Likewise, a motor may be substituted for the pulleys. 'A chain motor is simply a large electric motor with a gearbox and a chain drive mounted in one chassis. The chassis of the motor generally has a large hook mounted on its underside, to which loads are attached. An extremely heavy gauge chain with a hook at one end passes through the motor and into a chain bag. The hook of this chain is generally clipped to the shackle of a wire rope sling, which is attached to a load-bearing overhead beam (or it may be attached directly to the overhead beam or hanging point – author). Once the attachment has been made to an overhead hang point, the motors can have loads attached for flying' (Richardson, 2000). The motor is then controlled to raise or lower the truss by handheld controls, sometimes called *pickles*, located on the floor. It is important, notes Rick Smith of Riggit Services in Vancouver,

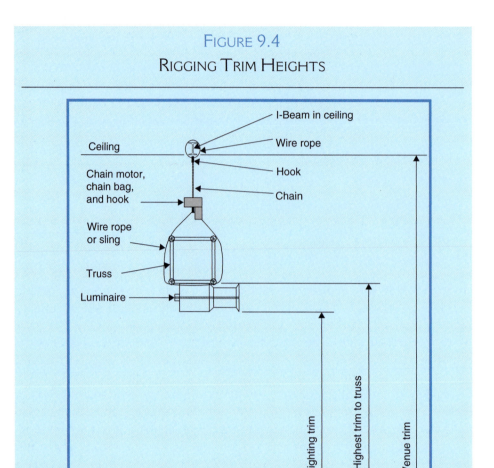

FIGURE 9.4

RIGGING TRIM HEIGHTS

Labels in figure:

I-Beam in ceiling

Ceiling

Wire rope

Chain motor, chain bag, and hook

Hook

Chain

Wire rope or sling

Truss

Luminaire

Lighting trim

Highest trim to truss

Venue trim

Floor

Courtesy: Doug Matthews

to ensure that all phases of a chain motor are in synch; otherwise the motor may inadvertently reverse when the switch is pushed, causing older motors with no safety mechanism to literally 'eat' the chain and hook. Figure 9.3 (right) illustrates trussing attached to slings and chain motors ready to be raised into position.

Smith also cautions that, when working with chain motor/truss combinations, technicians and producers must understand the exact definition of *trim height*, which is the final height above the ground or floor that the rigged equipment (e.g. lighting truss) must reside. He notes that there are as many as three different interpretations of the term and it is important that everyone involved understands the definition being used. As shown in Figure 9.4, the *venue trim* is the height above the floor to the lowest attachment point in the ceiling, the *highest trim to truss* or *low trim* is the distance from the floor to the bottom of a standard 16 in. (40 cm) truss, and the *lighting trim* is the distance from the floor to the lights or, in some cases, A-V equipment (e.g. projectors). Those involved have to understand that there must be space allowed for the wire ropes, hooks, chain motors, and chains between the ceiling and the truss (Rick Smith, Personal Communication, September 7, 2006). The 'War Story' in Chapter 5 illustrates what can happen when there is a misunderstanding of the term 'trim height.'

9.2.2.3   Trussing

We initiated a discussion about trussing in Chapter 5 and described how it is used in a variety of configurations for hanging luminaires. In this section, we will examine its design and safety.

Trussing as we know it, started to develop at the end of the 1970s in response to the entertainment industry's demand for lightweight, strong temporary structures that could span the width of a stage and be used to hang lighting and audio systems. Familiar with the spatial lattice structures found in bridges, scaffolding, and buildings, manufacturers used this as the basis for modern truss design. Today it is ubiquitous in the industry and comes in a wide variety of sizes, shapes, colors, and strengths.

Trussing must be able to withstand loads imposed on it in shear (i.e. force directed along the cross section, such as high loads on top of a vertical truss section) and in deflection (i.e. force directed down and perpendicular to its horizontal axis, such as too many luminaires clamped in one position). The amount it can withstand depends of course on its size and rated load. Each type and size of truss is rated by the manufacturer for specific maximum loads under these conditions. It is therefore critical that riggers know the exact loads that will be imposed on the truss in these conditions and what the total weight of the loaded truss will be so that the correct choice of supporting wire rope cable, slings, and chain motors may be made. Not only that, but the truss supplier for an event, usually the lighting company, is obligated to understand the load rating of their truss and to choose the proper truss accordingly, knowing in detail what the loading will be before the truss is ever rigged into position.

Particularly important are unique loading scenarios encountered outdoors. These include:

- *Wind*: Wind can cause damage to canopies and walls, it can overload trusses and towers due to the extra load of attached walls, and it can lift all or part of the complete structure.
- *Rain or snow*: This can make trussing slippery for climbing, it can cause overloading of rooftops due to accumulation of snow or water, it can cause short circuiting in control systems, and it can cause the support of saturated soils to weaken.
- *Lightning*: This can cause severe personal safety risk if it hits towers.

- *Temperature*: Solar heat can cause aluminum to become extremely hot, thus making it unsafe to the touch. It may also cause the safe temperature of any polyester sling covers to exceed their allowable limit (e.g. surface temperature can reach 150° C, greater than the normal safe limit for polyester of 100° C).

It is therefore imperative that such things as roofs be constructed properly and with due consideration of the expected weather conditions. For example, the inclusion of supporting guy wires, base distance frames (to minimize compression loads), and adequate ballast is absolutely necessary. Additionally, heights of towers and roofs must be restricted to recommended maximums, both indoors and outdoors. For example, the height of a tower grid system should be no more than 6 m (20 ft) if the width of the outrigger tower base is 2 m (7 ft). Outdoors, the height of a tower grid is generally three, and indoors four times the base width as a rule of thumb. A properly qualified rigger and the truss supplier should be able to certify compliance with these requirements. The accompanying war story describes the consequences of what can happen when proper design of trussing is not completed.

PRODUCTION WAR STORY: STAGE ROOF COLLAPSE IN TURKEY

When the roof first started going up for a multi-day festival in Turkey, I noticed a few things that worried me about the setup. Since all my rigging experience had been in ballrooms, tents, and convention centers and I had never worked with a self-climbing truss stage roof before, I didn't feel qualified to raise issue with the setup. However, some things that seemed unsafe included:

- The tower feet were placed on 6 in. × 6 in. pieces of 1/2 in. ply, not much bigger than the feet themselves.
- Truss was Thomas Supertruss and the crew wasn't using the safety clips on the truss pins.
- The roof was supported only at the peak. There were no support beams running from the peak to the sides, only a couple of steel cables in an 'X'. Thus the roof sagged and collected water. The crew used a pole to push the roof up so that the water would run off!!!

On the opening day of the festival, about an hour before the start, there was a sudden thunderstorm. There were massive lightning strikes in the mountains all around us (imagine my anger when I found the grounding stake was attached to the generator with 12-gauge wire!), and a massive amount of water started coming down. Everyone around the stage immediately got under the roof as the water coming down was as intense as anything I'd ever seen, including my times in the Amazon basin. Within minutes there were large puddles of water all over the field and everything not under the roof was soaked.

Continued

This went on for about 4–5 min. Suddenly, the rain turned to hail, about the size of dimes. And it was coming down hard! A cry went out to look at the roof. We looked up and there was a small lake on the roof, which was growing rapidly, with another on the other side but smaller. The sticks the crew was using earlier to clear water were now too short to reach the roof at trim, so they sent a couple of guys up into the truss to attempt to relieve the strain somehow. Within minutes the lake had grown to what I would estimate to be about 400 gal. The tarp was stretching between the peak and the side truss to allow this. One of the guys in the truss went to cut the tarp, but the company owner told him not to. It looked as if the tarp was going to break and dump a ton of water onto the stage.

Suddenly, there was a 'grrrunnnk' sound from the truss. I looked up to see that the truss piece creating the side of the roof had bent. At either end, near the corner blocks, the truss had bent, allowing the center section of the truss to pull inward about 2–3 ft. The upside-down boil on the tarp just kept growing as it stretched and filled with water and hail. At this point I decided to abandon ship and took a flying leap off the front of the stage. I turned around to see at least half the people still under the roof staring at the boil!!! I started screaming, 'The roof is going to fall! Get out of the way,' but they didn't listen. Thirty seconds later the roof collapsed on them. The bent section of truss gave way and we ended up with a huge mess. Amazingly, nobody died or was even hurt! And remember the two guys who were climbing the truss? They both jumped to safety! Thank God they weren't wearing safety harnesses.

Courtesy: Name withheld by request

9.2.3 Safety

Every year serious rigging accidents occur around the world, from workers falling off platforms, to trussing collapses, many resulting in serious injuries or death. Between 2002 and 2003, for example, four major stage and truss collapses occurred, including rigs set up for Justin Timberlake and Christina Aguilera, the Red Hot Chili Peppers, South African president Mbeki, and Christian rock group Godstock. Although nobody was killed in any of these, in most cases the damage was in the hundreds of thousands of dollars and for some, a tour cancellation and continuing litigation. The collapse described in this chapter's war story is another example from 2006. Indeed, there may be no other area of special event production that carries such a high-risk factor, including pyrotechnics.

According to Martin (1996), unlike the electrical industry, 'the entertainment rigging industry is almost universally unregulated.' Certainly, in recent years, some safety and design standards as listed below have evolved through the Department of the Environment (DOE), the American National Standards

Institute (ANSI), the Entertainment Services and Technology Association (ESTA), and the OSHA in the USA.

- *DOE-STD-1090–2004: Hoisting and Rigging Standard (Formerly Hoisting and Rigging Manual).*
- *ANSI Board of Standards Review, BSR E1.6–2: Entertainment Technology-Serial Manufactured Electric Chain Hoists.*
- *ANSI E1.1 – 1999: Entertainment Technology – Construction and Use of Wire Rope Ladders.*
- *ANSI E1.15 – 2006: Entertainment Technology – Recommended Practices and Guidelines for the Assembly and Use of Theatrical Boom & Base Assemblies.*
- *ANSI E1.2 – 2006: Entertainment Technology – Design, Manufacture and Use of Aluminum Trusses and Towers.*
- *ANSI E1.21 – 2006: Temporary Ground-Supported Overhead Structures Used to Cover Stage Areas and Support Equipment in the Production of Outdoor Entertainment Events.*

These standards, however, are far from complete, definitely less so than standards in Europe. In most cases, state or provincial health authorities have generated their own manuals and regulations for rigging, unfortunately not universally standard.

What is left for event producers is a very large responsibility for safety in a technically confusing and high-risk environment. We have already mentioned the criticality of using safety factors in rigging, and this is echoed strongly by Donovan (2002, 2003) and Glerum (1997). Donovan's position – and it is really the only rational one – is that the best way to eliminate liability is to avoid accidents, pure and simple. According to Donovan (2003), safety factors are established because of equipment degradation, unknown weights, dynamic loads (e.g. rig movement), shock loads (e.g. sudden stopping of motor chain hoists), unevenly distributed loads, incomplete knowledge, and human error. He recommends a minimum safety factor of five (European standards often call for 10), but with this modified by taking into account variables such as those mentioned (e.g. reduced strength and dynamic loads). The basic equation that is used by riggers to determine the allowable load for a specific support (e.g. a wire rope attached to a ceiling hanging point) is given by:

$$\text{Allowable load} = \frac{(\text{rigging strength})}{(\text{safety factor})}$$

where the rigging strength is the *breaking strength* or *rated capacity* of the wire rope and the allowable load is the total load to be lifted. However, Donovan also notes that this figure must be further modified by other factors to arrive at:

$$\text{Allowable load} = \frac{(\text{rigging strength}) \times (\text{strength reduction factor})}{(\text{safety factor}) \times (\text{load increase factor})}$$

where the strength reduction factor is a percentage based on the reduced strength caused by such things as a knot in the rope, and the load increase factor is a number greater than one caused by such things as dynamic loading caused by raising the load with a hoist.

According to Donovan, 'the importance of the strength reduction and load increase factors can be seen in the following exercise. Using a safety factor of five, find the allowable load for a ⅜ in. wire rope that has a breaking strength of 14,400 lb and supports a 16 ft/min chain hoist. The wire rope is bent over a tight turn, causing a strength loss of 30 percent (i.e. a strength reduction factor of 0.70 – author). When the hoist stops and starts, there is an increase of about 25 percent to the static load. If strength reduction and load increase factors are neglected, the allowable load might seem to be:

$$\text{Allowable load} = \frac{\text{(rigging strength)}}{\text{(safety factor)}} = \frac{14,400\,\text{lbs}}{5} = 2880\,\text{lb}$$

However, the equation above is incorrect because the true allowable load must include the strength reduction and load increase factors. Here is the proper equation:

$$\text{Allowable load} = \frac{\text{(rigging strength)} \times \text{(strength reduction factor)}}{\text{(safety factor)} \times \text{(load increase factor)}}$$
$$= \frac{(14,400\,\text{lb})(0.7)}{(5)(1.25)} = \frac{10,080}{6.25}\,\text{lb} = 1612\,\text{lb}$$

In this scenario, the difference of 1268 lb in actual strength is of great significance and illustrates the need for taking strength reduction and load increase factors into account.'

This means that everyone in the chain of command must ensure that the correct safety factors are used, and that they incorporate: the manufacturer's design loading for the equipment; the truss supplier's calculations for truss loading; the rigger's calculations for safety factors and choice of supporting material that ensures the right factor; and finally, the producer's guarantee that this has been done correctly. To avoid potential liability, this implies that the producer should demand a paper trail from the rigger and trussing supplier for all calculations and equipment load limits, preferably contractually, following the methodology explained in Chapters 6 and 7 of *Special Event Production: The Process*.

One positive recent development is the introduction of a North American, industry-wide certification program by ESTA. This program, called the Entertainment Technician Certification Program (ETCP), requires that riggers pass a 3 h knowledge exam set and scored by an independent body, the Applied Measurement Professionals, Inc. There are two certification categories: ETCP Certified Rigger – Arena, and ETCP Certified Rigger – Theater. For the special event industry, the arena certification is the desired one and it is strongly recommended that producers only work with such qualified individuals.

9.3   OTHER TEMPORARY STRUCTURES

For outdoor events, there is one final technical area that occasionally falls under the supervision of the event producer and that is temporary structures (other than tents and stages that have already been discussed). For this section, we will reserve discussion to scaffolding, bleachers, fencing or barricades, and portable washrooms, including a review of safety and design standards for each. By definition, the term *demountable structures* is often used in conjunction with temporary structures, particularly sectionalized ones that can be assembled and disassembled easily and quickly for portability (e.g. stages, tents, fencing, scaffolding, box truss arrangements, and bleachers).

9.3.1   Scaffolding

Although the term is used in other contexts, scaffolding in our industry is a temporary framework used to support people and equipment such as audio speakers, luminaires, special effects, performers, and technical crew as part of the operation of a special event.

9.3.1.1   Construction

Scaffolding is usually a modular system of metal pipes and wooden boards, although it can be made out of other materials. Pipes are either steel or aluminum. If steel they are either black or galvanized. The pipes come in a variety of lengths and a standard diameter of 1.90 in. (known as *1.5 NPS pipe* in North America), or 48.3 mm. *Couplers* are the fittings that hold the pipes together. *Boards* provide a working surface for users of the scaffold. They are made of seasoned wood and come in various thicknesses and widths. As well as boards for the working platform, there are *sole boards* that are placed beneath the scaffolding if the surface is soft or otherwise suspect.

'The key components of a scaffold are *standards*, *ledgers*, and *transoms*. The standards, also called *uprights*, are the vertical pipes that transfer the weight of the entire mass of the structure to the ground where they rest on a square *base plate* to spread the load. The base plate has a shank in its center to hold the pipe and is sometimes pinned to the sole board. Ledgers are horizontal tubes which connect between the standards. Transoms rest upon the ledgers at right angles. *Main transoms* are placed next to the standards. They hold the standards in place and provide support for boards; *intermediate transoms* are those placed between the main transoms to provide extra support for boards' (Wikipedia contributors, August 2, 2006) (see Figure 9.5 (left)).

'Other common components include guard rails for safety, ladders for access, and *cross braces* to increase rigidity. Cross braces are often placed diagonally from ledger to ledger, next to the standards to which they are fitted. If the braces are fitted to the ledgers, they are called *ledger braces*. To limit

Courtesy: http://en.wikipedia.org/wiki/Image:Scaff_t_01.png (left); Doug Matthews (right)

sway, a *facade brace* is fitted to the face of the scaffold at an angle of 35–55 degrees running right from the base to the top of the scaffold and fixed at every level' (Wikipedia contributors, August 2, 2006). Figure 9.5 (right) shows a fully constructed scaffold used to support performers, lighting, and special effects. Note the pipe construction, boards, bracing, and guard rails. Scaffolds may also be covered with custom roofs, polyvinyl chloride (PVC) panels, or windscreen panels for the sides. A general safety rule of thumb for freestanding scaffold construction is a maximum 3:1 height to base width ratio, as clearly shown in Figure 9.5 (right).

9.3.1.2 *Safety*

The US Department of Labor Occupational Safety and Health Organization (OSHA) has very specific standards for the construction and use of scaffolding in the workplace, and many large commercial and government construction projects require all workers to have scaffold training and OSHA certification. The main standard applying to general industry (i.e. special events) is *Title 29 Code of Federal Regulations (CFR) Part 1910.28: Safety Requirements for Scaffolding*. There are also a number of others that pertain to specific industries and producers should ensure that the correct standards are being followed by consultation with their subcontractors and the OSHA. Some of the OSHA regulations regarding construction of scaffolding include using specific types of lumber when not using steel, weight limitations based on the design of the scaffolding, and regular checks for weakened or broken sections.

In Canada, the responsibility for scaffold safety rests with each province and each one has individual standards that require compliance. General safety guidelines are available from the Canadian Centre for Occupational Health and Safety (CCOHS), but these are not enforceable, unlike the provincial standards. Producers should obtain copies of their provincial standards to ensure compliance.

Design standards are many, as they pertain to the various materials used in scaffold construction (e.g. wood, pipe, etc.). The British Standards Institute publishes numerous specific design and safety standards for entire scaffolds and scaffold components, including proper grounding. They can be found at http://www.bsi-global.com/index.xalter for those wishing further references.

9.3.2 Bleachers

Bleachers used for outdoor events are typically lightweight, aluminum portable units that are foldable. They are unlike the chair and riser combination that is used indoors mentioned in Chapter 7.

9.3.2.1 *Construction*

Although not completely consistent with all manufacturers, portable bleachers generally have a rise of 8 in. (20 cm), a horizontal depth of 24 in. (60 cm), and seats have a rise above the tread of 17 in. (43 cm). Seat sizes are 1.5 to 2.0 in. × 9.5 to 10.0 in. (3.75 to 5 cm × 24 to 25 cm), all usually constructed of anodized aluminum with end caps. Guardrails are usually anodized pipe, 1.5 to 1.675 in. (3.75 to 4.2 cm) diameter and 42 in. (106 cm) high. These are normally fitted to the backs, sides, stairs, and fronts of bleacher sections. Sections also come in more or less standard sizes of 3, 5, 10, and 15 row × 15 ft (4.5 m) sections, elevated or non-elevated, with various guardrail options, as well as accessibility options to meet Americans with Disabilities Act (ADA) requirements. See Figure 9.6 for an example of a 10-tier, elevated section.

9.3.2.2 *Safety*

The current guiding standard for the design, construction, and inspection of portable bleachers in the USA is contained in *ICC/ANSI 300-2002, Bleachers, Folding and Telescopic Seating, and Grandstands*. The International Code Council (ICC) initiated the development of this stand-alone standard to address bleacher safety, after the issue was highlighted when two US congressional representatives petitioned the Consumer Product Safety Commission to develop such regulations, following a study of deaths and injuries resulting from falls from bleachers. For example, in 1999 in the USA, there were an estimated 22,100 bleacher-associated injuries treated in hospital emergency rooms.

FIGURE 9.6

EXAMPLE OF ALUMINUM BLEACHERS

Courtesy: Bleachers International, Inc., www.getseating.com

Approximately 6100 of these injuries were a result of the person falling from, or through, bleachers, onto the surface below. Approximately 4910 of these falls involved children under the age of 15 years (US Consumer Product Safety Commission, 2000). Obviously, event producers must be aware of and meet the requirements of this standard to avoid liability.

In Canada, there appears to be no similar standard, although it would be prudent for event producers to follow the ICC standard as well. Accessibility for persons with disabilities is covered by standards in both countries, listed below, and must be followed for bleachers:

- *ADA Accessibility Guidelines for Buildings and Facilities (ADAAG)* for the USA.
- *Canadian Standards Association (CSA), B651-04 PDF: Accessible Design for the Built Environment* for Canada.

9.3.3 Fencing and Barriers

For special events, fencing and barriers are generally utilized for crowd control. Crowd control fencing and barriers come in many designs that fit into three main categories. We will briefly look at these and then at safety.

9.3.3.1 Categories and Construction

The first category is a low height, low strength, attractive sectional design typically used within an event space to delineate exhibits, ticketed sub-events, VIP areas, and such. This design is usually constructed of steel supports and wood, or steel supports and PVC. Sections are typically 6 ft (1.8 m) wide and 32–48 in. (80–120 cm) high and interlock (see Figure 9.7 (left)). Occasionally this design may be more functional and less attractive.

The second category of crowd control fence is a higher more durable design, used primarily as event perimeter fencing. This type is constructed of welded steel mesh and steel tubing of varying designs. Section heights are fairly standard at 7 ft 6 in. (2.25 m) and widths vary from 4 to 10 ft (1.2–3 m). Accessories include interlocking clamps, heavy bases, gates (with wheels), and privacy screens that can be installed over the entire fence surface. These screens are made of a PVC-coated nylon mesh with an open weave to allow wind to pass through (Figure 9.7 (center)).

Originally designed in Europe, the third category is often called a *barrier* and is used for heavy-duty crowd control typically at outdoor rock concerts in front of a stage. In this case it is called a *front-of-stage barrier* (FOSB) or *crowd barrier*. Barriers can come in lightweight or heavy-duty versions, usually constructed of aluminum or steel respectively, the steel type being used for larger events. Modern barriers are of A-frame construction in profile, and rely on a *tread plate* (ideally with a tapered lip to prevent tripping) in front to maintain their stability and to withstand the forces associated with crowd crushes and surges. They are normally freestanding but if used outdoors, they may be fixed to a stage using couplers, providing the stage is also built to withstand the lateral crowd forces. According to Petter Säterhed of XNSE Experience Enabling Services AB in Sweden who manufacture this type of barrier (Safe Barriers), 'a steel barrier section weighs about 65 kg (145 lb) so that a 100 m (110 yd) long barrier constructed of steel is very hard to move because it weighs about 6.5 metric tons (4850 lb) plus the weight of the crowd standing on the platform' (Petter Säterhed, Personal Communication, November 6, 2006). The rear of the barrier is usually fitted with a step to enable crowd control officials (called *event stewards*, who require certification in Europe) to monitor crowd activity and to assist with lifting crowd surfers and audience members in distress out of harm's way if necessary. Dimensions are nominally 4 ft (1200 + mm) high × 43 in. (1070 + mm) wide × 50 in. (1242 + mm) deep, although there might be slight differences amongst manufacturers. Railings should be rounded or covered to prevent injury to persons leaning on them or being lifted over them. Figure 9.7 (right) illustrates a single FOSB section. Sections lock together and fold up for easy storage and transport. The required minimum dynamic horizontal load resistance at railing height is 3.0 kiloNewtons per meter (kN/m or approximately 200 lb/ft) for the European manufacturers and most apply a design safety factor of at least 1.5 to this figure, with some authorities (e.g. Western Australia and the UK) demanding a minimum design rating of

FIGURE 9.7

EXAMPLES OF EVENT FENCING

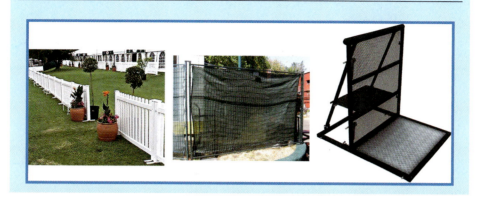

5.0 kN/m. Many of the better barriers can withstand over 15.0 kN/m, including the example in Figure 9.7, which can withstand over 22 kN/m.

Figure 9.7 illustrates the following types of event fencing:

- *Left photo*: Upscale event fencing (courtesy Signature Fencing & Flooring Systems, www.signaturefencing.com).
- *Center photo*: Perimeter fence with privacy screen (courtesy Doug Matthews).
- *Right photo*: FOSB (courtesy Safe Barriers, www.safebarriers.com).

9.3.3.2 *Safety*

For fencing and barriers, there are no current known specific safety or design standards in North America, although most fencing is manufactured using approved steel or aluminum products. The European design standard *NEN-EN 13200-3:2005 en: Spectator Facilities – Part 3: Separating Elements – Requirements*, appears to lead the way in this regard. In addition, in the UK, the guidelines *Temporary Demountable Structures: Guidance on Design, Procurement and Use* form the basis for the design and use of fencing and barriers. Another excellent reference, particularly for FOSB, is the publication *The Event Safety Guide: A Guide to Health, Safety and Welfare at Music and Similar Events*, published by the Health and Safety Executive in the UK.

Indeed, the most concern for crowd – and event worker – safety is associated not with the first two types of fencing described, but with FOSB and its use at live music – especially rock – concerts. Rutherford-Silvers (2004; pp. 185–187), Van Der Wagen and Carlos (2005; pp. 229–241), Tarlow (2002; pp. 85–109), and Fruin (1993) in particular, discuss crowds and the types of disasters that can result from crowd mentality. To put the seriousness of the potential for disaster in perspective, Fruin states, 'Crowd forces can reach levels that are almost impossible to resist or control. Virtually all crowd deaths are due to compressive asphyxia and not the "trampling" reported by the news media. Evidence of bent steel railings after several fatal crowd incidents show that forces of more than 4500 N (1000 lb) occurred. Forces are due to pushing, and the domino effect of people leaning against each other. Horizontal forces sufficient to cause compressive asphyxia would be more dynamic as people push off against each other to obtain breathing space. Experiments to determine concentrated forces on guardrails due to leaning and pushing have shown that a force of 30–75 percent of participant weight can occur. In a US National Bureau of Standards study of guardrails, three persons exerted a leaning force of 792 N (178 lb) and 609 N (137 lb) pushing. In a similar Australian Building Technology Centre study, three persons in a combined leaning and pushing posture developed a force of 1370 N (306 lb). This study showed that under a simulated "panic", five persons were capable of developing a force of 3430 N (766 lb).'

Suffice it to say, crowd disasters are a very real and serious risk at live events where music or other entertainment generates psychological pressures as well as physical ones. In Europe, studies have been ongoing for years about the best configuration for FOSB and have resulted in the optimum configuration – to date – of a convex or 'D-shaped' barrier arrangement in front of the stage, often with two or three layers of barrier (Upton, 2004). The minimum distance between the stage and the first barrier layer must, according to current regulations in many jurisdictions, be at least 1.0–1.5 m (3–5 ft) to permit event stewards, security, and emergency personnel free access and to permit the fast extraction of crowd members in distress. This shape also permits escape routes at either end of the convex shape and minimizes the locations where concentrated points of force may occur as would happen in a concave-shaped barrier. Figure 9.8 illustrates this configuration.

However, there is more than just pressure toward the stage to be concerned about. According to Säterhed from Sweden, one of the most potent dangers in a large audience is side-to-side movement. If crowd density exceeds approximately 7 persons/m^2, parrying a crowd surge (i.e. by taking a side step) gets difficult, resulting in the crowd *cratering* (i.e. many people falling, in a crater-like fashion). When the fallen audience gets up again, the crowd closes. This might – and has historically – trapped slow members of the crowd who are still lying down, putting them in severe danger of being trampled. In these cases, designing the FOSB with a *wavebreaker* – sometimes called a 'finger' – in the middle can be very effective (Figure 9.9).

For larger crowds, wavebreakers are combined with splitting up the crowd by creating 'cages' for smaller numbers of people. However, it is important to calculate the angles of the barrier correctly so that no audience member gets trapped in a dead-end against the barrier (Petter Säterhed, Personal Communication, November 6, 2006). This concept is illustrated

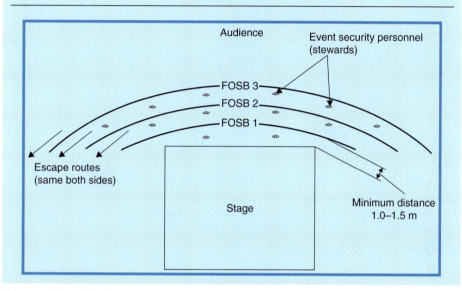

Courtesy: Doug Matthews

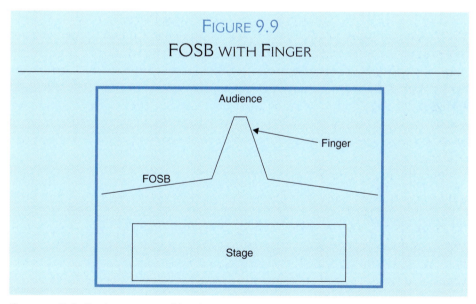

Courtesy: Safe Barriers, www.safebarriers.com

in Figure 9.10 which shows the cages along with the barriers and walkways between.

The number and spacing of FOSB arrangements are largely dependent on the total audience size and demographics as well as the nature of the event, and event stewards or security professionals with experience in this type of

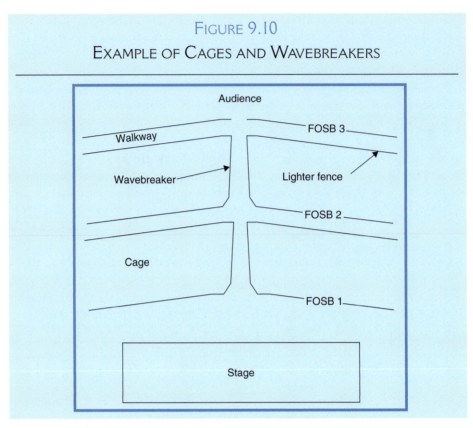

FIGURE 9.10

EXAMPLE OF CAGES AND WAVEBREAKERS

Audience

Walkway

FOSB 3

Wavebreaker

Lighter fence

FOSB 2

Cage

FOSB 1

Stage

Courtesy: Safe Barriers, www.safebarriers.com

event should be consulted before producers make the final decision on FOSB arrangements.

9.3.4 Sanitary Facilities

Creature comforts or rather the lack thereof, can form a lasting negative impression in the minds of event attendees. To prevent this, adequate sanitary facilities must be provided, no matter where the event is held. For outdoor events – and even large indoor ones – portable toilets may be rented on a short-term basis where sewer-connected sanitation and water are not readily available. It is often the responsibility of the event producer to estimate toilet needs and to make arrangements for their delivery, placement, and servicing.

9.3.4.1 *Equipment, Location, and Servicing*

According to the Portable Sanitation Organization International (www. psai.org), the basic equipment consists of the portable toilet units and service trucks. The toilet unit is a small toilet room built over a water tight waste holding tank. The service truck has a pump and a large tank which is divided into two compartments, one for fresh charge for use in cleaning the units and the other for receiving and transporting the effluent for proper disposal. At special events, toilet units are placed on a site and picked up when the event is completed. For big events with a large number of units, the service truck may remain on-site to provide continuous stand-by maintenance service, especially if the duration is long.

Portable toilets are large enough for a single occupant, usually about 90 cm (3 ft) on a side by 210 cm (7 ft) high. They are held upright by the weight of the disinfectant liquid in the holding tank at the bottom. Nearly all include both a seated toilet and a urinal. Most include lockable doors, ventilation near the top, and a stovepipe vent for the holding tank. Single sex units and larger units for wheelchair access compatible with ADA requirements are available. All are available in different colors and designs, depending on the manufacturer. Plastic, freestanding hand-washing units with four wash stations (one on each side) and equipped with paper towels and soap are now part of most portable toilet orders. Luxury units with more amenities are popular for smaller or VIP audiences. These incorporate separate stalls with doors, vanities and make-up areas, washbasins, and towels, all packaged within an attractive interior design.

The keys to the successful incorporation of portable toilets into an event are:

- *Correct estimation of the number of units needed*: HSE (1999) recommends that, when estimating the number of units required at an event, consideration be given to the duration of the event, the perceived consumption of food and beverages (particularly alcohol) by the audience, timing of breaks in entertainment performances, provision for children or elderly who make take longer to use a facility, and weather conditions and temperature. In addition, the ratio of women to men is essential to correctly estimating numbers. Figures 9.11 and 9.12 are combined averages of several sources (Government of Western Australia, 2004; Rutherford-Silvers, 2004; National Event Services, 2006), and can be used for general estimates of toilet units required based on event duration (8 h for both these graphs) and whether or not alcohol is consumed. Note that the straight lines in these graphs are the trend lines of the averages and it these lines that should be used. In addition to the number of toilet units, hand wash stations should be provided in the ratio of approximately 20 percent of the total number of toilets (i.e. for 100 toilets, 20 hand wash stations are needed). The Government of Western Australia (2004) in their extensive event guidelines, also further recommend that for more attendees:
  - Female toilets increase at the rate of one per 100 females with alcohol, or one per 200 without alcohol.
  - Male toilets increase at the rate of three per 500 males with alcohol, or three per 1000 without alcohol.

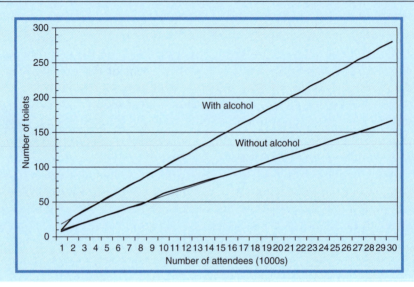

FIGURE 9.11

PORTABLE TOILET REQUIREMENTS FOR AN 8 H EVENT (TOTAL ATTENDANCE UP TO 30,000)

Courtesy: Doug Matthews

FIGURE 9.12

PORTABLE TOILET REQUIREMENTS FOR AN 8 H EVENT (TOTAL ATTENDANCE 25,000–100,000)

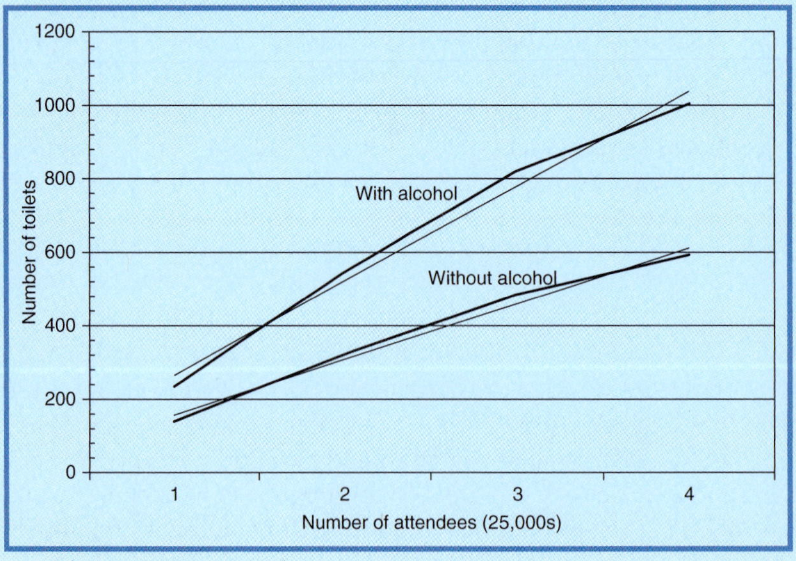

Courtesy: Doug Matthews

For events with different durations, they have the following recommendations for units:

- more than 8h, 100 percent increase over graph values;
- 6–8 h, 80 percent of graph values;
- 4–6 h, 75 percent of graph values;
- less than 4h, 70 percent of graph values.

According to National Event Services, in the USA, federal and state guidelines also require one ADA toilet unit for each 'cluster' of toilets, which works out to approximately 10 percent of the entire order that should be handicapped units. Event workers and employees must have their own dedicated facilities that should be located near work areas, specifically backstage, near the mixer tower, next to catering areas and car parks, and near first aid and children's areas. Toilets with hot and cold hand-washing facilities should be provided for food handlers.

- *Correct location of the units*: Where possible, toilets should be located at different points around the event site to minimize crowding and queuing problems. Attention should be given to accessibility for servicing and emptying. This may include temporary roadways and dedicated access routes, subject to the site layout.

- *Regular servicing schedule*: Depending on the type, portable toilet units have waste storage tank capacities ranging from about 150 l (40 gal) to 250 l (65 gal). On average, a single usage will deposit approximately 1.4 l (0.37 gal) of waste. Based on another average of 54–75 seconds per use (men versus women), smaller units may therefore require major service and emptying of toilet receptacles as frequently as every 2 h, or as infrequently as 4 h, but this may need to be monitored if some units receive heavier usage than others due to their location. At a minimum, units should be cleaned and checked for supply replenishment (e.g. toilet paper) at 2 h intervals, and a plumber should at least be on call for short events and on site for longer events. Major service procedure involves driving the service truck to within approximately 20 ft (6 m) of the portable toilet, pumping or evacuating the effluent from the portable toilet receptacle into the truck holding tank, recharging the portable toilet receptacle, and performing minor repairs to the portable toilet as needed.

9.3.4.2   Safety and Health Considerations

There are no known specific standards for portable toilets used at events; however standards do exist for portables used on construction sites. Some state and provincial jurisdictions now classify all portable toilet waste as *septage* (untreated waste that has not gone through a stabilization process, such as processing at a sewage treatment plant), and any group or organization that has portable toilets on site must use a licensed waste hauler to dispose of their waste. Clients have the right to demand that a waste hauler produce proof of a license.

As well, some jurisdictions (HSE, 1999) require stable and non-slip surfaces, protection from trip hazards, and adequate lighting (80–100 lx, depending on the jurisdiction).

Even with the estimates of required numbers of toilets as described in this section and the above safety considerations, producers should check with local authorities for the correct interpretation of local regulations, if any, for the numbers, locations, and servicing requirements of sanitation facilities.

PRODUCTION CHALLENGES

1. You want to check the calculations of your LD who has called for 100 A, three-phase service out of the following options presented by a venue in which you are producing a stage show:
   - 20 A, 120 V single phase;
   - 30 A, 120 or 208 V single or three phase;
   - 60 A, 120 or 208 V three phase;
   - 100 A, 120 or 208 V three phase;
   - 200 A, 120 or 208 V three phase.

   The lights he plans to use are 20 PAR64s @500 W, 16 PAR64s @1000 W, 10 Source Four ellipsoidals @500 W for gobo projection, and eight automated Vari-lites @1200 W for excitement. He plans to use a single dimmer system. Did he choose the correct option for electrical service?

2. Explain the different connection options for tying into house power in a way that your technically challenged client will understand.

3. You are producing an aerial ribbon act above a 3 ft high stage in a venue that has a 30 ft high ceiling. The ribbon must be suspended from a 16 in. square truss section that will be rigged from the ceiling using chain motors. The ribbon is 20 ft long and the performer needs a clear 16 ft of ribbon to work on. The chain motor, chain, and hooks require 4 ft of vertical space once they are fully trimmed. Will there be enough vertical space for the performer to work and what is the final highest trim to truss?

4. You are to produce a large outdoor festival for about 20,000 alternative music fans in an open farmer's field with a single road access. There will be six musical acts performing on a mobile stage during the festival which lasts for 4 h on a Sunday afternoon. It will be a non-alcoholic event. Consider what you might need in terms of scaffolding, bleachers (if any), fencing, FOSB, and portable toilets. Describe how these would all be used, how much or how many of each you might need, and where they might all be placed.

5. As a producer, you must be concerned with the safety both of your workers and of the audience. List at least one safety standard or guideline for each of the technical resources discussed in this chapter and describe for whom it is relevant.

REFERENCES

Amundson, M. (April 2006). Power Distro Connections. *Front of House Online*. Retrieved August 30, 2006, from http://fohonline.com/issue/archives.php? di=0604& fi=tech.txt.

Bloomfield, L.A. (August 29, 2006). Electric Power Distribution. *How Things Work. Virginia.edu*. Retrieved August 29, 2006, from http://rabi.phys.virginia.edu/HTW/electric_power_distribution.html.

Brain, M. (2006). How Power Grids Work. *How Stuff Works*. Retrieved August 29, 2006, from http://science.howstuffworks.com/power9.htm.

Candela, S. (April 12, 2006). How to Win Friends and Impress Power Engineers. *Projection, Lights and Staging News*. Retrieved August 29, 2006, from http://www.plsn.com/ Current-Issue/Technopolis/Technopolis-Apr06-1.

Donovan, H. (2002). *Entertainment Rigging: A Practical Guide for Riggers, Designers and Managers*. Rigging Seminars.

Donovan, H. (October 2003). What Goes Up Must Stay Up. *Pro AV Magazine*. Retrieved September 5, 2006, from http://proav.pubdyn.com/2003_October/2-ProAV-Old% 20Site%20Content-ProAVCopy-Current-2003-October2003-Currentproav-feature2.htm.

Electricians' Toolbox (1997). *Useful Formulas*. Retrieved August 29, 2006, from http:// www.elec-toolbox.com/.

ePanorama.net (August 27, 2006). *Rigging*. Retrieved September 1, 2006, from http:// www.epanorama.net/links/lights.html#rigging.

Fruin, J.J. (1993). The Causes and Prevention of Crowd Disasters. *First International Conference on Engineering for Crowd Safety*. London: Elsevier Science Publishers B.B.

Garber, N. (October 1, 2002). Tools of the Trade: Fresh Juice. *Special Events Magazine*. Retrieved August 30, 2006, from http://specialevents.com/supplies/meetings_fresh_juice/index.html.

Garber, N. (May 1, 2006). Tech Tips: Power Launch. *Special Events Magazine*. Retrieved August 30, 2006, from http://specialevents.com/eventtools/events_power_launch_20060516/index.html.

Glerum, J.O. (1997). *Stage Rigging Handbook*, Second Edition. Carbondale, IL: Southern Illinois University Press. Retrieved September 1, 2006, from Questia database: http:// www.questia.com/PM.qst?a=o&d=77477153.

Government of Western Australia (September 2004). *Guidelines for Concerts, Events and Organized Gatherings*. Perth, WA: Department of Health.

Health and Safety Executive (HSE) (1999). *The Event Safety Guide: A Guide to Health, Safety and Welfare at Music and Similar Events*. Norwich: Health and Safety Executive.

Martin, A.T. (December 20, 1996). Whose Law Is It Anyway? *Sound & Video Contractor*. Retrieved September 1, 2006, from http://svconline.com/mag/avinstall_whose_law_anyway/.

National Event Services (2006). *Portable Toilet Calculator for Events*. Retrieved September 11, 2006, from www.rentnational.com.

NEMA (2006). *About NEMA Standards*. Retrieved September 1, 2006, from http:// www.nema.org/stds/aboutstds/upload/StdationPolicies080706.doc.

Richardson, S. (July 6, 2000). Rigging. *WPI Technical Theatre Handbook*. Retrieved September 1, 2006, from http://www.gweep.net/~prefect/pubs/iqp/node43.html.

Rutherford-Silvers, J. (2004). *Professional Event Coordination*. Hoboken: John Wiley & Sons, Inc.

Tarlow, P.E. (2002). *Event Risk Management and Safety*. New York: John Wiley & Sons, Inc.

Upton, M. (January/February 2004). *Front of Stage Barrier Systems*. Paper presented to the Cabinet Office Emergency Planning College, Easingwold, UK.

US Consumer Product Safety Commission (2000). *Guidelines for Retrofitting Bleachers*, Publication No. 330-000011.

Van Beek, M. (August 2004). *Electrical Safety for Live Events*. Cambridge: Entertainment Technology Press Ltd.

Van Der Wagen, L. and Carlos, B.R. (2005). *Event Management for Tourism, Cultural, Business, and Sporting Events*. Upper Saddle River, New Jersey: Pearson Education, Inc.

Wikipedia contributors (August 2, 2006). Scaffolding. In *Wikipedia, the Free Encyclopedia*. Retrieved September 6, 2006, from http://en.wikipedia.org/w/index.php?title=Scaffolding&oldid=67278628.

Wikipedia contributors (August 10, 2006). NEMA Connectors. In *Wikipedia, the Free Encyclopedia*. Retrieved 03:30, August 30, 2006, from http://en.wikipedia.org/w/index.php?title=NEMA_connectors&oldid=68823247.

Index

M

W

X

Y

Z